Michael Smith is Defence Correspondent of the *Daily Telegraph*. His previous books include *Odd Man Out: The Story of the Singapore Traitor*, *Station X: The Codebreakers of Bletchley Park*, *Foley: The Spy Who Saved 10,000 Jews* and *The Emperor's Codes*. He lives in Henley.

The Spying Game

The Secret History of
British Espionage

Michael Smith

POLITICO'S

First published in Great Britain 1996 as *New Cloak, Old Dagger* by Victor Gollancz Limited

This revised edition published in Great Britain 2003
and updated 2004 as *The Spying Game* by
Politico's Publishing, an imprint of
Methuen Publishing Ltd
8 Artillery Row
London
SW1P 1RZ

10 9 8 7 6 5 4

Printed and bound in Great Britain by Creative Print and Design Wales, Blaina

Contents

Preface

This book was to have been an updated paperback version of *New Cloak, Old Dagger*, which I wrote six years ago and which was then generously described by Professor Christopher Andrew as 'the best up-to-date survey of British intelligence'. But so much information on Britain's spies has since flooded into the public domain – through releases to the Public Record Office, and as a result of leaks, both official and unofficial – that it required a completely new book. Apart from the mass of new information in *The Spying Game*, there is one other major difference from its predecessor. In order to persuade the publisher to bring out an expanded and updated paperback edition, I have been forced to agree to remove any notes on sources. Those who helped me by providing material that was not previously in the public domain would at any event have to remain secret. But where I can, I am happy to provide details of the origins of any individual piece of new information to anyone who e-mails me at michael.smith@telegraph.co.uk

I thank all of those who assisted me in the research for *The Spying Game*, many of whom cannot be named. Of those who can, I would like to single out Cees Wiebes, who allowed me to see key chapters of his new book *Intelligence and the War in Bosnia 1992–1995* prior to publication; Matthew M. Aid, whose forthcoming book on the US signals intelligence organisation, the National Security Agency (NSA), and its predecessors will reveal many more Cold War secrets; and David List, the most assiduous of PRO researchers. All three have been of immense assistance in the writing of *The Spying Game*. I am extremely grateful. I would also like to thank Richard Aldrich, Ralph Erskine, Paul Lashmar, Phil Tomaselli, Sean Magee of Politico's Publishing – without whom this book would never have appeared – John Schwartz, my agent Robert Kirby, and my wife and family.

Michael Smith
May 2003

Prologue

The Return of the Great Game

The dark green Puma helicopter had barely landed on the dusty airstrip at the north-eastern Afghan town of Khowja Bahauddin when the two men jumped out. Both were wearing Western clothes, the classic pale brown military shirts and battledress trousers affected by most male journalists in a war zone. They ducked down to avoid the rotor blades and ran towards a black Toyota 4x4 parked by the edge of the runway. Each man paused in turn to shake the hand of a bearded man in green fatigues and cap who had just climbed out of the Toyota. They exchanged a few brief words with him, shouting to make themselves heard above the noise of the Puma's engine, before getting into the back of the vehicle, which drove off towards the town at speed, disappearing in the cloud of dust thrown up in its wake.

After a short ride down a heavily pot-holed track, the Toyota stopped outside a brick-walled compound. The gates opened and the Toyota swept round the compound in a large circle, its wheels kicking up the dust, before stopping outside a brown rough-walled building, the temporary headquarters of Afghanistan's Northern Alliance. The two men slipped off their shoes at the door out of respect for their Muslim hosts, before being ushered inside to speak to the commander. It was late September. Little more than two weeks earlier al-Qa'eda terrorists had flown three airliners into New York's Twin Towers and the Pentagon and crashed a fourth, killing more than 3,000 people. It would be some days yet before America and its allies would begin bombing Afghanistan, wreaking a dreadful revenge on the Taliban regime that had harboured Osama bin Laden and his fellow members of the al-Qa'eda leadership. But already more subtle methods of regime change were underway.

Despite their appearance, the two men were not journalists. They were members of the British Secret Intelligence Service, MI6, and they were there to speak to the new commander of the Northern Alliance, General Mohammed Qasim Fahim. They and the rest of a small eight-man team of Dari- and Pashto-speaking MI6 officers had spent the last few days criss-crossing their way across Afghanistan. In the wake of the al-Qa'eda attacks on America, there had been criticism of both MI6 and the CIA for a perceived failure to maintain the agent networks set up inside Afghanistan during the Soviet occupation. The criticism was singularly misplaced.

Both had kept a number of networks inside Afghanistan, although the British, with a traditional interest in the area dating back to the Raj, not only had more than their US counterparts, their agents were more effective. They had been providing intelligence on the movements of Osama bin Laden since long before the attacks on the Twin Towers and were already proving their usefulness in the war on the al-Qa'eda leader and his Taliban hosts. The MI6 team's meetings with their agents across Afghanistan were designed to weave a web of networks that could be used to undermine the Taliban control over northern Afghanistan.

Not only did the British secret service have close links with Fahim's Jamiat-i-Islami, it had a large number of long-term agents spread right across Afghanistan. MI6 had friends among the Tajik Ismailis of northern Afghanistan and the Shi'ite Hazara, Mongoloid descendants of members of Genghis Khan's forces, whose mountainous central homeland, the Hazarajat, had never been subdued by the Taliban. It also had agents in the Pashtun south, who for several years had been providing important intelligence on al-Qa'eda and on the growth of the narcotics industry under the Taliban. Each group still controlled small areas of the country that the Taliban had yet to conquer. The plan was to expand those areas until all Taliban and al-Qa'eda forces had been forced out.

The two MI6 officers were reporting back to Fahim, keeping him briefed on their secret contacts. The Americans were carrying out similar operations, but with weaker networks they were forced to throw money at the situation. MI6 had a small budget – around seven million dollars – to help its agents to persuade others, some of them inside the Taliban itself, to switch their allegiances. But it was acutely aware of the adage of the British intelligence officers who fought the Great Game with Russia during the 19th century, 'You can't buy the loyalty of an Afghan, you can only rent it.'

The MI6 team was using similar techniques to those employed during the Great Game, working out what made the people they needed on their side tick. The key was rarely if ever money alone, sometimes it was the opportunity to avenge a long-held grudge, sometimes a promise of British support in the post-war carve-up of Afghanistan. Often the motive that might lead a key commander to switch sides was simply pragmatism, a wish to be on the winning side. Occasionally, but only when they were sure it would work, the MI6 officers team handed over money. Their aim was to create a situation where a few deft moves at the right moment would bring down the Taliban regime like a house of cards.

The foundations of this unsung MI6 operation had been laid 20 years earlier. It was the early summer of 1981. The snow had melted on the high mountain passes over the Hindu Kush, turning the river that ran through the small northern Pakistani town of Chitral into a raging torrent. A light aircraft circled above the mass of white flat-roofed houses surrounding the town's old imperial fort before landing on the nearby airstrip. Five men got out and climbed into a 4x4 pick-up truck that had been driven onto the runway to meet them. To the casual observer, their appearance was unremarkable. They looked like any of the other Mujahideen who regularly passed through the town on their way to and from the northern Pakistani city of Peshawar that was home to most of the Afghan resistance movements. All five wore beards, flat woollen *pakol* hats and *shalwar kamiz* – the traditional baggy shirt and trousers adopted like a uniform by the Mujahideen of north-eastern Afghanistan. All five were MI6 officers.

The pick-up took them along the road towards Garam Chasma, a tiny settlement nestling in a valley at the foot of the towering Hindu Kush mountain range. After about a mile, the road became a dirt track, skirting the mountainside above the heavily swollen river. They would spend the night in Garam Chasma before hiring guides and packhorses to help them find their way along the centuries' old smuggling route over the Dorah Pass and into Afghanistan.

It would take three days for their small caravan to climb over the Hindu Kush and down into the Panjshir Valley, 'the valley of the five lions'. Here they were to meet up with a young Mujahideen leader called Ahmed Shah Masood, a charismatic figure who was making a name for himself with a series of daring attacks on the Soviet troops who had marched into Afghanistan 18 months earlier. Born in the Panjshir village of Bazarak, Masood was the son of an Afghan army officer. He attended the French-run Lycée Istiqlal in Kabul before studying engineering at the city's university. In 1975, after taking part in an attempted Islamic revolution, he fled to Pakistan. There he was given guerrilla training by the Pakistani secret service, the ISI, and in the late 1970s, he slipped back across the border, initially to fight against the communist regime. Less than a year later, Soviet troops occupied Afghanistan and Masood began organising the resistance of the Jamiat-i-Islami in the Panjshir. His remarkable success in keeping the Russians out of the valley and taking the battle to within a few miles of the Afghan capital Kabul led to him becoming known as the Lion of Panjshir. It also attracted the attention of those in the West who saw the Mujahideen as a useful proxy force in the Cold War against Moscow, among them MI6.

The five MI6 officers were taken to see Masood near his family home in one of the side valleys of the Panjshir. They sat outside on a rug and cushions laid out under the shade of a walnut tree. Masood offered them green tea and listened as they explained that they worked for a right-wing European foundation. 'We like what you are doing to the Russians,' they said. 'We would like to help you. What do you need most?' It is unlikely that Masood was fooled by what was at best a 'light cover'. Five men, all British, and all working for a right-wing European foundation, it was not difficult to guess who had really sent them. The Mujahideen leader said that what he desperately needed was secure communications system that would prevent the Russians eavesdropping on his conversations with his commanders. MI6 had radios custom-built to evade the Russian intercept operators and sent a small team of communications experts to Pakistan to teach the Mujahideen how to operate them. Masood's forward observation post overlooking the major Soviet air base at Bagram used the radios to warn him whenever Soviet bombers were taking off to bomb the Panjshir, allowing him to withdraw his men to safety. One senior member of Jamiat-i-Islami later recalled that when the Russians tried to carpet bomb the Mujahideen out of the Panjshir during 1984 and 1985, the British radios repeatedly saved Masood's life.

By then MI6 was providing him with more than just secure communications. Initially Mujahideen were flown to remote camps in northern England and Scotland, where former members of the SAS trained them in guerrilla warfare and the use of explosives. But soon training teams were being sent into Afghanistan itself. The Russians realised what was going on in July 1983, when a Soviet *Spetsnatz* Special Forces team ambushed a group of Masood's men close to the Bagram airbase and discovered identification documents belonging to a Briton called Stuart Bodman. He allegedly worked for the Gulf Features Service, a front organisation that provided a useful journalistic cover. 'Bodman' was one of a group of MI6 officers infiltrated into Afghanistan three months earlier. The Russians claimed to have killed him but he was alive and well and already out of Afghanistan, his false name allowing the British government to deny any knowledge of his existence.

The *Spetsnaz* team also discovered an American AN/URS11 remote-controlled signals intelligence transceiver. The computerised device could intercept Soviet radio transmissions and send them back live via satellite to GCHQ in Cheltenham or to the US National Security Agency at Fort Meade in Maryland. Subsequent reports of British and US assistance to the Mujahideen focused on supplies of Stinger and Blowpipe hand-held surface-to-air missiles. But the remote intercept sets, planted on behalf of the CIA, were an important part of MI6 operations inside Afghanistan.

Another key role played by MI6 during the Soviet occupation was negotiating between the disparate Mujahideen factions in order to co-ordinate their operations. Perhaps because their relationships with MI6 were not simply about money, Masood and the other contacts inside the Mujahideen remained true friends to the British long after the Russians had left. When MI6 began operating against international crime, and in particular the drugs trade, their Afghan contacts provided details of shipments of raw opium moving across the border into Soviet central Asia. That intelligence helped considerably in cutting the amount of heroin reaching Britain's streets.

But soon there was a far more important MI6 target inside Afghanistan. Expelled from the Sudan in 1996 as a result of US pressure, Osama bin Laden had moved his al-Qaʻeda terrorist training camps to Afghanistan. The MI6 agents inside Afghanistan became invaluable. But Masood remained the most valuable by far. Briefly defence minister in the government that took over after the Soviet withdrawal, he was forced out of Kabul by the Taliban and retreated to the Panjshir from where he led the loose coalition of groups known as the Northern Alliance that was resisting the Taliban.

Just two days before the al-Qaʻeda attacks on New York's Twin Towers, on 9 September 2001, Masood agreed to meet two Arab journalists, a television reporter and his cameraman, who had been waiting more than a week to interview him. They claimed to be Moroccans whose families had moved to Belgium and they carried a letter of introduction from a London-based Islamic organisation. Masood insisted that they tell him before the interview what questions they would be asking. They all concerned his attitude to bin Laden. An aide warned Masood that the 'journalists' were almost certainly from al-Qaʻeda but he insisted on going through with the interview. 'You can start filming now,' he told them and at that moment the cameraman detonated explosives packed into his battery belt killing a number of people, including Masood. MI6 had lost a good friend, but perhaps more importantly the Northern Alliance had lost a leader whose ability and reputation had been the main thing holding it together.

His death could not have come at a worse time. The refusal of the Taliban to give up bin Laden in the wake of the 11 September attacks meant war. But the allied forces risked being dragged into a long debilitating Afghan campaign like those that had defeated the Russians and the British before them. With that in mind, British military planners favoured using the Northern Alliance as a proxy army. The allies would supply the air power, and special forces like the SAS would co-ordinate ground operations, but the bulk of the troops themselves would be Afghans. The US administration was initially sceptical. Only a few months earlier, it had dismissed the Alliance and Masood in particular as 'part of the problem, not part of the solution'. If the Americans were to be persuaded that the plan would work, then the various factions that made up the Northern Alliance would have to be truly united. But without Masood that was going to prove difficult, which was why the latest MI6 team had been sent into Afghanistan. Using their knowledge of the ground and the negotiating skills practised routinely by MI6 officers in trouble spots as varied as Northern Ireland and East Timor, they began contacting all the old agents and setting up new relationships with others, in particular the Uzbek warlord Abdul Rashid Dostum.

The real measure of the team's success was the astonishing four days it took for the Taliban to be forced out of northern Afghanistan. It began on 9 November, when the key northern town of Mazar-i-Sharif fell to a combined forces of Dostum's National Movement, Jamiat-i-Islami troops and Shi'ite Hazaras. The victory was set up in advance by the MI6 and CIA teams. Despite the gratuitous brutality of Afghan warfare, its proponents are pragmatists who will often switch sides rather than continue a fight they cannot win. The MI6 officers waited until precisely the right moment and then used their agents to press all the appropriate buttons. The next day, 10 November, the combined Northern Alliance force moved west, taking Sar-i-Pol and Shiberghan, Dostum's personal fiefdom. By 11 November, with the carefully laid plans of the MI6 and CIA teams encouraging a series of defections by key commanders, the Taliban retreat had turned into a full-blown stampede. In the west, the Northern Alliance captured the town of Qala-i-Now while in the north-east Fahim's men swept through Taloqan, Pol-i-Khomri and Bamiyan. The following day, the main western city of Herat fell and on 13 November, with the Taliban now in headlong flight, Fahim's men occupied the capital, Kabul. The Mujahideen were always inclined to exaggerate their capabilities but not even the most optimistic of the Northern Alliance commanders could have predicted the speed of their advance, which ensured that there was no need for the Allies to risk deploying large numbers of their own troops. It was the activities of the MI6 team pulling the strings behind the scenes that led Tony Blair to praise Britain's spies for the 'very important role' they played in bringing about the collapse of the Taliban. The British Prime Minister described them as 'unsung heroes' whose dangerous and risky work inside Afghanistan in the immediate aftermath of the 11 September attacks had helped to ensure that very few allied soldiers died removing the Taliban from power.

One

The Art of Espionage

Intelligence is a very imprecise art.

British diplomat David Gore-Booth in evidence to the Scott Inquiry

The popular fascination with the world of espionage has spawned a wealth of fiction ranging from Ian Fleming's highly romanticised version of Britain's MI6, in which James Bond's 007 designation gave him a licence to kill, to the more realistic style epitomised by John le Carré's George Smiley. As a result most people have a reasonable, if limited, perception of how spies work. They will understand terms like 'double agent', 'safe house' and 'tradecraft'. Pressed, they will even admit to being aware that there is much more to intelligence than the popular Cold War image of a secret agent nervously waiting in an east European café for the 'drop' that may never come. But very few will know the total scale of international espionage, an industry that costs the United States alone an estimated \$35 billion a year. Information is power, and governments are prepared to pay a heavy price to obtain it. The demise of the Warsaw Pact, which many saw as signalling the end for the spy, has only increased the need for intelligence as unpredictable terrorist groups plot mass murder, weapons-grade nuclear materials are traded on the black market, and Third World countries that were previously kept in check by their superpower mentors turn into dangerous mavericks.

Throughout history, war has followed peace as night follows day. Neither the League of Nations, set up at the end of the First World War amid a determination that such a conflict would never happen again, nor its successor, the United Nations, has been able to prevent states from using aggression to gain an advantage at their neighbour's expense or from redressing perceived grievances by force of arms. International relations might be governed by diplomatic etiquette, but there are few real rules. Those that do exist are observed only by countries which fear the consequences of others ignoring them, and when that happens the only truly effective sanction is war. In such circumstances, intelligence becomes indispensable and so for centuries spies have found useful employment with the state, according espionage a dubious reputation as 'the second oldest profession'. Governments and military commanders can make sensible judgements as to their future actions only if they know the other side's true position and intentions. In such a situation, diplomacy becomes like a game of poker, with each side protecting the details of its hand. It is the job of the spy to find out what cards the other side is holding. But, as well as gathering information on the enemy's secrets, the intelligence services must also protect their own from enemy attempts to uncover them.

The art of espionage can be divided into three separate categories. The first – strategic intelligence – is the collection of information which keeps political leaders and their advisers, be they civil servants, diplomats or soldiers, well informed on the situation in target countries and allows them a better chance of predicting how those countries will react in the future. It will include assessments of the political situation, the leaders and their potential successors, and economic and sociological factors that might influence policy, together with details of the target's economic activities and scientific and technological capabilities. The main British agency for gathering strategic intelligence, taking more than half of the £1 billion annual intelligence budget – traditionally called the Single Intelligence Vote – is the Government Communications Headquarters, based at Cheltenham in Gloucestershire. GCHQ monitors the communications of Britain's enemies and friends from a number of remote sites around the world, providing the British government with intelligence that will help it to formulate its security, foreign, defence and economic policies. The other main collection agency for strategic intelligence is the Secret Intelligence Service, better known as MI6. According to the Foreign and Commonwealth Office, under whose control both agencies come, MI6 collects exactly the same type of information as GCHQ, acquiring it 'through a variety of sources, human and technical, and by liaison with a wide range of foreign intelligence and security services'.

The second type of intelligence is tactical: simply put, that information which would be useful to military commanders in the field. It includes working out the precise order of battle of the enemy's armed forces, tracking the deployments of individual units, and monitoring and examining their peacetime training exercises in order to determine the type of tactics they will employ in war and how those tactics can best be countered. Not unnaturally, this information is collected in the main by the military intelligence agencies, whose activities under the British system are coordinated by the Defence Intelligence Staff. It is acquired by a wide variety of means, from the information collected by small infantry patrols probing the forward edge of the battle area, through the cocktail-party chat of the military attachés based in Britain's embassies abroad, to the most advanced technology that money can buy. These include spy satellites like the American Keyhole system, which is able to produce highly detailed pictures of what is going on far behind the enemy lines. Satellites are not just deployed to gather what is known as imagery intelligence; (IMINT) they can also be highly effective as remote platforms for the interception of signals intelligence, which provides a vital part of tactical intelligence, one reason why several thousand members of the armed forces work directly to GCHQ.

The last type of intelligence is counter-intelligence, famously defined in the post-war directive of Britain's domestic Security Service, MI5, as 'the defence of the realm'. Counter-intelligence is not purely confined to ensuring that a nation's secrets are secure against the machinations of foreign spies – an activity that is perhaps better described as counter-espionage or security. Counter-intelligence operations can in themselves yield a great deal of information about the enemy's intentions, the depth of his knowledge and the operations of his intelligence services.

The expulsion of a foreign spy, and the inevitable tit-for-tat gesture by his employers, will attract great interest in the media, but only infrequently will the full story behind the expulsion emerge. Before a spy is unmasked, his activities will have been monitored by the domestic security services. His contacts, quite possibly involving a network of agents, will have been noted, and the aims and successes of their operations will have been analysed. Some of these agents may even have been turned against him to feed him false information and provide more details of the enemy intelligence operations, thereby becoming double agents. This may have been going on for some time – in occasional cases for years – and the expulsion is unlikely to have come without a decision that the spy's presence is no longer useful for the collection of counter-intelligence. Once he is expelled, his masters must assume, unless they have very good information to the contrary, that the network he ran is also compromised and has been closed down – or, in the jargon of the spy, folded.

MI5's role in domestic counter-intelligence was laid down in a 1952 directive issued by Sir David Maxwell Fyfe, the then Home Secretary, as being 'the Defence of the Realm as a whole, from external and internal dangers arising from attempts at espionage and sabotage, or from actions of persons and organisations, whether directed from within or without the country, which may be judged to be subversive to the State'. The 1989 Security Service Act updated the Maxwell Fyfe directive, defining MI5's function as 'the protection of national security and, in particular, its protection against threats from espionage, terrorism or sabotage, from the activities of agents of foreign powers and from actions intended to overthrow or undermine parliamentary democracy by political, industrial or violent means'.

The rivalry between the domestic and foreign services over who controls counter-intelligence derives not from the traditional security role but from the potential for gathering exceptionally valuable intelligence. The information provided by well-placed double agents can justify budgets and earn knighthoods. It may even lead eventually to high-profile defections – the ultimate intelligence success. No agency would like to see its main rival gain the credit for an intelligence scoop that could have been its own. Although all spies fight shy of publicity – not unnaturally, since secrecy is the lifeblood of their profession – the plaudits that follow the acquisition of a defector and the information he can supply are valuable as a means of warding off the criticism that results from what at best is the public suspicion – at worst, opprobrium – which secrecy inspires. In part, the suspicion derives from a belief that the spies would not need to be so secretive if they were not doing anything wrong. The assumption is made – not always incorrectly – that behind their cloak of secrecy the spies must be wielding the dagger in an unnecessary and arbitrary way.

There has always been a moral streak in society that has considered espionage to be somehow unethical. It was epitomised in the reason given by Henry Stimson, the then American Secretary of State, for his 1929 decision to close down the Black Chamber, the predecessor of the National Security Agency, America's equivalent of GCHQ: 'Gentlemen do not read each other's mail.' The main ethical worry on foreign intelligence, however, concerns not the monitoring of enemy communications but covert action: special operations behind enemy lines, and in particular that type of operation which the KGB used to describe as *mokrye dela* – wet affairs – a graphic reference to the spilling of blood. Britain's 1994 Intelligence Services Act prohibits MI6 officers and agents, or anyone else who might act on behalf of MI6 (the SAS, for example), from taking part in any criminal activity for which they would normally still be liable in the United Kingdom even if it occurs abroad. They are thereby prevented from committing genocide, murder, kidnapping or indeed bigamy – unless the Foreign Secretary deems it necessary for the proper discharge of one of the service's statutory functions, in which case the agents will be absolved of all liability under British criminal law.

This appears to provide an easy opt-out solution, although Sir Gerry Warner, who as Intelligence Co-ordinator in the mid-1990s had responsibility for determining how Britain's intelligence requirements were met, said it would be 'unthinkable' for MI6 officers to be authorised to use violence in peacetime and that they do not carry weapons. However, given the nature of their work, which now includes not just espionage operations abroad but also 'the prevention or detection of serious crime', it is simply not credible that MI6 agents involved in that type of operation could be left unarmed in the face of what would inevitably be a serious risk of violence.

But the deep suspicion in which most secret services are held has little to do with their behaviour abroad, when to the vast majority of people they become 'our brave boys', but rather more with their potential use at home against their own citizens. The all-pervading domination of east European society maintained by the KGB, Stasi, Securitate et al. was far more effective than the sub-legal activities in this field of MI5 and the police Special Branch in Britain. But in their way the latter were infinitely more shocking and damaging to the public perception of the intelligence community. The KGB was expected to behave in that way; Britain's security forces were supposed to be the upholders of right and truth. The reputation of MI5 was badly damaged by the seemingly indiscriminate surveillance of a rag-bag collection of largely ineffective left-wing 'subversives' – including members of trade unions and groups like the Campaign for Nuclear Disarmament. While few people believed some of the more bizarre claims made by the former senior MI5 official Peter Wright in his book *Spycatcher*, the boast that 'for five years, we bugged and burgled our way across London at the state's behest, while pompous bowler-hatted civil servants in Whitehall pretended to look the other way' was entirely credible.

An expansion of such surveillance operations against British citizens – begun in the 1970s under the Heath government, largely as a reaction to the power of the unions, who were seen by politicians of both right and left as having become 'too mighty' – continued through both the Wilson and Callaghan Labour administrations. And reached its peak under the Thatcher government in the early 1980s, when, according to Cathy Massiter, an MI5 officer who left the service because she disagreed with what was going on, the Ministry of Defence was routinely asking MI5 to set up surveillance operations against CND members whose activities could not possibly have been regarded as posing a serious threat to the state. The damage that kind of over reaction to a perceived threat can do was shown most graphically by what emerged in the wake of the FBI's failure to combat the threat of al-Qaʿeda terrorists training inside America to fly aircraft into the World Trade Centre and the Pentagon. Previous operations that targeted among others the civil rights leader Martin Luther King had led to stringent restrictions on the FBI's surveillance activities. These prevented it from using the Internet or even public libraries to search for potential terrorist activities, and ensured that they could not even visit the mosques where al-Qaʿeda does most of its recruiting.

But the main focus of criticism was the way in which the human spy has been ignored with the increasingly costly spy satellites taking over as the main means of intelligence collection. Until the invention of radio and the realisation of its potential for military communications, information collected from and by human spies – known in the jargon of the intelligence community as

HUMINT – was by far the most important to the spymaster, whether obtained by using the secret agent as immortalised in spy fiction, traitors within the enemy camp, or information collected by diplomats and travellers. Tourists and businessmen were a common source of information before the information explosion dramatically increased the amount of data readily accessible in open sources like the Internet, books, periodicals, newspapers, and radio and television broadcasts. They remain useful in closed societies or remote areas where their genuine reasons for being in the country provide good cover for intelligence work and Britons abroad – expatriates and businessmen – are still seen by MI6 as its most reliable source of intelligence.

But HUMINT is more readily identified with the James Bond-style secret agent, who was previously thought to have been made redundant by the increasing use of technology to acquire intelligence. By the end of the First World War technical means had taken over from the man on the ground as the main source of information on enemy intentions, activities and capabilities, providing, according to some reports, as much as ninety per cent of the usable intelligence available to military commanders.

The part played in the Second World War by the Ultra 'special intelligence', collected by the Government Code and Cypher School (GC&CS) at Bletchley Park, is now universally known. There are those who, quite wrongly, have attempted to play down both its role in Hitler's defeat and the continued influence of intelligence collected from the interception of radio signals. But signals intelligence, or SIGINT – which includes information derived from the interception of numerous types of radio signal, not just straightforward voice communications – remains to this day one of the most important forms of intelligence, if not the most important. Signals intelligence divides into two main forms: communications intelligence, or COMINT and intelligence derived from the interception of electronic emissions, ELINT.

In recent years the interpretation of imagery intelligence – whether from straightforward photography or other methods such as infra-red thermal imaging – has assumed far greater importance with the introduction of the surveillance satellite. High-altitude reconnaissance aircraft, like the American U-2 and the SR-71 Blackbird, proved themselves particularly useful in the garnering of intelligence on developments in Soviet military missile technology during the Cold War. Their capabilities were as nothing compared to those of the modern surveillance satellite, which has proved indispensable for arms-control verification and as an early-warning system. But neither the capability to intercept mobile and satellite telephone calls nor the ability to produce immediate satellite imagery of events taking place on the ground in remote parts of the world such as Afghanistan was able to give the US administration warning of the 11 September attacks. The inevitable conclusion was that there had been a dramatic failure of intelligence and, in particular, of human intelligence.

Two

A New Order for the Spies

Next to the acquisition of information, its distribution to those who may be able to use it is the most important duty of the Intelligence Branch.
Lt-Col David Henderson, *Field Intelligence, Its Principles, Its Practices*, 1904

The most worrying aspect of America's apparent over reliance on technical intelligence to track the terrorist threat, at the expense of human intelligence, was that it was not the first time since the end of the Cold War that this had led to a so-called 'intelligence failure'. The immense cost of technical intelligence – around $30 billion of the US intelligence budget compared to a mere $5 billion for human intelligence – and the apparent inability of its expensive systems to detect the Iraqi invasion of Kuwait led many both inside and outside the intelligence community to call at the beginning of the 1990s for a return to the old world of James Bond, a revival of human espionage.

Brent Scowcroft, National Security Adviser in both the Ford and the Bush administrations, described the emphasis on technical means of collection as 'way overblown'. Following the demise of the Warsaw Pact and the end of the Cold War, 'we need a new kind of intelligence, a different kind of intelligence that is less directed at technical collection, where we are good,' he said. There is a need to go back to basics, 'back to human intelligence, where we don't do as well'.

But Admiral Stansfield Turner, a Cold War head of the CIA, dismissed this as just 'what one inevitably hears when there has been an intelligence failure', such as not predicting Iraq's invasion of Kuwait. 'The litany is familiar,' he said. 'We should throw more and more human agents against such problems, because the only way to get inside the minds of adversaries and discern intentions is with human agents. As a general proposition that simply is not true.

Not only do agents have biases and human fallibilities, there is always a risk that an agent is, after all, working for someone else.'

To a certain degree, both arguments are true. There is no doubt that America and its allies were caught cold by the invasion of Kuwait and the 2001 al-Qa'eda attacks on America because they had no human agents close enough to Saddam Hussein or Osama bin Laden to warn them of their plans. But, once the resultant wars began, their spy satellites and aircraft provided them with far more intelligence on what was going on in Iraq and Afghanistan, much of it crucial to the outcome of the two wars, than could ever have been acquired by human spies. The real lesson to be learned from the failure to predict the Iraqi invasion of Kuwait or the 11 September attacks was that both technical and human intelligence have their own roles to play and need to be very closely co-ordinated if they are to be truly effective. One or other on its own will only rarely be enough.

Despite the alleged failure to predict the 11 September attacks, the CIA had warned President Bush a month earlier that al-Qa'eda was planning a terrorist 'spectacular' inside America that summer with the intention of causing 'massive casualties'. This came from satellite telephone conversations picked up by one of either the US National Security Agency or Britain's GCHQ in the spring of 2001. There were no details from the intercepts of what form the attacks might take but the CIA report said al-Qa'eda had discussed the possibility of hijacking aircraft. This was in fact a classic use of Humint to complement SIGINT. Despite claims from a number of former CIA officers in the wake of the attacks that the agency did not have any agents in Afghanistan able to report on al-Qa'eda, it did. MI6 had even more, having reactivated old agents used during the Soviet occupation in the mid-1990s to help it to keep track of the heroin trail coming out of northern Afghanistan. Some of these agents had been reassigned to try to get close to al-Qa'eda and it was one of these who warned in 1998 of Osama bin Laden's interest in hijacking aircraft.

Nevertheless, if every member of al-Qa'eda maintained good operational security not even having very well-placed agents inside the organisation would necessarily translate into knowing what form its next operation would take. Some of the members of the al-Qa'eda hit squads who carried out the 11 September attacks were unaware that other aircraft were to be hijacked and may even have had no idea of what was to happen to the aircraft they were on. Much has been made of the ability of Westerners, including a number of Britons, to join al-Qa'eda but this ignores the fact that it is a large, layered organisation. It operates a very strict 'need to know' policy with regard to the details of its operations. Very few of the thousands of al-Qa'eda members given training in Afghanistan were selected to take part in terrorist operations. Those who reach the key decision-making and terrorist operation levels, rather than the vast majority who at most fought alongside the Taliban, have to be very highly trusted and willing to show that they will kill, or be killed, for the cause.

George Tenet, the US Director of Central Intelligence, and head of the CIA, admitted that the incident confirmed 'the importance of continuing clandestine human operations to penetrate these groups' but insisted that there were already agents out on the ground. 'Did we have penetrations of the target?' he asked. 'Absolutely. Did we have technical operations? Absolutely. Where did the secret for planning reside? Probably in the heads of three or four people, and at the end of the day, all you can do is continue to make the effort to steal the secret and break into this leadership structure, and we have to keep working at it. There will be nothing you do that will guarantee 100 per cent certainty. It will never happen.'

That is not to say that there were no avoidable intelligence failures, but on the whole they appear to have been much closer to home. The main villains of the piece were the appalling standard of security for internal flights, the complex US intelligence apparatus, which ensures that no one counterterrorism unit has access to all the available information on its targets, and excessively prohibitive legislation designed to protect the civil rights of the US population. Well-organised terrorists use 'lily-whites', people with no previous association with their group, to carry out their operations, isolating them in cells and allowing no contact with any other group members. Identifying the 19 terrorists who took part in the 11 September operation among the many Muslims working and studying in America ought to have been a near impossibility. They did not act like, or associate with, extremist Muslims. Most were in America legally. They drank alcohol, went out with women, and generally behaved in a secular way.

But some at least did make mistakes that drew attention to themselves and suggested to FBI officers that there was a suspicious number of Arabs trying to learn how to fly, at least one of whom was not at all worried about learning how to take off or land. Zacarias Moussaoui, a French Moroccan, was arrested 25 days before the 11 September attacks after the Minnesota flying school he was attending reported his lack of interest in how to take off or land aircraft. The FBI decided not to leave him in place and tap his telephone allegedly because of judicial complaints about the number of wiretaps they were making. Had they done so, they might well have managed to obtain warning of what was happening. While it is extremely unlikely that they would have discovered the scale of what was about to happen, even a warning that terrorists were planning to hijack an aircraft might have been enough to ensure an improvement in the lax security which was the key factor in their success.

Despite the flood of reports in the late spring and summer of 2001 that al-Qa'eda was planning an attack on America, the FBI continued to believe that the likelihood was that the attack would take place overseas. The Federal Aviation Authority (FAA), which was also warned of the danger, failed to improve the security surrounding domestic flights as a result of FBI advice to that effect. The utter ineptitude of the FBI counter-terrorism operations was shown most graphically by concerns raised by one of its officers in Phoenix, Arizona, two months before the attacks, over the number of Arabs being monitored for possible terrorist links who appeared to be interested in learning how to fly aircraft. It mentioned bin Laden by name and suggested that al-Qa'eda members could be using the school to train for terrorist attacks. It also called for the investigation to be broadened to all US flying schools to see if there was a wider pattern. Little was done in response to the report and, although FBI officials insisted that it was sent to the right desks, it was not sent to the joint bin Laden task force, nor was it sent to the CIA as specifically suggested by its author. One of the Arab pilots who learned to fly at a Phoenix flying school was Hani Hanjour, the pilot who flew a hijacked aircraft into the Pentagon.

The CIA was not totally free of blame. Not all of the terrorists were 'lily-whites'. One was linked by the CIA to al-Qa'eda by the beginning of 2001. It knew that he had visited America and it knew he was linked to another terrorist suspect who had also visited America. It did not know that they were living in America during 2001 and undertaking flying training, nor of course could it have known that they would both take part in the 11 September attacks. But it did not pass their details to the US Immigration and Naturalization Service (INS) until August 2001. When this revealed they were in America, the FBI began looking for them but they were not found in time. The fact that a nationwide search for them was underway and they still managed to board a civil aircraft is perhaps the most graphic illustration that the key problems lay not with the CIA but with the FBI and with US airport security.

Following the 11 September attacks, the system was revamped to ensure that intelligence operations against al-Qa'eda were centralised in the joint CIA–FBI bin Laden task force, which before the attacks had only around a dozen officers. but was now vastly expanded with the addition of officials from the Defense Intelligence Agency, the INS, the Treasury Department, and the FAA. The FBI meanwhile has admitted its failings, albeit only in response to a high-profile 'whistle-blower' and a congressional inquiry, more than doubling the number of officers working against terrorism to just under a thousand and borrowing 25 officers from the CIA to set up and manage its counter-terrorism intelligence centre.

Britain set up a similar multi-agency Joint Terrorism Analysis Centre under MI5 control. There was also an immediate increase of £108 million in the Single Intelligence Vote – or Single Intelligence Account as it is now known. It will rise to around £1.2 billion by 2005–6. This was a complete reversal of the initial post-Cold War position. Following the collapse of communism in eastern Europe and the former Soviet Union, western politicians looked for a 'peace dividend'. They demanded major restructuring of the intelligence agencies, and drastic budget cuts. The fight to maintain the intelligence budgets was not helped by large amounts of the information the agencies previously collected now being freely available in the open media or on the Internet. It is difficult to argue in favour of a surveillance satellite costing $700 million to build and a further $200 million to launch if the same information is available for the price of a few newspapers. One of the main criticisms in the Franks report into the Falklands War, which led to a major restructuring of the way Britain's spies are controlled, was that they ignored information freely available in the newspapers in Buenos Aires during late 1981 and early 1982. Lord Franks, whose committee saw all the intelligence available during the Falklands conflict, reported that 'the changes in the Argentinian position were, we believe, more evident on the diplomatic front and in the associated press campaign than in the intelligence reports'.

But spy satellites obtain far more information than can be found in newspapers, particularly when the target is a country such as Iraq, China or North Korea where the media is tightly controlled and information is not as readily available as it is in the West. Open source information can often supplement secret intelligence, whether gathered by technical means or by human agents, but it cannot replace it and the incorporation of the large amounts of material now available into intelligence assessments will cost money rather than save it.

If politicians hoped that the re-organisation of the secret services would lead to major cuts in the intelligence budgets, they were very quickly disabused of the idea. The Single Intelligence Vote plunged to a post-Cold War low of £693 million in 1998 before climbing rapidly as reality set in. While the major focus of the spies on both sides of the old Cold War had clearly gone, their governments' needs for intelligence had not, as the 11 September attacks vividly demonstrated. If anything, the Western agencies now found themselves facing far more complicated and less easily quantifiable problems.

Terrorism was not the only threat they now faced. The future of many old Warsaw Pact countries was and remains uncertain, a situation aggravated by the continuing turmoil in the various independent republics of the former Soviet Union and by the rapidly escalating influence of organised crime. The increasingly desperate economic situation as the old communist states attempt, with widely varying degrees of success, to adapt to capitalism has provided fertile ground for extremist politicians whose foreign policies may be more dangerous than the extremely conservative, and therefore highly predictable, stances of their communist predecessors. The governments of the smaller republics are also extremely vulnerable to organised crime, since the profits, particularly from drug-trafficking, are so large and the number of people who need to be bribed is so small. With such uncertainty over who is, or will be, in charge, the West still needs detailed intelligence on Russia's military strengths and, particularly in view of the apparent ease with which nuclear material stolen from the former Soviet Union can be purchased on the open market, its nuclear capabilities. In spite of the various treaties on arms control and destruction, there are still thousands of nuclear missiles in the former Soviet Union, all of which would be available to any future leader.

The situation in the Third World is no less volatile. Under the old super-power system, the Soviet Union and the United States were able virtually to dictate the foreign policies of their allies. Few such restraints now apply, particularly among former Soviet client states, over whom Russia has little or no control. The risk of being dragged into war – either directly, as in the Gulf, or indirectly, as in the former Yugoslavia – remains high. Even where Western countries do not become embroiled directly in such conflicts, they will need intelligence to ensure that they can protect or rescue their own nationals, or, as in Bosnia, mount effective peace-keeping missions. Nuclear proliferation in the Third World also creates an increasing risk of a cataclysmic conflict between traditional enemies, such as India and Pakistan, Iran and Iraq, or North and South Korea. Good intelligence can make the difference between detecting a nuclear-weapons programme in its early stages, when it can be curtailed by concerted diplomatic pressure or, if necessary, covert action, and having to respond to a new nuclear power by introducing costly modifications to nuclear-deterrent systems.

The end of the Cold War also led to far more openness about the activities of Britain's intelligence services. The 1989 Security Service Act, which put MI5 on a statutory footing, was followed by the 1994 Intelligence Services Act, designed to perform the same function for GCHQ and MI6, whose well-publicised existence previous British governments had consistently refused to confirm. Having named all the main officials involved in Britain's intelligence community, the government then published outlines of how they operated, in an astonishing reversal of the previously held position. This was epitomised by the farcical *Spycatcher* affair, in which the Thatcher government sought frantically to prevent the publication of a book which, once read, few totally believed.

The Intelligence Services Act also set up a committee of nine MPs to provide the first parliamentary oversight of the activities of Britain's intelligence community since its creation in the Middle Ages. The committee, the role of which is 'to examine the expenditure, administration and policy' of MI5, MI6 and GCHQ, meets once a week – 'inside a ring of secrecy' – in the Cabinet Office. It produces an annual report to Parliament through the Prime Minister, who under the Act is entitled to censor any part of the report if its publication 'would be prejudicial to the continued discharge of the functions' of any of the services involved.

The new acts also legalised a number of activities already undertaken by both GCHQ and MI6 which before the removal of the Soviet threat had not featured high in the public's perception of these agencies' work. These include counter-proliferation, counter-terrorism, combating of serious crime and gathering economic intelligence. The latter has been widely touted as the new justification for the intelligence services, although in reality it has been undertaken in various forms for a considerable time. Nevertheless, there is no doubt that, as the old superpower system is replaced by a new world order based largely on economic strength, the agencies' 'consumers' are becoming increasingly interested in the type of economic information the intelligence services can provide.

A recent review of US government intelligence requirements undertaken by America's policy-making National Security Council revealed that about 40 per cent of the information required by policy-making departments was 'economic in nature'. James Woolsey, Director of Central Intelligence from 1993 to 1995, said that, while the CIA would keep 'a rather careful eye on some foreign companies' and countries' efforts to bribe their way to contracts', it would 'not engage in industrial espionage to help American companies get a leg up on the competition'. His words were echoed by Sir Gerry Warner, Britain's former Intelligence Co-ordinator, who said, 'we are not businessmen' – adding in a peculiarly English fashion that such activities were 'not the right way' to go about advancing British business.

But the national intelligence priorities set by Britain's Joint Intelligence Committee (JIC) clearly indicate the increasing importance of economic intelligence. Although the continuing fears of a resurgent nuclear threat mean there is still a great deal of interest in the former Soviet Union – in particular the unstable republics of central Asia – there is as much if not more interest in Britain's economic rivals in western Europe than in the adversaries turned friends of eastern Europe. The real pointer to an increased interest in matters financial is in the priorities for the Far East, where the countries of the Pacific Rim – the so-called Tiger economies – are deemed to be as important as the communist dinosaurs of China, North Korea and Vietnam.

The inclusion in Britain's Intelligence Services Act of a reference to 'the detection of serious crime' led senior police officers to express concern that, in an attempt to justify their continued existence, the intelligence services will 'trample on our patch'. However, Warner said the role of MI6 and GCHQ in this regard, although not that of MI5, was limited to terrorism, drugs and money laundering – the last since it plays such a large part in raising funds for the first two and in concealing the profits from drug trafficking.

The arguments in Britain between the intelligence services and the police have been as nothing to the increasingly bitter battles that broke out in the United States between the FBI and the CIA in the wake of the Cold War. Bill Odom, a former NSA Director, said that during the mid-1990s the two agencies were embroiled in 'a turf war over counter-intelligence only slightly less bitter than the war in Bosnia'. National intelligence agencies are notorious for the bitter rivalries that rage between them. The relationship between the various American spy organisations has been so bad at times during the past 50 years that they have had far better relations with their British counterparts than they have enjoyed with each other. Ever since the beginning of the Second World War there has been a close link between the British and American agencies, based at first mainly on signals intelligence but also embracing other areas such as covert action. The British, having broken the German Enigma machine, initially approached the US Navy with an offer to exchange information on codebreaking in June 1940 but were rebuffed. A couple of months later, the US Army offered an exchange and in December 1940, a deal authorising a complete exchange on methods of breaking Japanese, German and Italian codes and ciphers was signed. A four-man US delegation visited Bletchley Park, bringing with them at least one Purple machine, designed to decipher high-level Japanese diplomatic ciphers and receiving a complete briefing on Enigma together with a full wiring diagram of how it worked. Stewart Menzies, the head of both MI6 and GC&CS (the Government Code and Cypher School), assured Winston Churchill, the British Prime Minister, that the discussion was 'confined to the mechanised devices we utilise and not to showing our results', a move reflecting the intense secrecy surrounding the British success and fears about US security. Nevertheless, the Americans were impressed. GC&CS noted that 'complete co-operation on every problem is now possible' and asked that a senior member of MI6 be sent to the British Embassy in Washington to liaise with the Americans.

Intelligence co-operation between the two sides inevitably grew, extending in 1942 to an agreement between the two special operations bodies, the Office of Strategic Services (OSS) and the Special Operations Executive (SOE), splitting up the world into traditional spheres of influence and thereby ensuring that neither side trod on the other's toes. Those two deals were to form the basis of the close working relationship between British and American intelligence that continues to this day. The arrangement was not without its initial difficulties. Senior members of the US Navy codebreaking operation were opposed to the deal from the start and there was often mutual suspicion between the two sides. But by 1943 the exchange of signals intelligence had become so well established that neither side could have operated effectively without it. In May 1943, the two sides agreed a formal exchange deal – the BRUSA Accord – linking their signals intelligence services.

The first three clauses of the accord summarised its intent:

1. Both the US and the British agree to exchange completely all information concerning the detection, identification and interception of signals from, and solutions of codes and cyphers used by, the Military and Airforces of the Axis powers, including secret services (*Abwehr*).
2. The US will assume as a main responsibility the reading of Japanese Military and Air codes and cyphers.
3. The British will assume as a main responsibility the reading of German and Italian Military and Air Codes and cyphers.

Quite how interdependent the two sides were to become was evident when they began to consider the post-war intelligence requirements. The agreement had given them access to a range of intelligence that it would have been virtually impossible for either side, and in particular Britain, to acquire on its own and which had made the analysis of enemy intentions child's play. There was no question but that it must continue. A joint conference was held in London in September 1944 to discuss the shape of future SIGINT exchanges. By mid-1945 the War Office and the US War Department were exchanging intelligence on the Soviet Union, and the two sides' photographic reconnaissance organisations had begun to share imagery of various parts of the world. But by October of that year the JIC was reporting that America had banned any exchange of intelligence. Problems had begun to creep into the exchanges, with clear signs of an American reversion to isolationism – 'although there are indications that the military authorities in Washington were not in sympathy with this policy which has probably been laid down by the State Department'. The McMahon Act, passed partly in reaction to the discovery of the Soviet agent Alan Nunn May, a British scientist on the allied atomic-weapons programme, prevented virtually any exchange of atomic information, the top priority of British intelligence at the time. But, despite the official policy, behind the scenes the close co-operation continued, partly as a result of the close personal relationships built up during the war but mainly because the two countries' intelligence systems were now inextricably intertwined. Any attempt by either side to withdraw from the BRUSA relationship would have seriously damaged the intelligence-gathering capabilities of both. Not only would their coverage of the world be seriously diminished, but since each knew the other's most vital secrets, the two sides must for security reasons remain permanently bound together.

Following a meeting of the British Chiefs of Staff held in late 1945 to examine the close relationship, Andrew Cunningham, the then Chief of Naval Staff, recorded in his diary that there had been 'much discussion about 100% co-operation with the USA about SIGINT. Decided that less than 100% was not worth having'. This was a feeling shared at the highest level on the other side of the Atlantic. The American military's willingness to continue with the relationship, despite its opponents, was bolstered not just by personal relationships but by a top-secret presidential edict. This gave the US Joint

Chiefs of Staff *carte blanche* 'to extend, modify or discontinue this collaboration, as determined to be in the best interests of the United States'.

So the relationship grew, and in 1948 the new Soviet threat led to the signing of the UKUSA Accord, a landmark agreement under which the two sides, joined as junior partners by Britain's imperial allies, Canada, Australia and New Zealand, carved up the world between them. The United States took responsibility for the Americas and much, although not all, of the Far East, while Britain covered its traditional spheres of influence in Africa, the Middle East and sub-continental Asia. The most important target areas – eastern Europe and the Soviet Union – were shared between Britain and America. The extent of the interdependency was evident in a report prepared by the US State Department's Bureau of Intelligence and Research in advance of a 1968 visit to America by the then Labour Prime Minister, Harold Wilson. The report, prepared for Dean Rusk, the American Secretary of State, said: 'In the intelligence field, the US and the UK give each other a greater volume and wider variety of information than either does to any of its other allies. The arrangements provide for exchange of information gathered both from overt and covert sources; for the swapping of estimates; and for the preparation of joint estimates. There is a division of labor in certain geographic and functional fields, and on some areas and subjects, each nation is dependent for its intelligence mainly on the other.'

But the ability to acquire such large amounts of intelligence does not necessarily aid consumers. Indeed, if too much information is passed on, it will only hamper their efforts to understand what is going on. So the raw intelligence information is analysed and reports are written. These are then passed further up the line, where they are in turn analysed in conjunction with material from other sources. Fresh reports are then compiled, pulling together all the available intelligence and presenting it to the consumers in a way that will provide them with only the information that they need to make policy decisions and not take up their time with material that is irrelevant to the decisions to be made. The maxim 'need to know' is primarily concerned with security: the fewer people who know about any individual source or the information it is providing, the safer it is. But it is also important that both consumers and initial analysts are not burdened with information they do not 'need to know'. If an intelligence reporter assessing the significance of a piece of information at the primary level of collection were to bring in material from a separate source his report would become tarnished, making it far more difficult for the analyst producing the final report for the consumer to assess the relative value of the information at his disposal. One source would gain extra credence by appearing to be backed up by information emanating from another. The effect would be like Chinese whispers, with inaccuracies introduced into the information on which the final intelligence assessment was made.

For this reason, an intelligence-reporting network has to be very carefully integrated. The British system has been repeatedly changed in response to perceived intelligence failures, and began to evolve into its present relatively well-integrated form shortly before the Second World War. Until the mid-1930s Britain had no system for co-ordinating the work of its various intelligence bodies or for providing assessments that drew together information from all available sources. But in January 1936 the War Ministry produced a report entitled *Central Machinery for the Co-ordination of Intelligence*, which recommended the setting up of a special body to perform precisely that function. Originally called the Inter-Service Intelligence Committee (ISIC), it was made up of senior members of the three service intelligence branches. But these organisations were themselves largely disorganised and the system was at best haphazard. Within six months came the first of many attempts to fine-tune it, with the ISIC made directly subordinate to the Chiefs of Staff and renamed the Joint Intelligence Committee.

The new system worked little better and there was a further reorganisation in July 1939, two months before the start of the Second World War, with the JIC coming under Foreign Office chairmanship. Its role was 'the assessment and co-ordination of intelligence' in order to improve 'the intelligence organisation of the country as a whole'. But it remained hampered by the fact that it had no intelligence analysts of its own. Far from co-ordinating and editing the incoming intelligence to produce a more accessible product, the JIC became overburdened by a variety of demands from various customers and ended up putting out bland and uninformative assessments, at one point adding to a particularly uninspired list of possible German moves the distinctly unhelpful caveat: 'which of these courses the enemy will select will depend less on logical deduction than on the personal and unpredictable decision of the Führer'. The committee was also distinctly amateurish in its approach. One JIC subcommittee, charged with getting under the skin of the enemy, produced reports which ended with the words 'Heil Hitler'.

But in May 1941, this subcommittee was replaced by the Joint Intelligence Staff, which provided the JIC with its first professional intelligence assessments staff. There was an immediate improvement in the standards of reports – helped in no small part by the fact that a large number of Ultra codebreaking reports were now being produced and by the introduction of more free-thinking civilian analysts. From then on most of the reports produced by the JIS could be passed on to the War Cabinet as so-called 'finals', without amendment. Assessing the reasons why Germany lost the war, the JIC pointed among other things to a failure of intelligence. 'The weakness and failure of the war were due to an ill-directed, badly organised and corrupt Abwehr and to the absence of any inter-service staff for the co-ordination and appreciation of intelligence.'

After the war the JIC continued in its role as an intelligence clearing-house, undergoing a number of changes before reaching its present form. The most important of these were the 1957 decision to bring it into the Cabinet Office and therefore closer to the decision-making process; the creation, in 1968, of the post of Intelligence Co-ordinator and of an assessments staff to write consolidated reports; and the removal, following the Falklands conflict, of Foreign Office chairmanship, in order to give the JIC 'a more independent and critical role'.

The JIC sets Britain's national intelligence requirements, reviewing them annually, and oversees the whole of the UK intelligence community to ensure that the target areas are covered as efficiently as possible. It co-ordinates intelligence from all the available sources, including the media, as part of its brief 'to monitor and give early warning of the development of direct or indirect foreign threats to British interests, whether political, military or economic ... to assess events and situations relating to external affairs, defence, terrorism, major international criminal activity, scientific, technical and international economic matters'.

According to Sir Percy Cradock, a former JIC Chairman, 'the committee gathers together all the information, secret and non-secret, and produces assessments of situations abroad or sometimes at home which are likely to be threatening to affect British interests – for example Iraq, the former Soviet Union, terrorist threats of various kinds.'

Intelligence from all sources is disseminated to a variety of customers, many of whom will have made specific requests for a certain type of informa tion and will receive detailed reports on those issues direct from the agencies. But if that detail were to be sent to every customer it would simply overload the system, so most reports also go to the JIC for incorporation into more general reports. 'The total number of intelligence reports is indeed huge,' John Major told the 1995 Scott Inquiry. 'The amount of intelligence reports reaching the Foreign and Commonwealth Office, for example, would be around 40,000 a year, and that would probably be – GCHQ and SIS split down – about two-thirds GCHQ and one-third SIS.'

The reports from the various agencies and outstations are then examined by the JIC's assessments staff. 'Some of that intelligence would be extremely valuable, some not so,' Major said. 'Quite a strong filtering process is needed. It is clearly absurd that ministers should read 40,000 pieces of intelligence, but it would be filtered through the appropriate machinery and, where intelligence was thought to be relevant, validated and reliable – reliable being a key point – the officials would endeavour to put that before ministers.' Clearly if a piece of intelligence is of urgent interest it will be put before the relevant minister as soon as possible. But, in terms of general strategic intelligence, the assessments staff collate it, analyse it, and where appropriate incorporate it into draft JIC reports. These include special evaluations of a particular situation or topic and the Weekly Survey of Intelligence for ministers known as the Red Book. But there will also be daily or more frequent reports on situations where Britain has a special interest, such as Bosnia or Sierra Leone, and occasionally, as in the Kosovo conflict and the wars in Afghanistan and Iraq, an unlimited number dependent only on the relative importance of the new information.

The drafts of the long-term and weekly reports are examined and, where appropriate, amended by Current Intelligence Groups, JIC subcommittees made up of specialists and experts on various areas or fields of interest, many of them seconded from other government departments. 'These groups tend to be geographical, for example, one on the Middle East, one on the Far East, one on the former Soviet Union,' Sir Percy Cradock said. 'But there are also functional ones dealing with terrorism and also dealing with economic matters. There is a staff of perhaps forty people plus a very high-powered secretariat to get the reports out in short order.' The long-term and weekly reports are then passed on to the JIC, which will decide how and to whom they should be disseminated.

The full JIC normally meets once a week in the Cabinet Office and is made up of senior Foreign Office and Treasury Department officials; the heads of MI5, MI6 and GCHQ; the Chief of Defence Intelligence and his deputy; the Intelligence Co-ordinator, and the Chief of the Assessments Staff. Liaison officers from the USA, Canada, Australia and New Zealand also attend some meetings. The committee 'tries to answer the first question in any crisis', Sir Percy, said 'namely, "What is the nature of the problem? What is the nature of the threat?", leaving it to ministers to decide the second question, which is, "What is the policy response to it?" It is a very flexible and efficient machine which serves British interests well and is much admired by our allies.'

Ministerial control over the intelligence machine is exercised by a Cabinet subcommittee, the Ministerial Committee on the Intelligence Services, comprising the Prime Minister, the Foreign, Defence and Home Secretaries, and the Chancellors of the Exchequer and the Duchy of Lancaster. Within the permanent government – the Civil Service – the top intelligence body is the Permanent Secretaries' Committee on the Intelligence Services, chaired by the Cabinet Secretary and including the permanent under-secretaries at the Foreign and Commonwealth Office, the Ministry of Defence, the Home Office and the Treasury. But the day-to-day running of British intelligence is carried out by the JIC's secretariat, led by its chairman, and by the Intelligence Co-ordinator. The committee reports to the Cabinet Secretary or, where military issues are directly involved, to the Armed Forces Chiefs of Staff. But the Intelligence Co-ordinator has direct access to the Prime Minister, as do the heads of MI5, MI6 and GCHQ.

The intelligence has arrived on the desk of the policy-makers, but how much influence it exerts on their decisions depends on a number of factors. A report will need to be easily accessible merely to ensure that it is read. Whether or not they are always busy, politicians see themselves as such, and any analysis that does not immediately make its point is likely to be discarded. Few people reach the elevated position of national policy-making without having a high opinion of their own abilities. Poorly worded reports will result in the consumers deciding that their own assessments are better informed. The best-known example of this was Winston Churchill, who at one point in the Second World War became so frustrated with the standard of reports he was receiving that he offered to do the analysis of the raw intelligence himself.

The Scott Inquiry into the Matrix-Churchill affair revealed a worryingly low regard for intelligence reports among British Cabinet ministers. 'They were significantly less riveting than the novels would have you believe,' said David Mellor, who as a former Home Office and Foreign Office minister would have had dealings with both MI5 and MI6. 'They were not as interesting as metal boxes marked "eat after reading",' recalled Lord Howe, Foreign Secretary under Margaret Thatcher. 'In my early days, I was naïve enough to get excited about intelligence reports. Many look, at first sight, to be important and interesting and significant. Then when we check them they are not even straws in the wind. They are cornflakes in the wind.'

Policy-makers frequently point a finger at the analyst for getting it wrong and, as in the Matrix-Churchill affair, usually have a vested interest in doing so. But the commonest failures of intelligence occur because it is disregarded by the consumer or because the policy it sought to help was itself wrong. Intelligence, however accurate it may be, will have little or no beneficial effect if basic foreign or defence policy is flawed. The intelligence reporter is in a no-win situation. If he is right and his analysis is accepted, policy will be changed and his 'negative' assessments will be shown automatically to be incorrect. If he is wrong, or if his assessment does not coincide with considered opinion, he becomes a convenient whipping-boy for those in charge. The inevitable result is that too often intelligence is diluted at various stages in the analysis process merely to match the perceptions rather than the requirements of the consumer.

It was ever thus. During the Israelites' exodus from Egypt, God told Moses to send spies into Canaan to discover whether it was safe to settle there. They returned with reports of 'a land flowing with milk and honey' but disagreed over the danger posed by the Canaanites. Caleb, the leader of the spies, reported that there was no significant threat, but the majority of the Israelites were afraid and Moses ignored his spymaster's advice in favour of popular opinion. His failure to trust the intelligence assessment led to the Israelites spending the next 40 years wandering in the wilderness. It is unlikely to have been the first time that the word of a spy was distrusted. It was certainly not the last.

Three

Britain's Three Great Spymasters

Spies you are lights in state, but of base stuffe, who, when you have burnt your selves down to the snuffe, stinke, and are throwne away. Ende faire enough.

Ben Jonson

The Israelites had more success with espionage once Moses had died. Joshua's demolition of the walls of Jericho was set up by two spies sent into the city where they were assisted by Rahab the harlot. She gave them lodgings in her home and, when the soldiers came looking for them, hid them on her roof under stalks of flax. In return, Rahab and her family were spared the widespread killing that followed the fall of the city. The early Chinese also knew the value of good intelligence. Sun Tzu, the sixth-century BC military tactician who wrote the classic book on warfare, *Bing Fa* (*The Art of War*), claimed that 'he who knows his adversary as well as he knows himself will never suffer defeat'. An examination of the ancient battle narrative *Tso-Chuan* (*Tradition of Tso*), which dates from some time between 770BC and 403BC, shows that the Chinese had already worked out a set of basic military and diplomatic intelligence requirements. These included not just enemy locations; strengths and weaponry, but also the morale of troops and the population as a whole; and biographical detail of enemy leaders. The spy should be valued highly, Sun Tzu said. 'No one in the armed forces is treated as familiarly as spies and no one is given rewards as rich as those given to spies.'

The ancient Greeks used their ambassadors, the *proxenia,* to gather foreign intelligence while in Athens the role of internal secret police was carried out by the *sycophants,* literally fig-informers, who acquired their name from their original role preventing illegal exports of figs. The Romans were fairly sanguine about the need for intelligence, but nevertheless kept a close watch on dissidence at home. Members of the fire brigade, the *speculatores*, were expected to keep an eye out for signs of dissent. This internal security role was later taken over by corn merchants, the *frumentarii*, who were considered to have their ears close to the ground in the markets. But not surprisingly the use of informants was unpopular. 'Rome of old plumbed the depths of slavery, robbed even of the interchange of ideas by the secret police,' complained the Roman historian Tacitus. The *frumentarii* were abolished in the third century AD by the emperor Diocletian, who replaced them with a more organised security service – the *agentes in rebus*, later given the appropriate title of *curiosi*.

Like the Romans, the great Muslim empires of the Middle-Ages employed spies to ensure that their populations were kept in check. In the ninth century, the Caliph of Baghdad paid 1,700 old women to inform on their fellow citizens while the 11th-century Persian Nizam al-Mulk wrote: 'Sending out police agents and spies shows that the ruler is just, vigilant and sagacious.' In 16th-century India, the Great Mogul Akbar's security service comprised an army of 4,000 scavengers, pedlars and merchants. Their reports were relayed to the Mogul via a central council of advisers and analysts, which presented him with a daily intelligence summary.

Despite King Alfred's famous infiltration of the Danish camp disguised as a minstrel, the British came late to spying. But by the beginning of the 14th century, King Edward II was ordering the seizure of 'all letters coming from or going to parts beyond the seas'. A royal writ dated 18 December 1324 reminded ports officials that it was part of their duties to 'make diligent scrutiny of all persons passing from parts beyond the seas to England to stop all letters concerning which sinister suspicions might arise'.

Cardinal Wolsey's open seizure of diplomatic correspondence sparked strong protests. Reporting back to the Doge in Venice, Sgr Giustiniani, the Venetian ambassador in London complained: 'The letters received by me from your Sublimity had been taken out of the hands of the courier at Canterbury by the royal officials and opened and read: the like being done by private letters from the most noble, the ambassador Badoer of France and others.'

Shakespeare alluded to the practice in *Henry V*, writing: 'The King hath note of all that they intend by interception which they dream not of.' There have even been suggestions that Shakespeare's knowledge of intelligence techniques stemmed from a role as a spy, one of a number of Elizabethan playwrights employed by Sir Francis Walsingham, Queen Elizabeth I's spymaster and the organiser of Britain's first really effective intelligence service. According to one biography, Shakespeare used the covername William Hall to undertake secret missions in Europe. The archives of Canterbury Cathedral record that a William Hall, one of Walsingham's agents, was sent on missions to Denmark, the Netherlands and Bohemia by Anthony Munday, himself a playwright but more importantly the Archbishop of Canterbury's *pursuivant*, or security chief. Although there is little evidence to back up the allegations that Hall and Shakespeare were one and the same, it might explain the previous mystery of Shakespeare's dedication of his sonnets to 'Mr W H all happiness'.

Under Henry VIII, Wolsey and Cromwell had run internal security networks aimed primarily at the Roman Catholic church but there was little real interest in collecting intelligence abroad. It was left to Elizabeth's spymasters to create Britain's first foreign espionage service, based around the English ambassadors across Europe. When Sir Nicholas Throgmorton was appointed England's ambassador to France in 1559, he began collecting intelligence for William Cecil, Elizabeth's chief minister, on French support for her half-sister Mary Queen of Scots and the Scottish rebels. But Throgmorton made the mistake of becoming too closely connected with Cecil's opponents at court and was replaced by Walsingham, a man widely recognised as the father of the British secret services. He developed a large network of secret agents, which he used against the banned Roman Catholic Church; to foil a series of plots to overthrow Elizabeth; and to prepare for the war against Spain. As Principal Secretary, his main role was 'to have care to the intelligence abroad' and so effective was he that it was said that 'not a mouse could creep out of any ambassador's chamber but Mr Secretary would have one of its whiskers'.

Walsingham set up a cipher department in his own home in London under the guidance of John Dee, the Queen's astrologer. Dee's intercepts of correspondence were so successful that the Spanish Governor of the Netherlands complained that the coded reports he sent home were read in London before they even reached Madrid. But perhaps Walsingham's main success was in foiling the Babington plot and providing the evidence that would lead to Mary's execution. One of Dee's cryptographers was a Catholic 'coney-catcher' or conman called Gilbert Gifford, whom Walsingham used as part of an operation aimed at incriminating Mary. He had her moved to Chartley Manor, near Titbury in Derbyshire, and sent Gifford to offer his services as a courier. Messages between Mary and her supporters were to be smuggled in and out in casks of beer delivered to the house by a Burton brewer. The plan worked and very soon Gifford was not only intercepting and reading all of Mary's correspondence; he had also obtained the keys to the main papal codes. Anthony Babington, a former page to Mary, wrote to her asking her to approve a hopelessly optimistic set of plans he and five incompetent co-conspirators had put together. The overthrow and execution of 'the usurper' Elizabeth was to follow an invasion carried out by troops sent from France and timed to coincide with an uprising by English Catholics. In a long response approving the plans, Mary wrote back to Babington detailing various points over which he should take special care and asking 'how the six gentlemen deliberate to proceed'. Walsingham could not be sure who all the conspirators were. But when news leaked out and Babington disappeared along with five other suspects, they were hunted down and executed.

Walsingham's intelligence network was also instrumental in the defeat of the Armada. A year before the Spanish fleet set sail, Walsingham drew up 'the Plot for Intelligence out of Spain'. This called for the interception of any correspondence from the French ambassador to Spain; the setting up of intelligence bureaux in various places around Europe; and the dispatch of agents to the main Spanish ports to report on any preparations for an invasion. One of Walsingham's agents even took confession from the French ambassador in London. Giordiano Bruno, the Italian philosopher and poet, was a priest in the ambassador's household who, under the covername of Henry Fagot, supplied Walsingham with detailed intelligence, including details of one ludicrous Spanish plan to assassinate the Queen by impregnating her underwear with poison. Bruno was not typical of Walsingham's agents. Most were criminals, recruited for their specialist skills or their willingness to do any kind of work, however dangerous, in order to avoid execution or prison.

Walsingham once said: 'If there were no knaves, honest men should hardly come by the truth of any enterprise against them'. A number of others were talent-spotted at Cambridge, a university that seems to have provided more than its fair share of spies.

One of these was Christopher Marlowe, the playwright, who interrupted his studies at Corpus Christi College to travel to the English Seminary at Rheims, where he infiltrated the ranks of those Catholic priests who were being trained to work undercover in England. Marlowe returned to England with the priests, who were disguised as Huguenot refugees, and promptly turned them over to the authorities. He then resumed his studies but was soon accused of treason. In a memorandum to the university authorities absolving Marlowe of any guilt, the Privy Council wrote that while it was true that he had 'gone beyond the seas to Reames', he had 'done Her Majesty a good service' and deserved to be rewarded not defamed 'for all his good service'.

He was not so fortunate some years later when he was again denounced in what may have been a campaign against Sir Walter Raleigh, the playwright's most prominent patron, by supporters of his rival for royal favour, the Earl of Essex. One of Essex's servants claimed that Marlowe had converted him to atheism. He also alleged that the playwright was the author of one of a number of anti-Protestant tracts which had appeared on posters in London, 'exceeding the rest in lewdness', and of a three-page treatise, 'denying the deity of Christ', which he had allegedly read to Raleigh. On 20 May 1593, Marlowe appeared before the Privy Council to answer the allegations. The council ordered a secret service agent called Richard Baines to produce a report on the playwright's activities. Baines claimed that Marlowe had described all protestants as hypocritical asses and had 'intent to go to the enemy', in this case the Scottish rebels. 'This Marlowe persuadeth men to Atheism willing them not to be afeared of bugbeares and hobgoblines and utterly scorning both God and his ministers,' Baines said. His report ended with a recommendation that 'the mouth of so dangerous a member may be stopped'. That report was delivered on 27 May. Within three days, Marlowe was dead, supposedly stabbed in a brawl over a bar bill. But behind the official records lies evidence of something quite different. The inquest was told that he had been at a private house in Deptford with three other men, Nicholas Skeres, Robert Poley and Ingram Frizer, his killer. The four men spent the day quietly 'alone together', taking lunch and walking in the garden. Skeres, Frizer and Poley told the coroner that they passed the evening playing backgammon while Marlowe rested on a bed. A row broke out over the bill or 'recknynge', Marlowe sprang from the bed, snatched a dagger from Frizer and beat him about the head with the handle. Frizer grabbed it back and drove the point into Marlowe's skull, killing him instantly. The coroner accepted a plea of self-defence and Frizer was granted a royal pardon. Nevertheless, there is more than a little evidence that Marlowe's death was in some way related to his undercover work and the recommendation to the Privy Council that his mouth be 'stopped'. At least two of his companions that day, Poley and Skeres, had been members of Walsingham's network of agents. Poley was a major player in the operation that uncovered the Babington plot and led ultimately to the execution of Mary Queen of Scots. He had also carried out secret missions to Denmark, France, Scotland and the Netherlands. Skeres, a petty thief and 'coney-catcher', had been involved on the fringes of the Babington operation. Ingram Frizer, Marlowe's killer, was a close associate of Skeres and like him a member of London's criminal fraternity. The long conversations and quiet walks in the garden of a private house bear all the hallmarks of the debriefing of an agent, presumably carried out by Poley, and having been debriefed, Marlowe would have known too much to have been allowed a public trial. The alleged row over 'the recknynge' would have been a simple method of disguising an assassination.

Walsingham himself had died three years before Marlowe, virtually penni-less. Elizabeth rarely provided substantial funds for intelligence-gathering and he had mortgaged his own estates to finance secret service operations. His will, made a year before his death, asked that he be buried simply and cheaply 'in respect of the greatness of my debts and the mean state I shall leave my wife and heirs in'. But despite the lack of funds, Walsingham was possibly Britain's most efficient spymaster. His death was reported back to Madrid by Spain's ambassador in London with the words: 'Secretary Walsingham has just expired, at which there is much sorrow.' King Philip noted in the margin of the report: 'There, yes. But it is good news here.' With his passing, English intelligence lapsed into its previous state of ineptitude, relying primarily on the efforts of its ambassadors abroad. But the interception of letters continued and in November 1641, there were again complaints from the Venetian ambassador, this time over 'the opening and detention of the letters coming from France and Antwerp'.

Under Oliver Cromwell, intelligence-gathering was given far greater resources than ever before. The Commonwealth's espionage network was centred on the postal system with John Thurloe, Cromwell's spymaster or Number One Argus, taking the role of Postmaster-General and installing a 'Secret Man' in the Post Office to open and examine any suspicious letters. The process was enshrined in an Act of Parliament which declared openly that the postal system was the best means 'to discover and prevent many dangerous and wicked designs . . . the intelligence whereof cannot well be communicated but by letter of escript'. Thurloe supplemented this intelligence-gathering system with an extensive network of 'subtil and sly fellowes'. Cromwell's willingness to provide the funds to support Thurloe's espionage system – Dr Samuel Pepys recorded in his diaries that the Commonwealth intelligence budget was £70,000 a year – contrasted sharply with the reluctance of Elizabeth I to part with any cash and undoubtedly ensured its effectiveness. 'Thereby Cromwell carried the secrets of all the princes of Europe at his girdle,' wrote Pepys. While his account of the sum allocated to the Commonwealth intelligence budget is almost certainly an exaggeration – the official records put the largest sum allocated to espionage during Cromwell's time as £2,000 – Thurloe's spy network was extremely effective. Cardinal Mazarin, the French Prime Minister, complained that whatever was discussed in his cabinet was known to Thurloe within a few days, and Sgr Giovanni Sagredo, the Venetian ambassador in London, said: 'There is no government on earth which divulges its affairs less than England, or is more punctually informed of those of the others.' Thurloe, Britain's second great spymaster, was particularly successful in infiltrating his agents into the Sealed Knot society, the secret Royalist council, and probably only survived the Reformation because of his claim to have 'a black book that would hang many that went for cavalries'. It was under Charles II that the dedicated intelligence budget that still exists today was first introduced. The Secret Service Fund appears in the main to have been used to pay for the services of various mistresses, although some of them almost certainly did act as spies.

Although both the Parliamentarian and Royalist forces had employed 'Scoutmasters' to gather intelligence during the Civil War, it was Marlborough who oversaw the birth of British military intelligence. His victory over a Franco-Bavarian force at Blenheim in 1704 was eased by a German spy who gave him a complete breakdown of the composition of the French force under Marshal Tallard and its battle plans. But following the Treaty of Utrecht, he was hauled before Parliament accused of defrauding the public purse. Marlborough's defence was that the allowances for secret service had been so pitiful that he had been forced to pay his spies out of other accounts. 'I cannot suppose that I need to say how essential a part of the Service this is,' Marlborough said. 'No war can be conducted successfully without early and good intelligence and such advices cannot be had but at very great expense. I affirm that whatever sums have been received on this account have been constantly employed in procuring intelligence. And I believe I may venture to affirm that I have in the article for Secret Services, saved the Government near four times the sum this deduction amounts to.'

During the same era, the writer Daniel Defoe was drawn into the world of intelligence, partly by a perennial lack of money. He was employed as a secret agent by Robert Harley, Earl of Oxford and Queen Anne's Northern Secretary. Defoe compiled a 'Scheme for General Intelligence' in 1704, outlining the need for a string of agents across the country, which would not just gather intelligence but also be involved in counter-espionage. 'For as intelligence is most useful to us, so keeping our enemies from intelligence among us is as valuable a hand,' he wrote. Posted to Edinburgh to run a network of agents against the opponents of the union of Scotland and England, Defoe told Harley: 'I have my spies and my pensioners in every place and confess 'tis is the easiest thing in the world to hire people here to betray their friends.' Robert Walpole, Prime Minister during the 1720s and 1730s, used the Secret Service Fund incessantly to bribe his fellow politicians. Walpole, who was credited with inventing the expression 'every man has his price', spent around £79,000 a year on so-called Secret Service, £40,000 of it on the 1734 election campaign alone.

Lord Chatham (Pitt the Elder) reorganised the British system of secret service again, placing the emphasis on the use of Britain's ambassadors abroad supplemented by the Post Office's interception of diplomatic correspondence. But it was under his son William Pitt the Younger that the next great British spymaster emerged. William Wickham came into espionage as a result of his friendship with Lord Grenville, the Foreign Secretary, whom he had met when they were both students at Oxford. The authorities were clearly pleased with his first mission abroad, 'in a secret foreign correspondence' for Grenville in 1793, because he was soon given a counter-espionage role keeping an eye on French spies in Britain. Wickham was appointed as a Superintendent of Aliens, working for the newly formed Alien Office, an early version of MI5, which was subordinate to the Home Office. Anyone suspected of coming into contact with French agents came under Wickham's surveillance. Defending the office's operations, he described it as 'a sort of System of Preventative Police. Without bustle, noise or anything that can attract Public Attention, Government possess here the most powerful means of Observation and Information . . . that was ever placed in the hands of a Free Government.'

Wickham's role was not confined to counter-espionage however, he also controlled Britain's foreign intelligence activities receiving considerable backing for a number of operations, most of which appear to have been unsuccessful. Their failure was not for lack of funds. Between 1793 and 1802, Wickham personally received a total of £187,494 9s 2d from the Secret Service Vote for the purpose of 'detecting, preventing or defeating treasonable or other dangerous conspiracies against the state'. Quite what he did with the money is difficult to gauge, although it seems likely that some of it was used to keep the Austrians and Russians on side against France. What he certainly managed to do was upset the French. Based initially in Switzerland, under the cover of 'Minister Plenipotentiary to Switzerland and the German courts', Wickham spent much of his time unsuccessfully attempting to start a Royalist uprising in France. In 1797, the Swiss demanded his expulsion from Berne on the grounds that he was acting 'not as a diplomatic agent but as a fomenter of insurrection'. Wickham moved to Frankfurt and then returned to England as an under-secretary of state in the Home Office, mixing his time between keeping an eye on the rebels in Ireland, searching for French spies in England

and continuing his foreign adventures. Having failed in an attempt to move the main centre of British foreign intelligence from Switzerland to either Vienna or Berlin – the Austrians and Prussians both refused to accept his credentials on the grounds that he was 'personally obnoxious to the French Government' – Wickham went to Dublin as Chief Secretary for Ireland. There he received praise from the Irish authorities for the way in which he quickly set up 'an alphabetical list of all persons against whom informations have been made, when given, by whom'. But countering revolution in Ireland involved a great deal of association with the lower classes and criminals, something Wickham had always resisted, to the detriment of his espionage operations both at home and abroad. He quit after his agents failed to predict the 1803 uprising. The work was 'distasteful', he said. He had not known of the revolt because the rebels 'were mostly all mechanics, or working people. If the higher order of society had been connected, they would divulge the plot for the sake of gain'. He was pursued into retirement by the Public Auditor's Commission, who found it difficult to accept that such a large proportion of the public purse could be spent by one man without so much as a single receipt being produced. Wickham was forced to swear three different affidavits to the effect that the money had indeed been spent on 'detecting, preventing or defeating treasonable or other dangerous conspiracies' before the frustrated accountants finally gave up their witch hunt.

Wickham's extensive control over Britain's intelligence activities would seem to qualify him as the third of the great spymasters, after Walsingham and Thurloe. But despite Pitt's willingness to fund Wickham's many abortive missions, the French secret service under Joseph Fouché, the Duke of Otranto, was so much more effective that the English used the French words *espionage* to describe the process of intelligence-gathering and *surveillance* for the main process of domestic security. Fouché himself was known as Europe's spymaster. *Espionage* was, the second Earl of Shelburne remarked grandly: 'a word which, I thank God, will not yet admit to an English interpretation'. Fouché ran an extremely efficient secret service bringing together the police and a widespread network of informers and secret agents. He perfected the late-night knock on the door that was to become the hallmark of the secret police throughout the world. Napoleon said of him: 'Intrigue was as necessary to Fouché as his daily bread. He intrigued at all times, everywhere, in all ways, and with everybody.'

Both Napoleon and his British opponent the Duke of Wellington were enthusiastic believers in good intelligence, spending a considerable part of each day reading the various dispatches from agents. The French Emperor was obsessed with intelligence, reportedly claiming that one well-placed spy was as valuable as several divisions. He set up a *Bureau d'Intelligence* within his own personal quarters or *Maison* with responsibility for obtaining intelligence from a wide range of sources, including agents infiltrated into all the important enemy cities. The French General Staff was responsible for the collection of intelligence in the field, principally obtained from forward patrols and from the interrogation of deserters or prisoners of war. This was supplemented by the work of staff officers briefed for special missions by the Emperor himself.

Wellington was so aware of the importance of good intelligence that he initially insisted all reports came to him alone. 'All the business of war,' he wrote, 'indeed all the business of life, is to endeavour to find out what you don't know by what you do. That's what I called: "guessing what was on the other side of the hill".' Shortly before the Napoleonic Wars, a Depot of Military Knowledge had been set up in the British Army's Quartermaster-General's Department at Horse Guards in Whitehall. Wellington also set up his own Field Intelligence Department in Brussels. French agents provided a constant supply of intelligence, according to one government account. 'At Ghent and in constant correspondence with Wellington was the Duc de Feltre and with him was M. Tabauer, late *Chef de Bureau* of the French War Ministry. At Paris, the Chief Clerk of the War Ministry was in our pay and in constant communication with us, while the mysterious "B" of the *Supplementary des Batches* kept us accurately informed of the march of events.' During the Peninsular War, he even had his own codebreaker, George Scovell, breaking the French ciphers. With this assistance and such good sources inside the French camp, it is scarcely surprising that Wellington claimed to have known 'everything the enemy was doing and planning to do'.

Not all the early 19th-century military tacticians were as enthused by espionage as Napoleon and Wellington. Carl von Clausewitz, author of the classic treatise *On War*, had a low regard for spies. 'Many intelligence reports in war are contradictory; even more are false and most are uncertain,' he wrote, before adding derisively: 'In short, most intelligence is false.' But his fellow military writer Baron Antoine-Henri Jomini disagreed, possibly as a result of his service on Napoleon's staff. In *The Art of War*, Jomini wrote: 'A general should neglect no means of gaining information of the enemy's movements, and for this purpose, should make use of reconnaissances, spies, bodies of light troops commanded by capable officers, signals and questioning deserters and prisoners.' He also stressed the need to confirm information from one source with that of another, by adding the rider that 'perfect reliance should be placed on none of these means'.

Throughout the Napoleonic Wars, British intelligence had been augmented by the continued espionage activities of the Post Office. By the 18th century, Thurloe's 'Secret Man' had become a Secret Department, charged with monitoring correspondence between foreign embassies and their governments, and in 1703 it was further strengthened by the creation of its own Secret Deciphering Branch, run by the Rev Edward Willes, an Oxford don who later became the Bishop of Bath and Wells. The Bishop and his sons ran the deciphering branch as if it were a family concern and, in 1844, when it was finally abolished, his grandson Francis Willes and great-grandson John Lovell, who carried out the deciphering at their home in Hanger Hill, west London, were pensioned off with secret service money, still protesting loudly at the great financial loss to their family.

The Foreign Office dismissed their complaints, pointing out that since taking over from his uncle, Willes had cracked 'scarcely any' codes. According to one official, there were great suspicions that he was merely 'a fraudulent trickster who leads a life of pleasure and relaxation at his house at Hanger Hill out of sight of the office'.

The Secret Department itself was housed in the Post Office headquarters but was similarly manned largely by members of one family. John Ernest Bode, 'Chief Clerk in the Secret Service of Hanover,' was brought to England in 1732 to forge new seals for the intercepted letters 'which was then badly done'. Two of Bode's brothers and two of his sons joined the Secret Department. It appears to have been a fairly efficient operation, surviving one parliamentary inquiry in 1742. John Barbutt, then Secretary to the Post Office, explained to the MPs why the Secret Department had been set up.

'The projectors of a General System of Postal Communication seem to have perceived the necessity for the public welfare of subjecting it to some control,' Barbutt said. 'They did not consider it to be the duty of Government to facilitate and protect the conveyance of treason from one end of the country to the other. Nor probably do right-minded people of the present day think it is good for the state that the Postmaster General should propel the correspondence of wicked and designing men from Shetland to Scilly at the price of a penny.'

The vast majority of material intercepted, and where necessary deciphered, was Russian, Swedish or French, reflecting Britain's main enemies at the time, although how much of it was of any great value remains far from clear. Successive heads of the Secret Department repeatedly protected its budget by stressing its deterrent effect. After intercepted correspondence led, in 1752, to the capture of a French spy, the then Chief Clerk of the department wrote: 'His conviction seems to have had so good an effect that the many spies then in London have been deterred as far as it appeared to me from giving intelligence to the enemy.'

But there were continued calls for the department to be axed to save money, particularly once the introduction of diplomatic couriers at the end of the Napoleonic Wars led to a dramatic reduction in the amount of intercepted material. In the late 1830s, under John Bode's grandson William, the department was persuaded by the Home Office to step outside its brief to report on diplomatic correspondence and to open the letters of private individuals who were seen for some reason as a threat to the state, starting in 1838 with the Chartists and continuing with the ringleaders of the industrial unrest of 1842–43. The move was to be its undoing.

When it was revealed in the House of Commons that Sir James Graham, the Home Secretary, had ordered the opening of letters addressed to the Italian nationalist Giuseppi Mazzini, a political refugee in Britain, another parliamentary inquiry was ordered into the activities of the Post Office. It proved to be one inquiry too many. William Bode mounted a courageous defence of the Secret Department. Praising his staff, he gave an interesting description of the type of person he considered to be best suited to intelligence work: 'They must obviously be men of great integrity as well as discretion and diligence. They must be men of good education for besides the delicate, difficult and sometimes hazardous manual operations which are to be performed, a knowledge of many foreign languages is required of them and that knowledge must be tolerably extensive to enable them to read and understand the worst writing.'

Bode was at pains to point out that his department had stuck to its brief not to open private correspondence 'with only very few exceptions'. 'If I occasionally examined a private letter it was because there was room to believe that it contained political matters,' he said. His testimony also revealed the existence in the Post Office of another interception department that did open private correspondence. The Secret Department had only examined the Mazzini letters at the request of 'the Private Office under the Home Department', he said. Col William Maberley, the Secretary of the Post Office, who was in charge of the Private Office, had asked Bode to look at them because they were written in Italian and he could not understand them.

In an impassioned plea on behalf of his own department, Bode told the inquiry: 'Whatever opinions may be entertained in the country, Foreign Governments will not desist from a practice which they all follow, nor will they believe that the English Government has abandoned all control over the Post Office. The motive of state necessity, which can alone justify the practice, will accordingly still exist. In my humble opinion it is expedient for the service of Government.'

The inquiry was effectively a whitewash, defending the opening of private letters. 'The information which has been derived from this source has been regarded as valuable and may have given better information upon dangers apprehended in particular districts than could be derived from local observation, or than might be collected from the vague and exaggerated rumours which in periods of disturbance very usually prevail,' the inquiry concluded. 'To leave it a mystery whether or no this power is ever exercised, is the way best calculated to deter the evil-minded from applying the Post to improper uses.' The Private Office, which had been responsible for the furore in the first place, was saved. But the Secret Department was already doomed, condemned not by the inquiry but by the Foreign Office's reluctance to continue to fund its operations. It was soon suspended on the orders of the Postmaster General and its Secret Deciphering Department was closed, to the chagrin of the Willes family. Two years later, on 1 January 1847, the Secret Department itself was abolished and Bode too was pensioned off.

The demise of the Secret Office epitomised the attitude towards intelligence-gathering in the period between the Napoleonic wars and the Crimean War. When the British Army sailed for the Crimea, it had no maps of the area, let alone any useful intelligence on the strengths of the Russian forces. Edwin Laurence Godkin, the correspondent of the *London Daily News*, described in one dispatch, from the Bulgarian Black Sea port of Varna, how a British officer had been sent to Romania and Bulgaria to find horses for the cavalry. 'The ignorance which dictated this step is scarcely conceivable,' Godkin wrote. 'A single interrogatory addressed to the consul here at Varna for example would have elicited the fact that there are not 500 horses in all European Turkey fit to mount an English dragoon. When mistakes such as these are made regarding matters in which information lies within the reach of the most careless observer, one is naturally led to fear that many blunders and oversights may be at first committed in departments where knowledge is more difficult of access.'

In some quarters at least, the need for better intelligence was recognised. The Secret Service Vote was increased to £32,000 a year while the Royal Navy appealed to British consuls in the Danish and Swedish Baltic ports 'to use the utmost diligence in collecting information that would be useful, and especially such information as regards the munitions of war for the enemy's use'. Shortly after the outbreak of the war, the ambassador in Stockholm, Sir Edward Grey, reported that he had asked a Swedish trader called Ekstrom to go to the Åland islands to find out about the Russian military garrisons there. 'This person's interests are entirely on this side of the water and he is fully aware of the danger of the service he has undertaken,' Sir Edward wrote. Ekstrom returned with detailed information on the Russian garrisons on the islands but despite being paid £1,000 for the information refused to return 'on account of the vigilance of the Russian agents', claiming that 'his neck was in too great danger'. Grey also received information on the Russian movements in Finland and the state of feeling there from two different sources, one 'a gentleman', the other 'a person' – the former presumably considered more reliable than the latter – and was provided by the Swedish Foreign Secretary, Baron Steinvald, with the Swedish government intelligence assessment of the strength of the Russian armies. But the lack of intelligence available to the British Army was alarming. Thomas Best Jervis, a retired Indian Army major, mounted a campaign to force the government to set up a department in the War Department to supply the British Expedition with maps and intelligence. The lack of any intelligence was, he said, 'the result of our overweening presumption, inattention to due precautions, sheer ignorance and contempt of an enemy by no means contemptible'. On 2 February 1855, the War Department finally bowed to his demands, creating the Topographical and Statistical Department from which the current British intelligence system would eventually evolve.

Intelligence-gathering and map-making were divorced in 1871. The newly independent Statistical Department was given a brief 'to collect and classify all possible information relating to the strength, organisation, etc, of foreign armies; to keep themselves acquainted with the progress made by foreign countries in military art and science, and to preserve the information in such a form that it can be readily consulted, and made available for any purposes for which it may be required.' Two years later, the department became the Intelligence Branch, with an increased staff of 27 and an expanded brief which included military planning based on the intelligence it collected. Its funds came from the Secret Service Vote administered by the Foreign Office, which had overall sanction over intelligence activities.

Four

Discarding Morality

Nothing is more revolting to Englishmen than the espionage which forms part of the administrative system of continental despotisms.

Erskine May, *Constitutional History of England*, Vol. 2, 1863

During the early part of the 19th century, British intelligence went into decline. But the resurgence of Irish nationalism in the mid-1860s led the Home Office to mount a number of 'secret service' operations, successfully infiltrating numerous agents into the republican movement and ensuring that an attempted rebellion in March 1867 was thwarted. The Fenians then took their campaign to the mainland, killing 13 people, including a police sergeant. Fearing the start of a widespread bombing campaign, the Home Office set up its own fully fledged 'Secret Service Department' under a young Anglo-Irish lawyer called Robert Anderson. By pure chance, Anderson was able to recruit a Briton who had close contacts with the Fenians in America to infiltrate their ranks. Thomas Billis Beach adopted the alias of Henri le Caron and set up a Fenian camp in Lockhart, Illinois, with himself as camp commandant. He was rapidly promoted, first to Military Organiser of the Irish Republican Army and later to Inspector General, feeding Anderson with every detail of the IRA's operations.

In the early 1880s, the Fenians began a new bombing campaign on the mainland, killing a seven-year-old boy and leading the Metropolitan Police Criminal Investigation Department to set up a Fenian Office. The rebel campaign escalated in 1882 with the assassination of Lord Frederick Cavendish, Chief Secretary for Ireland, and Thomas Burke, his permanent under-secretary, as they were walking through Phoenix Park in Dublin. It reached its peak in the Dynamite War of 1883, when some ten bombs exploded in London alone. Sir William Vernon Harcourt, the Home Secretary, called for the creation of what was eventually to become the Special Branch. 'This is not a temporary emergency requiring a momentary remedy,' he wrote. 'Fenianism is a permanent conspiracy against English rule, which will last far beyond the term of my life and must be met by a permanent organisation to detect and to control it.'

In March 1883, the Metropolitan Police set up an Irish Bureau with a network of agents and informers run by Major Nicholas Gosselin, whose main qualification for the job was that 'he understands these Irish scoundrels and can talk to them'. It did not have an auspicious start. Just over a year after its creation, in direct response to a series of mainland bomb attacks by Fenian Dynamitards, a bomb in the public lavatory below its Scotland Yard offices destroyed a large section of the building and caused considerable injury. But the bureau survived, and four years later it became the Special Branch, with responsibility for all political crime.

British attempts at intelligence-gathering abroad remained essentially amateurish. This was the period of the Great Game, when British fears of Russian expansion south into the Indian sub-continent led to an early version of the Cold War, with both sides seeking to subvert each other's influence in central Asia. It began in the 1830s, as a prelude to the First Afghan War (1839–42), when a British officer in the Indian Army's Bombay Horse Artillery entered Afghanistan disguised as a horse-trader. He returned with the news that a Persian army with Russian advisers was preparing an assault on the western Afghan town of Herat. The Great Game continued throughout the 19th century with Britain's insistence that it be allowed to set up 'listening posts' at Herat, Kandahar, and Kashgar in order to gather intelligence on the Russian expansion in Central Asia which led to the Second Afghan War (1878–80).

Britain's operations were centred on its consul general in the Persian town of Meshed. Colonel C S Maclean controlled a widespread network of agents and 'news writers' who provide intelligence on what the Russian troops were doing. Maclean also paid substantial sums from the Secret Service fund to mullahs, merchants, and local warlords in an attempt to ensure that Britain was preferred to Russia. Mullahs were seen as being particularly influential in Meshed, the site of a Muslim shrine and frequently crowded with pilgrims from across the region. Justifying payment of bribes to one clergyman, Maclean recorded in the Secret Service accounts that 'Mullah Bashi is specially devoted to our service and is busy advocating advantage of English friendship to Persia and damaging Russian influence among his own clan'. But the agents were unreliable, rarely filing reports 'either owing to snow, or treachery, or fear of discovery,' Maclean recorded. 'It appears that the Turkoman are now afraid to run the risk of detection. The Russians are making every effort to discover our agents and several men have already been arrested on suspicion at Samarkand.' They also frequently changed sides, selling their services to the highest bidder. At one point, Maclean was paying both the senior clerks in the Russian consulate to supply 'daily notes of what the Russian consul does . . . but neither is aware of what the other does.' He even attempted to recruit a Russian 'who is specially deputed by the Russians to Meshed to talk up Russian influence' as a double agent. 'He has not been sufficiently paid and is now about to return to his home in the Caucasus,' Maclean wrote. 'He is secretly an enemy of the Russians. I hope we shall be able to communicate with him by and bye and that he will send letters regarding the sate of affairs in the Caucasus.' Maclean's work was so well regarded that he was promoted to major-general.

Between 1876 and 1897, the Secret Service Vote remained static at £15,000, less than half the sum it had been in the years following the Crimean War. In an 1893 report on the threat from France, the then Director of Military Intelligence, General E. F. Chapman, wrote: 'Neither the Naval nor the Military Intelligence Departments have any system or machinery for securing secret information from abroad such as is possessed by the corresponding departments of every great state in Europe.' Nevertheless, the report concluded that any such system would be impracticable. 'We have considered the possibility of retaining the services of Frenchmen for that purpose, but even if natives of that country could be found who were willing to supply information under such circumstances, the service would be one of too great danger to be carried out with success.'

This belief that intelligence needed to be better organised was echoed two years later in the publication, by Colonel G. A. Furse, a British Army officer, of the book *Intelligence in War*. 'The intelligence service in war does not appear to us to have met with all the attention it rightly deserves,' he wrote. 'The very term 'spy' conveys to our mind something dishonourable and disloyal. A spy, in the general acceptance of the term, is a low sneak who, from unworthy motives, dodges the actions of his fellow beings to turn the knowledge he acquires to his personal account. His underhand dealings inspire us with such horror that we would blush at the very idea of having to avail ourselves of any information obtained through such an agency.' This distaste for the whole business of espionage had to be put aside, Furse said. 'In war, spies are indispensable auxiliaries and we must discard all question of morality. We must overcome our feelings of repugnance for such an unchivalrous measure because it is imposed on us by sheer necessity.'

The Boer War brought a new respectability to spying – at least within the military. Despite some initial criticism of the War Office Intelligence Branch for an alleged lack of preparation for the war – an allegation that was subsequently shown to be unfounded – it was raised in status to an Intelligence Division. A new section was formed with special responsibility for counter-intelligence and 'secret service'. Its budget was increased to £32,000, and a Field Intelligence Department was set up in South Africa, employing at its peak a total of 132 officers and 2,321 civilians. One of the department's most famous agents was Lord Baden-Powell, the founder of the Boy Scout movement, who as a young subaltern treated spying rather like cricket, a game for the gentleman amateur. His attitude was typical of the intelligence officers of the time. 'The best spies are unpaid men who are doing it for the love of the thing,' he wrote in his book *My Adventures as a Spy*. 'It is that touch of romance and excitement which makes spying the fascinating sport it is.'

When the Boer War came to an end, the Intelligence Division, by then based at Winchester House, St James's Square, in the heart of London's clubland, was again wound down. But the success of the South African department was to lead eventually to the creation of the British Army's Intelligence Corps. Lieutenant-Colonel David Henderson, Director of Military Intelligence, South Africa, returned to England to write 'an intelligence handbook', which he called *Field Intelligence, Its Principles and Practices*. It was used as the basis for the *Regulations for Intelligence Duties in the Field*, published by the War Office in August 1904. The most significant part of Henderson's handbook was his recommendation that 'all persons, except staff officers and secret agents, permanently engaged on intelligence duties in a campaign should be formed into an Intelligence Corps'.

Henderson painted a picture of the ideal intelligence officer. 'He must be cool, courageous and adroit, patient and imperturbable, discreet and trustworthy. He must have resolution to continue unceasingly his search for information, even in the most disheartening circumstances and after repeated failures. He must have endurance to submit silently to criticism, much of which may be based on ignorance or jealousy. And he must be able to deal with men, to approach his source of information with tact and skill, whether such source be a patriotic gentleman or an abandoned traitor.'

Field Intelligence also contained an interesting contribution on the work of female intelligence operatives. 'When women are employed as secret service agents, the probability of success and the difficulty of administration are alike increased,' Henderson claimed. 'Women are frequently very useful in eliciting information. They require no disguise. If attractive, they are likely to be welcome everywhere and may be able to seduce from their loyalty those, whose assistance and indiscretion may be of use. On the other hand, they are variable, easily offended, seldom sufficiently reticent, and apt to be reckless. Their treatment requires the most watchful discretion. Usually they will work more consistently for a person rather than a principle and a lover in the Intelligence Corps makes a useful intermediary.'

During the later part of the nineteenth century and even into the early twentieth century, the main threats to Britain were seen as France (the traditional enemy) and Russia. As late as February 1903, the Foreign Office was fighting off Treasury attempts to cut the Secret Service Vote, which following the Boer War had risen to £65,000, by arguing that 'most of our troubles are at present in Oriental countries where money is such a potent factor and our principal antagonist is Russia where such large sums are available for purposes of this kind.' Russia, France and the Fenians were all seen as far more dangerous to Britain than Germany. The threat from the IRA was at the heart of the close links between the War Office Intelligence Division, run by General Sir John Ardagh, and Scotland Yard's Special Branch.

General Ardagh believed that the main threat lay in a French invasion timed to coincide with an uprising in Ireland. 'The Irish Revolutionary Party, which has recently been very active in Paris, has in view the obtaining of French aid for a rising in Ireland in the event of a war with England,' he wrote in early 1901. 'There is reason to believe that such a project would command more support in France than it has done for many years past,' he added. The most likely route for the French invasion was via 'waters which cannot be so effectually observed. This naturally leads to the conception of an expedition starting from ports south of Brest with a destination west of Scilly, say to the west coast of Ireland.'

Obsessed with the threat of a French-IRA alliance, Ardagh devised a bizarre plan to set up an intelligence bureau in the Rue Gambon in the heart of Paris. Run by an H S Alexander, normally referred to only as A, the bureau's role was to gather information on both the French armed forces and Irish nationalists based in Paris. A front company was set up in New Jersey to provide the bureau with its cover as an American coal agency. The intention was to set up a chain of such agencies in all the major French ports and another in St Petersburg to spy on the Russians. But the plan never evolved beyond the Paris bureau, largely because it devoured a total of £20,600 over five years – virtually the whole of the military intelligence budget for that period – for little if any return in terms of useful intelligence. 'The original idea was that A should obtain agencies for leading American coal owners, which it was hoped would eventually bring him into close contact with the French Admiralty and lead to the establishment of sub agencies at the military posts,' one British officer said. It was supposed to be self-financing 'but in practice demanded more and more capital to be sunk into it.' Eventually, military intelligence cut its losses and paid Alexander off.

Given the failure of Ardagh's scheme, it was perhaps unsurprising that the status of military intelligence was subsequently downgraded under a radical reorganisation of the War Office. This abolished the post of Director of Military Intelligence and subordinated it to a new Directorate of Military Operations split into four sections. Only two were concerned with intelligence – MO2, the Foreign Intelligence section, and MO3, whose role was described as 'Special Duties' (a euphemism for covert intelligence activities).

The War Office agents were run by Major Nicholas Gosselin, the same man who controlled a network of Special Branch agents among the Irish rebels. In his application for the War Office agent-handler's job, Gosselin gave a brief description of his role with Special Branch: 'My work has been hitherto entirely or almost so with Irish Secret Societies in Europe and America. During the early stages of the dynamite scare, a good many Irish Constabulary and secret agents (private detectives) were employed.' When Gosselin decided to leave to concentrate on the Irish network, in 1903, he was replaced by Superintendent William Melville, the head of the Special Branch. Despite Melville's initial role as the 'controller' for the War Office agents and the fact that he was already in his early fifties, he appears to have been the main British secret agent in the period before the First World War. Born at Sneem in County Kerry, Melville was one of a long line of Irishmen recruited to watch their own. His enthusiasm for the job was not in doubt – he was very keen on disguises, his favourite being that of a sanitary inspector – but his methods were sometimes dubious.

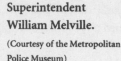

**Superintendent
William Melville.**

(Courtesy of the Metropolitan
Police Museum)

Melville had come to prominence in 1892 with the capture of the Walsall Bombers. The affair began with the arrest in London of Joseph Deacon, an anarchist from Walsall in Staffordshire, who had been under police observation for some time. Melville, then an inspector, was sent to Walsall to investigate the alleged ring of anarchists run by Deacon. He found bomb-making instructions, fuses and anarchist pamphlets, and five other men were arrested. Four of them were subsequently convicted of anarchy and imprisoned for up to ten years. The convictions ended the drive to cut back on the Special Branch, leading to widespread suspicion that those convicted had been set up by a police agent provocateur. At their trial, the anarchists claimed that the order for the bombs that they were making had come from one of their number who turned out to be a paid agent of Melville. The incident did no harm to Melville's career – rather the reverse: within a year he had been made head of Special Branch. But it may have coloured the response of Edward Henry, the Metropolitan Police Commissioner, when he was asked by the War Office to comment on Melville's suitability for the post of 'intermediary for the employment of secret service agents'. Henry said: 'He is shrewd, resourceful and although he has a tendency towards adventuring, he can keep this in check when it suits his interest to do so. For the purpose for which he is needed, to be an intermediary, no better person could be secured — probably no one nearly so good for the money. The Intelligence Dept will make it clear to him that he must abstain from taking a line of his own. We must arrange that he severs his connection with Scotland Yard as quietly as possible. His utility to War Office would be much lessened if it became known that he had taken service with them.'

The need for secrecy was paramount since Melville had become a popular hero for the Victorian press, which took delight in chronicling the activities of 'the ever-watching Chief Inspector' in his fight against anarchists and Fenians. *The Golden Penny* noted in July 1898 that 'To the journalist seeking information for publication, Mr Melville's lips are as a sealed book.' This may have made it necessary to fill in the odd gap. The most famous of his exploits, for example, was the arrest on Victoria Station in April 1894 of the French anarchist Theodule Meunier, who, according to the *Dublin County Telegraph*, shouted out as he was grabbed, 'To fall into your hands, Melville!

You, the only man I feared, and whose description was engraved on my mind!'

Melville, who was already receiving a police pension of £280 a year, was paid an annual salary of £400 by the War Office plus an allowance of 30 shillings a week for out-of-pocket expenses. He was also provided with enough funds to set up 'a small office doing the ostensible business of a

Meunier's arrest, as portrayed in the Illustrated London News.

(Courtesy of the Metropolitan Police Museum)

general agency and making enquiries nominally on behalf of commercial firms' as a cover for his activities.

'I started work in two rooms at 25 Victoria St, London, SW with the name of W Morgan, General Agent,' Melville recalled. 'I chose the offices specially for the reason that while the public entrance in Victoria Street showed almost innumerable offices in the building, immediately around the corner was another entrance – a great asset. Few men at this time were better known in London than I was yet during the five years I was there and although only about 400 yards from Scotland Yard I never met any person going in or coming out who knew me.'

As well as acting as general controller for the War Office agents in Africa, Germany and Russia, Melville, who to disguise his identity was known only as 'M', took on a role as a London-based 'fireman', undertaking a number of secret missions of his own around the world. Sent to Hamburg to investigate a suspected German-backed arms ring, which was allegedly smuggling weapons into South Africa, Melville proved his resourcefulness by blackmailing the city's chief of police into helping him to find the mysterious 'Herr Werner' who, along with a known gun-runner called Otto Busch, was allegedly behind the conspiracy. Melville investigated a number of different Werners, conning them into providing specimens of their handwriting, which he then compared with intercepted letters from 'Herr Werner'. The main suspect turned out to be 'not a man as originally assumed, but a woman with whom Busch appears to have had immoral relations'. But Melville's investigations eventually revealed that the arms ring had been 'a put-up job' dreamed up by a freelance agent in order to provide him with work.

Just over a year after his appointment, Melville was given a pay rise of £50 a year after complaining that Henry Long, his African-based agent, was better paid than he was. 'This last is an unfortunate circumstance and one which I always hoped he might not discover,' Colonel Davies said. 'It evidently rankled that a subordinate of comparatively little experience should get more than he does. He also fears that a change of Government might lead to his dismissal and he has got it into his head that a Liberal minister might disapprove of anyone being employed on such work as he is doing. In my opinion, M has worked very satisfactorily and I doubt very much if we could get anyone else for the money who would do as well. He is very resourceful and has a great capacity for picking up suitable persons to act as agents. Further he has a really good working knowledge of French, which is uncommon in men of his class and is most useful, in fact almost indispensable. His accent would certainly appal you but he is quite fluent and fully capable of transacting business in French.'

Few details of Melville's 'secret missions' survive, but he accumulated an impressive list of foreign decorations for his work on 'secret service', including the French Legion d'Honneur, the Crown of Italy, Spain's Order of Isabel la Catolica, the Order of Christ of Portugal, and the Danish Order of Danneborg. One contemporary said Melville had spent the period between 1903 and 1914 on 'responsible and spectacular duties which entailed extensive travel on the Continent during which he played an active part in the suppression of anarchism.'

By now the main potential threat was increasingly seen not as France or Russia but as Germany, and in 1905 the War Office was drawing up plans for a secret service in the event of 'a war in Europe'. Although no mention was made of Germany, details of the scheme were circulated among consular and diplomatic staff in Scandinavia and Switzerland, leaving little doubt as to the identity of the 'enemy territory' between them. 'Observers' based there were to collect intelligence which they would then hand on to 'carriers' – people who might travel in and out of the country without arousing suspicion, such as 'commercial travellers, gypsies and women'. The 'carriers' would take the information to the 'collectors', intelligence officers based in neutral countries, who would then pass it back to London via the local British consulates and embassies.

The plan caused alarm among some of the recipients. One diplomat in Denmark baulked at the idea of becoming involved in any way with such a scheme. 'I have always thought it undesirable that members of His Majesty's Embassies and Legations should be in any way connected with espionage,' he wrote. 'With earnest desire to be of every possible use to England, I think that the embassies and legations should have as little as possible to do with such matters which should be left to specialists.'

That attitude still permeated Britain's foreign service. In July 1901 Sir Ernest Satow, Britain's ambassador to China, wrote the following note to Sir

Thomas Sanderson, then the permanent under-secretary at the Foreign Office in charge of the Secret Service Vote.

My Dear Sanderson,

You know how often it has been said that this legation was not well informed as to what was going on and that it had no Secret Service. It seems to me quite natural that it should be so. The Chinese secretary is fully occupied with translations of notes and interviewing people. He cannot go around picking up information.

Even those Army officers posted as military attachés to Britain's embassies abroad saw espionage as below their station. Charles á Court Repington, who served as attaché, in Brussels and The Hague in the early 1900s, wrote: 'I would never do any Secret Service work. My view is that the military attaché, is the guest of the country to which he is accredited, and must only see and learn that which is permissible for a guest to investigate. Certainly, he must keep his eyes and ears open and miss nothing. But Secret Service is not his business and he should always refuse a hand in it.'

With war now inevitable, Sir William Everett, the British military attaché in Berlin was asked by the Intelligence Branch to continue in secret service after leaving Germany. He declined, saying: 'You will not have forgotten when we talked this matter over some months ago, that I mentioned how distasteful this sort of work was to me and how much more distasteful it would be to me when it no longer formed a necessary part of my duties. I so dread the thought of being compelled to continue in communication and contact with the class of man who must be employed in this sort of work, while the measures to which we are obliged to resort are repulsive to me.'

The Admiralty shared Everett's disparaging view of espionage. The Royal Navy had only reluctantly formed a Foreign Intelligence Committee in 1883, and even more reluctantly, on the orders of Lord Salisbury, the Prime Minister, had expanded it four years later into the Naval Intelligence Department. It was given the somewhat less than inspiring mission 'to collect, classify and record with a complete index all information which bears a naval character or which may be of value during naval matters, and to preserve the information in a form available for reference'.

By 1908, the NID was asking all British diplomatic and consular staff abroad to look out for intelligence on: 'Publications and printed matter such as the annual reports of the ministers of war and marine; lists of officers and ships of the Navy, Navy and Army estimates; code-lists of merchant-ships; progress reports of naval or military works; items of local or general interest having any connection with naval and military forces, fighting ships or permanent defences; and any change with regard to these either in equipment numbers or disposition.'

It was also sending officers to the main German ports to gather intelligence on 'naval policy, mobilisation, fleet dispositions and the like', according to a series of articles by 'A Former Member of the Secret Service' in the *Daily Telegraph* in September 1930. 'Although the writer feels some difficulty in praising his old service, he is satisfied that the British Naval Intelligence was incomparably superior to the much more elaborate, widespread, and expensive system of espionage which Germany built up in this country,' one article said. 'At any given moment, our Admiralty could have announced the number of submarines on the stocks or completing at Danzig, together with the salient features of each craft.'

But the Navy's low regard for intelligence was still evident. 'The work of our Intelligence correspondents in pre-war years was severely handicapped by the exiguous funds available,' the writer complained. 'Compared with the Secret Service budgets of the Continental powers, our expenditure on this branch was very small indeed. For reasons which to the writer are inexplicable, intelligence work, however hazardous it might be, and however valuable the results, was never sufficiently recognised by our home authorities as deserving of reward. It may be that this pointed neglect is due to an inherent prejudice against the whole business of espionage.'

By the beginning of 1909, the Special Duties section of the Directorate of Military Operations – by then known as MO5 – was busy building up a network of agents in Germany. Melville returned to Germany, travelling via New York so as to avoid detection, and recruited 'a retired officer of the army of a friendly power' living there on a salary of £600 a year as a spy. He also redeployed one of the junior agents from Russia to join a Mr Byszewski, the controller of the Russian network, who was based in Berlin.

Melville appears to have been the only British intelligence officer checking for spies. At first, he sought the assistance of former colleagues but to no avail. 'I had to travel to all parts of the country to make inquiries re suspected persons,' he said. 'In these duties, I found the police, whether in London or the provinces – absolutely useless. Their invariable estimate of a suspect as his apparent respectability and position. Just as though only blackguards would be chosen for espionage.'

His main adversary was 'the notorious Gustav Steinhauer', the leader of Germany's intelligence network, whom he had met when they were both protecting the Kaiser during a state visit to Britain. 'The Kaiser himself asked me one day at Windsor whether I knew Steinhauer,' Melville recalled. 'The latter having been many years in America spoke English fluently. He was in correspondence with many German spies in this country. He also travelled England as a Commercial man and visited his agents. On one occasion he had an exceedingly narrow escape of arrest in London. He did not venture to come here again.'

Melville was apparently extremely effective in countering German espionage. But this did not stop a near panic, orchestrated by the author William le Queux, who produced a series of books with titles like *The Invasion of 1910* and *Spies of the Kaiser: Plotting the Downfall of England*. He protested vigorously to anyone who would listen – and many influential people did – that the authorities were negligently ignoring the German threat. Lord Harmsworth, proprietor of the *Daily Mail*, serialised *The Invasion of 1910* in his newspaper, carefully re-routing the hypothetical marauding Hun troops through towns and villages where the *Mail*'s circulation was high.

'Among the thousands of Germans working in London, the hundred or so spies, all trusted soldiers, had passed unnoticed,' le Queux wrote in a work that deliberately set out to blur the lines between fact and fiction. 'But, working in unison, each little group of two or three had been allotted its task and had previously thoroughly reconnoitred the position and studied the most rapid or effective means.'

As the public excitement grew, so too did the number of largely imagined German spies. Lord Roberts, taking up the theme in Parliament, said, 'It is calculated, my Lords, that there are 80,000 Germans in the United Kingdom, almost all of them trained soldiers. They work in many of the hotels at some of the chief railway stations, and if a German force once got into this country it would have the advantage of help and reinforcement such as no other army on foreign soil has ever before enjoyed.'

The *Daily Mail* instructed its readers that they should 'refuse to be served by a German waiter. If your waiter says he is Swiss, ask to see his passport.' Even military intelligence was convinced by le Queux's claims, not least because Lieutenant-Colonel James Edmonds, the head of MO5, was his close friend. Edmonds asked the police what could be done about 'the systematic visits to this country by Germans who locate themselves with clergymen, farmers, and private persons' ostensibly to learn English.

The spy scare had the exact opposite effect that its originators had wanted. When a German spymaster, possibly even Steinhauer himself, arrived at Dover to recruit some new agents, the police refused to arrest him. There were clearly a large number of German officers taking 'holidays' in Britain. They included a series of Germans 'of soldierly appearance', who rented a house in Hythe, using the house as 'a centre for motoring' and spent an inordinate time watching the ranges at nearby Lydd. Two or three would stay for a month or so before being replaced by others. But Special Branch pointed out, quite accurately, that what the Germans were doing was actually not against the law. It made it clear that it was unconvinced by Edmonds's claim that German visitors to Britain were 'assiduous in collecting other information concerning the topography of the country, roads, dockyards, military magazines, which might be considered of value from the military point of view'. It told him that it doubted that they were really a source of danger. 'The really dangerous person is the foreigner possibly naturalised, settled in and British and carrying on some business or pursuit which shields him from suspicion, who has opportunities of collecting information and of transmitting it, probably at a time when it could be useful to some other country. If we could exercise some impression over these latter, it might be useful, but we cannot.'

But Edmonds and his direct superior, General John Ewart, Director of Military Operations, continued to lobby hard for some form of action, and in March 1909 Herbert Asquith, the British Prime Minister, instructed the

Committee of Imperial Defence 'to consider the dangers from German espionage to British naval ports'.

A subcommittee was set up, chaired by the War Secretary, and including the Home Secretary, the Metropolitan Police Commissioner, the Postmaster-General, the First Lord of the Admiralty, the Director of Naval Intelligence, the Director of Military Operations, and the permanent under-secretaries at the Treasury and Foreign Office, who between them administered the Secret Service Vote. At first, many of the sub-committee members were sceptical of the alleged German threat. Edmonds, who described himself as 'employed under the Director of Military Operations on secret service', was dismissed by Lord Esher, the Postmaster General, as 'a silly witness from the War Office'. Edmonds said a secret service's motto should be 'trust no one' and quoted Kipling's adage: 'trust a snake before a harlot and a harlot before a Pathan'. In a remark that may well have been the cause of Esher's anger, he added that 'though a mason myself, my experience is that even a mason is not to be safely entrusted.' Esher asked Edmonds sarcastically if he was not worried about 'the large number of German waiters in this country' and noted in his diary that 'Spycatchers get espionage on the brain.'

But despite the high level of scaremongering, the evidence of German spying was incontrovertible. On 24 July 1909 it reported: 'The evidence which was produced left no doubt in the minds of the sub-committee that an extensive system of German espionage exists in this country, and that we have no organisation for keeping in touch with that espionage and for accurately determining its extent or objectives. We have considered the question of how a Secret Service Bureau could be established to deal both with espionage in this country and with our own foreign agents abroad, and to serve as a screen between the Admiralty and the War Office on the one hand and those employed on secret service, or who have information they wish to sell to the British Government on the other.'

The sub-committee also called for the passing of a new Official Secrets Act to enable the police to prosecute spies and set the tone for the refusal of subsequent governments to acknowledge that Britain had any form of secret service. It published only one copy of its detailed recommendations, which it said were 'of so secret a nature that it is thought desirable that they should not be printed or circulated to the members'. The Secret Service Bureau was set up jointly by the War Office and the Admiralty on 1 October 1909 and made subordinate to the War Office's Directorate of Military Operations and Intelligence. According to popular mythology, the bureau consisted solely of Captain Vernon Kell, an officer in the South Staffordshire Regiment who would later become the first head of the Security Service. In fact it was slightly, although not much, larger than that. It was set up in Melville's offices under cover of his investigations as a 'private detective'. His work was to be supervised by Kell and by Captain Mansfield Cumming of the Royal Navy. Since the Admiralty's main requirement was for information on the Kaiser's rapidly growing navy, the naval section commanded by Cumming – or 'C', as he became known for security reasons – concentrated on gathering intelligence overseas, while the military section – under Kell, or 'K' – took responsibility for counter-espionage within the British Isles. In January 1916, a new Directorate of Military Intelligence was set up within the War Office claiming control of both sections of the Secret Service Bureau. Cumming's foreign department was designated MI1c – it was not until the Second World War that it would become MI6. But Kell's home department was given the name by which it is still generally known – MI5.

The Security Service MI5

Prologue

If the 'watchers' from *Urzad Ochrony Panstwa*, the Polish equivalent of MI5, had any doubts about the mysterious man seeking to buy a large consignment of arms, these were dispelled after the third change of taxi. He was clearly determined to shake off anyone who was following him across Warsaw to the southern commercial district of Mokotow and the offices of the newly established Eloks import–export business. 'We knew then that it could not be legal,' Gromoslaw Czempinski, the head of the UOP, said later.

Not that there had ever been any doubt in the first place. Eloks was a fake company set up by the Poles in mid-1993, part of a joint operation with the British aimed at preventing huge amounts of former Warsaw Pact weapons from being spirited out of the country to Northern Ireland. An MI5 agent inside the Ulster Volunteer Force, a small 'Loyalist' terrorist group of around 200 trained men, had reported that two of its members had been given £250,000 in cash with which to buy Polish arms and explosives. The Protestant paramilitaries were looking for the sort of firepower that would enable them to destabilise the fragile moves towards peace that were already underway.

Using the anti-terrorist links set up among Europe's security services during the Gulf War, T Branch, the MI5 department that handles Irish terrorism, had asked the UOP for its help. The Polish officer handling the Warsaw end of the operation was now about to meet the terrorists' intermediary – the man with the penchant for changing taxis – who would hand her their shopping list. For their £250,000, his UVF clients were to receive two tons of plastic explosive; a large number of detonators; 320 Kalashnikov assault rifles together with 60,000 rounds of ammunition; 500 hand grenades; and 53 Russian Makarov 9mm pistols with 14,000 rounds of ammunition.

The weapons – all supplied from the Polish authorities' own armouries – were loaded into a steel container and customs documents were discreetly arranged listing it as container number 2030255, a consignment of ceramic tiles destined for Frackleton and Sons, a Belfast company that had previously imported tiles from Europe but which knew nothing at all of this particular transaction. Another reputable company, the Szczecin-based hauliers Fast Baltic, was paid 40 million zlotys, about £1,400, to transport the container to the Baltic port of Gdynia where it was loaded on to the MV *Inowroclaw*.

The 6,300-ton Polish freighter set sail for Britain on 19 November 1993, stopping off at Tilbury to unload a number of its 230 containers, before heading north for Teesport where customs officers were lying in wait. T Branch had decided to seize the arms there before they could be unloaded and smuggled across the Irish Sea to Belfast. In the early hours of 24 November, the customs officers moved in, ordering container 2030255 to be removed from the ship.

Both sides held press conferences to announce their arms 'find'. Evidence that MI5 was operating just as much against Protestant paramilitaries as against their republican counterparts was no doubt helpful in persuading both the IRA and Dublin that London was serious in its search for peace in Northern Ireland. The Poles, anxious to show that they were responsible members of the new Europe, were more open about what had occurred. But even they were cagey about giving precise details of the operation. 'If these were to be revealed, it could cost eight lives on the British side alone,' Czempinski said. 'The UVF do not mess around.'

Five

Learning from the Crook

'Security is the mother of danger and the grandmother of destruction.'
Thomas Fuller, *The Holy State and the Profane State*, 1642

Among the mixture of real and imaginary evidence of German treachery, which Edmonds used to justify the creation of the Secret Service Bureau, was a map on which he marked the whereabouts of all the Kaiser's known spies. 'I made a map of England showing the positions of various spy locations which had considerable effect upon the Committee of Imperial Defence,' he wrote. 'I was opposed to the arrest of even undoubted espionage agents: it was better to let Germany live in a fool's paradise that we had no counter-espionage system. This was accepted: the agents were marked down and all but one (on leave) seized on declaration of war.'

Captain Eric Holt-Wilson, who was appointed as Kell's deputy in December 1912, recorded that Gustav Steinhauer's network was uncovered after a chance remark on a train by a loose-tongued German admiralty official. Melville discovered that Gustav Ernst, who was German by birth but had taken British citizenship was using his barber's shop at 402A, Caledonian Road, Islington, north London as the central 'post office' for the German network. All Steinhauer's agents in Britain sent their reports to Ernst through the post. He then sent them on to an address in Potsdam. Blanket interception of Ernst's mail allowed Melville to compile a list of 22 German spies active in Britain. On the advice of Melville, who pointed out that 'a bird in the hand is worth two in the bush', Kell decided to keep the bulk of Steinhauer's network in place, watching their movements and intercepting their correspondence. His men also used deception to hamper the German intelligence operations. 'Each German agent in this country received a small retainer, and the news he supplied was paid for according to its supposed value,' one British intelligence official later recalled. 'It is safe to say that 99 per cent of their reports were utterly valueless. But our own authorities, having access to the correspondence of most of these agents, may sometimes have found it convenient to insert items so circumstantial and convincing as to be calculated to deceive the shrewdest heads on the German naval staff.'

When war was declared on 4 August 1914 Steinhauer's network was rolled up, bar the one agent who had the good fortune to be on leave in Germany at the time. It is still regarded by the Security Service as one of its greatest coups. 'This sudden action had the effect of destroying the complete spy organisation built up by the enemy in peacetime,' wrote Holt-Wilson. 'As a proof of this statement, a German order came into our hands early in the war which disclosed the fact that as late as 21 August, the German Military commanders were still ignorant of the despatch or movements of our main expeditionary force, although this had been more or less common knowledge to thousands in this country.'

Many more German spies were discovered during the war. Messages were passed in newspaper small ads or written in secret ink on letters and even musical scores. Initially they used lemon juice, eau de Cologne and oil of peppermint. But the Germans gradually developed a number of inks that were more difficult to uncover. A total of 35 spies were brought to trial. Nineteen of these were condemned to death, although a number were later reprieved. Kell was somewhat irate to find that in the first of these cases it was because the condemned was a woman. He protested strongly, arguing that once the Germans realised that the British would not kill women they would flood the country with female spies. The Germans used a number of female spies, but Kell was unimpressed. 'Women do not make good Security Service agents,' he said. 'The difficulty with the female agent is her lack of technical knowledge of naval and military matters. The beautiful vamp, who removes secret treaties from the pockets of ambassadors after a couple of cocktails has I fear no counterpart in real life.'

The pre-war use of deception was improved on with one German agent who had been shot dead being impersonated by an MI5 officer who fed the Germans misleading intelligence and received substantial sums of money in return. There was also an early attempt to use Double Cross agents, turning captured German agents and playing them back under British control although this was largely aimed at agents sent into Britain to commit acts of sabotage. Minor acts of sabotage were arranged that did no real damage but could be reported as being effective and prevent the Germans from sending in more sabotage agents.

Although Kell insisted that MI5 should stay 'foursquare' within the law, Melville lectured new recruits on how to pick locks and break into houses. His course included practical training using the safe of the embassy of 'a so-called neutral power' and the services of 'a very experienced assistant who is out on a kind of compassionate leave from Parkhurst so that he can put his shoulder to the war effort for a few days.'

The aims of the operation were not to be compared to those of the common thief, as one of the trainees recorded in his diary: 'Melville paused. "So much," he said, "for the needs of the average crook." But if the same "operation" were to be envisaged by MI5 the whole pattern of the undertaking would need to be changed. The accent would no longer be on lifting the swag but on the identification of documents. When located they were likely to be photographed there and then and afterwards replaced so that they appeared to have been undisturbed. Finally in leaving the premises the marauders would need to obliterate every possible trace of their entry. The guiding principle, so far as an operation in this country was concerned, would not be the avoidance of conflict with the police but a clash with the vigorous security precautions made by the "other side" which could come into action at many points and nullify the exploit. This would lead at best to a showdown and at worst to the embarrassment of the Cabinet. Nevertheless, a house-break was always a house-break and there must remain much that the MI5 could learn from the crook.'

Melville warned his students against using the tricks they had learned for any more profitable activities. 'In case any of you should be tempted after the war to act up as a "gentleman burglar", I believe that is the term, I think I should point out that there is precious little in it for you. What you do for MI5 in wartime is strictly privileged. You may have to face risks because you are dealing with men who are potentially desperate. But there are positively no legal penalties, even if very occasionally you shoot to kill. In contrast, the peacetime "screwsman" can expect no government sponsorship and certainly no police protection ... sooner or later he gets convicted.'

With the help of the police, Kell had spent the pre-war years drawing up a list of 30,000 aliens. The Central Registry was a card index in which the subjects were classified on a bizarre scale that ran from AA for the least dangerous to BB for the most. AA was Absolutely Anglicised or Absolutely Allied, denoting someone who was definitely supportive of the British cause. A was Anglicised or Allied, i.e. supportive. AB was Anglo-Boche – allegiances unclear, but probably pro-British. BA was Boche-Anglo – allegiances also unclear, but probably pro-German. B was Boche, i.e. hostile. Where a subject's hostility to the British cause was not in doubt, he or she was graded BB or Bad Boche.

Once the war began, the number of registered enemy aliens swelled to an alleged 100,000, of whom 32,000 were eventually interned and a further 25,000 deported. Nor was it just German spies who provided scope for Kell's inveterate empire-building. From 1916, the Home Section – now officially known as MI5 – and Special Branch became increasingly involved in countering 'subversion', either from pacifists or from the left. This fuelled the growing rivalry between the two organisations, with Kell and Basil Thomson, the head of Special Branch, both lobbying furiously for control of what was expected to be the new post-war threat – the fight against Bolshevism.

MI5 officers had become openly resentful of Special Branch, complaining that, no matter how much work they put into uncovering German spies, Thomson always managed to take the credit for his own men. Captain Reginald Drake, the post-war head of MI5's counter-espionage department, wrote, 'BT [Thomson] did not know of the existence, name or activity of any convicted spy until I told him; but being the dirty dog he was he twisted the facts to claim that he alone did it.' It was to be the beginning of a long-running feud that has continued through to the present day.

Fears that industrial unrest would disrupt the war effort led to the creation of a 'Labour Intelligence' department within the Ministry of Munitions. Set up in 1916 with Kell's assistance, it was given the cover-name Parliamentary Military Secretary Department No. 2 Section (PMS-2) to disguise its real role.

But its amateurish attempts to capture alleged union subversives by using *agents provocateurs* served only to show the lack of any credible subversive threat and brought the intelligence services into public disrepute. PMS-2 was soon absorbed back into MI5, having tarnished not only its own reputation but that of Kell, who lost control over the fight against subversion to Special Branch at a crucial time – just months before October 1917 and Russia's Bolshevik Revolution.

The First World War saw a massive increase in the resources allocated to Kell's operations. At the start of the war he had the assistance of nine military officers, three civilians, three detectives and four clerks. By the time of the Armistice, MI5 had almost 850 employees. It had six branches: A – covering monitoring of aliens; D – Imperial Overseas Intelligence, which also covered Irish matters; E – Port and Frontier Control; F – Preventive Security; G – Investigation and H – Secretariat and Administration. Its activities had been bolstered by the catch-all phraseology of the 1914 Defence of the Realm Act, which effectively turned Britain into a military-controlled state and allowed unparalleled surveillance of the population, including the widespread inter-ception of postal communication. But with the threat now coming not from Germany but from Bolshevism, Thomson and Special Branch became the prevalent force in British domestic intelligence operations. When the govern-ment, fearful that Bolshevism was more rampant in Britain than anyone realised, set up a Directorate of Intelligence in March 1919, it was Thomson and not Kell who was appointed to head it. At the same time MI5 lost control of its Military Control network, the system of monitoring the movements of aliens. This was modified 'to exclude Bolshevik agents from the United Kingdom'; renamed the Passport Control Department; and handed over, together with the MI5 men who ran it, to Cumming's Secret Intelligence Service (SIS). To Kell's dismay, MI5's role was limited to military counter-espionage and preventing the spread of Bolshevism within the armed forces, and his budget was cut from £100,000 a year to £30,000.

Despite seeing his staff slashed by more than 800 to just 30, Kell fought a rearguard action to keep MI5 alive. He centred his activities on his registry of undesirable aliens, now renamed the Precautionary Index, using this to monitor the activities of all Russians and their sympathisers in Britain. MI5 expanded the list to include anyone who held or was suspected of having held left-wing views and might therefore pass them on to unsuspecting soldiers, sailors and airmen. In the mid-1920s, Kell also successfully beat off an attempt by the Secret Intelligence Service to absorb MI5. But his main turf battle remained with Special Branch over who should control civilian counter-espionage. 'The work of British MI5 is now carried on under the plea that revolutionary agents are attempting to create trouble in the British Army,' Major R. F. Hyatt, the deputy US military attaché, reported back to Washington in December 1920. 'Officially, MI5 is only concerned with civilian activities as they affect the army, but in reality and especially recently, they have concerned themselves in general with revolutionary and Bolshevik agents, using the Suspect List, built up during the war and since added to, as a basis for operations.'

As he strove to rebuild his empire, Kell made common cause with the private intelligence organisations set up by right-wing groups in the 1920s to counter the 'Bolshevik threat', even recruiting one of his most successful agent-runners, Maxwell Knight, from the British Fascisti, where he was Director of Intelligence. But the most significant link between MI5 and private intelligence agencies was that with Conservative Central Office, and it was this that led to the disclosure of the so-called Zinoviev Letter. The letter was supposedly written to the Communist Party of Great Britain (CPGB) by Grigory Zinoviev, President of the Comintern, the international body set up by the Soviet Union in 1919 to promote communism and revolution around the world. It called for the mobilisation of sympathetic forces in the Labour Party and the intensification of 'agitation-propaganda work in the armed forces'. The letter, which appeared to confirmed a widespread belief that the Labour Party was soft on Bolshevism, was leaked to the *Daily Mail*, which published it shortly before a general election called by Labour Prime Minister Ramsay MacDonald for 29 October 1924. The newspaper spread details of the letter across its front page with banner headlines: 'Civil War Plot By Socialists' Masters; Moscow Orders To Our Reds; Great Plot Disclosed'.

Much remains uncertain about the Zinoviev Letter – not least whether or not it was genuine and if it had any significant effect on the election, which the Labour Party had anyway seemed certain to lose. But documents in the archives of the Russian intelligence service suggest it was forged by a Russian émigré with connections to British intelligence. Reports from three separate Bolshevik intelligence officials sent to the Lubyanka in November 1924 all agreed that the letter was produced by Ivan Dmitrevich Pokrovsky, a member of the White Russian intelligence organisation based in Riga. Pokrovsky 'has in his possession Comintern stationery and made it up from extracts of Zinoviev's speeches with something extra added'.

The most comprehensive of the three accounts came from Aleksandr Gumansky, a Bolshevik agent who infiltrated the White Russian movement in Berlin. 'It was fabricated in Riga by a certain Pokrovsky, a really talented person, who worked for the British since 1920,' Gumansky claimed. Pokrovsky said he had been asked by a leading Russian émigré based in England for material that could be used against the British Labour Party in the forthcoming election.

Gumansky's report included a verbatim account of the affair in Pokrovsky's own words. 'My chief, Captain Black, suggested that I should compose a letter addressed to the British communists,' Pokrovsky said. 'I drafted it out on proper paper and without a signature, not knowing how it would be used. This was before the general elections.' Pokrovsky was paid a total of £1,360 for the letter, which was subsequently sent to the Bolshevik representative in London, Gumansky said. The police were tipped off that an important document would be arriving and it was intercepted, photographed and replaced with a blank sheet of paper which was delivered to the Soviet embassy with two policemen acting as witnesses while the postman obtained a signature to confirm receipt. The letter was then handed over to the Foreign Office.

Further evidence to back up the story that it was forged in Riga comes in the memoirs of Leslie Nicholson, a former MI6 head of station in the Latvian capital. Nicholson described how Artur Schmidkoff, the head of the Latvian political police, was fond of boasting to him how he had uncovered the man who forged the Zinoviev Letter. 'With a squad of men, he had raided the flat of a known ex-British agent and had discovered carbon copies of what he described as "the original Zinoviev Letter"', Nicholson said. 'These carbon copies had certainly been produced on the agent's typewriter, which was found in the flat. Although I tried to question Schmidkoff further, he refused to be drawn. All he would tell me was that he personally was convinced that the man was indeed the originator of the letter and he implied that it had been fabricated and passed to a "British organisation" for financial gain.'

But while that explains the letter's provenance, it does not explain how a copy of the letter came to be handed to the *Daily Mail*. The leak confirmed the right-wing nature of the intelligence services at the time, placing them firmly in collusion with Conservative Party Central Office. The key players in the affair were Thomas Marlowe, the *Daily Mail* editor; Colonel Frederick Browning, the former deputy chief of the SIS; and Donald im Thurn, a former MI5 member. But at least three other serving or former intelligence officials were also involved. They were: Kell himself; Admiral Hugh Sinclair, the head of SIS; and Admiral Reginald 'Blinker' Hall, the former Director of Naval Intelligence, who was by now Unionist MP for Eastbourne.

The precise roles of each of the men are far from clear, but Conservative Party Central Office had offered to pay im Thurn £5,000 to pass the letter to the press. Either Hall or Browning was almost certainly a man described by the *Daily Mail* editor as the 'old and trusted friend' who first told him of the letter's existence, while the other was the second 'friend' who confirmed its authenticity. According to im Thurn's diary, both Kell and Sinclair were involved in the decision as to when the letter should be leaked, with Kell pressing for its early release and Sinclair in favour of holding it back. Further proof of the intelligence services' close links with Central Office was to come in January 1927, when Joseph Ball, a senior member of MI5, who had been involved in black propaganda and is believed by some to have been the architect of the Zinoviev affair, resigned to take up a post as the Conservative Party's Director of Publicity.

How much influence this all bought Kell with the new Conservative administration is difficult to tell, but in 1931 he won a major victory in the long turf battle with Special Branch. Paradoxically, this was not as the result of any Special Branch wrongdoing. It resulted from an inquiry into the existence of Secret Intelligence Service operation against communists in Britain. The Home Office objected to SIS, which was supposed to operate abroad, running agents in Britain and as a result MI5, by then based in Cromwell Road,

Fulham, west London, was given control of civil and military counter-espionage throughout the United Kingdom and the British Empire. Both the SIS agents and Scotland Yard's civil intelligence staff were absorbed into Kell's organisation, and a new title, the Security Service, was adopted, although in practice the service was still known as MI5. Special Branch was left with the role of merely carrying out arrests and surveillance when MI5 directed. The new MI5 organisation consisted of four branches: A – Administration; B – Counter-Espionage; C – Security; and D – Liaison with the Military.

There followed an almost unparalleled piece of co-operation between MI5, the Secret Intelligence Service, the British codebreaking organisation GC&CS, and the Metropolitan Police. Operation Mask was targeted against the CPGB and the Comintern, the organisation set up in 1919 to promote communism and revolution around the world. It controlled all of the various Communist Parties around the world, each of which formed a so-called 'Section' of the Comintern and was bound to follow its direction. They were also required to set up parallel 'illegal', or more accurately underground, organisations that would be controlled by the Comintern in order to prepare for a general strike and armed insurrection that it was hoped would precede fresh revolutions. An additional role of these 'illegal' organisations was to carry out espionage.

The first sign of illicit transmissions linking the CPGB to Moscow came in early 1930, when various British wireless intercept units began picking up a large number of unauthorised radio transmissions between London and Moscow. The messages were deciphered by John Tiltman, a leading GC&CS codebreaker, and sent both to B Branch, which was responsible for Soviet subversion and espionage, and to a small SIS counter-espionage department known as Section V, which was led by Major Valentine Vivian, a former Indian police officer.

Jack Curry, who was in charge of MI5 operations against subversion for part of the 1930s, recalled that the messages dealt with a variety of subjects. 'The London/Moscow transmissions were part of a large network with a number of stations in different parts of the world and the material dealt with a variety of the affairs of the Comintern and its sections in different countries. Those from Moscow included directions and instructions regarding the line to be taken in propaganda and in party policy generally. They gave, among other things, details regarding subsidies to be paid by Moscow, a large part being allocated to the *Daily Worker*. They were also concerned with details regarding the despatch of students from this country to the Lenin School in Russia and with the movements of couriers.'

Many of the messages were obscure and difficult to understand without an appreciation of the context and the covernames of those to whom they referred, Curry said. 'Major Vivian was, however, able to extract useful intelligence from a number of messages and, in particular, obtained a certain picture of some of the details of Comintern finance and its measures for subsidising its Sections in other countries. Information about the names of couriers and active Communists, including certain British crypto-communists, was obtained from this source.'

Harold Kenworthy, the head of a small Metropolitan Police intercept team, set out with Leslie Lambert, the GC&CS technical expert, to track down the source of the London messages. Since the radio messages were always sent at night, their early attempts to home in on the signal met with suspicion from ordinary police officers and they were handicapped in any explanation by the need to keep what they were doing secret. Kenworthy recalled that they had to be provided with a special pass after the very act of loading the equipment sparked off a police investigation into an assumed robbery.

'Some exciting moments were experienced – particularly on one occasion, after going round a neighbourhood for some time a police car stopped us. On being asked: "What have you got in that parcel?" – the parcel being a portable short-wave set, Mr Lambert said: "I don't want to tell you." After that remark, there was nothing to it but for the pass to be shown. On another occasion, we spotted a PC waiting for us in the middle of a narrow crossing. We literally backed out of this by reversing round a corner and making off in another direction.'

They used a large direction-finding receiver in a van to find the general direction and then deployed the portable set to 'walk in' on the transmitter. 'It took a long time to get final results,' Kenworthy recalled. 'The search for the unauthorised wireless station went on for some months. We were only one and often after all the preparations the London station would be on the air perhaps two minutes only and then off until the following evening. These chancy sort of conditions made the effort a very long drawn out affair, but it was finally rewarded by locating the station in Wimbledon.'

An MI5 surveillance operation was set up. The house was found to belong to Stephen James Wheeton, a Communist Party member. MI5 officers followed him to regular meetings with Alice Holland, a prominent Communist Party member, at which the messages were handed over and collected. The transmitter was later moved to north London but it was not long before Kenworthy and Lambert again located it in the home of another party member, called William Morrison.

But the best source the British had within the Comintern was a 'walk-in', a spy who offered his services to the SIS head of station in Berlin. Johann Heinrich deGraff, codenamed Jonny X, was a German communist who was recruited by Soviet Army intelligence, the GRU. He walked into the SIS station in Berlin to volunteer his services and was run by its head, Frank Foley, who was to become far better known for his work in helping Jews to escape from Nazi Germany. Jonny X had been involved in the organisation of the Comintern 'illegal' network in Britain and was able to provide vital information on how it operated.

Foley recruited him in a Berlin Biergarten in the early 1930s. Jonny was attached to the Comintern. But he became disillusioned and upset after learning that his wife had been purged. Foley persuaded him to remain in the GRU as an 'agent in place'. He was to become one of the best agents the British ever had against the Soviet Union. Foley had gone against the rules in order to take advantage of the moment, a former SIS officer said. He should have contacted SIS headquarters in London before recruiting Jonny. 'It was some time before Frank sent a message to Head Office, saying: "I am in touch with Johann who is Comintern and can supply full breakdown of British and other communist parties." This was a maverick step. Head Office would have wanted to know before it had been taken this far. Vivian was sent out to Berlin to find out what was going on. Vivian was much maligned as a fusspot, which he was. But he had a policeman's eye for detail and note-taking that proved immensely useful.'

Shortly afterwards Jonny was sent back to London by the Comintern to sort out the British Communist Party which had failed to capitalise on the rising unemployment and hunger marches. 'Jonny visited the UK in 1931 and 1932,' said the former SIS officer. 'There was a lot of excitement about it all because of this. The details were passed to MI5 who took executive action on the basis of information supplied by Foley.' There was often no love lost between SIS and MI5 during this period, but Curry was full of praise for the 'close and fruitful collaboration' on the Comintern. The intelligence from the SIS agents, and particularly from Jonny X, whom he singled out as 'very valuable', was augmented and amplified by the intercepted Comintern messages.

B Division's operations against the Communist Party, run by M Section, were masterminded from an expensive apartment in Dolphin Square, Pimlico, by Maxwell Knight. An eccentric man with a passion for natural history, Knight would later present a BBC radio programme for children as 'Uncle Max'. But his fame within the intelligence services was based on a willingness to wait years for the 'sleeper' agents he placed inside the Communist Party to gain positions of influence, recalled one former MI5 officer. 'When I joined MI5, Maxwell Knight was one of the legendary people, the greatest agent-runner MI5 ever had, and his reputation was well founded. He had been very successful in the thirties. The secret of his success was his uncanny ability at getting on with people. He could persuade them to do things they didn't want to do, which is the secret of being a good agent-runner.'

The most successful of Knight's operations against the Communist Party involved the use of Olga Gray. In a typical Knight ploy, the nineteen-year-old began attending meetings of the Friends of the Soviet Union and in 1932 started working for the Anti-War Movement, a Soviet front organisation, as a typist. Eventually, four years into the operation, she had won the confidence of Harry Pollitt, the British Communist Party leader, who sent her on a secret mission to India.

Knight was insistent that at no stage was Gray to initiate a move deeper into the Communist organisation: advance was always to come at the invitation of the party. This patient approach paid dividends, and in 1938, seven years after first being recruited, Gray uncovered the Woolwich Spy Ring, which was smuggling details of the Army's secret weapons to the Soviet

Union. Percy Glading, the communist agent running the spy ring, and two co-conspirators were jailed after being convicted on the evidence given by Gray who was known throughout the trial only as 'Miss X'.

Despite his previous membership of the British Fascisti, from which he resigned only in 1930, Knight was equally successful at infiltrating right-wing extremist groups. Following the 1933 Home Office decision that the intelligence services should begin collecting data on Fascist movements, MI5 infiltrated a number of agents into Sir Oswald Mosley's British Union of Fascists. They included James McGuirk Hughes, who under the pseudonym P. G. Taylor became the BUF's head of intelligence and in an interesting side-operation used a number of unwitting BUF activists to burgle confidential documents from the home of a suspected Communist on behalf of MI5. But despite copious evidence that Mosley was being subsidised by Mussolini and almost certainly by Hitler, the Home Office persistently refused to allow MI5 to intercept his post or telephone calls.

MI5 moved to Horseferry Road, Westminster, in 1937 and in 1938 was reorganised into four branches: A – Administration and Registry; B – Counter-espionage and Anti-Subversion; C – Vetting; and D – Security of Defence Industry Establishments. Shortly before the outbreak of the Second World War it transferred its headquarters to Wormwood Scrubs Prison in north-west London. But the Victorian prison was not an ideal location, and in May 1940 all non-essential sections were transferred to Blenheim Palace in Oxfordshire, while those that had to stay in London moved to 58 St James's Street.

In the same month, Knight had success with another of his operations. Joan Miller had been told to infiltrate the Right Club, an anti-Semitic organisation set up by Captain Archibald Maule Ramsay, the Conservative MP for Peebles, who blamed the Jews for the war and wanted to reach an accord with Hitler. Knight succeeded in placing three female agents inside the Right Club: Miller herself; Marjorie Mackie, whom Miller described as 'a cosy middle-aged lady who will always remind me of Miss Marple'; and a young Belgian girl called Helene Louise de Munck. Miller discovered that Anna Wolkoff, a Russian émigre who was a member of the Right Club and a dressmaker for the Duchess of Windsor, was passing the Italians details of secret communications between Winston Churchill, the British Prime Minister, and Franklin D. Roosevelt, the American President. These were given to her by Tyler Kent, who was a cipher clerk at the American Embassy. The affair fuelled fears of attempts to replace King George VI with the Duke of Windsor and install a government willing to make peace with Hitler and a number of alleged Nazi sympathisers, including Mosley and Ramsay, were interned.

Despite the success of the operation against the Right Club, Churchill was singularly unimpressed by MI5's understandable failure to detect a mythical German fifth column that yet again had been largely dreamed up by the *Daily Mail*. In fact, most if not all of the fairly lightweight Axis intelligence operations in Britain before the war had been detected. But Churchill set up a Security Executive to ensure that British intelligence was operating efficiently. It was to be chaired by Lord Swinton, a former Air Minister, with the former MI5 member Sir Joseph Ball, now Director of Information at Conservative Party Central Office, as Vice-Chairman.

The Security Executive discovered that MI5 had been ill-prepared for the heavy workload the war would bring. Starved of funding it had only thirty officers at the beginning of 1939 and its surveillance section comprised just six men. Its problems had been exacerbated by a complete reversal in the approach of the Home Office, which swung from a blanket refusal to allow Mosley to be investigated properly to ordering the internment of around 26,000 Germans, Austrians, and later Italians. There was a public outcry, not least because many of those who now found themselves interned had fled their own countries for the 'freedom' of Britain. The Home Office now swung the other way and MI5 found itself blamed for the whole affair. The newly appointed Prime Minister Winston Churchill, who had initially encouraged 'a very large round-up', began to have serious doubts over the political wisdom of what he now described as 'the witch-finding activities of MI5'. The Home Office now decided that each and every internee should be investigated by MI5 with a view to releasing as many as possible. Impossibly overloaded by the increased workload, the MI5 system broke down completely.

Swinton only made matters worse. His initial reaction was to blame the hapless Kell, who was then sacked on Churchill's orders. The man who had created MI5 and had run it for thirty-one years was sixty-seven years old. He died less than two years later at his small rented cottage in Emberton, Buckinghamshire, a broken man. For six months, MI5 was in disarray as it sought to fight off attempts by Swinton to impose his own ideas on it. The introduction of William Crocker, a solicitor, as his representative with wide-ranging powers led many experienced and invaluable officers to contemplate resigning. Hearing of the problems, Churchill asked Sir David Petrie, a retired Indian police officer who had been in charge of the Indian Political Intelligence Bureau, to take over. Petrie was scathing of the attempts by Swinton's henchman to reorganise MI5. Crocker had gone but 'the evil that this man did lives after him'. He refused to take over as Director-General unless he was allowed to be 'master in his own house'. Churchill agreed and Petrie, who was by all accounts an exceptionally good man-manager, set about rebuilding MI5.

Six

The Double Cross System

For the greater part of the war, we actively ran and controlled the German espionage system in this country.

J. C. Masterman, *The Double-Cross System, 1939-1945*

Despite its initial problems, MI5 was to have a good war against both German and, to a lesser extent, Russian agents. On the outbreak of war between Germany and the Soviet Union in June 1941, Churchill ordered that all intelligence operations against Moscow should end. But MI5 continued to monitor Soviet activities, setting up a section based, with a number of other sections, at Blenheim Palace, near Oxford, that dealt with communist subversion and Russian espionage activities. Petrie's reorganisation split off a number of the tasks carried out by B Branch, setting up six separate branches or Divisions. A Division dealt with Administration; B was now purely Counter-Espionage; C – Vetting; D – Security and Travel Control; E – Alien Control; and F – Subversive Activities. Despite its counter-espionage role, the anti-communist section was part of F Division under Roger Hollis. Designated F2, it was split into three sections. F2A dealt with the CPGB. Thanks to the reports of Jonny X; the interception of post; telephone taps on party members; and a system known as the Special Facility (SF), it had a detailed knowledge of the party's organisation, personnel and methods of operation.

The Special Facility allowed the telephones at the CPGB headquarters in King Street, London to be converted into bugs. It was put in place in 1942, one former MI5 officer recalled. 'Normally when you put a telephone handset back on its cradle, it disconnects the mouthpiece microphone from the lines to the exchange,' he said. 'SF was a very simple device whose effect was to stop the disconnection of the line, so that the mouthpiece microphone remained active all the time. It then picked up any conversation within range and transmitted it to monitors at the exchange or on a line tap.' Kim Philby, then a Soviet agent inside MI6, was shown around the anti-communist section by Hollis, reporting back to Moscow that the MI5 officer 'said in a voice of triumph that they had got King St completely buttoned up'.

Philby was impressed with Hollis, who would later himself be accused of being a Soviet spy. 'Hollis struck me as being a man with a remarkable knowledge of his subject and with a good sense of bureaucratic organisation and technique,' Philby said. 'He was "broad-minded" on the subject of Soviet policy and himself put forward the view that Soviet policy might well be designed to attempt to make the Anglo-Soviet pact a reality, and consequently to temper the revolutionary spirit of the Communist Party. (This was in marked contrast to Vivian's usual view, which is to see something directly sinister in everything the Soviet Union does.)'

The other two anti-communist sections were F2B and F2C. F2B consisted of Millicent Bagot and three other women and dealt with Comintern activities on British territory. Hollis described Bagot, who had been dealing with the problem for more than 20 years, as 'a really outstanding character' with 'a postively encyclopaedic knowledge of the subject'. F2C, the Russian counterespionage section, was led by Hugh Shillito, who had achieved a major success in breaking a major nationwide spy ring controlled by the GRU, the Soviet Army's intelligence section.

The Green Ring was the GRU's equivalent of the Cambridge Spy Ring and, although ultimately not as successful, was described by MI5 as being 'welltrained and highly professional'. It was built up by Oliver Green, a printer who had been recruited by Soviet military intelligence while serving with the International Brigade during the Spanish Civil War. He began setting up the network after returning to Britain in 1938. Centred on Green's flat at 293a Edgware Road, north London, it was run by the GRU head of station, or *Rezident*, in London, assisted by two officers working under cover as trade representatives. All the agents recruited by Green were British subjects. They included a government official, a number of soldiers, a worker at an aviation plant, another source with access to an aviation plant, a merchant seaman and a pilot.

The prime role of the network was to gather political intelligence. One of the soldiers had access to the War Office's weekly summaries of military intelligence and passed these on. The other main target was details of British weapons and equipment. The network was also tasked to carry out sabotage, in the event of a British invasion of Russia or a German invasion of Britain. If the GRU *Rezident* was forced to leave, Green would take complete charge and would have authority to order CPGB members to carry out individual acts of sabotage. From the beginning of 1941, as Moscow began to suspect that Germany was planning to attack the Soviet Union, Green was also asked to gather information from British intelligence sources on German armaments and battle order.

Green travelled around the country collecting the agents' reports He then either passed them by hand to the GRU *Rezident* or had them sent by high-speed Morse from a number of radio transmitters dotted around the country. But Green's success in recruiting so many agents, and the subsequent amount of travelling he was forced to do, meeting around 15 agents a month, was to prove his downfall. He was warned against using his car by the GRU but ignored them and was driving so many miles in a week that he was forced to use forged petrol coupons. While travelling home from a meeting with one of his agents, Green was stopped by police officers who found the forged petrol coupons. A search of his flat uncovered a dark room with two rolls of film containing photographs of the weekly summaries of military intelligence. Green was arrested and confessed to Shillito, giving him full details of his network and how it operated.

The only other major case of Soviet espionage uncovered by MI5 during the Second World War was run by David Clark, the head of F2A, since the main agent was Douglas Springhall, a senior member of the CPGB, who was also in contact with the GRU *Rezident*. He was thought to have been carrying out espionage for some time before he was caught in 1943, when the flatmate of one of his female agents became suspicious. The woman, who worked in the Air Ministry, had given Springhall details of 'a new and highly secret device'. Notes in Springhall's diary revealed a number of agents, all of whom were Communist Party members. They included a secretary in the Secret Intelligence Service, which by now was known by its more familiar title of

MI6, and Captain Desmond Uren, an officer in the Special Operations Executive (SOE), who was arrested and gave a full confession. Philby told his masters in Moscow that according to Clark, 'Uren might easily have got away scot-free if he had realised the scantiness of the knowledge in the possession of the British authorities. If he had maintained steadily that, although approached by Springhall, he had refused to supply him with information, the authorities could never have broken him. He was however unable to stand the strain of the interrogation and ended up by confessing everything.'

As a result of the Springhall case, MI5 compiled a list of 57 members of the Communist Party who 'were in a position and willing to give to the CPGB or the Soviet authorities information about important secrets connected with new inventions and military operations.' Those removed from their posts as a result included one member of MI5, one member of MI6, and one member of the SOE. But in a number of cases, the relevant departments ignored MI5 advice. These cases included that of James Klugman, a member of the SOE who was playing a key role in liaison with the resistance in Yugoslavia. MI5 made repeated protests but it was only later, from a conversation picked up by the bug in the CPGB headquarters, that it obtained incontrovertible proof of Klugman's activities as a classic communist 'agent of influence'. Klugman had already helped convert Anthony Blunt, one of Cambridge Spy Ring, to communism and played a key role in the Soviet recruitment of John Cairncross, another member of the Cambridge Five. In a conversation monitored in full by MI5, Klugman told a senior CPGB member that he had been determined to use his SOE post to switch British support from Draza Mihailovic's Royalist Chetniks to Tito's communist Partisans.

'I was put into their Yugoslav section as what they call conducting officer, which was the man who did prepare [sic] the people, whether British or Yugoslav, to go to the country,' he said. 'The Yugoslav section had first of all four or five officers – it was supporting the Chetniks and that initiated about two years political work for me. The first political aim was to get permission for our Yugoslav section to learn from intelligence sources about Partisans, to show that there were Partisans as well as Chetniks. That took about three months, a fight with the Foreign Office and the War Office and GHQ Middle East. The second step was to get permission to send certain agents not only to the Chetniks but to the Partisans. That was another three months, fighting, persuading, documents, organising, every type of work. The next three months was to get permission to send arms to the people that were Partisans as well as Chetniks. The next three months, four months about, was to get permission to send people to support the Partisans in Serbia, which was the area where Mihailovic was strongest. Previously we had only been allowed to send them to other areas. The next stage, again for four or five months, was building up of reports we were getting from the Chetniks and the reports from the Partisans – no activity against the enemy on the Chetnik side, first-class activity on the Partisan side – to recall the missions from the Chetniks and to give support to the Partisans. And the last stage of my fight was to fight inside the organisation for political recognition of the Partisans. So finally in the country we had a dump of really bad types – people who supported Franco etc sending in ridiculous and ill-educated reports from the Chetniks and we had a network, really a dozen people, sending in first-class reports from the partisans. And on this basis you see we were able to go to the next stage to show that only in this area is work being done against the Germans.'

During the conversation, Klugman also claimed to have built up a group of people sympathetic to communism and to the partisans among the five intelligence organisations in Cairo that were dealing with Yugoslavia. 'We were able to act like a sieve. All information coming out of the country had to go through one of our departments, and to see what got back was satisfactory,' he said. 'We were able from our own British sources to prove what the Russian press, the communist press, had been saying for so long.' Klugman's activities were also alluded to in a bugged telephone conversation between two party members, in which one said the SOE officer was 'largely responsible for the improved relations, I mean as far as any individual worker can be, in improved relations with Tito.' Churchill decided in November 1943 to abandon the Chetniks and support the Partisans. How much effect Klugman's actions had is difficult to tell. By the time Churchill made his decision, the Partisans were certainly more effective than the Chetniks, a fact made clear by intercepted German messages. But it is difficult to believe that Klugman's efforts were not an important factor in the Partisans' success and by extension the creation of a communist post-war Yugoslavia.

But MI5 had no such problems dealing with Nazi agents. Its operations against the Abwehr, the German military intelligence service, were to evolve into one of the greatest intelligence successes of all time – the Double-Cross system. This was based on an operation carried out by the French *Deuxième Bureau*. Dick White, a future head of MI5, suggested that captured *Abwehr* agents should be left in place and 'turned' to work as double agents for British intelligence. MI5 would be able to keep complete control over all German espionage activities in Britain and as a welcome side-effect, the information the agents asked for would tell the British what the *Abwehr* did and did not know. At this early stage, this was the full extent of MI5's ambitions.

One of the earliest opportunities to turn a German agent came with the arrest of Arthur Owens, a Welsh businessman who travelled frequently to Germany and who had volunteered in 1936 to collect intelligence for MI6. But the intelligence he provided was of little use and he was soon dropped. He subsequently got back in touch with MI6 to inform them that he had managed to get himself recruited as an agent by the *Abwehr*, claiming to have done so in order to penetrate the German intelligence service on behalf of the British. But interception of his letters to his German controller suggested he was playing the two services off against each other. In September 1938, he announced to MI5 that he had now been appointed the *Abwehr*'s chief agent in Britain and that he had been given a special German secret service code with which to encode his messages.

On the outbreak of war, he was arrested at Waterloo station and agreed to work as a double agent under the covername of Snow. His controller was Lieutenant-Colonel Tommy 'Tar' Robertson of MI5, a remarkable man who was to become the key British figure in the Double Cross system, setting up an MI5 section (B1a) to run them. By the end of 1940, Robertson had a dozen double agents under his control. At the same time, MI6 was running a number of German spies abroad. 'Basically, MI5 was responsible for security in the UK and MI6 operated overseas,' said Hugh Astor, one of the B1a agent-runners. 'Obviously there was a grey area as far as double agents was concerned because they were trained and recruited overseas and at that point were the concern of MI6, while once they arrived here they became the responsibility of MI5.'

The other key players in the Double Cross system were the Radio Security

Service, an organisation originally run by the War Office and later by MI6 which monitored the agent messages, and the GC&CS codebreakers at Bletchley Park. A section was set up to at Bletchley under the control of Oliver Strachey to decipher the messages between the *Abwehr* and its agents in Britain. The decrypts became known as ISOS, standing either for Illicit or Intelligence Services (Oliver Strachey). They enabled MI5 to keep track of the messages of the double agents and spot any other German spies arriving in the country. It also meant that the agents' reports could be designed to allow the codebreakers to follow them through the *Abwehr* radio networks. Hopefully, this would help them break the keys for the Enigma cipher that the German controllers were using to pass the reports on to Hamburg.

A secret committee was set up to decide what information should be fed back to the Germans. Its small select membership included representatives of MI5, MI6, naval, military and air intelligence, HQ Home Forces and the Home Defence Executive, which was in charge of civil defence. The committee was called the XX Committee, although it swiftly became known as the Twenty Committee, or more colloquially the Twenty Club, from the Roman numeral suggested by the double-cross sign. It met every Wednesday in the MI5 headquarters, initially in Wormwood Scrubs prison, but subsequently at 58 St James's Street. 'The XX Committee was chaired by J C Masterman,' said Astor. 'Tar Robertson, who ran B1a, really developed the whole thing. He was absolutely splendid, a marvellous man to work for. He and Dick White were the two outstanding people I suppose and Tar collected around him some very bright people who actually ran the agents for him.' The Twenty Club's job was to decide what information could be fed back to the *Abwehr* without damaging the British cause. Initially, with the threat of a German invasion dominating the atmosphere in London, it was decided that the 'intelligence' provided by the double agents should be used to give an impression of how strong Britain's defences were. But by the beginning of 1941, it was clear that more could be done with the double agents.

'In the earlier years, the main aim was to block German attempts to infiltrate the UK with their spies,' said Kenneth Benton, one of the MI6 officers involved in the project. 'But it became clear that as well as keeping the *Abwehr* case officers content with their apparent coverage of events in wartime

Britain, we could use our *Abwehr* agents for a process of strategic deception. The object was not only to stop an enemy agent from operating, but where possible to "turn" him. He could be given the simple choice of either being tried and shot as a spy or agreeing to work entirely under the orders of the MI5 case officer. When a spy was successfully turned the profit was twofold. On the one hand the *Abwehr* case officer would believe that he had a useful agent on his books and thus have less need to recruit others. On the other, the false information which the British case officer would send to Germany through his agent's communication – e.g. radio messages or secret ink letters – could be useful for strategic deception.'

The MI5 officers handling the double agents needed to know what information they could give to their agents to build up their reputations with the Germans. Much of it was 'chicken-feed', unimportant information that would give the *Abwehr* a feel that its agents were doing something and had access to real intelligence without telling them anything really harmful to the war effort. But mixed among this were key pieces of specious or misleading information designed to build up a false picture of what the British were doing. The committee's task was to coordinate this work. They supervised the system. They did not run the individual agents, Astor said. 'They approved the overall plan. I was in touch with the Germans probably two or three times a day by radio and so I had to move fairly quickly. So the approving authorities were not the actual Twenty Committee, because it only sat once a week. I would get approval from people who were on the committee and every week I and others who were actually active would prepare a short report for the committee saying what we were doing and what we had done.'

But while the system appeared to be working, the Twenty Committee and the agent-handlers had a problem. They could not be sure the Germans were fooled. The *Abwehr*'s operations abroad seemed to be unbelievably incompetent. The agents were 'too amateurish' to be genuine. Capturing them and turning them round was so unbelievably easy that the British suspected that it might be part of an elaborate *Abwehr* deception. 'The position at the beginning was largely experimental as no one knew very much about the working of double agents or about the working and general incompetence of the *Abwehr*,' wrote Ewen Montagu, the naval intelligence representative on the

Twenty Committee. 'Later on, after we had had experience of the German Intelligence Service, no incompetence would have surprised us.'

While the response of the *Abwehr* controllers to the double agents' reports helped the Twenty Committee to work out where the gaps in the Germans' knowledge lay, it did not tell them whether or not the misleading intelligence picture they were attempting to build up was believed in Berlin. The only way of finding this out was by deciphering the messages passed between the *Abwehr* outstations in Paris, Madrid, Lisbon and their headquarters. But these links all used the *Abwehr*'s Enigma machine, which was completely different to those used by the other German services.

So the Twenty Club's confidence in their double agents was considerably enhanced in December 1941 when Bletchley Park's chief cryptographer Dilly Knox, who was dying of cancer and working from home, broke the *Abwehr* Enigma. The first of the messages, known as ISK for Illicit (or Intelligence) Services Knox, was issued on Christmas Day 1941. They were invaluable to the Twenty Committee, revealing that the Germans believed the false intelligence the Twenty Committee was feeding them and showing whether or not individual double-agents were trusted or under suspicion, in which case steps could be taken to remedy the situation. By the spring of 1942, the information collected from the Bletchley Park decrypts had built up such a good picture of *Abwehr* operations in Britain that Robertson believed MI5 now controlled all the German agents operating in Britain. The Twenty Committee was able to watch the Germans making arrangements to send agents to Britain and discussing the value of their reports, Robertson wrote. 'In two or three cases we have been able to observe the action (which has been rapid and extensive) taken by the Germans upon the basis of these agents' reports.'

But the breaking of the Enigma cipher had brought a new problem for the committee. The release of any material from Bletchley Park was controlled extremely strictly by MI6 in order to safeguard the Ultra secret. Nobody took this more seriously than Felix Cowgill, the head of Section V, who represented MI6 on the Twenty Committee. Cowgill was a shy, slightly built man in his mid-thirties. 'His face gives the impression of intensity coupled with a great weariness,' Kim Philby said in one of his reports to Moscow. 'Although normally quiet in manner, due to shyness, he is combative in his work, always prepared to challenge an office ruling.' Cowgill protected the Ultra decrypts vigorously to the extent of refusing to allow the Home Forces and Home Defence Executive representatives on the Twenty Committee to see them at all, while anything that referred to MI6 agents was held back even from MI5. 'Cowgill was so imbued with the idea of security that when he was put in charge for C of this material, he was quite willing to try entirely to prevent its use as intelligence lest it be compromised,' Montagu said. 'These views inevitably caused friction.' Cowgill's attitude made the Twenty Committee's operations almost impossible. Some members were not privy to vital information on which the others were basing their decisions. The result was potentially far more detrimental to security than the widespread dissemination that Cowgill was trying to prevent. His controls were soon being ignored on a wholesale basis. 'A good deal of bootlegging of information had to take place,' said Montagu. 'Many undesirable "off the record" and "under the table" practices were essential unless work was to stop entirely.'

The situation came to a head over the case of a man who was to become the most valuable of all the Double Cross agents – Juan Pujol Garcia, better known by his codename: Garbo. The Bletchley decrypts had revealed an *Abwehr* agent who claimed to be running a network of agents in Britain. His reports were ridiculously inaccurate. He was clearly a fraud, reporting 'drunken orgies and slack morals in amusement centres' in Liverpool, and Glasgow dockers who were 'prepared to do anything for a litre of wine'. It ought to have been obvious to the Germans that, not only had he never met a Glasgow docker in his life, he had never been to Britain. Yet they believed him wholeheartedly. MI6 became concerned that his false reports might damage the Twenty Club's own plans.

Then in early February, the MI6 head of station in Lisbon was approached by a Spaniard claiming to be a top *Abwehr* secret agent. He said he had been disaffected by the Spanish Civil War and was keen to help Britain to fight the Germans. Having been turned down by the MI6 station in Madrid, he had gone to the *Abwehr* equivalent, persuading the officers there that he was a Spanish intelligence officer who had been posted to Britain and offering to act as a German spy. In fact, Pujol went to Lisbon, where armed with a Blue Guide to Britain, a Portuguese book on the Royal Navy and an Anglo-French vocabulary of military terms, he produced a series of highly imaginative reports built on his alleged network of agents. Pujol was vehemently anti-Nazi and his reports were apparently designed to disrupt the German intelligence service, he was in effect a freelance double-cross operation in miniature. Cowgill kept him secret from MI5, on the basis that although sending reports ostensibly from British territory and therefore notionally under MI5 jurisdiction, he was actually abroad and the responsibility of MI6.

The fact that an important German agent was sending uncontrolled reports about Britain, however inaccurate, could have caused immense damage if it were not taken into account in the overall deception plan. So when, at the end of February, senior officers in MI5 discovered that his existence had been hidden from them, they were furious. A few weeks later, they discovered that Cowgill had also been holding back ISOS messages thought to refer to MI6 agents. It was the final straw. Sir David Petrie used the row to lobby for MI5 to take over control of Section V. He added all the arguments over the distribution of deciphered intercepts, MI5 criticism of the apparent lack of basic knowledge about Germany among a number of Section V officers, and the fact that it was based in St Albans, too far away from London to make liaison with MI5 as easy as it should have been. Menzies agreed to set up a new department within Section V called VX to deal exclusively with the Double Cross system. It would be based in London to allow easy liaison with MI5 over the work of the double agents and would be headed by Frank Foley, who, having been head of station in Berlin throughout the 1920s and 1930s, had an unrivalled knowledge of Germany. 'He was not a member of the establishment clique,' said Desmond Bristow, one of Foley's MI6 colleagues. 'But he was a pretty serious chap, feet on the ground, solid, very much the elder statesman, giving useful advice whenever called upon. His exceptional knowledge of the workings of, and personalities in, the *Abwehr*, acquired during years of service in Berlin, made him a tower of strength.'

Foley replaced Cowgill as the MI6 representative on the Twenty Committee. 'There was an obvious qualitative difference in the way in which the committee worked from then on,' one former MI5 officer said. 'For the first time, the MI6 representative was speaking authoritatively because he was a real operational officer. He knew what he was talking about and it showed.' Masterman, who as secretary of the Twenty Committee was in the perfect position to know, also pointed to the mid-1942 changes as the moment that the Double Cross system really began to take off. 'Broadly speaking, bad men make good institutions bad and good men make bad institutions good,' Masterman said. 'It cannot be denied that there was some friction between MI5 and MI6 in the early days, but this disappeared when the MI6 representative on the committee was changed.'

The running of the Double Cross operations was helped immensely in July 1943 when Section V moved from St Albans to Ryder Street, a stone's throw from the MI5 headquarters in St James's Street. This meant that, if there were any problems, MI5 officers could simply walk across the road to discuss them with their opposite numbers in MI6. 'One always gets the impression of a tremendous rivalry and that sort of thing,' said Astor. 'And I suppose at the top, there can be rivalry. But at the lower level, one just has to get on with the job and I always found everybody very helpful. Even at the top, one can exaggerate the degree of thigh grabbing. The time scale was so short you couldn't really have a long battle with anybody. I don't think there was really enough time for bad blood to be created. I knew all that I needed to know about those organisations and the style and characteristics of the agents I was running, the techniques that they used and of course assisted very much by Ultra. One usually got advance information about the arrival of agents through Ultra, so one knew what training they had been through.'

MI5 succeeded in turning more than forty *Abwehr* agents. They included 'Tate', Wulf Schmidt, a Dane who parachuted into East Anglia in September 1939 and was given his cover name because of a striking resemblance to the famous music-hall artist Harry Tate. Despite being a member of the Nazi Party, Schmidt continued operating until Hamburg fell in May 1945. He was so successful that the *Abwehr* described him as 'the pearl' in its British network, sent him large sums of money, and awarded him two Iron Crosses. Another agent was Dusko Popov ('Tricycle'), an urbane, womanising Yugoslav who is thought to have been the model for James Bond. Popov had been recruited before the war by MI6 and was later to claim controversially that the

FBI ignored intelligence he provided which indicated that an attack on Pearl Harbor was being planned.

By now the main thrust of the Twenty Club's operations was in preparing for D-Day. Churchill was as fascinated with deception as he was with espionage. At the Teheran Conference in November 1943, when the final decision was made to launch the invasion of Europe in mid-1944, the British Prime Minister told Stalin that 'in wartime, truth is so precious that she should always be attended by a bodyguard of lies'. From that point on, the overall deception plan for D-Day was known as Operation Bodyguard. The double agent handlers now had to think continuously about the various elements of the deception plan and how the agents could be used to convince the Germans they were true. The Double Cross system became like a game of chess with the agents resembling pieces, each being carefully moved into a position where it could contribute to the opponent's demise.

The key agents in the deception plan to cover the actual D-Day landings, which was to be called Fortitude South, were to be those who were controlled by wireless. Although the reports of the letter-writing agents would also be used to point the Germans away from the Allies' real plans, it was only those with wireless sets who could send messages in 'real time'. Fortitude South evolved rapidly during the early months of 1944, but the bare bones of the plan remained the same. The Germans were to be led to believe that the Normandy landings were a feint attack aimed at drawing German forces away from the main thrust of the allied invasion, which would be against the Pas de Calais. This would ensure that the bulk of the German forces would be held back from the Normandy beaches, allowing the Allies time to establish a strong foothold in northern France from which they could break out towards Paris and then on to the German border.

A completely mythical formation, the First United States Army Group (FUSAG) was allegedly commanded by General George Patton, a hero of the invasion of Sicily and a man whom the Germans would believe must be heavily involved in the invasion of Europe. FUSAG was supposedly grouped in East Anglia and south-eastern England and it was vital that the agents' reports were coordinated to show that this was the case, and to downplay the mass of troops waiting in the south and south-west to attack the German defences in Normandy.

The most spectacularly useful of the wireless agents used in the Fortitude South deception plan was Garbo. Although he had now been moved to Britain, his network was so large and so vital to the overall deception picture that virtually everything had to be closely coordinated on a day-to-day basis. The most important of the other agents who, in the parlance of the Twenty Committee, 'came up for D-Day' was the triple agent Brutus. Roman Garby-Czerniawski, a Pole, had led the Interallié resistance network in France and, once it was uncovered, volunteered to work for the *Abwehr* in London in order to save the other members of his group from execution. On arrival in Britain he immediately told the authorities of his mission and was turned against the Germans. Two others were also important to Fortitude South: Tricycle, and Natalie 'Lily' Sergueiv (Treasure), a French citizen born in Russia whose family had fled in the wake of the Bolshevik revolution.

All four of these helped in building up Fortitude South, the false picture of the intended target of D-Day. Tricycle and Brutus, who was run by Astor and was supposedly a member of a Polish unit attached to FUSAG, provided an order of battle for the fictitious formation so detailed that the Germans were not just supplied with details of individual units, strengths and locations, but even with reproductions of the insignia painted on the side of their vehicles. Treasure's role was to report from the West Country that there were very few troops there, further pushing the Germans towards the view that the main thrust of the attack would be against the Pas de Calais. But by far the most important and complex role was played by Garbo. At one point he had a network of 27 agents, including a Swiss businessman based in Bootle who had reported 'drunken orgies and slack morals in amusement centres' in Liverpool and an enthusiastic Venzuelan living in Glasgow who had noted the willingness of Clydeside dockers to 'do anything for a litre of wine'. The Swiss businessman died of cancer in the autumn of 1942. But his widow continued working for Garbo, becoming virtually his personal assistant. The Venezuelan also grew in stature, becoming Garbo's official deputy and developing his own ring of agents in Scotland, one of whom was an ardent communist who actually believed he was working for the Soviet Union. The *Abwehr* codenamed this group of agents the Benedict Network. Garbo's mistress, a secretary working in the offices of the War Cabinet, provided useful opportunities for valuable pillow talk. She, like the wireless operator, believed that her lover was a Spanish Republican. Garbo had also successfully set up a large network of agents in Wales, mostly Welsh Nationalists but led by an ex-seaman, 'a thoroughly undesirable character' who was working for purely mercenary reasons. They were all figments of either his imagination or that of his MI5 controller Tomas Harris. Nevertheless, they all contributed to the German dependence on him as their most reliable source for intelligence on the allied plans setting the scene for Garbo's, and arguably MI5's, greatest triumph.

In the early hours of D-Day, 6 June 1944, Garbo made repeated attempts to warn his *Abwehr* controller that the Allied forces were on their way. It was too late for the Germans to do anything about it but ensured they still believed in Garbo as their best-informed secret agent even after the invasion had begun and paved the way for the next stage of the deception. Shortly after midnight on 9 June, as the Allied advance faltered and with the elite 1st SS Panzer division on its way, together with another armoured division, to reinforce the German defences in Normandy, Garbo sent his most important message. Three of his agents were reporting troops massed across East Anglia and Kent and large numbers of troop and tank transporters waiting in the eastern ports, he said. 'After personal consultation on 8 June in London with my agents Donny, Dick and Derrick, whose reports I sent today, I am of the opinion, in view of the strong troop concentrations in south-east and east England, that these operations are a diversionary manouevre designed to draw off enemy reserves in order to make an attack at another place. In view of the continued air attacks on the concentration area mentioned, which is a strategically favourable position for this, it may very probably take place in the Pas de Calais area.' Garbo's warning went straight to Hitler who ordered the two divisions back to the Pas de Calais to defend against what he expected to be the main invasion thrust. This ensured the success of the Allied invasion. Had the two divisions continued to Normandy, the Allies might well have been thrown back into the sea.

MI5 did not just enjoy some notable successes against Soviet and German agents. It also managed to run a number of agents of its own inside the embassies of neutral and allied countries based in London. These were run by by a Soviet agent within MI5, Anthony Blunt, who was put in charge of B1b by Dick White. Blunt set about expanding MI5's operations, ostensibly to extend the amount of intelligence available to the British but in fact to help his Soviet masters. He obtained material from: diplomatic intercepts deciphered by GC&CS; taps on embassy telephones; agents; and the opening of diplomatic bags, a system known as 'Triple X', which was carried out by a small unit in MI6, called N section.

'White asked me to investigate the question of diplomatic communications which had not up till then been studied systematically by MI5,' he told Moscow Centre. 'First I had to find out what mechanisms already existed, and then what could be found or invented. The existing ones were nearly all in the hands of MI6. For instance, the breaking of ciphers by GC&CS is in effect directed by MI6 and the opening of diplomatic bags is also in their hands. The listening to embassy telephones is also done by MI6. The reason is that MI6 is technically under the Foreign Office and diplomats are supposed to be primarily of interest to the Foreign Office. My first job – and by no means my easiest – was to persuade MI6 to let MI5 see the material which was of interest to us. By managing to see their old files I discovered that there was a mass of material of the greatest interest from the counter-espionage point of view which we had never seen.'

MI5 expanded the network of agents by persuading Hunt's, a domestic agency that specialised in providing servants to foreign missions, to cooperate. Whenever Hunt's had a request for a domestic servant from one of the embassies where MI5 needed intelligence, an agent run by Maxwell Knight's M Section was placed in the post. This operation was run by a J G Dickson, an employment specialist who was on loan to MI5 from the Ministry of Labour, and a Mrs Gladstone, a specialist in domestic personnel, who liaised with Hunt's. 'She has built up a certain group of servants, mostly people she knew before and she could get hold of through friends,' Blunt told Moscow. 'These are planted, as opportunity offers. What usually happens is that she rings me up and says that, let us say, the Argentine embassy are looking for a housemaid and asks me if I am interested. I say yes or no according to the interest in the embassy and the suitability of the post offered. Certain jobs are almost useless. For instance, a housemaid in the ambassador's house as opposed to the chancery. Others, such as the position of the man who burns the waste paper are obviously ideal. One way or another, we have a constantly changing series of people in certain of the embassies. In some cases, we only leave them there for a short time and then take them away if we find they cannot get anything of interest. In others we have got people who constantly get us really good stuff, for instance in the Spanish embassy. The useful material they get is of different kinds. Our best agent of all, who is a secretary and not a servant, in the Spanish embassy, gets us cipher tape, clear versions of cipher telegrams, drafts of the ambassador's reports, private letters, notes on dinner parties and visitors, and general, gossip about the members of the embassy. Others only get us the torn letters from the waste-paper baskets, but even these are sometimes of interest.'

Spain was one of the highest-priority targets because of Franco's alleged neutrality but tacit support for Hitler and MI5 had at least three agents in the Spanish embassy. But it also had agents in the Portuguese, French, Dutch, Belgian, Lebanese, Turkish, Swedish, Swiss, Polish, Persian, Brazilian, Chilean, Colombian, Peruvian and Argentine embassies.

Some of these agents, including those placed in the Brazilian; Chilean; Colombian; Portuguese; Spanish and Swiss embassies, were kept in place at the end of the war but Blunt warned his bosses that the ability to use the domestic servants in particular was likely to decline sharply in peacetime. 'Whole series of agents wanted to do this kind of work during the war out of patriotic motives but, after the war, either agree reluctantly to carry on for moral reasons or want to find themselves better paid and more permanent work. Generally speaking, embassy domestic staff are not able to obtain intelligence information of any great quality. In some cases, they have been of great service by obtaining the contents of waste-paper baskets, which has provided either valuable documents or material of use in breaking ciphers. Most embassies, however, are very careful to burn such material and we cannot rely on many of them being as usefully careless as the Spanish were during the war.'

Yet for all its success, in detecting communist and Nazi agents, and running agents into neutral and friendly embassies, MI5 never uncovered the presence deep inside the British Establishment throughout the war of a ring of five top

KGB agents including Blunt. Claims by Maxwell Knight, the veteran anti-Communist campaigner, in a 1941 report entitled 'The Comintern is not Dead', that there was a Soviet agent inside MI5 were ignored at an horrific cost. The Double Cross system was an unqualified success, but it did nothing for MI5's reputation. By the time the details emerged, that had already been damned by the failure to detect the Cambridge spy ring.

Seven

Subversion, Terror and Crime

MI5's political surveillance role involves above all a fine judgement between what is subversion and what is legitimate dissent, which in my experience is unlikely to be found in those who live in the distorting and Alice-through-the-Looking-Glass world in which falsehood becomes truth, fact becomes fiction, and fantasy becomes reality.

Roy Jenkins, former Home Secretary on his impressions of MI5

MI5 was deeply distrusted both by the Labour Party, which still harboured bitter memories of the Zinoviev Letter, and by the Conservatives. During the 1945 election campaign Churchill played on fears of the idea of a British secret police, warning that a Labour government 'would have to fall back on some form of Gestapo'. When Clement Attlee came to power, he ignored the internal favourite, Guy Liddell, and appointed Sir Percy Sillitoe, the Chief Constable of Kent, to head the service. No doubt it was a reassuring choice for the Labour leader. In his introduction to Sillitoe's autobiography, Attlee wrote that one of the key requirements for a Director-General of MI5 was 'a very lively appreciation of the rights of the citizen in a free country'. R. V. Jones, who, as Director of Scientific Intelligence, sat on the JIC with Sillitoe in the early 1950s, recalled once asking him if he would like support for more draconian powers. 'No,' he replied. 'If I had more power, it would turn Britain into a police state. That would be the worst thing for England.'

Less reassuring was the secret report of the inquiry by Brigadier Sir Findlay Stewart, Chairman of the Security Executive, into the future of the intelligence services. 'The purpose of the Security Service is the Defence of the Realm and nothing else,' it said. 'From the very nature of the work, need for direction except on the very broadest lines can never rise above the level of Director-General. There is no alternative to giving him the widest discretion in the means he uses and the direction in which he applies them – always provided he does not step outside the law.'

The London headquarters of MI5 had by now moved to Leconfield House in Curzon Street, Mayfair, and the staff evacuated to Blenheim during the war transferred there. It was to be the service's main base until 1972. One of MI5's biggest post-war headaches was the number of refugees coming in from Europe, many of whom were expected to be Soviet agents. Between 1950 and 1952 the service carried out a mass investigation into their backgrounds, interrogating more than 200,000 émigrés, the vast majority of whom had come from what had become the Soviet Bloc. Of those interrogated, 3,023 were earmarked for internment should there be war with Russia. Operation Post Report was not just about looking for Soviet spies: MI6 was keen to send some of the refugees back into the Soviet Union as British agents. What it was definitely not about, however, was finding war criminals. In order to encourage the émigrés to tell the truth, they were given an assurance that they had 'nothing to fear by disclosing the facts about their past history and true identity'.

The end of the war also brought the first details of the extent to which the British Establishment had been penetrated by the Soviet intelligence services with the defection of Igor Gouzenko, a cypher clerk at the Soviet embassy in Ottawa, and a failed attempt at defection by Konstantin Volkov, the KGB's deputy *Rezident* in Ankara. Volkov claimed to have the names of seven Soviet wartime moles in British intelligence, and Gouzenko revealed that Alan Nunn May, a British atomic scientist, was working for the GRU, Soviet military intelligence. The fact that Nunn May, a communist, had been allowed to work in such a secret field and the resultant American fears over poor British security led to the United States Congress passing the 1946 McMahon Act, which severely restricted exchanges of atomic information.

In 1947, Attlee set up a Cabinet committee on subversive activities, GEN183, and this began the process of weeding out communists and Fascists from sensitive government posts. But it was a slow job, and even after the 1950 discovery of another atom spy, Klaus Fuchs, Attlee refused to sanction stronger measures. It was not until 1951 that the defections of Donald Maclean and Guy Burgess led to the more comprehensive process of 'positive vetting' being introduced for all sensitive posts. At the same time a re-examination of MI5's role by Sir Norman Brook, the Cabinet Secretary, recommended that the service be made responsible to the Home Secretary, ending an anomaly under which it had been responsible to no single government ministry and at the mercy of inter-departmental wrangles – in the words of Brook's predecessor, Maurice Hankey, 'something of a lost child'.

Informing Sir Percy Sillitoe of the change, on 24 September 1952, Sir David Maxwell Fyfe, the new Conservative Home Secretary, laid down the ground rules which were to apply to MI5 until the Security Service Act was passed in 1989. 'The Security Service is part of the Defence Forces of the country,' he said. 'Its task is the Defence of the Realm as a whole, from external and internal dangers arising from attempts at espionage and sabotage, or from actions of persons and organisations, whether directed from within or without the country, which may be judged to be subversive to the State.'

Although the Maxwell Fyfe directive stressed that the Director-General should ensure that MI5's operations were apolitical and limited to what was absolutely necessary, it left the decisions on what actually constituted subversion or a threat to the Defence of the Realm entirely up to MI5 itself. It said, 'You and your staff will maintain the well-established convention whereby Ministers do not concern themselves with the detailed information which may be obtained by the Security Service in particular cases, but are furnished with such information only as may be necessary for the determination of any issue on which guidance is sought.'

While many of Peter Wright's allegations in *Spycatcher* were simply not credible, his description of MI5 in the immediate wake of the 1952 Maxwell Fyfe directive certainly was. The training he received on joining the service in 1955, which included 'regular classes run for MI5 and MI6 in its lock-picking workshop', seemed remarkably similar to that given to earlier recruits by Inspector William Melville. Although the very broad outlines of the Maxwell Fyfe directive may have been adhered to in Wright's MI5, Sir Findlay Stewart's exhortation that the Director-General should not 'step outside the law' clearly was not. Sir John Cuckney, who went on to become chairman of a number of prominent British companies, including Brooke Bond, Thomas Cook and Royal Insurance, began the training with a lecture on MI5's legal status, Wright alleged. "'It hasn't got one," he told us bluntly. "The Security Service cannot have the normal status of a Whitehall department because its work very often involves transgressing propriety or the law." He made it very clear that MI5 operated on the basis of the 11th Commandment – "Thou shalt not get caught" – and that in the event of apprehension there was very little that the office could do to protect its staff.

Wright's description of how, in Operation Party Piece, his colleagues burgled the British Communist Party's membership files from a flat in Mayfair to photocopy them may appear scandalous today. But, with Churchill's Iron Curtain speech still ringing in people's ears, the operation doubtless seemed entirely reasonable to the 'pompous bowler-hatted civil servants' of the early 1950s. Communism was seen as the main threat to the Defence of the Realm. The next two decades were to be dominated by Soviet penetration of the British Establishment and even of the intelligence services themselves. That was of far greater public concern at the time, and questions would more likely have been asked if MI5 had not 'bugged and burgled its way across London' to prevent it.

The service's reputation was badly damaged by a series of spy scandals in which it was seen as not doing enough to stop Soviet penetration. Between the defections of Guy Burgess and Donald Maclean in 1951 and that of Kim Philby twelve years later, came the arrests of the Portland Spy Ring, which was passing on submarine secrets from the Portland naval base; George Blake, an MI6 officer 'turned' by the Russians; and William Vassall, a homosexual Admiralty official blackmailed into passing secrets to the KGB. There was also the Profumo affair, when an MI5 operation to recruit the Soviet naval attaché, in London became embroiled in the public scandal surrounding the relationship between Christine Keeler, a call-girl, and John Profumo, the Defence Secretary.

There were some successes, during the counter-insurgency campaigns that marked the retreat from empire in the late 1940s and the 1950s. But these were mainly orchestrated by MI5's security liaison officers in its colonial outposts – Security Intelligence Middle East (SIME) in Cairo and Security

Intelligence Far East (SIFE) in Malaya – and were anyway seen as being successes for the British Army rather than for MI5, which until the Denning Report into the Profumo affair was not even officially acknowledged to exist.

Dick White, MI5 Director-General from 1953 to 1956, instigated a major reorganisation of the Security Service. Henceforth the divisions would be known by their old name of branches. Technical Support – including the 'watchers', the officers in charge of target surveillance – remained the responsibility of A Branch; B Branch became Personnel; C Branch was Security; D Branch took over Counter-Espionage; E Branch was in charge of Security and Intelligence in the Colonies, which under the so-called Attlee Doctrine was solely an MI5 responsibility; and F Branch was charged with Counter-Subversion, with orders from White to infiltrate left-wing organisations, including the Labour Party and the trade unions.

White, who as head of both MI5 and MI6 and later as Britain's first Intelligence Co-ordinator dominated post-war British intelligence, had hoped that the reorganisation would expunge the memory of the failures of the post-war era and restore morale within the service. But it was not to be. The Cambridge spy ring was to haunt MI5 for years to come. Following the defection in December 1961 of Anatoly Golitsyn, a KGB officer who told startled British intelligence officers that there were not three members of the Cambridge ring but five, and the 1964 discovery that Anthony Blunt, a wartime member of MI5, was one of this so-called Ring of Five, the service turned in on itself in a series of investigations supervised by a joint MI5–MI6 working party known as the Fluency Committee. If the KGB had been happy to let Blunt leave MI5 at the end of the war, the mole-hunters reasoned, they must have had another Soviet agent in place. A number of the committee's mole-hunters – Wright among them – became inordinately influenced by the views of James Angleton, the head of the CIA's counter-espionage division, sharing his obsession that the British intelligence services were riddled with Soviet agents. Their main suspicion, that Roger Hollis, Director-General of MI5 from 1956 to 1965, was a long-term KGB agent, was eventually ruled out. It was Wright's refusal to accept the vindication of Hollis that eventually led to the publication of *Spycatcher*. But Wright was by no means alone in his continued belief that Hollis was a spy. Oleg Gordievsky, a former KGB colonel and long-term MI6 double agent, recalled that 'when the KGB saw the chaos caused by the allegations against Hollis, their laughter made Red Square shake'.

MI5 fought back, however, and, following the defection in 1971 of Oleg Lyalin – a KGB officer charged with identifying British targets for Spetsnaz (Soviet special forces) sabotage squads – it gained a significant success. Sir Martin Furnival-Jones, the Director-General of MI5, told a meeting of senior officials from across Whitehall chaired by Sir Denis Greenhill, the Cabinet Secretary, in May 1971 that over the past 15 years there had been evidence of widespread Soviet penetration of important British organisations. These included the Foreign Office, the Ministry of Defence, the Army, the Royal Navy, the RAF, the Labour Party, the trade unions and the Board of Trade. He produced a list of more than 100 known Soviet intelligence officers based in London. His evidence led to the expulsion of ninety Soviet diplomats and the exclusion of a further fifteen who were on leave. The expulsions were made on the grounds that the diplomats were *personae non gratae* – the traditional code for spies. The bulk of the KGB's London *Rezidentzura* had gone. 'In 1971, the golden age of KGB operations came to an end,' Gordievsky claimed later. 'The London residency never recovered from the expulsions. Contrary to the popular myths generated by media "revelations" about Soviet moles, during the next fourteen years ... the KGB found it more difficult to collect high-grade intelligence in London than in almost any other Western capital.'

If MI5 was looking around for something to compensate for the dearth of Russian spies, it soon found it. Within months of coming to power in June 1970, the Conservative government of Edward Heath was engaged in a bitter battle with the trade unions, declaring a state of emergency in response to strikes by dockers and power workers. The 1971 Industrial Relations Act, designed to curb union power, merely precipitated further stoppages, and more days were lost to strikes in 1972 than at any time since 1919. When the 'flying pickets' deployed during the 1972 miners' strike prevented coke from reaching the power stations and Britain's industry had to be placed on a three-day week, the government was close to panic.

'At this time, many of those in positions of influence looked into the abyss and saw only a few days away the possibility of the country being plunged into a state of chaos not so very far removed from that which might prevail after a minor nuclear attack,' Brendan Sewill, a special adviser to Anthony Barber, the then Chancellor of the Exchequer, would later recall. 'If that sounds melodramatic I need only say that – with the prospect of the breakdown of power supplies, food supplies, sewage, communications, effective government and law and order – it was the analogy that was being used at the time. This is the power that exists to hold the country to ransom: it was fear of that abyss which had an important effect on subsequent policy.'

One of the measures taken by the Heath government was to ask MI5, which was in the process of moving its headquarters to Gower Street, Euston, north London, while retaining offices in Curzon St, to increase surveillance of the trade unions and left-wing organisations. Sir Michael Hanley, the new Director-General of MI5, called a meeting of key members of F Branch, the counter-subversion department, 'to discuss the changing shape of MI5's priorities', Peter Wright would claim. 'The meeting began with a presentation from Hanley on the climate of subversion in the country and the growth of what he termed the "far and wide left". The Prime Minister and Home Office, he said, had left him in no doubt that they wanted a major increase in effort on this target. Hanley began to pour resources and men into F Branch and away from K Branch. Obtaining intelligence about domestic subversion, as opposed to catching spies, became our overriding priority.'

The Maxwell Fyfe directive, which still ruled MI5's operations, allowed it to act against 'persons and organisations, whether directed from within or without the country, which may be judged to be subversive to the State'. But by the mid-1970s there was growing concern over what exactly constituted subversion in MI5's eyes. Unlike many of Peter Wright's allegations, the expansion of activities against 'subversive' organisations and individuals had already been confirmed by other former MI5 officers.

Periodic claims, mainly in the left-wing press, that MI5 indulged in widespread bugging of the telephones of union leaders and organisations like the National Council for Civil Liberties were largely unsubstantiated and dismissed by most people as 'conspiracy theory'. One of the more bizarre claims was an allegation made by Sir Harold Wilson that, while Prime Minister, he had been the subject of a smear campaign by a group of right-wing MI5 officers. A subsequent claim that Wilson's office in 10 Downing Street had been bugged led to the whole story being dismissed as yet another conspiracy theory.

But in April 1984 a spectacular court case set in train a series of revelations which showed that not every allegation made against MI5 could so easily be dismissed. Michael Bettaney, a young officer in K Branch, the counter-espionage branch, was found guilty of attempting to pass secrets to the Russians. He had been arrested the previous September, having made three unsuccessful attempts to offer himself as a potential double agent, contacting Arkady Guk, the KGB's London *Rezident*, or head of station, directly. In messages dropped through the letter-box of Guk's London home, Bettaney employed typical agent tradecraft to lay out a complicated system of dead-letter boxes and methods of communication that were to be used should Guk decide to accept his offer. In the first letter, Bettaney 'instructed Guk that he would find in the first-floor gents lavatory at the Academy One Cinema in Oxford Street, taped under the lid of the cistern, a canister containing exposed film of classified information,' Sir Michael Havers QC, the British Attorney-General, told Bettaney's Old Bailey trial. 'If he did decide to accept, he was to place a drawing-pin (any colour) at the top of the right-hand banister of the stairs leading from platforms three and four at Piccadilly Circus Underground Station. When the defendant checked the banister at Piccadilly Circus Underground, there was no drawing-pin and he concluded 'that after consultation with the KGB's headquarters in Moscow a decision had been taken that my offer should not be accepted.'

In fact Guk had decided that Bettaney's approach was an attempted MI5 provocation, and he ignored both it and the next two attempts. But he mentioned it to fellow KGB officers, including Oleg Gordievsky, a long-term MI6 agent-in-place. Gordievsky informed his British handlers, and Bettaney was subsequently arrested. Fortunately, he had not been one of five K Branch officers who were aware of Gordievsky's existence and working with MI6 to ensure that the KGB officer's cooperation was not inadvertently disclosed. Following his conviction, Bettaney issued a prepared statement which, among other things, alleged that MI5 'cynically manipulates the definition of subversion and thus abuses the provisions of its charter so as to investigate and interfere in the activities of legitimate political parties, the Trade Union Movement and other progressive organisations'. The statement, which was full of pseudo-Soviet rhetoric, was widely discounted as an attempt by Bettaney to justify his attempted treachery and sparked little debate. But there was considerable discussion of the way in which senior MI5 officers had apparently ignored Bettaney's serious drink problem and the fact that he had become disillusioned to the point where he was openly denouncing MI5's activities to his colleagues. The Security Commission, set up in the wake of the Profumo affair to investigate such scandals, subsequently ordered a comprehensive overhaul of the service's personnel system.

The debate led two of Bettaney's former colleagues to complain that he was not alone. There was widespread disillusionment among the service's younger officers, partly due to the intractably right-wing attitudes of its senior officers but mainly as a result of the role of F Branch. Miranda Ingram, a former colleague of Bettaney's in K Branch, wrote that while the counter-espionage branch is 'the acceptable face of MI5 ... it is in the area of domestic surveillance that problems can occur. This comes under F Branch. Working here means monitoring one's fellow-citizens.' There was concern among some officers over what was considered to be subversion, she said. But, 'in the prevailing right-wing atmosphere, an officer who dissents from the official line does not feel encouraged to voice his concern. He feels that it will be futile or detrimental to his career.' Ingram expanded on the theme in a subsequent newspaper article. 'Then come the doubts about the nature of your work. Reading private letters, listening to telephone calls – which to some is distasteful. Suddenly, at the age of 24, you have to decide whether to open a file on a fellow citizen. Your vetting assessment may ruin somebody's career. There are doubts about the legality of some of the work. It can be alarming for a recruit to be party to deliberate law-breaking, and particularly worrying to discover that it is "wrong" to question such activity.'

The second officer, Cathy Massiter, had served in F Branch but had left after becoming 'increasingly at odds with myself over the nature of the work and its justifications'. Massiter alleged that she and other MI5 officers had been 'violating' the rules on political bias in an operation against the Campaign for Nuclear Disarmament. In March 1983 Michael Heseltine, the

Defence Secretary, had set up an organisation called Defence Secretariat 19, or DS19, to counter CND unilateralist propaganda. The unit approached MI5 for information on CND activists, and Massiter was ordered to help it. She expressed the view that it contravened the Maxwell Fyfe order to be 'absolutely free from any political bias or influence', but was told to get on with the job. 'It did begin to seem to me that what the Security Service was being asked to do was to provide information on a party political issue,' she said. 'Unilateral nuclear disarmament had been adopted as a policy by the Labour Party, a general election was in the offing, and it had been clearly stated that the question of nuclear disarmament was going to be an important issue there. It seemed to be getting out of control. This was happening not because CND as such justified this kind of treatment but simply because of political pressure. The heat was there for information about CND, and we had to have it.'

Massiter described how any union taking strike action would routinely be subjected to MI5 surveillance. 'Whenever a major dispute came up – something at Fords or the mines, or the Post Office – immediately it would become a major area for investigation: What were the Communists doing in respect of this particular industrial action? And usually an application for a telephone check would be taken out on the leading comrade in the particular union concerned.' She also revealed that two prominent members of the National Council for Civil Liberties, Harriet Harman and Patricia Hewitt, who both later became leading Labour politicians, had been the subject of MI5 surveillance. Files would be routinely opened on anyone who was active within the NCCL. Her revelations led the NCCL (now known as Liberty) to take the government to the European Court of Human Rights and – indirectly, since the government anticipated that the court would rule MI5's activities illegal – brought about the 1989 Security Service Act. It was clear from the testimony of Massiter and Ingram that not only was MI5 bugging people's telephone calls and opening their letters but many of those put under surveillance were not even guilty of the very broad definition of subversion that the service was using as a benchmark.

'You couldn't just concentrate on the subversive elements of CND,' Massiter said. 'You had to be able to answer questions on the non-subversive elements, and the whole thing began to sort of flow out into a very grey area. It highlights very clearly this extreme ambivalence between what the Security Service is there to do – what it perceives itself as being there to do: to study subversion – and what actually happens in practice, which is in effect to broaden this study quite a long way beyond those basic guidelines.'

Her allegations led to Leon Brittan, the then Home Secretary, admitting that people did not have to be behaving illegally or even contemplate doing so to find themselves the subject of an MI5 surveillance operation. 'Tactics which are not in themselves unlawful could be used with the aim of subverting our democratic system of government,' Brittan said. With MI5's reputation at an all-time low, it emerged that further revelations would appear in a new book by a former MI5 officer. Peter Wright's motives for writing *Spycatcher* were not to expose alleged 'dirty tricks' – far from it. Despite starting his career in 1955 as a scientific officer, apparently producing useful gadgets much in the manner of James Bond's fictional colleague 'Q', Wright had been on the Fluency Committee and remained convinced that Hollis was a long-term Soviet agent. But when *Spycatcher* was finally published, after a protracted and, for the British government, ignominious battle through the Australian and British courts, it was Wright's allegations of an MI5 plot to destabilise Harold Wilson that made the headlines rather than the oft-repeated claims against Hollis.

Wright and Arthur Martin, the two leading mole-hunters, had given considerable credence to a claim by the KGB defector Anatoly Golitsyn that Hugh Gaitskell, Wilson's predecessor as Labour Party leader, had been murdered to allow Wilson to become Prime Minister. But the allegations of a plot against Wilson were damaged by Wright's own subsequent testimony. Interviewed by the BBC, he admitted that the *Spycatcher* claims of a plot were 'unreliable'. Asked about the figure given in the book of thirty officers who approved of the plot, he conceded that it was 'exaggerated'. 'The maximum number was eight or nine,' he said. 'Very often, only three.' Wright, who had written in *Spycatcher* that he was not involved in the plot, was then asked, 'How many people, when all the talking died down, were still serious in joining you in trying to get rid of Wilson?' He replied, 'One, I should say.'

Even taking Wright's admission of exaggeration into account, *Spycatcher* only added to the impression of a security service that if not totally out of control was already a good way along that road. The inevitable concentration on the alleged Wilson plot and the fact that Massiter had already blown the whistle on F Branch's counter-subversion activities meant that little attention was given to Wright's account of the 1972 Hanley order to root out the 'far and wide left'. But several senior politicians who had direct experience of working with MI5 while in government during the 1970s and had no record of subscribing to conspiracy theories expressed serious doubts over what was going on. Roy Jenkins, Home Secretary from 1974 to 1976, called for MI5 to 'be pulled out of its political surveillance role'.

'I had been doubtful of the value of that role for some time,' he told a 1989 House of Commons debate prompted by the *Spycatcher* allegations. 'I am convinced now that an organisation of people who live in the fevered world of espionage and counter-espionage is entirely unfitted to judge between what is subversive and what is legitimate dissent.' Even Edward Heath, who as Prime Minister had ordered the increase in the surveillance of 'subversives', said there were officers within MI5 'whose whole philosophy was ridiculous nonsense. If some of them were on the tube and saw someone reading the *Daily Mirror*, they would say, "Get after him, that is dangerous. We must find out where he bought it."' The politicians and the public had lost faith in MI5, and within the service itself there was widespread dismay both at the low esteem in which it was held and at its inability to respond to the various allegations being made in the press. John Day, a former K Branch officer who had left the service in 1982, described many of the allegations made at the time as 'stupid rubbish', adding, 'while some of the criticism levelled at MI5 was undoubtedly deserved, often it was ill-informed.'

Stella Rimington, who was in charge of MI5's counter-subversion section F2 at the time, confirmed Massiter's claims that trade unions and CND were under surveillance, admitting that she had run operations against the National Union of Mineworkers during the 1984–5 Miners' strike. 'The thing people fail to understand is that subversive organisations by definition target areas of society that have the most influence – unions or whatever,' she said in defence of the operations. 'What the service was doing was very clearly set out by the definition of subversion. I think, in the past, some of our predecessors may have been a bit over enthusiastic but by the time I got there we were very focused on this definition and what we were doing. But it's not always an easy judgement to make.'

MI5 had targeted Arthur Scargill, the NUM President, Mick McGahey, the Vice-President, and Peter Heathfield, the General-Secretary, because they 'had declared that they were using the strike to try to bring down the elected government of Mrs Thatcher', and because the union was 'actively supported by the Communist Party'. Rimington described her period in charge of counter-subversion as one of 'very considerable upheaval – the miners' strike, the Greenham Common protests, the height of CND, the growth of Militant Tendency, and a Socialist Workers Party very active in universities'. She claimed that 'we in MI5 limited our investigations to the activities of those who were using the strike for subversive purposes'. MI5's targeting of leading CND activists was justified on the grounds that the movement was 'of great interest to the Soviet Union', which 'encouraged members of the Communist Party of Great Britain to infiltrate it'.

Following the Bettaney case, Prime Minister Margaret Thatcher appointed Sir Antony Duff, the Chairman of the Joint Intelligence Committee, the body which co-ordinates British intelligence assessments, to be the new Director-General of MI5, with a brief to stop the rot. He spent the next two years replacing the emphasis on counter-subversion with a major drive against terrorism. He also began pushing for a more clear-cut system of legal accountability and some form of oversight. Duff's reforms, with their avowed emphasis on dragging the Security Service out of the old-boy network and into the real world, included the recruitment of more young people and promoting women to senior posts – among them Stella Rimington, who was appointed to the prestigious post of Director of K Branch, in charge of counter-espionage.

Mrs Thatcher was adamantly opposed to any suggestion that the intelligence services should be subjected to parliamentary oversight. Even getting her to set up the Franks Committee which looked into intelligence-gathering during the Falklands War had, according to David Owen, the former SDP leader, been 'like dragging teeth'. She did agree to the Security Service Act – which was seen as imperative, given the NCCL's case in the European Court –

but insisted there should be no further moves towards openness. 'I believe we should continue to enable the security services to run in a secret way,' she said. 'After all, those against whom they operate have the benefit of secrecy.'

The Security Service Act reiterated that MI5 was responsible to the Home Secretary and laid out its role as being 'the protection of national security and, in particular, its protection against threats from espionage, terrorism and sabotage, from the activities of agents of foreign powers and from actions intended to overthrow or undermine parliamentary democracy by political, industrial or violent means'. While that was a reiteration of MI5's traditional role, two other parts of the Act would later lead to further debate over MI5's future role. These were an additional task to 'safeguard the economic well-being of the United Kingdom' and a reference to passing on, presumably to the police, any information that the service might come across which might be useful in 'preventing or detecting serious crime'.

The Act also included an immunity clause to the effect that 'no entry on or interference with property shall be unlawful if it is authorised by a warrant issued by the Secretary of State' and, in a limited move towards oversight, provided for a Commissioner and a tribunal of three lawyers to investigate complaints. They would have to meet in camera and, although the Commissioner had the power to award compensation against the Home Secretary, the government was not obliged to take any notice of what the tribunal decided. Nevertheless, the report would be published and, if adverse, might be expected to lead to criticism from politicians and the media. Sir Patrick Walker, who took over from Duff in 1987, had maintained his reforms. MI5 was reorganised, with the responsibilities of the old F Branch, by now the basis of most of MI5's work, forming three separate branches: Counter-Terrorism (International); Counter-Terrorism (Irish and Other Domestic) and Counter-Subversion. The new role of counter-proliferation was included among the tasks of the Counter-Espionage Branch and the old A Branch, which provided technical support, such as expertise in breaking and entry, bugging, and surveillance – the 'watchers' – remained much as it had been before.

MI5's computer records were soon shown to be little better than Kell's Precautionary Index. In an operation reminiscent of the Second World War 'witch-finding activities' against German, Austrian and Italian refugees, the threat of Iraqi terrorism during the 1991 Gulf War led to deportation notices being served on a total of 167 Iraqi, Jordanian, Lebanese and Yemeni nationals. No doubt a number of the Arab nationals served with the notices had represented some form of risk. Eight were Iraqi diplomats, among whom were almost certainly members of *Da'irat al-Mukhabarat al-Amah*, the Iraqi intelligence organisation. But, as in 1940, the vast majority were innocent. A total of 81 left Britain without exercising their option to appeal. Most of the remaining 86 were held either in police cells or behind barbed wire on Salisbury Plain until they were released on appeal, which occurred in 33 cases, or until the end of the war. Their quasi-internment raised a political storm when the paucity of the evidence against them began to emerge.

Sir Philip Woodfield, the Security Service Commissioner, held an inquiry into the affair. His report was kept secret, but the Foreign Office, which had bitterly opposed the detentions, let it be known that he had been severely critical of MI5 over the poor quality of information in its files on the detainees, although in fact the operation against suspected pro-Iraqi terrorists was conducted by a joint MI5–MI6 Middle-East terrorism unit, which was subsequently disbanded. The controversy over the Gulf War internments was an embarrassing glitch amid the internal changes that were intended to modernise MI5 and ensure there was no repeat of the public-relations débàcle of the mid-1980s. The second stage of that rehabilitation process was not to be enacted until Sir Patrick's successor, Stella Rimington, took over as Director-General in 1992.

Eight

Fresh Challenges for MI5

It is almost inevitable that national security intelligence work which is based on covert sources and techniques will involve some infringement of the civil liberties of those under investigation.

Stella Rimington, then MI5 Director-General, James Smart Lecture,
3 November 1994

The appointment of Stella Rimington as MI5 Director-General was the first such appointment to be announced publicly. She issued a statement saying that, despite the end of the Cold War, the service still had a difficult job to do. She was pleased to have been given 'the responsibility of leading the service in facing up to the challenges which the coming years will bring'. The first challenge MI5 faced if it was to maintain its empire in the post-Cold War world was to find a new lead role. Counter-terrorism, and in particular the fight against the IRA, seemed to fit the bill. The Security Service had for some time been lobbying hard to take control of all activities by the police, military and intelligence services directed against Irish terrorism. Amid complaints of chronic lack of co-ordination between the various factions fighting the IRA and its 'loyalist' counterparts, the Home Office had been considering taking responsibility for counter-terrorism intelligence operations on mainland Britain away from the police and giving it to MI5. Several times the move was rejected, but with a full-scale turf battle being waged in the pages of the national press, and following substantial private lobbying by Rimington herself, MI5 won control over all operations against the IRA both on the mainland and abroad, but not in Northern Ireland where the RUC remained in charge. In May 1992 Kenneth Clarke, the Home Secretary, told the House of Commons that 'political change' – an apparent euphemism for the collapse of the Warsaw Pact and the resultant drop in espionage activity – had made it possible for MI5 to devote more resources to countering the IRA. There would be no conflict with the police, who would remain responsible for the collection of evidence and the arrest and prosecution of suspects. As part of the takeover, known in the service by the codeword Ascribe, MI5 would share its intelligence on IRA activities with Special Branch and the Anti-Terrorist Squad, Clarke said. It had been important to draw a line in the sand to prevent relations between MI5 and Special Branch 'festering'.

With the battle to keep its resources secured, MI5's management board moved on to the next stage in the rehabilitation process. On 16 July 1993, Rimington held a press conference to launch a government brochure describing the role of MI5 and how it worked. In the introduction, she admitted the information it provided on the service was limited. 'There is, of course, a clear limit to what can be made public without either undermining its [MI5's] effectiveness, or else endangering its staff, and others who work closely with it.' But the brochure was being published 'to dispose of some of the more fanciful allegations surrounding its work'. In fact the booklet, which looked for all the world like a company prospectus, did not do very much to dispel the 'fanciful allegations', apart from a denial that MI5 monitored the behaviour of people just because they were well known or held responsible positions – presumed to be a reference to allegations that it had been watching Princess Diana – and a rejection of Wright's claims of a plot against Harold Wilson. Nevertheless, the fact that only five per cent of the service's resources were taken up with subversion – it has since been reduced to just a watching brief – would have gone a long way towards reassuring left-wing and trade-union activists. Even former MI5 officers conceded that the booklet was a step in the right direction. 'If MI5 is moving towards more openness, two cheers,' said one. 'It may be a public relations exercise but if it makes the public aware of the good things the service is doing what is wrong with that? At least this might bring worthwhile criticism instead of the stupid rubbish that appeared during the *Spycatcher* episode to which nobody in the service could respond.'

Clarke's hopes that giving the Security Service primacy in the battle against terrorism would prevent a 'festering' rivalry between MI5 and the police had meanwhile proved to be false. During a 1991 visit to Moscow, when she was

Deputy Director-General (Operations), Rimington held detailed discussions with her Russian opposite numbers on what the TASS news agency described as 'the fight against international terrorism and drug trafficking'. The reference to 'drug trafficking' had set alarm bells ringing among senior police officers, a number of whom, having noted the clause in the Security Service Act on 'preventing or detecting serious crime', already suspected that Rimington had a hidden agenda to turn MI5 into a British version of the FBI. Both the Home Office and Rimington herself denied that there were any plans for MI5 to become involved in the investigation of organised or drugs-related crime. But the service's involvement appeared to be confirmed by Baroness Park, a former member of MI6, who in December 1993 told the House of Lords that both MI6 and MI5 were reporting on 'the potentially destabilising threat posed to our economy and that of some dependent territories by drug trafficking and the consequent laundering of dirty money'.

As the moves towards greater accountability continued, with the announcement that a new cross-party committee of Privy Councillors would provide a limited form of oversight of MI5's activities, Rimington kept up her efforts to improve the service's public reputation, appearing on television to give the 1994 Richard Dimbleby Lecture. It was a careful mix of candour and Civil Service-speak which flitted between the past and present tenses in order to put the best possible gloss on the service's image and also included touches of dry humour. Rimington worked hard in her lecture at dispelling the lingering 'fanciful allegations'. The service now always operated within the law, she said. It did not keep watch on people simply because it disagreed with their politics, nor did it subcontract operations out to evade legal controls or monitor the activities of people with a high public profile 'on the off chance ... that they might be at or even pose a risk'. This was all said in the present tense, of course – and, given MI5's dubious past, much of it could only have been honestly stated if it were. She acknowledged this briefly, conceding that, yes, there may have been occasional 'rotten apples' in the past, but in her MI5 there was no group of 'mavericks' pursuing its own agenda, she said. Nor was the service using the resources previously deployed in the Cold War to turn its attention to the general public 'or for that matter anyone else about whom we, or perhaps the government, feel uncomfortable. The idea is quite frankly ludicrous. Just as ludicrous as the allegation that the service carries out murder.' In the only apparent allusion to the counter-subversion activities of the 1970s and early 1980s against organisations like CND and the National Council for Civil Liberties, she said simply, 'The allegation that the service investigated organisations which were not in themselves subversive is quite untrue. Our interest was in the subversives, not in the organisations they sought to penetrate.'

At best that last statement was highly subjective. It scarcely squared with Massiter's sworn affidavit on the work of the old F Branch. Nor presumably would it have met with much sympathy from Roy Jenkins, who had a few months earlier told Parliament that he retained grave doubts over the service's ability to distinguish between subversion and legitimate dissent. 'I experienced in the Security Service what I can best describe as an inherent lack of frankness, an in-growing mono-culture and a confidence-destroying tendency to engage in the most devastating internal feuds,' he said. The political surveillance role involved 'a fine judgement . . . which in my experience is unlikely to be found in those who live in the distorting and *Alice-through-the-Looking-Glass* world in which falsehood becomes truth, fact becomes fiction, and fantasy becomes reality'. But, in the real world of spin-doctored public relations, it was not what Rimington or anyone else said that mattered. It was the fact that she had been prepared to stand up in front of the television cameras and justify her existence – albeit without anyone questioning her statements – that would grab the headlines, take MI5 a step further down the road to public rehabilitation and, perhaps more importantly, improve her stock still further among the politicians and senior civil servants who would decide the service's future role. For, as Rimington would already have known, covert negotiations on a peace settlement with the IRA were by now well advanced, and, with some 40 per cent of the service's resources devoted to domestic terrorism, peace in Northern Ireland represented a considerable threat to MI5's future. The announcement of the IRA cease-fire and the official start of the Northern Ireland peace process, in September 1994, brought renewed speculation that the service was about to move into the area of serious crime and on to the police's patch.

As MI5 prepared to move from the various offices it had occupied during the past thirty years, mostly dotted around its Gower Street headquarters, into the new home at Thames House on Millbank, which had been refurbished and specially kitted out at a cost of £245 million, it found itself at an important watershed. There were inevitable parallels between similar situations in 1919, 1946 and 1972. On all three occasions MI5 had lost a major part of its work at a stroke: in 1919 and 1946 by the end of the two world wars, and in 1972 by the expulsion of the bulk of the KGB's London *Rezidentzura*. In 1972, the fear of left-wing subversion had provided a replacement activity for MI5; in 1946 it was the Soviet threat and the coming Cold War. The salutary lesson, to be avoided at all cost, was 1919, when the new role of countering Bolshevism had gone to the police Special Branch – albeit in the guise of Basil Thomson's Directorate of Intelligence – leading to horrendous cuts in MI5's budget and staff. The Security Service now found itself under a similar threat. The drop in counter-espionage activities resulting from the end of the Cold War had been adequately compensated for by the increase in counter-terrorism and the 1992 take over of the war against the IRA. But, with both the republicans and the government apparently moving inexorably towards a peace agreement, it was clear that MI5 had the choice of making drastic cuts in staff or finding a new role.

In November 1994 Rimington emerged from the shadows again, to deliver the 1994 James Smart Lecture – and with it the first shots in a campaign to ensure that this time MI5 did not lose out to the police. Addressing an audience of senior police officers, she suggested an expanded role for MI5 in areas that would normally be the territory of the police. Senior police officers defended their patch by stressing that their role of collecting evidence and then making arrests was very different from that of the Security Service, which tends to keep suspects in place rather than have them arrested. Intelligence officers regard having a comprehensive picture of what is going on as more important than preventing crime, and at the time at least had a poor record of collecting evidence. But Rimington said it was wrong and misleading to make too sharp a distinction between the spy and the detective. 'The Security Service is fully committed to supporting the police in detecting and preventing crime and preserving law and order,' she said. 'Criminal investigation can be a valuable focus for intelligence work, and equally intelligence can be converted into evidence.'

It was those two carefully phrased sentences that convinced senior police officers that she aimed to move into other areas such as combating organised crime, drug-trafficking and money-laundering. They knew they were vulnerable to attack. Rimington had proved to be an extremely effective Whitehall infighter, and she was able to argue with justification that, like the various agencies fighting the IRA before the 1992 MI5 takeover, police intelligence was poorly co-ordinated, with no acknowledged overall supremo. Their concern was not eased by an endorsement from Michael Howard, the Home Secretary, of Rimington's sentiments. While the secret service and the police had distinct roles and functions 'these differences should not be exaggerated,' he said. 'The two services should be seen as complementary and ... operating in a broadly similar field.' A secret Home Office report had just denounced the National Criminal Intelligence Service, which was supposed to be co-ordinating police intelligence, as ineffective and impotent, dependent on other parts of the police force to carry out actual operations.

But police officers argued that the MI5 officers they had worked with seemed to have no real understanding of what would be required in terms of evidence if a case were to come to court. Rimington had assured senior police officers that MI5's procedures for gathering, recording and collating intelligence had been tightened to ensure it could be used effectively as evidence. But Special Branch officers said that, despite Kenneth Clarke's 1992 insistence that the police would remain in charge of evidence, attempts to give the increasingly young and highly ambitious MI5 desk officers advice on the difficult process of collecting evidence frequently led to 'friction'. As speculation over MI5's search for new roles mounted, Deputy Assistant Commissioner John Howley, the head of Special Branch, accepted that the Security Service had a part to play in the investigation of serious crime. But he insisted that 'There would need to be a difference of attitude on the part of MI5 in coming to terms with the different standards of accountability.' Unlike its sister organisation, the Secret Intelligence Service, which had to seek ministerial permission before undertaking any major new operations, MI5 was self-tasking. Having been given its remit in terms of the Security Service Act, it was the service's own management board that sanctioned the individual branches' proposed operations, having satisfied itself that each falls within the

Act, that was is a cost-effective method of achieving the aim, that where necessary the evidence would stand up in court, and that it did not pose unnecessary risks. But the lack of any ministerial, or even Home Office, control over the decision to undertake a specific operation and the broad, if not open-ended, mandate to protect national security left the service itself to decide what constitutes a security threat.

In early October 1995 Rimington again laid out her stall for MI5's participation in operations against organised crime, stressing the service's experience in dealing with trans-national terrorism through co-operation with other agencies. 'The changing international climate means that everywhere perceptions of the threats to national security are being re-examined,' she said. 'This new world order has created conditions which also encourage the growth of what is increasingly being called organised crime. There seems little doubt that crime of this sort will grow, feeding on the increasing ease and speed of communications and travel and the weakening of controls. Countering the threat successfully will require the same methods, which have been developed to deal with the more familiar threats such as terrorism. This means the same strategic approach, the same investigative techniques. But above all it means the same close national and international co-operation between security intelligence and law-enforcement agencies.' It later emerged that those comments had also been designed to reinforce the case for her chosen successor, Stephen Lander, amid suggestions that a senior police officer might better cope with the changes required if MI5 were to take on organised crime. Mr Lander, as a former director in charge of counter-terrorism, had been responsible for setting up the close links with other agencies that Rimington said would be vital in combating serious crime.

A week after Rimington's lecture, John Major announced that the government was planning to change the legislation to give the Security Service the role it wanted in fighting crime, working with the National Criminal Intelligence Service under the control of the newly created Home Office Directorate of Organised and International Crime. 'The police really had no reason to worry,' one MI5 officer said. 'There were always going to be problems. When you get two people fishing in the same pool, there are bound to be tensions. But we just felt there was something we could bring to the party.' Even before the legislation was introduced, MI5 had mounted a number of criminal operations in support of the police. Serious crime is now a growth area for MI5. It may investigate crime if it 'involves the use of violence, results in substantial financial gain or is conducted by a large number of persons in pursuit of a common purpose; or the offence or one of the offences is an offence for which a person who has attained the age of 21 and has no previous convictions could reasonably be expected to be sentenced to imprisonment for a term of three years or more.'

There may just be a few too many ors in that brief, since it appears to sanction operations against a wide variety of criminals, including wife-batterers and bosses with their fingers in the company pension fund, people few would regard as a threat to the security of the state. There are also legitimate concerns over MI5's large armoury of highly sophisticated electronic surveillance equipment, most of which is so top secret that it has to be protected in court by the frequent use of public immunity certificates – so-called gagging orders. How far do these new high-tech surveillance gadgets infringe on our civil liberties?

Telephone taps and postal intercepts are authorised by government ministers under the 1985 Interception of Communications Act and their use is recorded in an annual report by the Security Service Commissioner, a senior judge. But the report is far from informative and the public concern over such matters was increased considerably by the 2000 Regulation of Investigatory Powers Act (RIPA). Section 12 of this act requires mobile telephone network and Internet providers to provide 'the interception of the entire contents of the communication and the related communications data going from or intended for a warranted person or premises, and transmission to government/the intercepting agencies in near real time'. They are also required to provide all mobile telephone numbers, email addresses, Internet logons and passwords. They must provide 'sufficient security so that the chance of a warranted person or other unauthorised persons becoming aware of any interception is minimised.' The National Technical Assistance Centre, a Home Office organisation based inside the MI5 headquarters at Thames House, decrypts emails and other intercepted encrypted computer transmissions.

The tapping of ordinary landline telephone calls is controlled by computers based at the BT switching centre at Oswestry, in Shropshire, which instruct the local digital exchange to send them simultaneously to the nearest telephone-tapping centre. Monitoring of mobile telephones, which is carried out by GCHQ, is extremely useful to MI5 since it also allows those tracking a subject to locate him or her to within a certain relatively small area. A national mobile telephone system is made up of a series of base stations controlling small roughly circular areas, normally about 12 miles in diameter. These are designed to overlap slightly in order to provide cell-like coverage of the whole country. The base stations are controlled by a mobile telephone switching office (MTSO). Once a mobile telephone is turned on, its trans-ceiver automatically searches for the local base station with the strongest signal and begins passing it information on its identity, which is then passed back to the MTSO to allow any incoming calls to be routed to the telephone. As its owner moves, it constantly seeks out the strongest base station, switching from one to another as it moves from cell to cell. All this informa-tion is passed back to the MTSO to allow it to redirect calls to the appropriate base station, allowing the movements of the telephone's owner to be tracked to within 12 miles. The control channels used to pass all this information between the telephone and the base station also create a very simple bugging system, regardless of whether the owner of the phone is making a telephone call. Simply switching the telephone on allows anyone who has obtained the right information from the network provider to listen in to what is being said in the telephone's immediate vicinity.

In the mid-1990s, a reorganisation of MI5 split responsibility for the service's work between two deputy director-generals: one in charge of intelli-gence operations, and the other covering administration. But in early 1996 one of these posts was abolished, leaving the other deputy controlling four operational branches. A Branch, intelligence resources and operations, provides technical support, such as expertise in breaking and entry, bugging, and surveillance. D Branch, counter-espionage, also covers other non-terrorist threats such as organised crime, subversion and protective security, providing vetting for government departments and defence contractors, advising on security and investigating breaches of security. G Branch handles international terrorism and counter-proliferation; while the fourth, T Branch, covers domestic terrorism and in particular Irish paramilitary activity. Two other branches come under the direct control of the Director-General: B Branch, personnel, training and office services; and H Branch, dealing with strategy, finance, planning and information management.

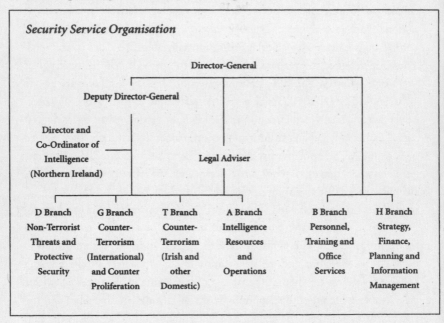

Security Service Organisation

Director-General

Deputy Director-General

Director and
Co-Ordinator of
Intelligence
(Northern Ireland)

Legal Adviser

D Branch	G Branch	T Branch	A Branch	B Branch	H Branch
Non-Terrorist	Counter-	Counter-	Intelligence	Personnel,	Strategy,
Threats and	Terrorism	Terrorism	Resources	Training and	Finance,
Protective	(International)	(Irish and	and	Office	Planning and
Security	and Counter	other	Operations	Services	Information
	Proliferation	Domestic)			Management

Each branch is headed by a director, and these directors together with the Director-General and his deputy make up the service's management board. There are around 2,000 staff, roughly half of whom are women, and this figure is expected to rise to around 3,000 by 2007. But only around 15 per cent of the staff are general intelligence officers (GIO), the actual Security Service officers who form the core management structure and are responsible, for example, for monitoring intelligence investigations, running agents, and carrying out policy work. Each branch consists of a number of GIOs as well as a wide range of administrative, technical and other specialist staff. The vast majority of the service's work is now aimed at terrorism, with domestic terrorism, mainly Irish and including both 'loyalist' and republican activities, taking up 30 per cent of the service's resources. International terrorism, dominated by Islamic groups and in particular by al-Qaʻeda, take up a further 30 per cent. But this is seen as likely to increase. While the likelihood of an IRA bombing in the UK is greater, the damage of an al-Qaʻeda attack would be far greater, both in terms of the numbers killed and its impact on the public consciousness. The continued terrorist threat in the wake of the 1998 Omagh bombing and the 2001 al-Qaʻeda attacks on America has also led to an increased effort at protective security, taking up 10 per cent of resources. The scale of the threat has had to be 'recalibrated' following the 11 September attacks, one official said. Whereas previously MI5's protective security effort was aimed purely at government departments, now a number of areas of the private sector that are part of the 'critical national infrastructure' receive MI5 advice. These include the utilities, the gas, water and electricity industries; banks; telecommunications companies; and the air and rail transport organisations. Counter-espionage now only takes up 16 per cent of resources with the other targets being proliferation of nuclear, biological and chemical weapons, three per cent; and serious crime, eight per cent. The remaining 3 per cent of resources is dedicated to liaison and examining potential new threats.

Stephen Lander continued Rimington's attempts to revamp MI5's image. But this process was disrupted by the decision of a junior officer to take his complaints about the service to a Sunday newspaper and Rimington's surprising decision to publish her memoirs. The junior officer was David Shayler, who had joined MI5 in 1991 and left in 1997 after becoming disaffected over what he saw as excessive bureaucracy within MI5. Shayler initially discussed writing a book but publishers were wary and legal advice stated unequivocally that under Section 1 of the Officials Secrets Act 1989, it was an offence for anyone who had served in MI5 to reveal any information about intelligence or security obtained during that service without permission. Shayler was also not what publishers expected from a rebel MI5 officer. He was not arguing that civil liberties were being infringed, far from it. In fact, he was prepared to defend the service against such charges. 'Unfortunately,' he said, 'what's happened with MI5 is they didn't quash a number of stories in the Eighties, which they should have quashed, some of the more outlandish idiocies, and they gained some ground. So everybody had this idea of MI5 being this incredibly out of control organisation but in fact that is not the case. It certainly, in the past, had a very strong bias against the Left. But people would argue that the Left was where certain bits of subversion were happening.' The problem was over-bureaucracy and waste, he said. It was this he wanted to expose.

Determined to make his concerns public, he then decided to make his allegations through the newspapers. In August 1997, the *Mail on Sunday* published a series of allegations by Shayler. They included the fact that MI5 had files on two government ministers, Peter Mandelson and Jack Straw, who as Home Secretary at the time was also in charge of MI5. The other main allegations related to Shayler's most recent experience in the section of G Branch that dealt with operations by Libya in support of terrorism. One of them contained details that MI5 believed could have endangered the life of one of its agents. An injunction granted against the *Mail on Sunday* and preventing it from publishing any further allegations by Shayler did not however, suggest this. It merely stated that the information disclosed might have made MI5 targets aware of surveillance, allowed them to identify sources and thereby jeopardised the usefulness of those sources, or adversely affected the confidence of current or potential agents and informants in MI5's ability to protect their identities.

Shayler fled to France where he made a number of further allegations. Most notably and, more important, most credibly, he claimed that the 1993 Bishopsgate bomb, which killed one person and caused £350 million worth of damage, could have been avoided. It had already emerged that an MI5 surveillance team following a Provisional IRA Active Service Unit walked past a lorry bomb parked in the Bishopsgate district of the city of London only minutes after another ASU had parked it and primed it. Shayler was subsequently arrested and held in La Santé prison in Paris for three months pending an extradition hearing, which in the event failed. He eventually returned to Britain of his own volition and was charged under Section 1 of the Official Secrets Act. His lawyers argued that, as a 'whistle-blower' attempting to reveal bureaucracy and inefficiency within MI5, which would not otherwise be made public, he should be allowed to mount a public interest defence of his actions. This was rejected by the British courts on the grounds that he had gone to a newspaper rather than make his complaints through the staff counsellor, a post created in the wake of the Massiter allegations to look into concerns expressed by ordinary officers. Neither did he attempt to complain to the Security Service Tribunal, three senior lawyers appointed to investigate complaints about MI5 from members of the public, or even to the Parliamentary Intelligence and Security Committee, although after the newspaper articles appeared he did send a list of complaints to the committee. As the legal arguments were unfolding, it emerged that Stella Rimington intended to publish her memoirs. MI5 was put in a very difficult position. Rimington's case was different to Shayler's in that she offered her book, entitled *Open Secret*, to the Defence Press and Broadcasting Advisory Committee, perhaps better known as the D-Notice Committee, for vetting. But she nevertheless made it clear that, although she would take note of any changes she was asked to make, she was determined to publish. Rightly or wrongly, it looked as if it was alright for a former director to go public but not for a junior officer to do so. Given that she had written to all former MI5 officers in the wake of the *Spycatcher* affair warning that they should not write their memoirs, she was vulnerable to a charge of double standards.

Lander managed however to dispose of the Rimington book with fewer problems than might have been expected, largely because she accepted his suggested cuts. She admitted that initially 'emotions rose quite high on both sides'. But although there is no doubt that MI6 and GCHQ were furious over the affair and Rimington was initially roasted by the Cabinet Secretary, Sir Richard Wilson, she was told that if she agreed to the cuts she could publish.

The main feature of Lander's period in charge was the apparent success of the Northern Ireland peace process, a greater sharpness in MI5 operational capability and a major improvement in MI5's ability to produce evidence that stands up in court, a key factor in both anti-terrorist and criminal investigations. This is largely due to the fact that it now employs seven lawyers who assist in surveillance operations to ensure that the evidence collected will pass muster in court. The first major operation in which the lawyers' participation was revealed in court was the capture of three Real IRA terrorists.

David Rupert, a US lorry driver who infiltrated the Real IRA on behalf of MI5, had discovered that its leaders were anxious to establish links with Iraq.

Strapped for cash and short of weaponry, the Real IRA believed Saddam Hussein would support them as a means of attacking the British. In the autumn of 2000, in Operation Samnite, a joint operation with MI6, British intelligence officers and agents posing as Middle Eastern journalists contacted the press officer of the 32 Counties Sovereignty Committee, the political wing of the Real IRA. They used a statement on the committee's website condemning British bombing of Iraq as an excuse to seek more information about the Real IRA. Only later did they claim to be Iraqi intelligence agents offering arms, explosives and cash as part of an attempt to wreak vengeance on Britain for the RAF's part in policing the no-fly zones over Iraq. On 19 January 2001, one undercover intelligence officer rang a 'secret' telephone number they had been given. The call was answered by 'Karl', who Woolwich Crown Court heard was Michael McKevitt, leader of the Real IRA. A number of telephone conversations followed, leading to a first meeting in the Hungarian capital Budapest on 7 February, which was attended by Fintan O'Farrell and Declan Rafferty, two leading members of the Real IRA, and a British intelligence officer, posing as an Iraqi called Samir. It was one of several meetings designed to establish each other's *bona fides*. In a move aimed at correcting MI5's poor reputation on the collection of evidence, lawyers were part of the back-up team for each meeting making sure that nothing happened that might cause problems in court. It was particularly important to ensure that the terrorists made the first moves in terms of asking for weaponry, to avoid any suggestion that any of the British intelligence officers were acting as *agent provocateur*. 'All the initiative had to come from them,' one insider said. 'They were asking for weapons and money.' At this first meeting, O'Farrell and Declan Rafferty were keen to impress the Iraqis with their willingness and ability to damage British interests, admitting responsibility for a rocket attack on MI6's Vauxhall headquarters. They could do better with more advanced kit, they said. They appeared to accept Samir as a serious Iraqi representative but were nevertheless wary. A second meeting took place a month later, again in Budapest. It was a success and the Real IRA decided it was ready to give the 'Iraqis' a detailed list of the weapons and explosives it needed.

The key meeting took place in the small Slovakian spa town of Piešt'any on

9 April and was attended by Rafferty and Michael McDonald, a more senior member of the Real IRA standing in for McKevitt, who had been arrested in the Irish Republic. McDonald was taped boasting that the 'struggle' would continue until the British completely withdrew from Northern Ireland. 'They are still occupying our country. They have not left and until they have left the thing goes on. It does not stop, whether I die or get jailed, whatever, it doesn't make any difference.' He also explained the composition of the Real IRA's leadership. 'There's a board of directors,' he said. 'There's eight people who make decisions, not just one person. Inside, there's me and McKevitt. McKevitt's doing the weapons, that's his job.' Rafferty explained that the Real IRA was formed in 1997 but that the bulk of the Republican funds remained in the hands of the Provisional IRA. 'They had control of everything including finance and weapons so we had to start from nothing,' he said. 'When we heard about the help your people were willing to give, we were only too delighted.'

McDonald wrote down their requirements on a paper napkin. They wanted 10,000lb of explosives, 2,000 detonators, 200 rocket grenades and 500 guns, plus a million dollars. He was not keen on the 'Iraqis' taking the list away with them but one of the two MI5 officers reached over, picked up the napkin, blew his nose on it and stuffed it into his pocket. It would provide a crucial piece of evidence against the Real IRA men. But still it was not enough for the MI5 lawyers. Samir arranged a further meeting with Rafferty in the Austrian capital Vienna in May to finalise details for a further meeting at which the Real IRA's demands would be agreed. It took place in an Arab restaurant in Piešťany. McDonald, Rafferty and O'Farrell were all there to meet Samir and another British intelligence officer posing as a senior Iraqi intelligence officer who could OK the Real IRA's requirements. When McDonald asked if they were able to provide the weapons and explosives they needed, the two British intelligence officers offered them a choice of three different types of plastic explosive. McDonald said: 'We used to work in Semtex all the time but maybe this is better.' Given a list of weapons, he asked for 250 RAK 9mm sub-machine guns and 250 Browning 9mm pistols, adding that the latter was 'as good as any'. McDonald also asked for a high-powered sniper rifle capable of penetrating body armour 'to kill British soldiers' at a range of up to 2,000 metres, and a Russian-made anti-tank guided missile which could penetrate 'substantial armour'. Arrangements were made for the handover of a million dollars in four instalments and for various shipments of weapons and explosives to be delivered by lorry to Belgium or Holland. 'We can control that area,' McDonald said. 'We have people there in that area.' It was enough for the lawyers. Armed Slovak police set up a roadblock to stop the van carrying the three Real IRA men and the undercover British intelligence officers. 'It the arrest was just like you see in films,' one Slovak police officer said. 'It came as an absolute surprise. All three were taken down in a matter of seconds.' They were extradited to Britain and, after admitting their guilt in order to prevent more information about the Real IRA from emerging, sentenced to 30 years' imprisonment.

A short time later it was announced that MI5 was to have its second female Director-General. Eliza Manningham-Buller, Lander's deputy and a former head of both T Branch, which deals with Irish terrrorism, and A Branch, which mounts surveillance operations, would take over in October 2001. Early on in her career, she had worked in K Branch, the counter-espionage division, and was involved in the handling of Oleg Gordievsky, then a British agent-in-place inside the KGB. Gordievsky described her as an 'exceptional' operational officer.

'Eliza's ability to keep secrets saved my life. In 1983, she was MI5's senior officer dealing with Soviet affairs. I was deputy head of the KGB's London station, but also working for MI6. She and her two assistants were among the few who knew about me. Her assistants shared an office with Michael Bettany, the traitor who offered his services to the KGB. Despite being in daily contact with Eliza and staff, Bettany knew nothing about me – which is a tribute to Eliza's ability to keep secret information secret. Had she not had that ability, Bettany would have certainly betrayed me to the KGB, and I would have been shot. We met for the first time in early 1986, at a major meeting to discuss the KGB. I was astonished by the extent of her knowledge: she knew more about some areas of Russian intelligence-gathering than I did. The threat has changed. Osama bin Laden has said that acquiring nuclear and chemical weapons is a "religious duty"; his lieutenants in al-Qaeda have echoed that, insisting that "we are not fighting so the enemy will offer us something. We are fighting to wipe out the enemy". It is a new and terrifying challenge for MI5 – but I have no doubt that Eliza Manningham-Buller will rise to it.'

The Secret Intelligence Service MI6

Prologue

As he watched the heavily armed thugs arriving at the house on al-Jumhuriya Street, Karim realised instantly that he needed to call a crash meeting with the men from MI6. He had recognised some of the paramilitaries trooping past the colourful mosaic of Saddam Hussein at the gates of the grey concrete building. They were leading members of the Special Security Organisation and the Saddam *Fedayeen*, the paramilitaries who held Basra in the grip of fear. If they could be eliminated, the city's 1.3 million inhabitants would begin to believe they were at last free and the uprising that everyone had hoped for might begin.

Karim was one of a number of British spies inside the city, some of them long-term penetration agents, others developed in the months before the war. He had been given a short-range communications system and a series of times when he should send his reports. But there was no time for that. He needed to find the two strangers who called themselves Ali and Hashim, and fast. With their closely cropped hair, their beards and their grubby *dishdasha* robes, they could easily pass for locals. Karim had been surprised when they told him they had been sent by MI6. He was even more surprised to discover that they were British commandos, members of the Special Boat Service.

It was Friday 28 March. British troops had been on the outskirts of Basra for nearly a week. Their presence had been expected to spark the uprising. But the paramilitaries' reign of terror had ensured it failed to materialise. Not that the pressure wasn't beginning to tell. A couple of days earlier, the Ba'ath Party had split in two after the Iraqi regional commander, Ali Hasan al-Majid, ordered the execution of a wavering party leader. There had been a series of clashes between the two sides but the paramilitaries had put down the resistance. Al-Majid, better known as Chemical Ali for his use of chemical weapons against the Kurdish town of Halabja, had called this meeting at the local Ba'ath party headquarters, the house on al-Jumhuriya Street, to re-impose his authority.

The SBS commandos reported the news back to Karim's MI6 handler by radio, before making their way swiftly to al-Jumhuriya Street. They knew they had to act fast. In a revolutionary move, designed to ensure that the intelligence gathered on the ground by its agents in Basra was available to the military in 'real time', MI6 had sent its 'Camel Corps' of Arabic specialists out to the Gulf. A number of officers were on the ground handling the agents inside the city and one was sat alongside the British commander, in his headquarters south of Basra. Even now, Maj-Gen Robin Brims was ordering up an air strike on the paramilitaries. By the time the two US Air Force F15E Strike Eagles roared in, the British commandos were in place, training the laser designator on the party HQ, guiding the three JDAM delayed-action bombs onto their target.

It was a devastating strike, taking the flat roof down to ground level on much of the house. Nevertheless, despite coalition claims that all those inside were killed, some at least survived, including Chemical Ali. But a week later, in a similar operation, he was spotted going into another house and this time it seems that if he was not killed, he was at least persuaded it was time to leave. With the man orchestrating the city's defences gone, the *Fedayeen* paramilitaries melted away and Brims made plans to take the city. The men of the 7th Armoured Brigade, the Desert Rats, were to make an armoured thrust into the city in the early hours of Tuesday 7 April. But when the MI6 officers said their agents inside Basra were reporting that there were virtually no paramilitaries left he brought the operation forward by a day. 'The MI6 agents were very brave people reporting in real time,' one defence source said. 'They realised that Saddam's grip on the population had gone and allowed us to go in a day early. It was their intelligence that gave us the keys to the city and ensured we lost just three men in the entire operation.'

Nine

Sharp Practice and Green Ink

Between the wars, the profession and practice of espionage did not much change. Invisible inks and false beards were still standard issue.

Robert Cecil, 'C's War', in *Intelligence and National Security*,
Vol 1, No 2 (May 1986)

When the foreign and home departments of the Secret Service Bureau were split from each other in 1910, Captain Mansfield Cumming, head of the Foreign Department, set up his headquarters in his own flat in Ashley Gardens, Vauxhall Bridge Road, under the cover of Rasen Falcon & Co, Shippers and Exporters. His budget was a relatively paltry £2,700 and, like Walsingham before him, he was at times forced to dip into his own pocket to supplement the funds of his new secret service. His initial orders were 'Organise an efficient system by which German progress in Armaments and Naval construction can be watched . . . Obtain information of any movement indicating an attack upon this country . . . Obtain information of interest to this country as to hostile action or preparations for such . . . Organise a scheme of permanent correspondents both at home and abroad, who will furnish information within enemies' lines in time of war.'

Cumming subsequently moved into his own offices at 2 Whitehall Court, a stone's throw from the Admiralty and War Office buildings. 'A lift whisked us to the top floor, above which additional superstructures had been built for war emergency offices,' wrote Sir Paul Dukes, probably one of Cumming's best recruits, of his first meeting with 'the Chief', who was known within Whitehall as 'C', from the initial of his surname. 'I had always associated rabbit warrens with subterranean abodes,' Dukes wrote. 'But here in this building I discovered a maze of burrow-like passages, corridors, nooks and alcoves, piled higgledy-piggledy on the roof.' Despite an abrupt manner, Cumming was regarded with a great deal of admiration by his officers, Dukes recalled.

'From the threshold, the room seemed bathed in semi-obscurity. Against the window everything appeared in silhouette. A row of half a dozen extending telephones stood at the left of a big desk littered with papers. On a side-table were maps and drawings, with models of aeroplanes, submarines, and mechanical devices, while a row of bottles suggested chemical experiments. These evidences of scientific investigation only served to intensify an already overpowering atmosphere of strangeness and mystery. But it was not these things that engaged my attention as I stood nervously waiting. My eyes fixed themselves on the figure at the writing table. In a swing desk chair, his shoulders hunched, with his head supported on his hand, sat the Chief. This extraordinary man was short of stature, thick-set with grey hair half covering a well-rounded head. His mouth was stern and an eagle eye, full of vivacity, glanced – or glared as the case may be – piercingly through a gold-rimmed monocle. At first encounter, he appeared very severe. His manner of speech was abrupt. Yet the stern countenance could melt into the kindliest of smiles, and the softened eyes and lips revealed a heart that was big and generous. Awe-inspired as I was by my first encounter, I soon learned to regard "the Chief" with feelings of the deepest personal admiration.'

Initially, the highest priority was to obtain intelligence on German naval activity, and the foreign department was subordinated to the Admiralty. One former member of Cumming's staff recalled that it was 'severely handicapped by the exiguous funds available' and by the hostility of the Foreign Office, which remained reluctant to allow its staff abroad to involve themselves in secret service work. But, in spite of this handicap, the British intelligence system was, 'on the whole, wonderfully efficient" and was particularly good at detecting movements of German ships into and out of the Baltic. 'Every "surprise" which the Germans sprang upon us at sea was foretold and elucidated in full detail,' the former officer said. 'Practically complete diagrams of every German capital ship down to the *König* class, showing the extent and thickness of their armour, the layout of their underwater compartments and bulkheads, and every other protective feature, were obtained by our intelligence service. It was thus known, long beforehand, that the German ships were built to withstand the severest punishment, and it is a thousand pities that this knowledge was not taken into account by the Admiralty officers who were responsible for the design of our armour-piercing projectiles.'

The German network was based around three or four British officers and a network of agents, a number of whom remained in place after the war began and whose work was 'by no means as melodramatic as certain writers have pictured them. A great deal of information, and that not the least valuable, was collected by perfectly legitimate means. The newspapers often contained, in spite of careful censorship, service news, which conveyed useful facts to the trained reader. Again a trip round Kiel harbour, or along the waterfront of Hamburg or Bremen, where the great shipyards are situated, rarely failed to bring to light some new development of importance. Occasionally, however, it was necessary to resort to less overt measures.' At least some of the reports on Baltic shipping movements were provided by Captain Walter Christmas, an officer in the Danish navy. He passed on reports from its coast-watching service on condition that a 'pretty girl' was always available to act as his go-between. When he was discovered and the British were forced to 'exfiltrate' him, he was given a flat in Shepherd Market in London's Mayfair, where some of the 'pretty girls' he worked with almost certainly carried out their more regular employment.

Cumming had four agents based in Brussels, controlled by Henry Dale Long, or 'L' – an experienced officer who had previously served under William Melville as the military intelligence department's man in Africa. There was also a Rotterdam bureau headed by Richard Tinsley, or 'T', the owner of a successful shipping business. When war broke out in August 1914, the networks in Brussels and Germany collapsed and T's Rotterdam base became the centre of the European operations, although 'there still remained in the enemy's country a few courageous men, who taking their lives in their hands continued to keep German and Austrian naval affairs under observation'.

The best of those 'few courageous men' was almost certainly Herman Karl Krüger, a marine engineer who had been court-martialled while serving with the German navy for insulting a relative of the Kaiser. Determined to extract revenge, he offered himself to the British legation in The Hague and was taken over by Tinsley. Krüger's profession secured him access to all the German naval bases and dockyards. He could travel freely within Germany and Holland, passing as a neutral Dane. Krüger provided Tinsley with detailed reports as agent TR16. He was regarded as an 'absolutely reliable source' and a post-war assessment of his work described it as always accurate, up to date and of the 'very greatest possible value'. So well was he protected that Henry Landau, who worked as Tinsley's deputy in Rotterdam, did not even realise he was German.

'I knew him as the Dane,' Landau recalled. 'What his name was, or where he came from, I do not know, although I met him several times. Slight of build, fair, with blue eyes, he looked the reserved, well bred Scandinavian of cultured and professional interests. He certainly did not look the arch-spy that he was. When I came to know him better, however, I realised why he was so successful. He was a marine engineer of exceptional quality; he was a man without nerves, always cool and collected; nothing escaped his austerely confident eye; and he was possessed of an outstanding memory for the minutest detail of marine construction.'

The problems caused by the loss of many of C's European networks were exacerbated when he was involved in a serious car crash while driving back from a visit to the headquarters of the British Expeditionary Force in France. Cumming's son was killed, and he himself was so badly injured that one of his legs had to be amputated, putting him out of action for several months. In his absence both the Army and the Navy set up their own independent 'secret services', and by the time Cumming had recuperated there were three separate and largely unco-ordinated bodies all vying with each other to produce intelligence. He set about rebuilding his own intelligence system, with networks in Holland, Belgium and Switzerland supplementing the information provided by those agents left behind in Germany. Among the most productive networks were the train-watching units which monitored the movement of German troops towards or away from the front. 'From the composition of the train, it could be seen if it was a leave train, a freight train or a train carrying what we called a "constituted unit",' wrote one of the agent runners. 'About forty trains of constituted units were required to move a division. So a study of these traffic returns could show how many divisions were moving along the Belgian and French railways and in which direction.' Perhaps the best of the networks was *La Dame Blanche*, an extensive train-watching system named after the legendary White Lady of the Hohenzollerns whose appearance was supposed to signal the dynasty's downfall. One of the agents operating for Cumming behind enemy lines was Edith Cavell, an English nurse who was matron of a Brussels hospital, and who was shot by the Germans in 1915 for aiding Allied soldiers to escape from behind enemy lines. Other networks included Felix, a group of Belgian prostitutes run from Rotterdam and paid for the information they garnered from their German clients with drugs smuggled in from London. There was also a train-watching network based in Luxembourg which passed on its intelligence in coded knitting patterns published in a local newspaper, a plain stitch for a coach carrying men, a purl for a wagon full of horses. Reports were sent using the prefix CX in front of the serial number, the CX is believed to indicate that the report should be passed to C expeditiously. Its first recorded use was in 1914 when an agent in Brussels was told: 'If you have urgent material you want to get to us quickly you should put CX CX CX CX on the report.' By 1917, it was routinely used as the prefix for the serial numbers on all SIS reports and this remains the practice to this day.

The author Somerset Maugham, one of the British spies working in Switzerland, created the fictional hero Ashenden based on his wartime service. Ashenden, who shared a cover name, a London address and a number of agents with his creator, was based in Geneva, sending freelance stringers into Germany to collect information from which he compiled 'long reports which he was convinced no-one read, till having inadvertently slipped a jest into one of them he received a sharp reproof for his levity'. If the intelligence reports were at least read, they were seldom passed on to the departments that needed them. Even when they were, the intelligence was frequently not believed. When one agent based in Germany reported, entirely accurately, that the Kaiser's naval gunners had developed a superior new targeting system, the Admiralty was dismissive, claiming that 'shooting of the quality detailed in his report was absolutely impossible ... and that, in effect, he had been hoodwinked'.

Cumming's department also maintained a number of agents in the United States, where, despite a Royal Navy blockade, the Germans were attempting to obtain supplies and war *matériel*. Controlled by Sir William Wiseman, the station chief in New York, and his deputy, Major Norman Thwaites, the British spies kept a close watch on German commercial activities and the cargo ships trapped inside the blockade. Wiseman developed close relations with both American intelligence and President Woodrow Wilson, pioneering the links that still exist to this day. 'Persons in the employ of the British Intelligence Service were stationed at every port on the Atlantic coast of the United States,' one former agent revealed. 'In consequence no movement of any enemy ship could take place without almost instant notification to British headquarters, the locality of which had better not be divulged. Many of the people who kept watch and ward at these ports were humble individuals who performed a very dangerous duty from purely patriotic motives. The writer has in mind one person who was responsible for observing enemy shipping at a port not a hundred miles from New York. Although a working man, his despatches and memoranda sent to headquarters were standard examples of terse English, reflecting the keenest powers of observation. For two and a half years, he performed his duties admirably, though in constant danger from the machinations of the Central European agents, who swarmed in the Eastern States. Then one morning, his body was found floating in the dock, riddled with bullets.'

Wiseman warned in March 1917 that a young revolutionary called Leon Trotsky had been in America collecting money to fund a socialist revolution. 'An important movement has been started here among Socialists backed by all Jewish funds, behind which are possibly Germans,' he reported to London. 'Main leader is Trotsky who was principal speaker at a mass meeting here on 20 March. 'The aim of the movement was to return "revolutionary Socialists into Russia with object of overturning present Government and establishing a republic and initiating peace movement." It was also aimed at "promoting Socialistic Revolutions in other countries, including United States."

A week later, Wiseman reported that Trotsky had sailed for Russia on board the SS *Kristiania Fjord* with '$10,000 subscribed by socialists and Germans to start revolution against present government.' He warned the authorities in Canada that the ship was stopping off in Halifax, Nova Scotia, and that it should be held until it had been decided what to do about Trotsky. The Russian revolutionary was arrested by the Canadian police and held in a camp for German PoWs, where the commandant said he immediately began preaching revolution to the other inmates. 'He is a man holding extremely strong views and of most powerful personality, his personality being such that after only a few days stay here he was by far the most popular man in the whole camp,' the camp commandant said. But Lieutenant-Colonel Claude Dansey, who was then in charge of the War Office intelligence department liaising with Cumming's secret service, dismissed the claims of an intended revolution. Dansey examined the evidence against Trotsky and decided that it had been invented by 'a Russian *agent provocateur* used by the old Russian Secret Police'. He ordered that he should be released at once, taking the funds needed to launch the Bolshevik revolution with him to Russia.

Dansey had the power to overrule Wiseman because of a 1916 reorganisation of intelligence operations that had absorbed Cumming's 'Secret Service' into the War Office Directorate of Military Intelligence as MI1c. But the War Office in particular remained unhappy with the way the secret service was organised and at the end of 1917 forced through a number of changes designed to give it and other consumer departments more say in what the agents did. The geographically structured operations sections were replaced by six liaison, or 'Circulating', sections, each led by a representative of the relevant consumer department. Section I, liaison with the Foreign Office, was named 'Political'. Section II was 'Air' intelligence. Section III was 'Naval'. Section IV was 'Military', under the command of MI1c, i.e. Dansey. He was also in charge of Section V, 'Counter-Espionage'. Section VI was 'Economic'.

By the end of the war, no doubt bolstered in his rivalry with the War Office by Dansey's dismissal of Trotsky and the subsequent October Revolution, Cumming had fought off its attempted takeover, and the service was subordinated to the Foreign Office. Its official title had now become the Secret Intelligence Service (SIS), as it remains today, although it was still often referred to as MI1c. The main target for its operations was now Russia, where its agents included Dukes and the legendary Sidney Reilly. Dukes, a fluent Russian-speaker, managed during a brief ten-month mission to the Soviet Union not only to join the Communist Party but also to pass himself off as a member of the *Tcheka*, the early Soviet predecessor of the KGB. He had been talent-spotted during a spell as a diplomat in the Soviet Union, and he described how he was shipped back home to be recruited by Cumming's deputy, Lieutenant-Colonel Freddie Browning:

'The Colonel, to my stupefaction, informed me immediately that I had been recalled to London because I was to be invited to work in the Secret Intelligence Service. "We have reason to believe that Russia will not long be open to foreigners," he explained. "We want someone to remain there to keep us informed of the march of events." Besides general conditions, he told me, I should have to report on changes of policy, the attitude of the population, military and naval matters, what possibilities there might be for an alteration of regime, and what part Germany was playing. As to the means by which I should re-enter the country, under what cover I should live, and how I should send out reports, it was left to me to make suggestions.'

The lack of funding remained a problem and Cumming resorted to using British businessmen travelling to Russia to collect intelligence. In the summer of 1919, Cumming wrote to the Hudson Bay Company agreeing to pay all expenses for H A Armitstead, the company's representative in Moscow, who has 'temporarily placed his services at my disposal for a journey through Russia'. Cumming probably regarded Dukes as his best agent in post-revolutionary Russia, the most famous was undoubtedly Sidney Reilly. Despite his Irish name, Reilly was in fact born in Odessa in March 1874. He came to Britain in his twenties, acquiring a British passport and his new identity by claiming to be the son of an Irish father and a Russian Jewish mother. By the early 1900s, he was combining extremely dubious business activities with even more dubious espionage activities on behalf of a variety of governments. There have been suggestions that at one time or other between 1903 and 1917 he worked for the Japanese, Russian, German and British governments – in some cases simultaneously. He is supposed to have been working undercover for British Naval Intelligence as a businessman in Port Arthur in the Russian Far East in the early part of the century. Certainly the Russians and the British

Sir Francis Walsingham, Queen Elizabeth I's Principal Secretary, who is widely regarded as Britain's first spymaster. (Getty Images)

Vernon Kell, MI5's first Director-General, known within the British establishment by his initial of K.

Thames House, the MI5 headquarters in London.

Dame Stella Rimington, the first female Director-General of MI5.

(*Financial Times*)

Eliza Manningham Buller, who took over as MI5 Director-General in 2002.

(Home Office)

Mansfield Cumming, the first head of Britain's Secret Intelligence Service (MI6).

Sir Stewart Menzies, the wartime 'Chief' of MI6.

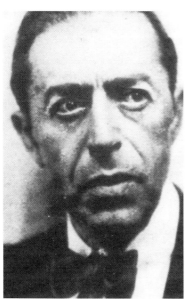

Sidney Reilly, the so-called Ace of Spies, who worked for Cumming in Bolshevik Russia. (Getty Images)

Frank Foley, who is credited with saving tens of thousands of Jews from the Holocaust and is still regarded as one of the best agent-runners ever to serve in MI6.

Harold 'Perks' Perkins, the former SOE officer who set up many of the early Cold War MI6 networks in Eastern Europe.

Sidney Cotton, the maverick Australian pilot who set up the British photographic reconnaissance operation at the start of the Second World War, initially as part of MI6 and later with the RAF. He is shown here briefing Air Marshal Sir Arthur Barrett, the British air commander in France at the beginning of 1940.

Anthony Blunt. (PA Photos)

John Cairncross. (*Sunday Telegraph*)

Donald Maclean. (Camera Press)

Guy Burgess playing the piano at a
friend's house in Moscow.

(private collection)

Kim Philby giving a press conference in November 1955 after he had been 'cleared' in parliament by Harold Macmillan, the then Foreign Secretary, of being the Third Man in 'the Burgess and Maclean spy ring'.

Oleg Penkovsky, the GRU officer and MI6 agent whose information was regarded as crucial during the Cuban Missile Crisis. (*Sunday Telegraph*)

Ahmed Shah Masood, the Mujahideen leader who benefited from MI6 attempts to undermine the Soviet occupation of Afghanistan.

(Itar-Tass/Reuters)

were engaged in a full-scale espionage war – the Okhrana, the tsarist prede-cessor of the KGB, even had a mole in the British embassy in St Petersburg providing it with secret documents. There is little evidence to back up Reilly's claims to have been spying for the British at this early stage in his career, although he may have been spying for other countries. Former SIS officers who have examined the service's records insist he was not recruited into the service until 1917, a suggestion backed up by evidence of MI5's shambolic attempts to follow him during the vetting process, losing him on the way between his lodgings off St James's Street and the Ritz. But this does not preclude his earlier use as an agent.

Getting to the truth is difficult with Reilly. His activities – in goverment service, in business, and in love – were exaggerated beyond belief, both by himself and by his biographers. But they were nevertheless colourful, one former SIS officer said. 'He's been written off by historians by and large. But he has been greatly underrated. He was very, very good – a very able agent and a far more serious operator than the impression given by the myth. Historians do have this tendency to write off something that has been made to appear glamorous. He was unusual but I don't think he was glamorous. He was a bit of a crook, you could almost say, certainly sharp practice. But as an agent he was superb.'

After spending the years before the war in St Petersburg – supposedly combining the job of Russian agent for a firm of German shipbuilders with intelligence work for the British – Reilly had sailed for America, where he is alleged to have spent much of the war mixing weapons procurement for the tsarist government with sabotage operations against US factories that might be blamed on German agents and thereby hasten America's entry into the war. When Wiseman was asked by American intelligence in July 1917 what he knew of Reilly, he replied: '[He] claims to be a British subject but doubt has been cast upon this. For the last two years, he has been mixed up with various scandals in connection with the purchase of Russian munitions here and his reputation is a bad one. Reilly is said to have been at Port Arthur in 1903 where he is suspected by the Russians of acting as a spy for the Japanese. While in this country, during the present war, he has been mixed up with various undesirable characters and it would not be the least surprising if he was employed by enemy agents in propaganda or other activities.'

Since the available evidence suggests that by now Reilly was, at the very least, in close contact with SIS, this could only be disinformation and strongly suggests that his sabotage activities were undertaken on behalf of the British. So too does the fact that, with America now having entered the war, Reilly returned to London with the assistance of Thwaites and within months was in Russia working for Cumming. The October Revolution had ended Russia's part in the war, allowing the Germans to concentrate on the western front, so the British were anxious to bring the new government back on board, Reilly recalled. 'In the spring of 1918, on returning from a mission, I found my superiors awaiting me with some impatience. I was instructed to proceed to Russia without delay. The process of affairs in that part of the world was filling the allies with consternation. My superiors clung to the opinion that Russia might still be brought to her right mind in the matter of her obligations to her allies. Agents from France and the United States were already in Moscow and Petrograd working to that end.' Reilly was having none of it. Fanatically anti-communist, and ever anxious to increase his own importance, he reported back to Cumming that defeating Germany was of minor significance compared to preventing the spread of Bolshevism. 'Will the people of England never understand? The Germans are human beings; we can afford to be even beaten by them. Here in Moscow there is growing to maturity the arch-enemy of the human race. At any price, this foul obscenity which has been born in Russia must be crushed out of existence. Peace with Germany? Yes. Peace with Germany, peace with anybody. There is only one enemy. Mankind must unite in a holy alliance against this midnight terror.'

Robert Bruce Lockhart, the head of the British mission to Russia, was horrified when Reilly sparked off a diplomatic incident by marching up to the Kremlin gate and demanding to see Lenin. 'Asked for his credentials, he declared that he had been sent specially by Mr Lloyd George to obtain first-hand news of the aims and ideals of the Bolsheviks,' Lockhart wrote. 'The British government was not satisfied with the reports it had been receiving from me. He had been entrusted with the task of making good the defects.' Told of the incident by a furious Bolshevik Commissar for Foreign Affairs, Lockhart at first thought that Reilly must be a madman masquerading as a

British agent, but promised that he would investigate. 'That same evening, I sent for [Lieutenant Ernest] Boyce, the head of the Intelligence Service, and told him the story. He informed me that the man was a new agent who had just come out from England. I blew up in a storm of indignation.'

Nevertheless, Lockhart and Reilly were to become involved in one of the greatest spy scandals of all time – the so-called Lockhart Plot. The British Head of Mission confessed to a grudging admiration for Reilly's style. 'He was a man of great energy and personal charm, very attractive to women and very ambitious. I had not a high opinion of his intelligence. His knowledge covered many subjects, from politics to art, but it was superficial. On the other hand, his courage and indifference to danger were superb.'

By mid-1918 most of the allied representatives in Russia had given up all hope of persuading the Bolsheviks to join the fight against Germany, and a number of plans were being made to try to subvert the new government. Two Latvian soldiers then made contact with the British naval attaché in Petrograd asking for British support for the anti-Bolshevik underground. The two 'walk-ins' were sent to Lockhart, who claims to have simply passed them on to Reilly. The full extent of Lockhart's involvement is far from clear. His own published account seeks to distance him from the whole affair – and indeed from anything but the most insubstantial involvement in espionage and covert operations – but his reports to the Foreign Office portray a different picture, recording various attempts to fund and support the anti-Bolshevik underground. Since the Latvian regiments were being used to police Moscow, Reilly saw the two officers as a golden opportunity and held a series of meetings with them, trying to persuade them to help overthrow Lenin. Lockhart, who admitted discussing the plans with his French counterpart, claimed to have 'categorically turned down' any such suggestion. 'Reilly was warned specifically to have nothing to do with so dangerous and doubtful a move.'

But this seems to have been another in a long history of 'deniable operations' carried out by the intelligence services – a tactic in which Reilly clearly specialised. Lockhart was in fact present at a number of meetings with the two Latvian officers, and it was his request to meet a senior officer of Moscow's 'praetorian guard' which drew the British irrevocably into a Russian trap. The two Latvian 'walk-ins' were in fact Tcheka *agents provocateurs*. Their mission had been to infiltrate the underground, but by now Feliks Dzerzhinsky, the head of the Tcheka, had spotted an opportunity to dismantle not only the resistance but also the allies' spy networks by means of a 'provocation', a sting operation designed to entice foreign agents into illegal activities that could be used to discredit their employers.

In theory, Dzerzhinsky had banned such practices, chiefly because of their widespread use against the Bolsheviks themselves by the Okhrana, the tsarist secret police. But with both Reilly and Lockhart convinced that the Latvians were genuine the opportunity was clearly too good to miss. When Lockhart demanded to speak to a senior officer, another Tcheka agent, Colonel E. P. Berzin of the Latvian Special Light Artillery Division, was brought into the scheme with a brief to draw the conspirators into a plot to assassinate Lenin. There is some evidence to suggest that British intelligence seriously considered killing the Russian leader, although George Hill, a War Office agent who was also involved in the plot, claimed Reilly was insistent that, if at all possible, none of the Bolshevik leaders was to be killed. 'He proposed to march them through the streets of Moscow bereft of their lower garments in order to kill them by ridicule.' Whatever the extent of Reilly's real plans, Dzerzhinsky's were brought to a premature halt by an apparently unrelated, but very nearly successful, assassination attempt on Lenin. The Tcheka began rounding up all those involved in the plans to overthrow the Bolshevik leader. Reilly and Hill both evaded capture and made their way back to Britain on false passports. But their Russian agents and the counter-revolutionary underground were less lucky. The Tcheka executed many hundreds of opponents of the regime and wiped out all of Hill's fourteen agents and couriers. Reilly was sentenced to death in absentia. *Pravda* announced the discovery of a widespread Anglo-French conspiracy to overthrow the Bolsheviks, shoot Lenin and Trotsky, and set up a military government allied to the West and hostile to Germany. Lockhart had provided a total of a million roubles to fund a counter-revolution, *Pravda* said. 'The intention of the allies as soon as they had established their dictatorship in Moscow was to declare war on Germany and force Russia to fight again.'

On their return to Britain, Reilly was awarded the Military Cross and Hill the Distinguished Service Order. Lockhart meanwhile set about distancing himself from the whole affair. 'My experiences of the war and of the Russian revolution have left me with a very poor opinion of secret service work. Doubtless, it has its uses and its functions, but political work is not its strong point. The buying of information puts a premium on manufactured news. But even manufactured news is less dangerous than the honest reports of men, who, however brave and however gifted as linguists, are frequently incapable of forming a reliable political judgement.'

SIS believed that Lockhart was to blame for the collapse of the scheme. 'He very quickly involved the French and there seems little doubt that the French then brought in a French correspondent who was actually in touch with the *Tcheka*,' a former SIS officer who had studied the files said. 'In a sense, Reilly was landed in it by Bruce Lockhart. I think Bruce Lockhart was very glad to have got away and not got tarred with Reilly's brush as it were. There is a slight smell around that whole period. The French were probably the culprits in that they were very slack about security and they produced this correspondent who was supposedly working for them but was also working for the Russians. It all came unstuck then.'

Despite his Military Cross, Reilly found that he was no longer held in high regard either by the Foreign Office or even by Cumming. His rampant anti-Bolshevism and his taste for *Boy's Own* schemes made him at best unreliable, at worst dangerous. Reilly applied for a full-time post with SIS, telling Cumming, 'I venture to think that the state should not lose my services. I would devote the rest of my life to this wicked work.' But his fame, his tendency to exaggerate his exploits and his womanising embarrassed Britain's spymasters. His discarded wives became 'tiresome' and, by 1923, when a further bigamous marriage to Pepita Bobadilla, an actress, hit the headlines, he had already been discarded by SIS. He spent the early 1920s mixing his business schemes with intermittent freelance jobs, mainly involving further hopeless plots to overthrow the Soviet government which – despite a consistent record of failure – convinced the Russian intelligence service, by then known as the OGPU, that he was a top British agent.

Seven years after the Lockhart Plot, Soviet intelligence lured Reilly, now 51, into a second, and this time fatal, deception operation. The Trust – supposedly a secret White Russian opposition group – had been created by the OGPU in order to penetrate the pro-monarchist émigré groups, to control their activities and to uncover the remaining opposition contacts inside Russia. Reilly, working with Ernest Boyce, now the secret service station chief in Helsinki, agreed to go to Russia to meet the Trust's leadership. Reilly disappeared. He was supposedly shot dead by Bolshevik border guards in October 1925 as he tried to cross the Finnish border into Russia. But an SIS report obtained from Russian émigré sources described how he was, in fact, shot in the back at Stalin's insistence after days of being interrogated in the Lubyanka, the OGPU's Moscow headquarters. 'The Bolsheviks wished to conceal his arrest, but the English found it out, and the Bolsheviks, in order to escape the possible demands by the English of his release, murdered him,' the report said. Four OGPU officers took him to woods north-east of Moscow on the evening of 5 November 1925. On their way they stopped, claiming that the car had broken down. All four OGPU officers, together with Reilly, got out of the car to stretch their legs. One of the OGPU officers, named only as Ibrahim, lagged behind the party and then 'put several bullets into Reilly'. He fell but was still alive and another officer fired the shot that killed him. SIS was pursued by a number of his wives, including Pepita, for compensation. But it insisted that 'all Reilly's activities after 1921 were his own private affair' and, given Reilly's 'somewhat complicated matrimonial tangles', they had no intention of paying up.

Cumming had moved his headquarters to 1 Melbury Road, West Kensington, in 1919 and in 1921, a Secret Service Committee set up to consider the post-war future of intelligence handed control over all foreign espionage operations to Cumming's department, resolving the War Office's continued claims on ownership by placing SIS firmly under the Foreign Office. It retained the title of MI1c, probably for cover, in correspondence within Whitehall and had a total of 65 headquarters staff, 132 staff at stations abroad and 484 agents, producing around 40 reports a day. Little attempt was made to analyse the product collected on behalf of the consumer departments. Raw intelligence was passed on direct without interpretation. The War Office's interests and that of the other main customer, the Admiralty, were protected by a promise that they would take turns in providing the Chief of the Secret Service.

The Secret Service Committee also placed SIS in charge of the Passport

Control Department, thereby allowing its overseas heads of station to use the cover of passport control officer, albeit with no diplomatic status. But just as Boyce remained remote from Reilly's activities in Russia, the station heads initially acted as little more than post-boxes while 'the secret service work itself continued to be carried out by private individuals paid out of Secret Service funds' and by members of the service acting under commercial cover. The operations were controlled by C from London with the assistance of a small group of officers, one of whom was Frank Stagg, who was in charge of Section III, naval intelligence, and an operation to intercept German diplomatic bags and extract any intelligence. 'The latter was a quite a big proposition as the German bags on the Siberian mail train were being extracted and opened, and yielded much useful stuff which was dealt with by the Board of Education.'

A secret history of Cumming's era written by Stagg provided a glimpse of Cumming's sense of humour. He was a keen advocate of the use of invisible ink, which was normally exposed by those intercepting the letters with the assistance of iodine vapour. 'Secret inks were our stock-in-trade and all were anxious to obtain some from a natural source,' Stagg wrote. 'I shall never forget C's delight when the Chief Censor, Worthington, announced that one of his staff had found that semen would not respond to iodine vapour, and told the Old Man that he had had to remove the discoverer from the office immediately, as his colleagues were making his life intolerable with accusations of masturbation. The Old Man at once asked Colney Hatch [lunatic asylum] to send female equivalent for testing – and the slogan went round: "Every man his own stylo." We thought we had solved a great problem. Then our man in Copenhagen, Major Holme, evidently stocked it in a bottle, for his letters stank to high heaven and we had to tell him that a fresh operation was necessary for each letter.'

Cumming died in 1923, sat on the sofa in his office, having quite literally given his heart to the service he founded. He was succeeded not, as he should have been under the inter-service rules, by an Army officer, but by Rear-Admiral Hugh 'Quex' Sinclair, Director of Naval Intelligence, who was appointed Head of the Secret Service and at the same time acquired control of the British codebreaking organisation GC&CS. Sinclair had a reputation among his friends as a man with a taste for the high life. He moved GC&CS to the Strand in central London so that it was close to the Savoy Hotel, his favourite haunt, and he acquired the nickname Quex from the title character in Arthur Pinero's then highly popular play *The Gay Lord Quex*, who was supposedly 'the wickedest man in London'. One of his officers recalled meeting him for the first time. 'I was put in a small room and left. Shortly, in came the most unusual person I had ever seen. He was a short man with a Jewish face and keen eyes. He had a hard-brimmed hat in his hand and, below a blue suit with a red tie, he had light brown shoes. My first impression was that how clever the authorities were to head their SS [secret service] with an Armenian gangster.' Sinclair kept his predecessor's soubriquet of C and the practice of signing all memos in green ink – a tradition that continues to this day. Cumming had resisted a 1918 War Office attempt to amalgamate SIS and MI5. But Sinclair saw counter-espionage as a valuable tool in the intelligence battle against the Soviet Union and lobbied hard to be allowed to absorb MI5 into his operations. When this failed, he strengthened the role of Section V, his own counter-espionage section, placing it under a former Indian police officer, Valentine Vivian, with a brief to obtain advance notice of espionage operations mounted against Britain from abroad. Sinclair's SIS also continued the practice of opening diplomatic bags, setting up a unit called N Section to carry it out.

The main target of British intelligence operations throughout the 1920s was Bolshevik Russia, with all six circulating sections involved in running operations against it. Two agents in particular stood out. The first was an agent at the heart of the Politburo, the Soviet Communist Party's top decision-making body, who during the early 1920s was producing exceptional intelligence on the Bolsheviks' attempts to subvert Britain and the Empire. One report included an account of a 'stormy' Politburo session in which Leonid Krassin, the commissar for foreign trade, clashed with Trotsky over the use of the Comintern to subvert India. Krassin believed that his attempts to reach a desperately needed trade agreement with Britain were being damaged by the concerted attempts at subversion both in Britain and Asia. Trotsky's response was that 'India, Afghanistan, Persia, Egypt constitute Great Britain's heel of Achilles and we would be great blockheads if we did not wound her there'. The agent's report revealed the Politburo decision that Krassin should go ahead with the vital trade talks and promise that Moscow would not attempt to undermine Britain while at the same time the subversion should continue unabated.

The identity of the agent, who continued reporting on the Politburo's machinations at least until 1924, is not clear. It may be that he was subsequently uncovered and executed. But another intriguing possibility is that he was Boris Bajanov, who defected to the West in 1928. Bajanov had been private secretary to Stalin and then secretary to the Politburo in the early 1920s. But he was under investigation by the OGPU when he crossed the border into Persia on New Year's Day 1928, persuading his minder that he might as well come with him rather than face the music for letting his charge defect. Pursued by other OGPU officials, they managed to make their way to India where Bajanov was interviewed by British intelligence officials. But despite his detailed knowledge of the workings of the Soviet leadership, OGPU operations and the use of the Comintern in coordinating communist activities around the world, SIS insisted he could not come to Britain. It dismissed his defection as a Soviet 'ruse'. This appears, however, to have been a ruse itself, possibly designed to throw the OGPU investigation off the scent and prevent it from realising that Bajanov was a long-term British agent. For at the same time, SIS was in 'delicate negotiations' with French intelligence over a scheme under which he would be allowed to live in Paris, where he could be debriefed safely by British officials who in return would allow the French a share in the valuable intelligence he provided.

The other particularly valuable agent against the Bolsheviks was Jonny X, the agent inside the Comintern recruited in Berlin by Frank Foley. Although his extensive information on communist operations and activities inside Britain was the most valuable intelligence he provided, he was a leading GRU officer who was sent to sort out the Communist Parties in a number of countries, including Austria, Belgium, China, Czechoslovakia, France, Romania, Argentina and Brazil. The intelligence he was able to provide was therefore of incalculable use, not only helping to build up a picture of Soviet subversion and espionage but also allowing important exchanges with other services, such as the French. His most spectacular role came in 1935 when he foiled an attempted coup in Brazil which was to be led by Luis Carlos Prestes, a Brazilian folk hero who had been secretly groomed in Moscow. Jonny X was sent in to oversee the coup but successfully ensured it failed while at the same time making it appear that he had done more than anyone to make it succeed. He was subsequently recalled to Moscow and investigated for 15 months but was eventually cleared of any wrongdoing and continued as a British agent-in-place within the GRU until the outbreak of the Second World War. New recruits to SIS were subsequently told that Jonny X was 'an example of an outstanding success in penetration of Russian secret organisations'. To this day, and despite the defection of a number of senior KGB officers during the Cold War, he is regarded by SIS as one of its best catches.

SIS and GC&CS both moved to Broadway Buildings, at 54 Broadway, Westminster, in 1935, but the headquarters operation of SIS itself was now relatively small, comprising Sinclair and around 25 'G officers' who controlled the collection process, looking after the stations abroad on a regional basis. The six 'Circulating Sections' remained those formed in late 1917. The only other headquarters elements were the diplomatic-bag interception unit; a financial and administration section; and the Passport Control Department based in Queen Anne's Gate at the back of Broadway Buildings. SIS was badly underfunded throughout the inter-war period. The disdain felt within the Foreign Office for anyone involved in the 'dirty business' of intelligence continued until the Second World War and many ambassadors refused to sanction any SIS presence within their missions. 'Right up to the outbreak of war, cases had occurred in which a head of mission was hostile to secret intelligence and other arrangements had to be made,' said one Foreign Office official who worked with SIS. 'Hostility arose partly because some heads of mission objected to transmission of intelligence to London from an unknown source and partly because of fear that the activities of the passport control officer might land the mission in trouble.'

The work of the heads of stations was also hampered by the fact that they had to carry out passport control on top of their own duties, often with little or no knowledge of either consular duties or indeed espionage. When Leslie Nicholson was sent to Prague in 1930 to run SIS operations there, he was given no training in tradecraft and had not the faintest idea of how to run a network of agents. 'Nobody gave me any tips on how to be a spy, how to make contact with, and worm vital information out of, unsuspecting experts.' An attempt by Nicholson to draw on the experience of Captain Thomas Kendrick, the Vienna station chief and allegedly one of the service's top field men, provides a useful insight into the abilities of many of the SIS old hands. Asked if there were any standard rules or practical hints he could pass on, Kendrick replied, 'I don't think there are really. You'll have to work it out for yourself.' As a result of such inefficiency, and despite undoubted successes against both the Bolsheviks and Nazi Germany, a number of SIS customers appear to have been disatisfied with the service they received in the inter-war period. 'It is beyond question that the system produced frustration in the user departments,' noted the official historian with a measure of understatement. 'There was some substance in the departmental criticisms.'

Ten

Turning On the Tap

Of the great intelligence triumphs of the war, not one was directly or exclusively due to the Secret Service proper.

Hugh Trevor-Roper, The Philby Affair, 1968

The above statement by a distinguished member of Britain's wartime intelligence establishment reflects popular assumptions about SIS and its work during the Second World War. In the post-war period, a number of former members of rival British intelligence organisations made such allegations. Determined to protect its secrecy and thereby its sources, SIS did not counter these claims. But as more details begin to emerge of its wartime operations it is clear that there needs to be a re-evaluation of how effective it really was during the Second World War. It certainly had its problems at times early on. These were caused partly by an inefficient recruiting system based on the flawed concept that only those within the establishment could be trusted and partly by the severe curtailment of funding during the inter-war period. The impossibility of running an efficient service on the resources that were being allocated came to a head in 1935, when Sinclair complained that the SIS budget was 'so reduced that it equalled the normal cost of maintaining one destroyer in Home Waters'. A report on the parlous state of affairs noted that demands on SIS were increasing as awareness of the Nazi threat grew. If its budget was not 'very largely augmented, this country will be most dangerously handicapped'. The urgent call for funds brought a virtual doubling in the size of the Secret Service Vote, from £180,000 to £350,000, allowing Sinclair to increase his preparations for war against Nazi Germany. Sinclair used some of the money to set up a number of special departments, including Section D – the D allegedly standing for 'destruction' – to investigate 'every possibility' of carrying out 'irregular' warfare (a euphemism for terrorist attacks) behind enemy lines. Richard Gambier-Parry was recruited from Philco to set up a communications department. Sinclair also encouraged the air section, run by Frederick Winterbotham, to carry out a series of secret Anglo-French aerial photo-reconnaissance missions across Germany and the Mediterranean, under the cover of civilian flights on behalf of the so-called 'Aeronautical Research and Sales Corporation'. With the passport control officers' cover already blown, Sinclair used a large proportion of the extra funds to set up a series of parallel 'fallback' networks in Germany and Italy. The members of the 'Z' Organisation were recruited by Colonel Claude Dansey, the former station head in Rome, who was believed by everyone except Sinclair to have been sacked over one of the many financial scandals – largely caused by inefficiency rather than fraud – that bedevilled the passport control offices.

The role of the passport control offices was to issue visas to anyone wanting to come to Britain or anywhere in the British Empire, including Palestine, which at the time was administered by Britain under mandate from the League of Nations. As war loomed, British passport control offices across central Europe were swamped by requests from Jews for visas to go to Palestine. A few officials undoubtedly took advantage of the situation but most of the scandals appear to have been the result of incompetent accounting and many passport control officers did what they could to help. One man however went much farther. Frank Foley, the SIS head of station in Berlin, is estimated to have saved 'tens of thousands' of Jews from the Holocaust. Most wanted to go to Palestine but the very strict quotas imposed by the British meant that few were eligible. Foley realised the danger they were in and tore up the rulebook, giving out visas that should never have been issued, hiding Jews in his home, helping them to obtain false papers and passports and even going into the concentration camps to obtain their release.

'He was a quite outstanding character,' one former SIS officer said. 'Schindler pales into insignificance besides his work on getting Jews out of Germany and he was also an outstanding officer. There would be lots of people waiting for Foley to hand out the visas so the Gestapo would come round and try and frighten them away. Foley would come out and say: "You gentlemen have come to apply for a visa I suppose. Could you join the queue?" And when they said: "No we haven't," he'd reply: "Well, could you kindly get out because this room's a bit crowded." He went on to Norway and organised the evacuation of the Norwegian Royal Family and then got out himself. He was later involved in running operations into Norway and he interrogated Hess, whom he already knew. A very, very able man, who I don't think ever got the recognition he should have done, outstanding.'

During the 1961 trial of Adolf Eichmann, Benno Cohen, former Chairman of the German Zionist Organisation, described the reign of terror under which Germany's Jews lived in the run-up to the Second World War and how few people reached out to help them. 'There was one man who stood out above all others like a beacon,' Cohen said. 'Captain Foley, Passport Officer in the British Consulate in the Tiergarten in Berlin, a man who in my opinion was one of the greatest among the nations of the world. He brought his influence to bear to help us. It was possible to bring a great number of people to Israel through the help of this most wonderful man. He rescued thousands of Jews from the jaws of death.' This is not to be taken lightly either in human or espionage terms. Foley operated at considerable risk to himself. His main role in Berlin during the 1920s and early 1930s had been to keep track of Soviet and Comintern agents attempting to infiltrate Britain and the empire. Under the so-called 'Third Party Rule' of SIS operations, stations abroad were supposed to operate against neighbouring countries and not against the country in which they were based, not least because SIS officers were not allowed diplomatic immunity. But as Hitler and his generals prepared for war, the Third Party Rule was abandoned and Foley began to collect intelligence on the Nazi war machine. As a result, helping the Jews put himself, his operations, and, since he was hiding 'four or five a night' in his home, his family at risk. But such was his willingness to help that he even put Jewish activists in touch with his agents on the German borders, most of them clergymen opposed to Hitler, who could spirit people out of Germany.

Foley's espionage achievements may have been dwarfed by his efforts to help the Jews but they were nonetheless considerable. For a long time, it was accepted as fact that SIS had no agents of any great use inside wartime Germany. We now know that, largely thanks to Foley, this was not true. A

number of senior German officials had been unhappy about Hitler's preparations for war and during the mid- to late-1930s some of these were recruited
by Foley. They included a *Luftwaffe* colonel working in the German Air
Ministry who volunteered his services in return for cash. Given his access to
high-grade intelligence from Goering's office and the panic in London over a
claim by Hitler that the *Luftwaffe* had reached parity with the RAF, SIS agreed
to pay him. Budgets had been urgently increased in the wake of Hitler's
decision to build up his armed forces, so there was hard cash available for
good intelligence.

Initially, his information was not believed in London, largely because it
contradicted the more conservative estimates of the RAF. Lord Londonderry,
the British Secretary of State for Air, dismissed it – a typical example of the
difficulties SIS faced in putting across information where the source could not
be disclosed. 'He [Londonderry] doubted whether the opinion of the Secret
Service in a matter of this kind, which had some technical aspects, was as
good as that of the department concerned,' the cabinet minutes record. 'The
Air Ministry interpretation and deduction was more likely to be the correct
one.' The Air Ministry was wrong. Over the next three years, Foley met the
Luftwaffe officer every two weeks, regularly receiving photocopies of top-
secret documents with details of both the structure of the rapidly expanding
Luftwaffe and its strategy. But when Nevile Henderson, the British ambassador in Berlin, found out about the source, Foley was ordered to drop him. 'I
had an agent who was a very friendly colonel in the *Luftwaffe* HQ,' Foley later
told a colleague. 'He passed me reports twice a month – all top level stuff. But
at the end of 1938, I was instructed by the Foreign Office to drop this chap.
Just imagine, the best source we had in Germany and in a strategic position.'

The *Luftwaffe* colonel was not the only good SIS source to be disbelieved by
the intelligence departments of Britain's armed forces. Herman Krüger, agent
TR16, handled from Holland, was still operating right up until shortly before
the Second World War. In November 1934, he reported that Germany was
constructing submarines. It was the first evidence that German was rebuilding
its U-Boat fleet but the Admiralty dismissed it on the grounds of 'improba-
bility'. In April 1938, Krüger was arrested while trying to collect intelligence
on a secret airfield. He managed to talk his way out of it but was now under

suspicion and eventually was arrested for a second and final time. Shortly after the outbreak of the Second World War, the Germans announced that Krüger had been executed by axe after being found guilty of 'working against Germany in favour of foreign powers'.

Despite what were clearly good sources of intelligence inside Germany, the three armed services repeatedly complained that the SIS was unable to produce any reliable intelligence. The Air Ministry discounted SIS reports as 'normally 80 per cent inaccurate' although this appears to have been more a reflection of rivalries and the fact that the reports did not concur with unrealistic air intelligence assessments. A measure of the credibility of some of the criticism can be had from a somewhat naïve reluctance within the British establishment to believe that Nazi Germany was as bad as it was painted and fact that much of the SIS reporting was dismissed as 'rumours planted by international Jewry'.

Nevertheless, there is no doubt that SIS had a number of early problems, caused by the lack of funding and a series of intelligence disasters between August 1938 and late 1939. They began with the arrest of Captain Thomas Kendrick, the head of station in Vienna, while observing German troops carrying out manoeuvres on the Czech border. 'Kendrick had been double-crossed by two of his agents,' a former SIS officer said. 'They told all to the Gestapo about his military reporting on the German Army in Austria.' His expulsion 'because proofs are to hand that he engaged in espionage' led Sinclair temporarily to recall the passport control officers in Berlin and Prague for fear that similar action might be taken against them.

Under pressure from the Foreign Office to find political intelligence on German opposition groups willing to form an alternative government to Hitler's, SIS was gradually drawn into an elaborate deception operation set up by the *Sicherheitsdienst* (SD), the Nazi Party's internal intelligence organisation. Sigismund Payne Best – a First World War Intelligence Corps officer and the Z network's Dutch representative – attempted to recruit what he thought were members of an anti-Nazi opposition group. It was to be a disastrous mistake. The alleged dissidents were in fact SD officers. For reasons that remain inexplicable, on the outbreak of war, the Z network was merged with long-blown SIS stations across Europe and Best was ordered to work with the passport control office in The Hague, which had already been infiltrated by the Germans. He and Major Richard Stevens, the Hague head of station, were lured to a café at Venlo, on the Dutch–German border, for negotiations with opposition 'emissaries' and were smuggled across the border by an SD snatch squad. Not only did German intelligence claim a major propaganda victory by alleging that Best and Stevens were part of a British-led plot to assassinate Hitler, but, more crucially, the secret of the Z Organisation was blown and a number of European networks compromised. In the middle of the Venlo débâcle, Sinclair died and Stewart Menzies, the head of the military circulating section, was put in charge – possibly in an attempt to improve the poor reputation of SIS among the military. Dansey was made Vice-Chief with responsibility for operations.

It appears to have worked initially. An inquiry into SIS under Lord Hankey, Minister without Portfolio, which reported in March 1940, largely exonerated the service. The Foreign Office and the Ministry of Economic Warfare were 'quite happy with the amount and quality' of the material they were receiving. The main complaints of the service intelligence departments concerned a lack of technical intelligence. The Navy was unhappy with the level of reporting of German ships leaving the Baltic, comparing it unfavourably, and perhaps unfairly, to that produced by Christmas during the First World War. There was in fact a well-established MI6 ship-watching service in place with reports coming from agents in Norway, Sweden, Denmark, the Baltic republics and even Kiel.

The Army told Hankey it wanted more detailed information of the production figures for weapons factories, no easy task. Meanwhile, the Director of Air Intelligence complained that the last useful technical intelligence report produced by SIS 'was at the start of 1937 when he received a very valuable document, which described plans to expand the German air force'. Ironically, this appears to be a reference to the *Luftwaffe* source Foley had been ordered to drop. Hankey added that the RAF was 'generally speaking well informed about the deployment of the German air force from a source that should not be divulged here'. This is a reference to either signals intelligence from Bletchley Park – which was just beginning to produce reports from *Luftwaffe* Enigma traffic – or the photographic reconnaissance section, which was now producing such good results that the RAF had decided to take it over. Hankey revealed that

SIS funding for the period 1939–40 had been £700,000, four times the 1935–36 figure, and that this had been increased since the start of the war to £1,100,000. The initial budget estimate for 1940-41 was £1,600,000. He rightly concluded that the biggest problem was actually the poor relations between SIS and the service intelligence departments, and recommended that there should be closer co-ordination, ideally through membership of the Joint Intelligence Committee. Despite resistance from both Menzies and the Director of Military Intelligence, in May 1940, SIS became a member of the JIC, a move that began to improve matters. It was also around this time that SIS first acquired the title by which it is now more popularly known. This followed a re-organisation of military intelligence in which the title of the War Office section liaising with SIS was changed from MI1c to the now legendary MI6.

The service departments' criticism of the lack of technical intelligence appears distinctly misplaced given that this was precisely the period when MI6 was beginning to produce exceptionally good intelligence on German technological advances. This again was the result of Foley's pre-war work in Berlin, which had resulted in the recruitment of the head of research and development at the German electronics company Siemens to the anti-Nazi cause. Hans Friederich Mayer opposed the Nazi's treatment of the Jews and before the war had asked Cobden Turner, a representative of the British General Electric Company, to help the daughter of a Jewish neighbour to escape. Turner had gone to Foley, who produced a British passport on the pretext that the girl was Turner's daughter, asking in return if Mayer felt able to share any information on Siemens research programmes with the British. Mayer declined but did not rule out helping if things became worse. Shortly before war broke out, Foley was recalled from Germany and sent to Oslo as Chief Passport Control Officer (Scandinavia). The intention was to try to run his German agents from there. A message was passed to Mayer that if he had any information to pass on, he should send it to the British embassy in Oslo. In November 1939, while on a business trip to Oslo, Mayer typed up two separate letters and posted them to the British embassy. They were to become known as the Oslo Report.

The two letters were passed to R V Jones, the principal scientific adviser to MI6. 'It was the most amazing statement I have ever seen,' Jones said. 'It included information that the Germans had under development two kinds of radar, one of which was already in use. It also told us of important experimental stations, that rocket and glider bombs were being developed, and other things too.' One of the two letters contained an actual electronic proximity fuse that was much better than anything the British had at the time. The letters also included details of: a new long-range bomber; the first German aircraft carrier; two new types of torpedo; and a remote-controlled glider carrying a large explosive charge – the prototype of the V1 flying bomb which, the report said, was being developed at Peenemünde in north-east Germany. But despite their complaints over a lack of technical reports from MI6, the information in the Oslo Report was largely ignored by the service intelligence departments. It was not until four years later and only after more intelligence collected by MI6 that major air raids were launched against Peenemünde.

Foley's operations in Germany and the shipwatching service were disrupted briefly by the German invasion of Norway, which yet again forced MI6 back on its feet. It now had no stations in Europe outside of the neutral capitals of Madrid, Lisbon, Berne and Stockholm. The Broadway-based operations organisation under Dansey, which was centred around the G officers, was restructured into a series of G Sections, dealing directly to those stations still in existence, and A sections, dealing with operations inside Nazi-occupied territory. A1, under Foley, covered Germany and Norway; A2 covered Holland and Denmark; A3 ran operations into Belgium; A4 covered France and Poland. Among the G Sections, the responsibilities of G1 were Sweden and Finland; G2 was the Far East, North America and South America; G4 covered Aden, Iran, Iraq, and Africa; G5 covered Iberia; G6 was the Balkans; G7 was Egypt, Malta, Palestine and Turkey; and G8 was the USSR. The circulating sections remained as they had been since 1917, i.e.: Section I, Political; Section II, Air; Section III, Naval; Section IV, Military; Section V, Counter-Espionage; Section VI, Economic. These sections liaised with the customers, providing advice to the G and A Sections on tasking and disseminating the CX reports. Communications with agents abroad was controlled by Section VIII, under Gambier-Parry, which according to Hankey had developed 'remarkably compact equipment for the particular needs of the Secret Service'. Its main wireless station was at Whaddon Hall, close to Bletchley Park where it had its own cipher section encoding and decoding messages to and from agents. Messages were ferried between Whaddon Hall and Bletchley by dispatch rider and once deciphered taken by dispatch rider to the Central Registry, which had been evacuated to St Albans to protect it from German bombing. The other main elements were Section VII, which provided finance for operations; D Section, also known as Section IX; N Section, which specialised in opening diplomatic bags in conjunction with MI5; an operational transport section; a section providing false documents; and a technical aids section, run by the real life equivalent of James Bond's 'Q'.

The service suffered a further blow in mid-1940 when D Section was hived off to form the basis of the Special Operations Executive, against Menzies's wishes – a move that created an acrimonious relationship with SOE that was to continue throughout the war. Philip Johns, who joined SOE from MI6 midway through the war, said: 'I was indoctrinated into the belief that SOE was rash and untrustworthy, lacking in security. I was briefed that in "setting Europe ablaze" our own agents might well be compromised and endangered so that caution was the watchword with the Baker St irregulars. It was emphasised that their intelligence originated from sources untrained and consequently unreliable. In short, SOE was suspect.' The distrust of SOE was not confined to MI6. A naval intelligence history of the war said it 'was a little blinded by the cloak and dazzled by the dagger. Some time was to pass before the fierce young animal became house-trained.'

The competition between MI6 and SOE extended to battles over transport needed to infiltrate agents into occupied territory. As a result of their disenchantment with MI6, both the RAF and the Royal Navy saw any assistance rendered to secret service work as a wasted effort, and the JIC was forced to insist that 'all possible priority should be given to any request from MI6 for transport facilities'. At one stage, MI6 and SOE were running rival private navies of French fishing-smacks and small motor torpedo boats, based a few miles from each other on the Cornish coast, in order to infiltrate agents into France. But these were eventually amalgamated under joint naval command at Helford, five miles south-west of Falmouth.

Despite the inevitable loss of overseas stations and networks, by the beginning of 1941 successful relationships with the intelligence organisations of the

Polish, Czech, Norwegian and French governments-in-exile as well as with the Vichy French *Deuxième Bureau*, some members of which were prepared to work with the British, had extended the reach of MI6 considerably. The Poles, who were exchanging intelligence on the Soviet Union with the Japanese, even had an intelligence officer sat in the Japanese embassy in Berlin, passing information out to Stockholm in the Japanese diplomatic bag. The close links with Czech intelligence and its head General Frantisek Moravec, produced a number of agents inside Germany, including the particularly valuable Paul Thümmel, a senior *Abwehr* officer. Known to the British as agent A54, Thümmel provided comprehensive details of German order of battle and plans, including those for the invasions of Poland, France, Britain and the USSR, before being arrested by the Gestapo in October 1941. Moravec claimed his organisation was 'the first of the European intelligence services to operate from London and the only one to have maintained a continuity of professional staff, established field stations, and agents active in Germany and elsewhere'. Working with the Norwegian intelligence service, Foley set up a coastal watching service in occupied Norway, ferrying the Norwegian agents via the Shetland Bus, a fleet of Norwegian fishing boats, based as its name suggests in the Shetland Islands. The Gaullist *Bureau Central de Renseignements et d'Action* set up a fledgeling coast-watching operation in the French Atlantic ports.

The end of 1940 and beginning of 1941 also saw a build-up of information from Germany, including more intelligence on the experimental rocket site in Peenemünde, via refugees arriving in Switzerland, said Sir Harry Hinsley, the official historian of wartime intelligence. 'We did not have an agent there,' Sir Harry said, 'but we did have these neutrals – Luxembourgers and Swiss – who were working there, some of them in Peenemünde, and information from them would come into Berne.' But the Swiss station's prize source for information from inside Germany was Halina Szymanska, the Polish confidante of the head of the *Abwehr*, Admiral Wilhelm Canaris. The JIC described the material dispatched to London by the Berne station as 'most valuable and amongst the best reports received from any quarter'. Madame Szymanska turned out to be a very significant contact, one former MI6 officer said. 'Canaris was violently anti-Nazi and was involved in plotting against Hitler.

He took a very dim view of what the Nazis were up to and as head of the *Abwehr*, where he could, he managed to commute death sentences to life sentences where agents were involved, including some British agents. He had a penchant for attractive ladies. He is supposed to have placed four at various posts overseas. Madame Szymanska was the wife of the Polish military attaché in Berlin before the war. They were both very friendly with Canaris. She was rescued by him after her husband had been captured by the Russians during the Soviet occupation of Poland. Canaris was able to arrange for her and her children to travel in a sealed railway carriage across Germany from Poland to Switzerland, where he maintained contact with her. Indeed, he himself visited her in Berne a number of times.'

On arrival in Berne, Madame Szymanska had reported her story to the Polish embassy, which passed it on to Polish intelligence officers based in London with the government-in-exile, said another MI6 officer who was actually involved in the case. A senior Polish officer 'brought it to Dansey and said, "This is a very hot potato. It is the best I can ever give you and it is so secret that I don't trust my own people to handle it, so I am giving it to you," he said. Dansey then sent Frederick van den Heuvel out to Switzerland and told him: "Your number one mission in life is to handle this woman. Everything else is second class." Canaris talked very freely to Madame Szymanska about German intentions. He was either extremely indiscreet or using her as an intentional conduit to pass information to the allies. Dansey was determined to keep the information totally secure, and at the Berne station only van den Heuvel was briefed on what was going on. Dansey kept the whole of the Swiss station and its activities in his own hands in headquarters. He wouldn't let the files go out. He wouldn't give them the general circulation that they should have. His story was: "I started the Swiss station. It's my station and I'm running it from here". The product of Source Warlock, as Madame Szymanska was known, began spectacularly at the end of 1940 with a full rundown of German plans to invade Greece via Bulgaria and Yugoslavia, which would be occupied 'with or without' its government's permission.

'The most important item Szymanska reported was in January 1941, when she was able to tell us that an irrevocable decision had been made by Hitler, against the advice of his staff, to attack Russia in May of that year. At this time the main German military effort appeared to be preparing the invasion of England in the spring. This valuable nugget of intelligence foretold a relaxation of the pressures on England and a future sharing of the war burden with Russia. This information – suitably disguised, together with some other, probably Ultra, items on the subject – was passed to the Russians by Sir Stafford Cripps, our ambassador in Moscow. Unfortunately, Stalin discounted it as misinformation from the British intelligence service.' Menzies believed to his deathbed that more use might have been made of Szymanska's links to Berlin, telling a colleague that Canaris had made an offer of talks that he had been ready to accept 'but Eden [the British Foreign Secretary] stopped me'. Shortly before he died, Menzies disclosed that he had hoped 'to open discussions with Admiral Canaris on the removal of Hitler as a means of shortening the war and negotiating peace. But this biggest intelligence coup of all time ... was thwarted in certain Foreign Office quarters "for fear of offending Russia".'

Some of the British agents inside Germany were foreign workers; others were trade unionists. MI6 appears to have taken over links to the International Transport Federation set up by Naval Intelligence before the war, collecting large amounts of information, including details of weapons production. One Norwegian agent run by the MI6 station in Stockholm had such good contacts in Germany that he was given the run of its military facilities. Among the intelligence he supplied was the crucial report that the *Bismarck* was leaving the Baltic, allowing the Royal Navy to hunt her down. 'He has been given facilities to visit German military areas, Baltic provinces, naval ports, etc.' the naval attaché in Stockholm told London. 'On occasions this information has been of great value ... including the passage of the *Bismarck* through the Kattegat in 1941.' But such was the reputation of MI6 that his report was initially ignored. 'It wasn't believed by the Admiralty,' a former MI6 officer said. 'That was commonplace. Some of the best reporting we produced was not believed by the recipients.'

In 1942, with the services still calling for reform but apparently unwilling or unable to be specific about what changes should take place, Menzies agreed to the appointment of three deputy directors, one from each of the services, thereby relieving himself of some of the more onerous management duties while at the same time keeping the critics off his back. He also accepted a

Foreign Office representative, initially Patrick Reilly, but later Robert Cecil, as personal assistant to 'C'. After the space of a year during which the service deputy directors – known within MI6 as the Commissars, because of their blatantly political role – were forced to experience at first hand some of the difficulties Menzies faced, their new roles were 'abandoned by mutual agreement' and each took over their respective service circulating section, albeit remaining members of an overall management board.

By now the A and G Sections had been replaced by production sections with precise geographical responsibilities numbered simply with Arabic numerals from P1 through to P15. P1 was France; P2 Iberia; P3 Switzerland; P4 Italy; P5 Poland; P6 Germany; P7 Belgium; P8 Holland; P9 Scandinavia; P10 Balkans; P11 Sub-Saharan Africa; P12 MI6 Stations in Western Hemisphere; P13 Baltic Republics; P14 was Instruction in Codes and Ciphers. P15 was Liaison with MI9, the military intelligence organisation set up to collect intelligence from British prisoners of war and run the European PoW escape lines. MI9 came under Dansey's control because it involved running agents abroad who in addition to assisting British PoWs to escape also provided intelligence. Norman Crockatt, the head of MI9, later complained that the German discovery of Edith Cavell, one of the agents in its First World War *La Dame Blanche* network, appeared to colour the attitude of MI6 towards his operations. Cavell, the matron of a Brussels hospital, had been uncovered and shot as a result of helping allied soldiers to escape from behind enemy lines. Anxious to keep control of as many secret networks as possible to protect his own, Menzies helped Crockatt to set up his escape lines, with the agents effectively working for both organisations. The PoWs themselves also provided intelligence from inside the camps, dispatched in coded letters home, and on the general situation on the ground inside Germany, during debriefings back in Britain. How much useful intelligence was collected from PoWs is not altogether clear, although as the Allies closed in on Germany the JIC said it had been of 'vital importance' and was reluctant to order prisoners not to escape for fear of losing their contribution. 'If escaping stopped,' it said, 'there would be a certain loss of intelligence gained by men at large, for example on general conditions, on raid damage and on questions affecting the Ministry for Economic Warfare.'

MI6 also had a number of regional outposts abroad. The 1940 expansion of its apparatus in America to create British Security Coordination, a New York-based organisation run by William Stephenson, helped to ensure the service had strong links with American intelligence. This was due in no small part to Stephenson's close relationship with Colonel William 'Wild Bill' Donovan, who later founded the Office of Strategic Services, an American organisation that combined the roles of Britain's MI6 and SOE and was a predecessor of the CIA. By December 1941, the two sides were sharing intelligence extensively. British output was passed on either to a US liaison officer in London or to Donovan himself via a Washington-based Joint Intelligence Committee, which included Stephenson among its members.

There were only a limited number of SIS officers in the Middle East at the start of the war. This and the fact that they were frequently required to cover both security and intelligence roles left them 'overworked and unable to devote adequate time and consideration to either role', and here again there were complaints that their product was inadequate. The situation was improved by the creation in Cairo of an independent security and counter-espionage organisation, Security and Intelligence Middle East, and a separate MI6 body, the Inter-Services Liaison Department (ISLD), which set up new stations in Tehran, Damascus, Baghdad and Beirut and controlled secret service operations in the Balkans.

Intelligence from the Far East was based before the outbreak of the war with Japan at stations in Shanghai, Hong Kong and at the Far East Combined Bureau in Singapore, which was a joint operation with Naval Intelligence, GC&CS and MI5. But here too MI6 had a poor reputation. As late as January 1941, Air Chief Marshal Sir Robert Brooke-Popham, C-in-C Far East, was complaining of the poor quality of British intelligence in the region: 'Weakest link undoubtedly is SIS organisation. At present little or no reliance is placed upon SIS organisation by any authorities here and little valuable information in fact appears to be obtained. I am satisfied that identity of principal officers at Shanghai, Hong Kong and Singapore is known to many. Their chief subordinates are in general local amateurs with no training in intelligence techniques nor adequate knowledge of military, naval, air or political affairs.' That view was shared by Admiral John

Godfrey, the Director of Naval Intelligence, who said: 'From the intelligence point of view, the Far East had always been difficult, particularly in Japan where SIS depended almost entirely on one source who could not be checked. SIS reports were somewhat better outside Japan, there being a useful link with the French in Indo-China, but it has to be admitted that in general Far Eastern intelligence, particularly after Singapore, depended too much on Special and Y [communications intercepts].' With the fall of Singapore, an Inter-Services Liaison Department (Far East) was set up in Delhi, later moving to Ceylon on the creation of South-East Asia Command in 1944. Separate ISLD operations were set up in Algiers for the Torch landings in North Africa in November 1942 and for the advance through Italy in the second half of 1943 through to May 1945, working direct to the military commands and subordinated to ISLD Cairo.

Gradually the service's reputation began to turn around, helped partly by the reconstruction of the network's across Europe and Section V's role in the Double Cross system but in the main by the increasing exploitation of special intelligence provided by Bletchley Park. To protect the fact that the codebreakers had broken the Enigma cipher, their decrypts were distributed by MI6 as CX reports, and their origins were disguised by giving the impression that they came from human intelligence. RV Jones recalled that this resulted in a growing admiration for MI6 abilities:

'At first those decrypts that were deemed important enough to justify some degree of circulation were disguised to appear as reports from secret agents operating under MI6, their cryptographic origin being disguised by some introduction such as "A reliable source recovered a flimsy of a message in the wastepaper of the Chief Signals Officer of Fliegerkorps IV which read...", or, in the case of an incomplete decrypt, "Source found a partly charred document in the fireplace of..." I can remember myself handing such a disguised decrypt to Air Commodore Nutting, the Director of Signals, who exclaimed: "By Jove, you've got some brave chaps working for you." Inevitably, there was speculation about the identity of the supposed secret agent or agents who were sending back such valuable reports. Gilbert Frankau, the novelist, who had a wartime post in the Flak Section, told me that he had deduced from internal evidence that the agent who could so effectively get into German headquarters must be Sir Paul Dukes, the legendary agent who had penetrated the Red Army so successfully after the Russian Revolution.'

As the number of Bletchley Park reports grew to a level where it was difficult to disguise them all as HUMINT, special liaison units had been set up in all the key commands under the control of MI6 to distribute them. But the continued assumption by those who were not indoctrinated into the Ultra secret that its product was the work of MI6 helped to improve the service's reputation. Although this was of course undeserved and coloured the impression among those who were aware of Bletchley Park's role, it is clear even from the extremely limited material now available that MI6 did have a number of excellent agents inside Germany and occupied Europe, producing far better intelligence than is generally believed.

Madame Szymanska's importance as an agent inside Germany was rivalled by Paul Rosbaud, a scientist recruited before the war by Foley. Rosbaud was a Catholic but he had a Jewish wife, whom Foley helped to escape to London. Rosbaud was close to a number of leading German scientists and as the scientific advisor to the Springer-Verlag publishing house, was kept abreast of all the latest scientific developments in Germany. He was run by the MI6 station in Stockholm, using letters from his wife sent via the German Jewish scientist Lise Meitner, who was living in exile in Sweden. In one of the letters from his wife, he was told that a young Norwegian 'friend of the family' who was studying at the *Dresdener Technische Hochschule* would be in touch. It was therefore no surprise when Sverre Bergh, a Norwegian agent sent by MI6, telephoned Rosbaud at the Springer-Verlag offices in Berlin's Linkstrasse. Rosbaud handed over further information on Peenemünde but it was not enough and Bergh was himself sent there to gather more intelligence. The young Norwegian came back with a description of a 'cigar-shaped projectile' – the A4 rocket, the first guided missile to exceed the speed of sound and a prototype of the V2 flying bomb that was to cause widespread damage in London. He also produced a plan of the central cluster of experimental buildings where the main work was being carried out under the direction of Wernher von Braun, the top German rocket scientist and later the man behind America's Nasa space programme. The material was passed back via a Swedish diplomat to the Stockholm station. But like so many MI6 agent

reports, it was not believed. It was not until 1943, following two corrobora-
tive, although far less detailed, reports by another British agent, that the RAF
was persuaded to mount major air raids against Peenemünde, forcing the
Germans to pull the rocket base back into Poland.

The information on Peenemünde was not the only important scientific
intelligence produced by Rosbaud. As the man in charge of the country's
leading scientific journals, he saw reports on every significant German scientific advance before they were sent to the censors and was able to pass on
anything interesting to the British. He also remained on close terms with all
the leading Nazi scientists. They were ever eager to curry favour with him
since they needed the publicity provided by the Springer journals in order to
enhance or maintain their own reputations and prestige. Gathering the intelligence was not so much of a problem as smuggling it out of the country.
Whenever one of the students at the *Dresdener Technische Hochschule* went
home to Norway he would take reports back, one of those involved in the
operation recalled. 'They occasionally got some help from Swedish diplomatic
couriers, who would take an envelope with them in the bag, and then hand it
on to one of the student group who 'happened' to be travelling north on the
same train, as soon as they reached Swedish territory. But more often they had
to carry the material all the way themselves.' Bergh developed his own ingen-
ious method of getting the intelligence back to London. One of the
Norwegian's friends was the Swedish journalist Olle Ollen, a very keen tennis
player. Every so often, he would send his racquets back to Stockholm to have
them re-strung. Bergh persuaded Ollen to let him hollow out the handle of
one of the racquets that needed new strings so material could be smuggled
safely out of Germany. The hollowed-out tennis racquet was frequently sent
back to Stockholm for re-stringing, taking with it valuable intelligence for the
British, including details of the new jet engine under development for the
Messerschmitt Me-262.

But perhaps the most important information that Rosbaud provided to
MI6 was from within the *Uranverein*, or Uranium Club, the small group of
German scientists attempting to build an atomic bomb. In the early summer
of 1942, Rosbaud was able to travel to Oslo himself where he passed on the
news that the *Uranverein* had given up any hope of building an atomic bomb.

'Rosbaud's wartime reports were particularly valuable because they helped us correctly to conclude that work in Germany towards the release of nuclear energy at no time reached beyond the research stage,' said R V Jones. 'His information thus calmed fears that might otherwise have beset us. His contributions were considerable and, in nuclear energy at least, approaching crucial.'

Rosbaud and Sverre were not the only British agents inside Germany run by MI6 from Sweden. There was extremely good intelligence from inside Hitler's entourage, particularly on his health, dating back to 1923 and continuing until his suicide in Berlin in April 1945. The Stockholm station also ran a number of intelligence networks in Berlin, Hamburg, Bonn, Königsberg and Vienna. The most extensive description available of these networks comes from the German interrogation of MI6 agent R34. Carl Aage Andreasson, a Danish businessman who was able to travel in and out of Germany, was captured by German intelligence in January 1944. He told his interrogators that there were four separate British networks in Berlin alone, while in Hamburg, Hampton had some eighty people working for him. CX reports from this period include good intelligence from inside Hitler's personal circle on the Führer's increasingly idiosyncratic behaviour. Reports were sent in microfilm inside crates of goods exported to Sweden. In what looks like a major breach of security, particularly since he was run from Stockholm, Andreasson's capture appears to have robbed MI6 of its best source inside Germany, Madame Szymanska. He told his interrogators that the most important British agent was a woman who had a relationship with a senior German and who had provided the British with continuous information from inside Berlin, including warning of Operation Barbarossa, the invasion of the Soviet Union. It was on 12 February 1944, shortly after Andreasson's arrest, that Canaris fell out of favour and Hitler ordered him to stay out of Berlin.

Apart from the large amount of intelligence MI6 was collecting from inside Germany itself, the networks in France were also important producers of intelligence, mainly naval and military. Some of the French networks were controlled by the Gaullist *Bureau Central de Renseignements et d'Action*, some by the Poles and some, like the large Alliance network, directly by MI6. They provided extensive details of German naval movements. All of the U-boat ports on the French Atlantic coast were covered extensively and the networks also provided vital intelligence for the 1942 commando raids on Dieppe and Saint-Nazaire. Some of the best intelligence provided by the Vichy *Deuxième Bureau* came from Source K, a French telephone engineer called Robert Keller, who for most of 1942 managed to tap into the long-distance telephone line between the German command centre in Paris and Hitler's headquarters in eastern Prussia. The French intelligence networks and guerrilla fighters on the ground produced extremely useful order-of-battle intelligence in the run-up to the D-Day. French agents stole the plans for the Atlantic Wall and provided detailed sketches of the beaches where the landings were to take place. Other members of the Free French forces were part of Operation Sussex, a joint enterprise with the *Bureau Central de Renseignements et d'Action* and the American Office for Strategic Services (OSS), in which two-person teams, including female agents, were trained by MI6 before being dropped into Normandy to provide up-to-date tactical intelligence. The French and Polish networks also provided intelligence that allowed the RAF to pre-empt a number of V-1 attacks on England. Polish agents from the Monika network, which was an SOE-type operation whose intelligence material was handled by MI6, identified 103 V-weapon sites in Northern France and Belgium between June and August 1944. A single French agent identified the location of 37 separate V1 launch sites, preventing an unknown number of British civilian casualties.

The main problem for MI6 appears to have been its lack of credibility within the service intelligence departments, much of which can be put down to petty jealousies and a refusal to believe intelligence that did not tally with their own, often false, assessments. At the start of the war, SIS certainly had a number of failings. The pre-war policy of recruiting from among 'clubable' members of the Establishment was deeply flawed and led to some very poor desk staff in London. But the main cause of its problems was the refusal of successive peacetime governments to put sufficient money into intelligence gathering. Robert Cecil, Foreign Office advisor to Menzies for much of the war, apportioned a large part of the blame for this situation to the Treasury and the Foreign Office 'which did not understand that intelligence requires a long-term perspective and cannot be turned on, like a tap, when crisis impends'. But better organisation in London, the recruitment of staff on the basis of ability rather than background, and a willingness to cut the coat according to the cloth would surely have produced better results, and created greater confidence among its customers. As the Russians advanced inexorably across eastern Europe, there were those within the service and within its 'junior half-sister', SOE, who were determined it should not be so badly prepared for the next war.

Eleven

The Next Enemy

Long before the end of the War with Germany, senior officers in SIS began to turn their thoughts towards the next enemy.

Kim Philby, *My Silent War.*

British intelligence had been aware for some time, from messages intercepted by the Radio Security Service, that the NKVD was briefing its agents within the resistance movements on 'the next war'. Some British officials harboured grave reservations about an agreement by the SOE liaison mission in Moscow to infiltrate Soviet agents into western Europe, fearing that they would form the basis for post-war subversion and intelligence networks working to create communist governments.

A post-war British intelligence briefing on NKVD resistance operations confirmed these fears. 'Though resistance to the Germans was the unifying force in these movements,' it said, 'an equally important motive was to seize power from the ruling cliques on the defeat of Germany. Through their communist leadership the Partisans received encouragement from the Russians while Russian propaganda and the successes of the Red Army caused the Partisans to look to Russia for inspiration and support when the time came to seize power.' But in 1942–43, most SOE officials were unaware of the Soviet Union's Cold War preparations and in their eagerness to secure Moscow's co-operation for their own schemes, they were happy to back its repeated demands for British help in placing agents into various parts of the world. They naïvely advocated placing NKVD agents at various strategic points of the British Empire like Singapore and Hong Kong, to ensure that if the Soviet Union collapsed 'there would be sufficiently senior NKVD officials at key points in British territory who would continue to control and direct for our purposes NKVD agents in various parts of the world.' The Foreign Office pointed out the rather obvious dangers of helping Soviet intelligence agents infiltrate the cornerstones of the Empire, but Gladwyn Jebb, then executive head of SOE, defended the proposal. In a remarkably naïve assessment of the organisation that would soon change its name to the KGB, Jebb said: 'These agents will not be Comintern men but agents of the Russian National State Police. I really do not think therefore that there need be any apprehensions.' Both the Foreign Office and MI6 rightly rejected the suggestion as suicidal. 'We must guard against requests which contribute nothing towards winning the war and are put forward only to further Russia's own post-war political aims,' one official wrote. 'We could be unwittingly building up an enemy organisation under our very noses and far from collaborating in attack on the Axis, we may be subscribing to the doctrine of *hari-kari* [*sic*].' Long before the end of the war, MI6 recognised that the Soviet Union would soon cease to be an ally. In October 1943, Valentine Vivian, MI6 Deputy Chief, wrote to a senior Foreign Office official suggesting that MI6 set up an anti-communist section to infiltrate foreign Communist Parties and gather intelligence on how they were controlled by Moscow. Despite MI5's continuing watch on Russian espionage in Britain, MI6 had been prevented from operating against the Soviet Union. But the Foreign Office was happy to agree to Vivian's suggestion 'on condition that the necessary caution is exercised and you do nothing directly inside the USSR. We believe our task to be finding out as much as possible about the aims and the activities of the NKVD and other Soviet organisations abroad. The Russians would simply take us for fools if we did not make use of these opportunities when it is perfectly clear that they have their own wide network of agents in Britain.'

MI6 set up a new Section IX to cover the Soviet Union, in May 1944. By August it had drawn up a plan whereby MI6 officers would be sent into a post-war Soviet Union either under 'official cover' as members of trade delegations or under 'natural cover' as businessmen, engineers, and industrialists. British spies could also be part of exchanges with the Russians on music, ballet, drama and sport, one official suggested. 'A start could be made now by preparing the ground with the Football Association to get them to be prepared to start work straight away.' Using the contacts gained in setting up his Z Organisation, Dansey lined up a number of companies who might be persuaded to allow MI6 officers on to their staff. These included the Hudson Bay Company, which had lent Cumming its representative in Russia in 1919; the Henry Lunn travel company (now Lunn Poly); the Harland and Wolff shipbuilders, who were about to start talks on the construction of icebreakers for the Russian merchant fleet; and Johnson Matthey, who 'have entered into preliminary talks with the Russian Trade Mission on the processing and distribution of Russian platinum and other rare metals.'

Despite the early enthusiasm of its Moscow mission for co-operation with the Russians, SOE was if anything preparing even more vigorously for the Cold War. 'The chief threat to world peace is now the increasing divergence becoming evident between Russian aims and the policies of the western allies,' wrote Harold Perkins, head of SOE's Polish Section, in a confidential memo in October 1944. He suggested keeping the section's operatives in Poland in place and even sending others back to set up networks to collect intelligence and organise resistance to a Russian-controlled regime. 'There are very few Englishmen who possess a first-hand knowledge of Russia, of Russian mentality, and of Russian methods,' Perkins added. 'The Poles on the other hand have several thousand persons having those qualifications and being at the same time bitterly hostile to Russia, although friendly to us. In the event of war with Russia they would be of inestimable value to us. They represent an asset, which should not lightly be discarded.'

The idea was taken up by Sir Colin Gubbins, the head of SOE, who ordered that a list of all its agents in Central Europe be drawn up. 'With the European war drawing to a close, many SOE agents who have served the Organisation well have been or will shortly be stood down,' Sir Colin said. 'It is considered most desirable that contact should be maintained with them to form a nucleus of tried and experienced agents capable of rapid expansion in the event of another war.' He also suggested that sympathetic businessmen should be approached to provide the agents with cover. The Board of Trade and other government departments should be enlisted 'to obtain priority for them over their competitors,' he said. 'There are many people both within and outside SOE who have wide business and commercial contacts and will be willing to anxious to help in this scheme.' The plans were co-ordinated with similar activities by the American OSS. As the war in Europe drew to a close, Perkins, now in charge of SOE's operations in Poland, Czechoslovakia and Hungary, travelled to Prague to contact its agents there. In signals back to London, he recorded their wartime cover, stressing that 'the continuity of the stories should not be broken'.

MI6 began making exploratory attempts to infiltrate members of the anti-Russian resistance movements into the Baltic republics. The JIC discussed plans to work with the anti-communist resistance movements to set up networks inside eastern Europe. Menzies said 'it was essential the Soviet authorities should not become aware of the nature of the measures'. This was a somewhat vain hope given that Kim Philby, the so-called Third Man in the Cambridge spy ring, had been appointed head of Section IX and Major Anthony Blunt of MI5, another key member of the Cambridge ring, was a frequent participant in JIC discussions.

Despite his communist allegiances, Philby began preparing for the Cold War with apparent enthusiasm. 'In late February or early March 1945, there arrived on my desk the document that Philby describes as "the Charter" of Section IX,' wrote Robert Cecil. 'It included a substantial number of overseas stations to be held by officers under diplomatic cover who would be directly responsible to the Head of IX. With hindsight, it is easy to see why Philby pitched his demands so high and why he aimed to create his own empire within SIS. Quite apart from his covert aims, it is clear that he foresaw more plainly than I the onset of the Cold War, bringing with it more menacing surveillance and making necessary more permanent use of diplomatic cover.'

The archives of the Russian Foreign Intelligence Service, the SVR, contain a number of MI6 papers passed to Moscow by Philby at this time. They include plans to revive the Double Cross system for use against the NKVD after it attempted to recruit a Hungarian who was already working for the British. What happened to the luckless agent as a result of Philby's treachery is not recorded but could be easily guessed.

With the end of the war, intelligence officers were needed en masse in Germany to assess the information from Nazi files and interrogation of former German officers. The Nazi stay-behind units, the so-called Werewolf organisation, failed to materialise in any strength and it soon became clear that the main problem for those MI6 officers posted to the British Control Commissions in Germany and Austria was the huge number of Russian espionage agents who had been infiltrated into the British sector. Intelligence exchanges with the Soviet Union were cut to an absolute minimum as the post-war predictions came to fruition.

As Menzies negotiated with the services over their post-war intelligence requirements, MI6 was told that its most urgent priority was information on the Soviet Union's attempts to produce an atomic bomb. MI6 agents in Germany began recruiting low-level scientists in the Russian zone. 'We are convinced,' one official said, 'there is an opportunity now to obtain high-grade intelligence from these men which will enable us to build up an almost complete picture of Russian scientific and technical activities in Germany and so make it possible to forecast more accurately than we can at present the progress of Russian development of weapons during future years.'

With the Cold War already in full flow in the occupied zones, Gubbins and Menzies made their peace. But SOE's independent attitude and its determination to 'resort to and encourage every form of terror' had made it unpopular within Whitehall where the enthusiasm of SOE officers working with the British Control Commissions in Austria and Germany for freelance 'activities of a cloak and dagger variety' was viewed with undisguised horror. 'Their activities in Germany seem to me to be of a somewhat dangerous political character,' one official wrote. He expressed alarm at an SOE plan to mount an operation into the Russian zone of Austria to 'lift' film of German rocket technology. 'We have to watch our step,' the official said. 'The Russians are watching us and we must be particularly careful not to allow any activities of a cloak and dagger variety to continue under our auspices.'

Although the need for some form of slimmed-down peacetime special operations branch was recognised, there were genuine fears that if it remained an independent body it would turn into a loose cannon. It was decided that special operations should be put back under MI6 control. Even before it's 'liquidation' and absorption into MI6 as the Special Operations Branch, at the beginning of 1946, SOE officers like Perkins began working effectively for their new boss, handing their networks over to MI6 control to protect them from Foreign Office demands that they be closed down to appease the

Russians. 'Perks' – described by one colleague as 'the only man I have ever seen bend a poker in his hands' – subsequently become head of the Special Operations Branch, running a number of covert operations into eastern Europe. How successful the networks were is not clear. But the Baltic operations were quickly compromised and, by May 1946, many of the Polish agents were under arrest.

As a result of the propaganda of the war years, 'Uncle Joe' Stalin was still regarded with affection by the British and American public. But in February 1946, Canadian police arrested 22 members of a Soviet spy ring revealed by the defector Igor Gouzenko. A week later George Kennan, the US Chargé d'Affaires in Moscow wrote an influential telegram outlining the view that the Russians were intent on world domination, subverting capitalism by means of 'an underground operating directorate of world communism, a concealed Comintern tightly coordinated and directed by Moscow'.

The British position was outlined by the JIC, which noted that 'Communism is the most important external political menace confronting the British Commonwealth and is likely to remain so in the foreseeable future' and that 'Russian policy will be aggressive by all measures short of war'. Stalin was unlikely to start a major war unless he unwittingly pushed America or Britain too far, but 'we cannot exclude the possibility that Russia may pursue a policy, which will present the West with local *faits accomplis*.'

Four days later, Churchill, now out of office but still well briefed on intelligence matters, made a speech at Fulton, Missouri, that was to herald a radical sea change in the public perception of the Soviet Union. 'From Stettin in the Baltic to Trieste in the Adriatic, an Iron Curtain has descended across the continent,' he said. 'Behind that line lie all the capitals of the ancient states of central and eastern Europe. Warsaw, Berlin, Prague, Vienna, Budapest, Bucharest and Sofia, all these famous cities and the populations around them lie in the Soviet sphere and all are subject, in one form or another, not only to Soviet influence but to a very high and in some cases increasing measure of control from Moscow.' Amid all this concern about the danger from the Soviet Union came a moment of pure farce, recalled by R. V. Jones, then head of the scientific section: 'One morning just before a weekend, the Security Officer rushed round the MI6 offices telling everyone to take down all maps off their walls. It turned out that the MI6 offices were all rented and the landlord had heard that we were thinking of moving. Anxious to re-let the premises in such an event, he had somehow made contact with the Russian Trade Delegation and he wished to take them round on the Saturday afternoon. Could it happen anywhere but Britain that representatives of its major prospective opponent should be allowed to tour the offices of its Secret Service?'

By now, Menzies was already submitting proposals for special operations, along the lines of those carried out during the war. One of the earliest and, perhaps fortunately, more short-lived was devised by Perkins and involved planting explosive devices below the waterline of ships carrying Jewish refugees from Italy to Israel. A single, empty ship was blown up before the plan was abandoned. But there was little doubt about the main target of the MI6 special operations. Menzies told the JIC he intended to make good use of a report, compiled for the Germans by a captured Russian officer and inherited by the British at the end of the war. It contained 'suggestions for political warfare against the Russians, and plans and a map for military action in support of this policy.'

The first MI6 attempt to set up a network in Latvia had taken place shortly after that country was annexed by Moscow in June 1940. Kenneth Benton and his wife, Peggy, then posted to the service's Riga section, trained a stay-behind agent to use a small wireless, but after sending three messages detailing Russian activities he disappeared. 'There were no more messages from our agent and we concluded that the Soviet police or NKVD had traced his signals and located him,' Benton said.

MI6 resumed its attempts to set up networks in the Baltic republics in 1945. But unbeknown to Harry Carr, the MI6 Controller Northern Area, they had quickly become compromised. Major Janis Lukasevics of Latvian state security organised a deception operation. 'We had to know the MI6 plans and the only way we could do that was by successfully infiltrating our men into the MI6 networks,' Lukasevics said. Once the networks were infiltrated, they were to be left in place, feeding back false information to London and providing Soviet intelligence with details of what the British were trying to do. 'There was a decision not to touch them, to continue finding out what their specific tasks were. Well, we quite quickly found out that their job was not just spying but also to prepare the way for other spies, to set up a link and new points of support and to establish contact with resistance groups.' More than 30 British agents, most of them emigrés, were dispatched to Lithuania, Estonia and Latvia over a period spanning a total of ten years. Anthony Cavendish, who as an MI6 officer based in Germany, helped to ferry some of them into Latvia, recalled that all the missions ended in failure, as did similar attempts to link up with the Ukrainian nationalist movement. None of this would have surprised those British and American intelligence officers who had worked in Germany at the end of the war. As they interrogated their German counterparts and Soviet defectors, it became clear that since the 1920s, most of the Russian, Ukrainian and Baltic emigré groups had been penetrated by Soviet agents. Arnold Silver, a US intelligence officer who served in Germany before going on to join the CIA, described the evidence of such penetration as 'staggeringly convincing'. Silver found it 'astonishing' that both MI6 and the CIA nevertheless decided to use the emigré groups to set up networks inside the Soviet Union. 'Given the scale of Soviet penetration of the groups, it could not be expected that such operations would benefit anybody but the KGB and of course CIA and MI6 suffered one disaster after another. There was not one successful operation. The mass of information militating against this kind of blindness on the part of those responsible for the decision to operate with emigré groups was simply ignored, resulting in many lost lives of emigré agents.'

Britain's Cold War activities against the East Bloc were coordinated by a high-level Foreign Office committee, the Russia Committee, which in November 1948 decided on a more offensive policy, using limited 'special operations' that would stop short of full-blown hot war. 'Our aim should certainly be to liberate the countries within the Soviet orbit by any means short of war,' the committee decided. Sir Ivone Kirkpatrick, the Foreign Office official responsible for secret service activity, suggested an attempt to foment insurrection in Albania, again using emigrés to link up with resistance groups that were assumed to be operating inside the country, in a joint operation with the Americans that was to be run for MI6 by Harold Perkins.

With Philby as the MI6 representative on the committee co-ordinating Operation Valuable, it was doomed to failure from the start. But even without his involvement it would surely not have worked. It was not only poorly conceived – there was no resistance group to link up with – it was also hampered by inter-service rivalry between the Americans and the British. Over the next four years a succession of emigrés were ferried across the Adriatic or parachuted into Albania to stir up revolt. Most were discovered immediately and executed. A few managed to make it across the border into Greece. 'The information they brought was almost wholly negative,' Philby wrote. 'It was clear, at least, that they had nowhere found arms open to welcome them.' The final phase of the operation, an 'invasion' by around 1,000 armed emigrés to firm up the revolt, like the revolt itself, never materialised.

Another of the early Cold War operations occurred in Vienna, where in 1949, the British discovered they could tap into the telephone lines of the Imperial Hotel, the Red Army headquarters. In order to disguise these activities, MI6 dug tunnels to the points at which the lines could be tapped. As cover for one 70-ft tunnel, the house from which it led was turned into a shop selling Harris Tweed, recalled Andrew King, who was in overall charge of all operations in Vienna. But it became so popular that MI6 officers found themselves spending more time attending to customers than monitoring Soviet telephone calls and the cover was abandoned.

Simon Preston, who as a young Royal Marines subaltern was attached to MI6 was involved briefly in one of the operations:

In late 1952 I was sent up to Vienna for a week because they wanted someone to help in pretending to dig the road up. We were actually listening in on the Russian communications, which had to go through that part of our sector. We dug a hole, and a long way down there was a chap with earphones on tapping the Russian telephone lines. My job was simply steering people on the surface away – police, curious passers-by – and that went on every day for a week. I was working with an MI6 character in his mid-thirties. He and I were put up by an eccentric landlady in the south end of Vienna, and every day we used to come back covered in mud. For some reason he had told her that he played football, and she used to ask, quite incredulously, 'Wieder Fussball spielen, Herr Oberleutnant? Wieder Fussball spielen?'

The telephone-tapping operations continued until 1955, when the wartime allies withdrew from Austria. But it provided complete details of the Soviet order of battle as well as vital intelligence on Soviet intentions towards Yugoslavia. 'We had a total of three tunnels at various times,' recalled King. 'They were important operations and the customers became very excited about them, particularly the defence establishment. They really thought they were in on something.'

Peter Lunn, then station head in Vienna, successfully repeated the operation in Berlin, in 1955, on this occasion digging a 600-yard tunnel underneath the Soviet zone in conjunction with the CIA. For nearly a year, until it was revealed at a Soviet press conference, it provided a wealth of information on the Soviet military and, most importantly, details of Khrushchev's denunciation of Stalin at the Twentieth Party Congress. But even here, there was to be failure. The minutes of the meeting to set up the Berlin tunnel were recorded on the British side by George Blake, who was soon to be revealed as a Soviet agent.

'Blake had given the whole thing away from the beginning, and the Russians knew perfectly well we were tapping these lines,' King said. 'They probably said, "Nobody's to say anything important and keep the buggers busy. It's a waste of their money and manpower mounting an operation like this." And it was a tremendous operation. It was shared with the Americans – the CIA finance went to I should think about 75 per cent of the thing – and there was enormous manpower put into it on processing the results, which were brought back on tapes. We had something like fifty or sixty Russian emigrés going through all these tapes.'

Throughout the late 1940s and early 1950s the British and Americans set up stay-behind units in western Europe in preparation for the expected Soviet invasion. Simon Preston and Michael Giles, another Royal Marine officer, were among those selected to take part in the operation and were sent to Fort Monckton, the MI6 training base on the Solent, where they were given instruction in codes, the use of a pistol, and covert operations. 'We were made to do exercises, going out in the dead of night and pretending to blow up trains in the railway stations without the stationmaster or the porters seeing you,' Preston said. 'We crept about and pretended to lay charges on the right part of the railway engine with a view to blowing it up.'

Not all the sabotage was simulated. Michael Giles took part in an exercise at the Eastleigh Marshalling Yards, part of the Southern Railway:

We laid bricks inside railway engines to simulate plastic explosives. I remember rows and rows of steam engines all under thick snow, standing there in clouds of vapour. There were troops out with dogs. The guards came past and I was actually hiding among the cylinder blocks of these engines as they went past. We were also opening up the lubricating tops of the axle boxes and pouring in sand. What happens is that after about fifty miles the sand in the axle box starts to turn them red hot and they all overheat.'

Preston was dispatched to London for an additional course on tradecraft. 'I had to do a ten-day course in Greenwich, learning about following people in the street and shaking off people following me – the practicalities of being in the intelligence world. They were then sent to Austria, where as part of the Gladio network set up to provide stay-behind units in the event of western Europe being overrun by Soviet forces, MI6 and the CIA had set up a number of underground bunkers, filled with weapons, clothing and supplies. 'We spent a lot of our time up in the mountains, learning all about the terrain, learning German, meeting other potential agents, recruiting agents if possible, identifying and plotting dropping zones,' Preston said. 'The whole object was that we would all form the nucleus of a partisan or a guerrilla army should the Russians invade. It was thought that within five years there would be a conventional war. We would be dropped back into the area we knew and immediately we would be among friends. The food, arms and explosives would be all there in the bunkers. It doesn't take much imagination to work out that the Russian Army would have hunted us from pillar to post. It would have been a short but interesting life I suspect. But I can't remember ever worrying about that. There was one nasty moment. We'd been up in the mountains for about a week, when early one morning there was an enormous number of explosions down in the valley which sounded like the beginning of something. It turned out to be some kind of saint's day, and the villagers were just letting off fireworks.'

MI6 embarked on a series of reorganisations in the immediate post-war period. Five separate directorates were created: D1: Finance and

Administration; D2: Production; D3: Requirements; D4: Training and Development; and D5: War Planning. The Requirements Directorate, equating to the old circulating or liaison sections, remained much as before. The roman numerals were dropped in favour of Arabic and the importance of science was reflected by it being given its own section, with R1: Political; R2: Air; R3: Naval; R4: Army; R5: Counter-Espionage – an amalgamation of Section V and Philby's Section IX; R6: Economic; R7: Scientific; R8: SIGINT and, briefly, R9: Atomic Intelligence.

Production was split on geographical lines initially under five Controllers. Controller Northern Area was in charge of Scandinavia and Holland; Controller Western Area covered Belgium, France, Italy and the Iberian peninsula; Controller Eastern Area oversaw Germany, Austria and Switzerland. There was a single Controller for eastern Europe and just one for the whole of the Middle East and Far East. But this format was clearly unsuitable for the Cold War era and after a series of minor reorganisations during the late 1940s and early 1950s, the management structure settled on three Chief Controllers, the so-called Robber Barons: CC(E), covering Europe – split into three, North, East and West; CC(M) for the Mediterranean (Middle East and Africa), and CC(P) for the Pacific (Far East and the Americas) with a fourth controllerate, Production Research, covering operations carried out from the United Kingdom under the auspices of London Station, based at Londonderry House, Victoria.

Menzies retired in 1951 to be replaced by his deputy Sir John Sinclair, a former Director of Military Intelligence. The highlight of Sinclair's period as C was Operation Boot, the overthrow of Mohammed Mossadeq, the Iranian Prime Minister, who in 1951 had nationalised the Anglo-Iranian Oil Company. The Great Game – Britain's rivalry with Russia for control of the region – had continued into the Cold War, given added significance by the importance of oil to the Western economies. By August 1944, the JIC was identifying Iran and Iraq as the area where friction between the two sides might most easily arise, reporting: 'It is clear that if it came to war, Russia would be likely to strike at Persia and Iraq in order to gain depth of defence for the Caucasian oilfields, to deny us most important sources of oil and to secure an outlet to the Persian Gulf.'

British interests in Iran were centred on Anglo-Iranian, in which Churchill had bought a majority stake for the Government in 1914. As well as ensuring a steady supply of cheap oil, it was an important source of intelligence and since 1946, when the refusal of Russia to withdraw its troops from northern Iran had sparked fears that Moscow might provoke confrontation there, the company's employees had included an MI5 officer. Mossadeq certainly had left-wing tendencies but it was the loss of Anglo-Iranian that led to British action. A plan to seize control of the Abadan refinery with an amphibious landing while an airborne force provided a diversion in eastern Iran was abandoned, partly as a result of the fact that large numbers of British troops were needed to keep control of the Suez Canal, but in the main because of an American veto on the use of force. Although willing to be persuaded that Mossadeq might let in the Russians, the Americans had no interest in supporting Britain's domination of Iranian oil supplies.

So Monty Woodhouse, the MI6 head of station in Tehran, and George Kennedy Young, who as Controller (Middle East) was based in Nicosia, hatched a plot under which Mossadeq was to be overthrown by orchestrated street violence – fomented by the main MI6 agents in Tehran, the Rashidian brothers – followed by a coup. With the plans well underway, Mossadeq broke off relations with the British, leaving MI6 with no base inside Tehran. Woodhouse flew to Washington to bring the CIA into the action. 'I decided to emphasise the Communist threat to Iran rather than the need to recover control of the oil industry,' he wrote. 'Two separate components were dovetailed into the plan, because we had two distinct kinds of resources: an urban organisation run by the brothers, and a number of tribal leaders in the south. We intended to activate both simultaneously. The urban organisation included senior officers of the army and police, deputies and senators, mullahs, merchants, newspaper editors and elder statesmen, as well as mob-leaders. These forces, directed by the brothers, were to seize control of Tehran, preferably with the support of the Shah but if necessary without it, and to arrest Mossadeq and his ministers. At the same time, the tribal leaders were to make a show of force in the direction of the major cities in the south.'

For almost a week, the mobs, incited by CIA dollars, ran riot through the streets of Tehran, trampling several hundred people to death. Behind the scenes, the Rashidian brothers' influential contacts in the army and the police pulled the strings ensuring that anyone who might oppose the prime minister's removal was quietly disposed of. The operation was an undoubted success although perhaps not an unqualified one. The downside of bringing the Americans in was that Anglo-Iranian, renamed British Petroleum, was left with just 40 per cent control of the newly formed National Iranian Oil Company, with various American companies taking a further 40 per cent. The CIA also claimed the credit for the success of the operation. But the Shah knew who to thank and, right up until the 1978 Islamic Revolution, Woodhouse's successors were accorded privileged access to the Peacock Throne. The Shah was not the only grateful party. Both MI6 and the CIA have been able to make good use of oil companies as cover for their agents. There are few countries willing to turn down the potential revenue offered by an exploration team from a major oil company. Like its predecessor, Anglo-Iranian, BP is among a number of British companies with close relations with MI6, to the extent that senior executives have been on the distribution lists for its reports.

Despite the success of Operation Boot, Sinclair's time in charge was to become known as 'the Horrors', in part because of ineffectual leadership but largely due to the failures in eastern Europe and the knock-on from the Third Man affair. The Americans found the determination to protect Philby incomprehensible and wondered if British intelligence was not riddled with communist spies. While there was a good deal of respect among individual American officers, dating back to the war years, there was also a lot of resentment at the patronising, superior attitude of some of the British counterparts. As early as 1943, Donovan had made it clear that, while he was 'perfectly willing to coordinate on a higher level', he was 'determined not to tolerate any tutelage' from the British. America's post-war tendency to isolationism and its determination to undermine the British position in the world as a means of improving its own had already strained the relationship. The Third Man affair placed it close to breaking point.

The lowest point of 'the Horrors' came in April 1956 with the Buster Crabb affair. Comander Crabb, a veteran diver who had been used in the past by MI6 for special jobs, was to dive into Portsmouth harbour to gather intelligence on the Russian destroyer *Ordzhonikidze*, which had brought the Soviet leader Nikita Khrushchev on a state visit to Britain. Following his second dive, Crabb failed to return. His body was not found for more than a year, by which time it was impossible for the coroner to determine the cause of death, although there was inevitable speculation that he had been murdered by the Russians. It was a nightmare moment for MI6. Crabb's death came literally as the Russians announced that they had found the Berlin tunnel. The affair grabbed the headlines for days, with MI6 inevitably depicted as a bunch of bungling amateurs, and Anthony Eden, the British Prime Minister, went so far as to dissociate his ministers from it in parliament. Sinclair was forced into early retirement and Dick White, the head of MI5, was switched across to replace him and clear up the mess. He was immediately presented with a further problem. Eden, believing that Britain's control of the Suez canal was 'the lifeline to the empire', was obsessed with removing Gamal Abdel Nasser, the Egyptian President. With the military deeply sceptical about Eden's plans 'to knock Nasser off his perch', his main instrument had become MI6. George Young, one of the so-called robber barons, and Patrick Dean, initially MI6 Foreign Office Adviser and then chairman of the JIC, told Eden what he wanted to hear. Nasser was a dangerous dictator, who was taking arms from Moscow and was determined to overthrow the Middle East monarchies on which Britain depended for its influence in the region.

MI6 recruited a senior Egyptian air force officer, Squadron Leader Assam ul-Din Mahmoud Khalil, giving him valuable intelligence on Israel as cover for meetings with his controllers. Julian Amery, an MP and former member of SOE who had been heavily involved in the Albanian fiasco, was drafted in to find dissidents who could be counted on to form a pro-British government. A senior MI6 officer, Nicholas Elliot, was sent to Tel Aviv to liaise with the Israelis, whose involvement in the affair was to be kept unknown to all but a few British officials, even at the highest levels. The Israelis were to invade Egypt across the Sinai. The British and the French would then intervene, ostensibly to separate the two warring sides, in reality as part of what was effectively a joint British, French and Israeli invasion force aimed at replacing Nasser with someone more amenable to all three.

For the British at least, deposing the Egyptian leader was not enough. Various schemes were devised to assassinate him: an exploding electric razor;

poison gas in the ventilation system; or even a straightforward hit squad. White vetoed them all. Young laughingly told one planning meeting that 'thuggery is not on the agenda'. It was. While the collusion with Tel Aviv was known to only a few, the suggestion that Nasser should be done away was widespread. After a meeting with one senior treasury official, Humphrey Trevelyan, the British ambassador to Egypt, complained: 'High officials in the Treasury seem to have been very free with their proposals on what to do with Nasser, which included the most extreme solutions.' Meanwhile, Eden ordered the BBC to stop broadcasting even-handed reports of the crisis and the MI6-owned Near East Arab Broadcasting Service, which ran a genuinely successful commercial radio station, al-Sharq al-Adna, from Cyprus, began pumping out blatant anti-Nasser propaganda so unsubtle that one commentator has suggested it 'could well have been conceived by Dr Goebbels'.

The MI6 contributions were no more successful than the operation as a whole. Intelligence out of Cairo both before and during the crisis was at best highly optimistic if not downright misleading, particularly with regard to Nasser's popularity and the lack of any viable opposition. The main network, founded around another black-propaganda organisation, the Arab News Agency, was rolled up by the Egyptian security police and a number of MI6 officers arrested. Khalil turned out to be a double-agent who apparently had kept Nasser completely informed of what the Egyptian leader dubbed 'the Restoration Plot'. There was an element of irony in this failure, since Egyptian intelligence held MI6 in such high regard that its training school used James Bond books as textbooks in tradecraft. 'The Egyptians had a thing about 007,' a former MI6 officer said. 'Their representative in London in the days of Nasser was instructed to go and buy every book by Fleming on James Bond because they wanted to have it as compulsory reading for the training course for their intelligence service. At that time, we happened to have a good connection with the Egyptian intelligence service of which they were not aware, and indeed this chap went and bought them all and was congratulated on subsequent visits to Cairo for having done so.'

The Suez Crisis served to draw MI6's attention away from events in eastern Europe, where, at the same time, the Hungarian uprising was taking place and food riots were sweeping across Poland. The immediate catalysts for these events could not have been predicted – most being associated with the de-Stalinisation campaign that took place in the Soviet Bloc following Khrushchev's secret denunciation of his predecessor. But MI6 had been active behind the scenes for some time providing covert assistance to potential Hungarian rebels and knew they were planning an uprising.

The mid-1950s were regarded by both British and American intelligence as the last chance to challenge the Soviet domination of eastern Europe. The Eisenhower administration had been elected on a platform of liberating the Soviet satellites – the so-called 'Rollback' policy – but in the ten years since the end of the war, the Russians had considerably strengthened their hold over eastern Europe. All reports from inside the satellite states spoke of high levels of dissatisfaction, but the presence of 100,000 Russian troops held out little hope that any revolt was likely to succeed. Nevertheless, the CIA had stepped up its covert operations in eastern Europe in the twelve-month period leading up to the Hungarian uprising, training the 'Red Sox' teams of Polish, Hungarian, Czech and Romanian emigrés for covert action inside their home countries. Allen Dulles, the head of the CIA, told the National Security Council that 'developments in the satellites present the greatest opportunity for the last ten years both covertly and overtly to exploit the situation'.

MI6 had been in close contact with dissident elements inside Hungary for some time, spiriting them across the border into the British zone of Austria for resistance training in preparation for a future uprising. Paul Gorka was one of a group of Hungarian students recruited in the early 1950s to gather intelligence on Soviet activity inside Hungary and equipped with 'enough weapons to shoot our way across the border'. They were sent 'coded messages from Vienna asking us for information about Russian troop movements, index numbers of military vehicles, so that a picture could be built up of details of Russian occupation units. We replied with information written in invisible ink in innocuous letters to special addresses.' But Gorka and his fellow students developed the unfortunate habit of meeting in a popular Budapest coffee bar to discuss their activities and were swiftly rounded up. 'I was interrogated for seven weeks, sometimes in the presence of a Soviet major' Gorka said. 'I was tortured several times. Sometimes I was left in my cell with both feet immersed in icy water, other times I was hung from a beam by my arms handcuffed together. When I was cut down after several hours, my hands were black and so swollen that it was impossible to remove the handcuffs. Under torture, I confessed and after a brief trial was sent to prison for 15 years.'

Some Hungarian dissidents were smuggled across the border for resistance training, rendezvousing with their contact in true Cold War fashion, often quite literally under a certain lamp-post in a back street of a border town. Michael Giles was one of those training the dissidents for resistance work. 'I had this battered old Volkswagen and I was picking up agents on the Hungarian border. We were taking them up into the mountains and giving them a sort of three- or four-day crash course. I would be told to pick somebody up from a street corner at a certain time of night in the pouring rain. Graz was our staging point. Then, after we'd trained them – explosives, weapons training – I used to take them back. This was in 1954, two years before the uprising. But we knew it was going to come. We were training agents for the uprising.' The expectation that an uprising would take place is surprising and – given that there were riots going on in Poland in support of reform at the same time – raises the possibility of outside co-ordination, even that some of Perkins's old networks were still in place. Certainly MI6 planned to support resistance fighters in both Hungary and Czechoslovakia. The service's representatives in Prague and Budapest went out into the woods burying stay-behind packs like those that were being hidden in the Austrian Alps by Preston and Giles.

No one could have expected quite such propitious circumstances for an uprising as those caused in Hungary by the forced resignation in 1955 of the liberal Prime Minister Imre Nagy and the news a few months later of Khrushchev's denunciation of Stalin, which had a powerful effect across eastern Europe. Neither MI6 nor the CIA had been able to get hold of the full text of the speech, but a Mossad agent in Warsaw seduced a secretary working in the Polish Communist Party headquarters and persuaded her to let him make a transcript, which the Israelis then passed to the Americans. Thousands of copies of the speech were distributed clandestinely throughout eastern Europe.

As details of the secret speech became more widely known, the clamour for reforms began to grow. On 23 October 1956 a student demonstration calling for free elections, the withdrawal of Russian troops and the return of Nagy brought a quarter of a million people on to the streets of Budapest. Large numbers of weapons began to appear in the crowd, many of them from British and American arms caches in Austria or Hungary itself. Fighting broke out with the security forces. In an attempt to placate the demonstrators, Nagy was reappointed Prime Minister. There was sporadic fighting for several days, followed by a series of reforms introduced by Nagy, including the disband-ment of the AVH secret police and the abandonment of the one-party system. On 1 November the Red Army invaded Hungary. The uprising was suppressed, Nagy was arrested and the reforms were brought to an early end. Whether or not Western intelligence was aware that there was to be an attempted uprising, no one seems to have been expecting anything on quite the scale that occurred. Allen Dulles told the National Security Council, 'In a sense, what had occurred there was a miracle. Events had belied all our past views that a popular revolt in the face of modern weapons was an utter impossibility.'

Throughout the Cold War, MI6 special operations were closely co-ordinated with the dissemination of propaganda. It was produced by the Foreign Office Information Research Department (IRD) – a direct descendant of an earlier secret Foreign Office department known simply as EH, because it was located in Electra House on the Embankment. At the start of the Second World War, EH had been amalgamated with Section D and a War Office special operations organisation to form SOE. But it was soon hived off to form a separate psychological-operations department, the Political Warfare Executive, led by Sir Robert Bruce Lockhart, Sidney Reilly's co-conspirator in the Lockhart Plot. At the end of the war, the PWE's intelligence-gathering responsibilities were taken over by the Foreign Office's Political Information Department. It was not until three years later that the propaganda function was reactivated, when Christopher Mayhew, then a junior Foreign Office minister, set up the IRD 'to discourage the Slavs from using the UN for black-guarding us, by occasionally pulling a skeleton out of their cupboard for a change'. It prepared briefs for politicians and journalists that were specifically designed 'to stimulate subversive activities in the Soviet orbits'.

The Russia Committee had already enthusiastically advocated a co-ordinated policy of propaganda and special operations to counter Soviet influence in eastern Europe. 'We have a good analogy in our successful propaganda campaign during the war directed towards stimulating resistance movements in Europe,' Kirkpatrick recalled. 'The V-sign was emblazoned all over the world. But at the same time we acted. We parachuted men, money and arms into occupied territory. We were not inhibited by fear that the Germans would find out what we were doing or that they might react, or that we might be criticised. Propaganda on the larger scale was co-ordinated with our policy. The result was success.'

The IRD's first use in conjunction with MI6 special ops came during Operation Valuable and the attempts 'to detach Albania from the Soviet orbit'. But its attentions were soon attracted from 'the Slavs' to anywhere in the world where forces regarded as anti-British were operating. Long before Suez, al-Sharq al-Adna carried IRD-inspired news reports, as did the Arab News Agency, which had offices in all the major Middle East capitals and numbered most of the major Arab newspapers among its subscribers. Africa and southeast Asia were also flooded with IRD propaganda.

One of the most interesting aspects of the IRD's work with journalists was its relationship with the BBC, and in particular with the Overseas Service, whose director, Major-General Ian Jacob, was a member of the Russia Committee. Jacob had been drafted onto the committee after approaching the Foreign Office 'for guidance' on British policy towards Moscow. Thereafter the BBC was 'extremely helpful and co-operative'. Its coverage of the Soviet Bloc was 'tempered' so much that there were worries that if anything it was pushing propaganda too hard. In his twelve years in charge, White succeeded in moving MI6 away from the cowboy behaviour of the Robber Barons, who in the old days had met up every evening in the bar below Broadway Buildings to share a drink and dream up new targets for 'special political action'.

Under a further reorganisation which more sensibly reflected MI6 coverage, four production directorates were formed, with the chief controllers becoming directors: DP1 to cover Western Europe; DP2, the Middle East and Africa; DP3, the Far East and the Americas; DP4, the Soviet Bloc and operations carried out from London Station. But the old problems of Foreign

Office funding remained. 'We were underfunded from the start,' recalled Kenneth Benton. 'The KGB was streets ahead of us in almost every way. They were extremely well trained and well manned and they had absolutely unlimited money. We had none. We had very, very little. The only way we could have got penetration agents right into Russia would have been a long-term process. It would have been putting in sleepers over a long period of years costing money. We never got the money from the Foreign Office. They had a stranglehold over us, not only on our finances, but over the way we went about our work. Every time we produced a scheme that looked promising the Foreign Office wouldn't agree.'

It was the KGB's willingness to spend time and money on long-term penetration that would lead to Britain's biggest spy scandal.

Twelve

The Ring of Five

It is possible to hate treason without making a caricature of a traitor.
Robert Cecil, *The Cambridge Comintern*, 1983

Walter Krivitsky, a Russian defector, arrived in London in early 1940 to tell MI5 what he knew of Soviet espionage against Britain. He brought with him a long list of KGB* agents, including 'a young English journalist' who had covered the Spanish Civil War for a London newspaper. The journalist was Kim Philby but the case was not followed up. The Krivitsky debriefing provided no information that could help in the war against Hitler. It was soon filed and forgotten.

H A R Philby had followed in the footsteps of his father, the noted Arabist Harry St John Bridger Philby, with an education at Westminster and then Trinity College, Cambridge. Shortly before coming down in 1933, he approached Maurice Dobb, one of his tutors and a well-known communist, for advice. He had decided to travel in Europe and wanted to become a member of the party. How should he go about it? Dobb referred him to 'some French comrades who may be able to help you'. The 'comrades' were the members of a KGB front organisation, the World Committee for the Relief of Victims of German Fascism. They told Philby to go to Vienna to help the communist underground. Philby's desire to become a communist was not unusual at Cambridge. During the 1930s the effects of the depression, the overwhelming power of the British class system, and the rise of Hitler and Mussolini led many politically active undergraduates to see communism as the only answer. 'The Wall Street Crash seemed to herald the end of

---

* The Soviet state intelligence and security service underwent a number of name-changes during the period covered by this chapter. For ease of understanding it is referred to throughout as the KGB.

capitalism,' said Robert Cecil, another graduate of Trinity in the 1930s and a contemporary of Philby at MI6. 'In Germany and Italy fascism was in power and by 1936 was threatening to take control also in Spain. The USA remained aloof and in Britain and France the democratic trumpet gave a very uncertain and wavering sound. To this hard core of young intellectuals the schematic and revolutionary message of Marxism seemed to hold all the answers; it was a cause to which they could devote their idealism, a cause that would assuage their despair.'

Within months of Philby arriving in Austria the right-wing Christian Social government had organised a putsch, declaring the Social Democrats who controlled the city government in Vienna illegal. The private armies of the two political parties clashed on the streets of the capital, and more than a thousand people were killed. Philby worked as a courier for the communists and helped those socialists and communists who were on the government's wanted list to flee the country. 'I greatly admired Kim Philby,' wrote one of those helping the refugees. 'Here was a young Englishman, determined to risk much to help the underground freedom movement in a small country which must have been of very limited interest to him. But doubts began to dawn on me when Philby appeared as a communist go-between and when he declared that he could provide all the money we needed for our work. The money Philby offered could only have come from the Russians.'

He had not actually been recruited as a Soviet agent at this time, but his potential had been noted by Teodor Maly, a Soviet intelligence officer based in Vienna. Philby married Litzi Friedmann, his lover and a leading Communist Party activist, to get her out of Austria safely. Maly sent Arnold Deutsch, a fellow KGB officer, to London to oversee the recruitment of Philby, codenamed Söhnchen (Sonnie). It was to be carried out by Edith Tudor-Hart, an Austrian communist married to a British doctor who as a friend of Litzi had the perfect excuse for visiting the Philbys. Maly and Deutsch used Tudor-Hart as a 'cut-out' to protect themselves, standard KGB practice in case the target turned the offer down and went to the authorities. She was brilliantly successful, helping them to recruit the first members of both the Cambridge and Oxford spy rings. 'Through Edith we obtained Söhnchen,' they told Moscow Centre in October 1936. 'In the attached report, you will find details of a second Söhnchen who, in all probability, offers even greater possibilities than the first.' The second agent, codenamed Scott, went on to lead the Oxford Ring. But contrary to the initial KGB assessment, this ring was never to be as important as its Cambridge counterpart.

Deutsch sent Philby back to Cambridge with instructions to recommend a number of his former fellow students who would make good recruits for the KGB. Top of his list was a young man who was about to join the Foreign Office. Donald Maclean was the son of a Liberal Cabinet minister. Tall, dark and athletic, he had won an exhibition at Trinity Hall, where he became part of a left-wing circle at Cambridge, which already included Philby, Guy Burgess and Anthony Blunt. It was Philby who made the initial approach to Maclean, who swiftly accepted the offer to work for Soviet intelligence.

One of the other names on the list, almost as an afterthought, was that of Burgess, an Old Etonian who had won a scholarship in modern history to Trinity College. 'He had the reputation of being the most brilliant undergraduate of his day. Indeed he did not belie his reputation,' wrote Goronwy Rees, a fellow of All Souls, Oxford, who under Burgess's influence had a brief flirtation with communism. 'His conversation had the more charm because he was very good looking in a boyish, athletic, very English way; it seemed incongruous that almost everything he said made it quite clear that he was a homosexual and a communist. Among the multitude of his diverse activities, social and political, he spoke most freely of his success in helping to organise a recent strike of busmen in the town of Cambridge.'

Blunt was the eldest of the four and, by the time Burgess persuaded him to join the Comintern, already a fellow of Trinity. His father was a clergyman who had served as chaplain to the British embassy in Paris, where Blunt acquired a passion for French art. He went to Marlborough before going up to Trinity on a scholarship in mathematics, later switching to modern languages. He was elected a fellow in 1932 on the basis of his work on *The History and Theory of Paintings with Special Reference to Poussin*. It was Blunt who got Burgess elected to the Apostles, an exclusive dining-club centred on King's College but including a number of Trinity scholars. Its values, based in part on the teaching of the philosopher G E Moore, included a belief in freedom of thought and expression and a denial of all moral restraints other than loyalty to one's friends. A significant number of its members were, like both Burgess and Blunt, homosexual. John Cairncross, the Fifth Man, was recruited later and was never closely associated with the other four, who remained unwisely linked through their continued mutual friendship with Burgess.

On arriving back in Britain, Philby had attempted to join the Civil Service, but it soon became clear that his referees felt obliged to suggest that his political loyalties might be questioned. Rather than have that negative assessment placed on the official record, he withdrew his application and settled for a job in journalism with the *Review of Reviews*. Blunt remained at Trinity. But Burgess and Maclean were now also seeking employment, and they and Philby carefully set about creating political personae that would expunge all memory of their 'youthful dalliances' with communism. Burgess and Philby joined the Anglo-German Fellowship, a pro-German organisation with close links to the German Ministry of Propaganda.

This was not just an attempt to create what one former colleague described as their 'unbreakable cover'; it was also a valuable source of intelligence for their Soviet masters. 'No one has so far suggested that I had switched from Communism to Nazism,' Philby later wrote. 'The simpler, and true, explanation is that overt and covert links between Britain and Germany at that time were of serious concern to the Soviet Government.'

Burgess made a trip to the Soviet Union and a number to Germany, which allowed him to announce to those friends – who were baffled by his membership of the Anglo-German Fellowship and his acceptance of the post of personal assistant to the far-right Conservative MP Jack Macnamara – that, having seen both countries for himself, he now realised that his student infatuation with communism had been misguided.

Meanwhile Maclean was telling his mother that he intended to take the Foreign Office entry examination. When she asked whether this might not conflict with his communist beliefs, Maclean replied, 'You must think I turn like a weathercock, but the fact is I've rather gone off all that lately.' He passed the entry exams with flying colours and recalled having had a good final interview, but that he stumbled momentarily at the end. 'I thought they'd finished when one of them suddenly said: "By the way, Mr Maclean. We understand that you, like other young men, held strong Communist views while you were at Cambridge. Do you still hold those views?"' Maclean later told his mother. 'I'm afraid I did a double take: Shall I deny the truth, or shall I brazen it out? I decided to brazen it out. "Yes," I said. "I did have such views – and I haven't entirely shaken them off." I think they must have liked my honesty because they nodded, looked at each other and smiled. Then the chairman said: "Thank you, that will be all, Mr Maclean."' He thus became the first of the Ring of Five to fulfil his mission, entering the Diplomatic Service in October 1935.

Burgess had more difficulty finding employment, but he was eventually accepted by the BBC, where he worked himself into a role as producer on *The Week in Westminster*, which gave him access to a wealth of political gossip. He also developed widespread contacts through the so-called 'Homintern', his network of well-placed homosexual friends, passing on what he could to friends in MI6. This and his BBC experience made him an ideal candidate when the service decided to create a special-operations organisation which, among other things, would set up radio stations broadcasting black propaganda into Germany.

Philby meanwhile had gone to Spain, ostensibly as a freelance journalist but in fact on the instructions of Maly, who in early 1936 had been sent to London to take overall charge of the KGB networks. Maly had been ordered by Moscow Centre to send one of his British agents to Spain under journalistic cover. Once there his task was to help to assassinate General Franco. Philby acquired a letter of accreditation from a London news agency and arrived in Spain in early 1937. Reporting from the areas controlled by Franco's forces, he bombarded *The Times* with unsolicited dispatches until the newspaper agreed to take him on.

He swiftly became one of the best-informed correspondents on Franco's side, with a detailed knowledge of the involvement of German and Italian forces, which he communicated to Moscow through regular meetings with Soviet contacts across the border in France. An incident in which a shell landed on a car in which Philby was travelling, fatally wounding the three other occupants, led to his acceptance by Franco's forces as a hero and the award from the General himself of the Red Cross of Military Merit. But by now the plan to assassinate Franco had been aborted.

On the outbreak of the Second World War *The Times* sent Philby to France. But he was soon back in London with little to occupy his time. He attempted to get into the Government Code and Cypher School at Bletchley Park, but was turned down. Burgess manoeuvred a position for him in MI6 as his assistant. When the newly formed Special Operations Executive swallowed up Section D in June 1940, Burgess was pronounced surplus to requirements. But Philby retained his position, becoming an instructor at SOE's Beaulieu training school. When MI6 was looking for new recruits to beef up the Iberian operations of its counter-espionage unit, Section V, which was based in St Albans, Philby's experience in Spain earned him the job of head of the Iberian subsection, which was designated Vd.

'My new job would require personal contacts with the rest of SIS and MI5,' Philby wrote in an assessment of its usefulness to his Soviet masters. 'There was also a suggestion of Foreign Office interest, not to mention the service departments. By accident, I discovered that the archives of SIS were next door to Section V.' Shortly after his arrival in Section V, Philby persuaded the archivist to allow him to look at the files on the Soviet Union and was able to provide his new controller, Anatoly Gorsky, codenamed Henry, with details of the pre-war MI6 agents there.

Maclean had rapidly become a rising star within the Foreign Office and by 1938 was third secretary in the Paris embassy, where he would have seen most of the correspondence of Sir Eric Phipps, the ambassador and a staunch advocate of appeasement. It has to be assumed that he was passing the ambassador's views on to his Soviet control, Robert Cecil said. 'Such reports can scarcely have failed to influence Stalin during the critical period in the summer of 1939 when he was making up his mind to ditch the democracies and throw in his lot with Hitler, as he finally did in August. After the war broke out, it would have been possible for Maclean to report the existence of Anglo-French military plans to support Finland in her winter war against the USSR, and to attack Soviet oil wells in Baku, in order to reduce the volume of oil flowing into the Nazi war machine.'

After leaving MI6, Burgess had gone back to the BBC, where he had responsibility for liaison with both MI6 and SOE and the organisation of propaganda. His contacts within the political world were invaluable to him in collecting information from indiscreet friends, and ensured that news of the proposed D-Day landings reached Stalin 'well before either of his two allies saw fit to inform him'.

Burgess spent much of the war living with Blunt in the Bentinck Street flat of Lord Rothschild. Blunt had resigned his Cambridge fellowship in 1936 and joined the Warburg Institute to continue his art studies, before applying for a job with the Field Security Police, the fledgling Intelligence Corps, the role of which was to hunt down suspected enemy agents behind Allied lines and interrogate them. He received two replies, one rejecting him, the other accepting him, and ripping up the former he reported for training. Halfway through his course, MI5, which was vetting all applicants for such posts, ordered him to be recalled, because he had visited Russia and had once sent a contribution to a left-wing journal. But military intelligence, with its in-built mistrust of MI5, sent him back again to continue his course.

Following the fall of France, Blunt was taken in by his friend Rothschild, who was himself working for MI5, and despite the previous ruling that he was not to be employed in any sort of intelligence work, he was soon recruited by Guy Liddell, one of its most senior officers. He spent much of the war collecting intelligence by intercepting the diplomatic bags of neutral missions based in London. But he worked hard to ensure that he could provide the KGB with as much intelligence as possible through liaison with MI6, the War Office and GC&CS. 'I have spent a good deal of my time arranging for various kinds of most secret documents to come through me,' Blunt told Moscow Centre in one of his reports. 'I get in the ordinary course of my job the deciphered diplomatic telegrams, the diplomatic telephone conversations, and the product of the various agents in the embassies.' He had access to the deciphered intercepts concerning the Double Cross system 'although in fact it has nothing to do with my work'. He was also briefed on a number of other MI5 operations 'on the grounds that I have to watch for leakages in the diplomatic channels, which I watch'. But perhaps his most spectacular coup was to persuade the Soviet counter-espionage section based at Blenheim Palace to use him for liaison with London.

Shortly before the evacuation of Paris, Maclean had met and married Melinda Marling, the eldest daughter of a Chicago businessman. They returned to London together, where he was promoted to second secretary and posted to the General Department, which liaised with the Ministries of Shipping and Economic Warfare – the latter being in charge of the SOE. How much high-grade information he was able to pass to his Soviet control is not clear. But Moscow Centre apparently regarded him as a valued agent since when he was transferred to the Washington embassy in April 1944 his London case officer was sent to the US capital to handle him.

John Cairncross had joined the Foreign Office in 1936, topping the entrance examination. At the outbreak of the war, following a spell in the Treasury, during which he passed on documents on the organisational structures of MI5 and GC&CS plus details of the construction of a chain of radio intercept sites around Britain, he was made private secretary to Lord Hankey. It was here that the Cambridge spy ring had its most spectacular success. Cairncross not only passed on all the details of Hankey's 1941 investigation into the intelligence services, he also produced a series of documents on Tube Alloys, the Anglo-American project to create the atomic bomb known to the Americans as the Manhattan Project. Cairncross denied ever being an atom spy, but according to Pavel Fitin, the KGB's then head of intelligence, this was the first information the Russians had on the atomic bomb and 'formed the basis' for the construction of their own atomic weapons programme. One particular memo from Fitin on the origins of *Enormoz*, the Soviet operation to uncover the Allies' atomic secrets, not only demolishes Cairncross's claim that he never betrayed atomic secrets but also makes it clear that the information he provided gave a significant boost to Moscow's own atomic weapons programme. 'Extremely valuable information on the scientific developments of *Enormoz* reaches us from the London *Rezidentura*,' Fitin wrote. 'The first material on *Enormoz* was received at the end of 1941 from John Cairncross. This material contained valuable and highly secret documentation, both on the essence of the *Enormoz* problem and on the measures taken by the British government to organise and develop the work on atomic energy. This material formed the point of departure for building the basis of, and organising the work on, the problem of atomic energy in our country.'

Cairncross was later transferred to Bletchley Park, where he passed the decrypt 'flimsies' directly to his Soviet control. It is possible to accept his argument that when he handed over details of the German Tiger tank and the complete plans for the Wehrmacht's 1943 offensive Operation Citadel he was helping the war effort in a way the British authorities seemed reluctant to do. In fact the information was being passed to Moscow in a disguised form but Stalin was suspicious of official British reports. The intelligence provided by Cairncross was invaluable in the Soviet victory at the Battle of Kursk, the turning point on the eastern front. But the Red Army and the KGB had been widely infiltrated by German agents during the period before June 1941 when Berlin and Moscow were working in tandem, and he could easily have compromised the whole of the Ultra operation.

Philby's new job in Section V of MI6 was mainly concerned with following the trail of *Abwehr* agents arriving in Spain and Portugal as a prelude to infiltrating Britain. As such he was a key recipient of the *Abwehr*'s radio traffic deciphered by GC&CS. One of the items that passed his desk was a decrypt revealing that Admiral Canaris, the head of the *Abwehr*, was planning to go to Spain. Philby, unaware of the links with Madame Szymanska, sketched out a plan to assassinate him, which to his chagrin was swiftly vetoed by Menzies. Philby also volunteered for regular stints as duty officer in Broadway Buildings, which gave him access to much more information. 'It was an instructive occupation,' he wrote. 'In the course of a single night, telegrams would come in from all parts of the world, throwing new light on the operations of the service. One file available to night-duty officers in Broadway was especially valuable to me. It contained telegrams from the War Office to the British Military Mission in Moscow, sent over SIS channels.'

Philby provided the KGB with complete breakdowns of MI6, SOE and what he knew of MI5 and GC&CS. But when he told Gorsky that British intelligence was not operating any agents in Moscow, having been ordered to stop all operations against the Soviet Union following the German invasion, Moscow Centre apparently found it impossible to believe. For two years, Philby was suspected by the KGB of being an MI6 plant. 'He is lying to us in a most insolent manner,' one report concluded. When Blunt confirmed what Philby said, that only led Moscow Centre to conclude that he too must be a plant. The other three seem to have been similarly damned.

But in 1944, following a reshuffle in Moscow Centre, they were all rehabilitated. It was to be a good year for the Cambridge Five. Maclean was posted as a First Secretary to Washington, where he had access to a wealth of information on Anglo-American relations and their secret post-war agreements, including the exchanges of intelligence and atomic secrets. Philby took charge of Section IX, the MI6 department handling the Soviet Union. Blunt began attending JIC meetings, which increasingly discussed ways of countering the future Soviet threat. Burgess succeeded in getting a job with the Foreign Office News Department where he had access to a wealth of material, taking dozens of secret files home for Gorsky to copy. Cairncross was transferred to Section V of MI6 and was supplying a great deal of useful material.

In early 1945, Philby presented Robert Cecil, then personal assistant to C, with his proposals for the organisational structure of Section IX. 'It included a substantial number of overseas stations to be held by officers under diplomatic cover, who would be directly responsible to the Head of IX,' Cecil wrote. 'With hindsight, it is easy to see why Philby pitched his demands so high and why he aimed to create his own empire within SIS. Quite apart from his covert aims, it is also clear that he foresaw more plainly than I the onset of the Cold War, bringing with it more menacing surveillance and making necessary more permanent use of diplomatic. My vision of the future was more opaque and optimistic; I sent the memorandum back to Philby, suggesting that he might scale down his demands. Within hours, Vivian and Philby had descended upon me, upholding their requirements and insisting that these be transmitted to the FO. I gave way. But I have since reflected with a certain wry amusement on the hypocrisy of Philby who, supposedly working in the cause of "peace" (as Soviet propaganda always insists), demanded a larger Cold War apparatus, when he could have settled for a smaller one.'

Philby's new job as head of the Soviet section of British foreign intelligence boosted his reputation to 'almost God-like proportions', according to Yuri Modin, who was working on the British desk at Moscow Centre. But in the late summer of 1945 two defectors claimed that the Soviet Union had infiltrated British intelligence. Igor Gouzenko, a cipher clerk at the Soviet embassy in Ottawa, exposed the British atom spy Alan Nunn May, a contemporary of Maclean's at Trinity Hall, and provided evidence of a Russian mole in British intelligence. While nothing Gouzenko said pointed directly to Philby, the other defector was far more dangerous. Konstantin Volkov, a KGB officer working under consular cover in Turkey, contacted the British embassy, saying he wanted to defect. Volkov, who had served on the Moscow Centre British desk, sought asylum and a large sum of money in return for a wide variety of intelligence. This included information on a number of unnamed Soviet agents in Britain: two inside the Foreign Office (Burgess and Maclean) and seven who had served in wartime intelligence, one of whom was 'fulfilling the function of head of a section of British counter-espionage in London'. For security reasons, Volkov insisted that the offer be relayed to London in a hand-written communication addressed to a high-ranking official, but this could not prevent it landing on Philby's desk. 'Two Soviet agents in the Foreign Office, one head of a counter-espionage organisation in London!' Philby wrote. 'I stared at the papers rather longer than necessary to compose my thoughts. The only course was to put a brave face on it.' Volkov had put a three-week time limit on his offer. Eight days had already elapsed. Philby needed to play for time. He also needed to warn Moscow. 'That evening I worked late,' he wrote. 'The situation seemed to call for urgent action of an extra-curricular nature.'

Philby suggested to Menzies that an experienced officer be dispatched to Istanbul to deal with Volkov direct, hoping that he himself would be sent. He was disappointed when Menzies suggested that Brigadier Douglas Roberts, head of Security Intelligence (Middle East), be sent instead. But, since Roberts was scared of flying and would travel only by land or sea, this added a useful delay. Menzies then agreed that Philby should go himself, but the flight was delayed by weather and when he finally arrived in Istanbul the deadline was nearly up. All attempts to contact Volkov failed. 'The exact details of what happened to the wretched Volkov in Moscow are unknown to me,' said Modin. 'Suffice it to say that he was summarily tried and shot. The official line was that he had fallen ill in Turkey. I imagine he was simply given an injection to put him to sleep and then sent home on grounds of ill-health. It was the usual practice.'

In his role in overall charge of operations against the Soviet Union, Philby was able to provide the KGB with details of the agents the British were sending into the Baltic republics. 'We knew in advance about every operation that took place by air, land or sea, even in mountainous and inaccessible regions,' Modin said. 'We knew who was coming, and when, and we neutralised these spies and saboteurs; most were arrested and imprisoned. The KGB let some of the agents go free temporarily, to avoid jeopardising Philby, while others were turned and became our double agents.' Philby was himself posted to Istanbul, as head of the MI6 station, in early 1947. His main job was recruiting agents to send into the southern Soviet Union. It was a difficult task, Robert Cecil would later recall – not least because Stalin had ordered large numbers of the ethnic minorities who might be persuaded to side against Moscow to be deported to central Asia. 'Some Armenians were found, however, who would be induced to venture into the Soviet part of their homeland, and these were pitilessly sacrificed to the vengeance of the KGB.'

Maclean's Washington posting appeared to be going well, both for his Foreign Office career and for the KGB. The amount of information he was able to supply was phenomenal. He was appointed as one of the joint secretaries of the Anglo-American Combined Policy Committee, which was responsible for liaison on atomic matters. Despite the restrictions imposed by the McMahon Act, which prevented British involvement in the production of nuclear weapons, Maclean was able to tell Moscow how much uranium the Americans were acquiring, allowing the Russians to make a remarkably accurate assessment of the US nuclear arsenal. He was also able to provide his control with details of the British-led plans for a West German state, comprising the French, American and British zones; the blueprint for the new North Atlantic alliance; and vital information on the allied reaction to the Soviet blockade of Berlin. Secure in the knowledge that, despite the American sabre-rattling, Truman had decided not to resort to force unless the Russians fired first, Stalin held the whip hand throughout the 1948 Berlin crisis.

Melinda Maclean was living with her mother in New York, so 'Homer', as the KGB had now code-named her husband, had the perfect excuse to leave Washington each weekend, meeting Gorsky to pass on the week's take away from the routine surveillance of Soviet diplomats in the federal capital. The information he produced also included the content of top secret exchanges, in March 1945, between Churchill and Truman over the fate of the leaders of the

Polish Home Army who, while *en route* to London, had been 'diverted' to Moscow and incarcerated in the Lubyanka. Although this was by no means the most important information he was reporting to Moscow, it would ultimately prove to be among the most significant.

Burgess, now codenamed 'Hicks', was also becoming extremely useful to Moscow. In 1946, he managed to get himself a job as private secretary to Hector McNeil, Foreign Office Minister under Ernest Bevin, the British Foreign Secretary and a key figure in the negotiations over the future of Europe and the creation of NATO. He provided the KGB with briefcases full of Top Secret Foreign Office documents detailing Britain's positions, and disagreements with its American ally, on the partition of post-war Germany, ways of countering the Soviet domination of eastern Europe and the formation of NATO. At one point, he was taking so many documents out of the Foreign Office, in a damning indictment of security procedures, that he suggested the London *Rezidentura* provide him with a suitcase in which to carry them. His KGB handler reported that Hicks's carelessness had led to 'a fairly unpleasant incident'. Normally, they met in the street but on their last meeting, it had been raining and they had gone into a pub. 'As I left the pub, I noticed that H was not coming out. I opened the door and saw him gathering up documents on the floor. II said that as he went up to the door some documents had fallen out of the package of Foreign Office telegrams. He added that the telegrams had fallen blank side up and nobody had noticed because the door was screened off from the pub by a curtain. Only one telegram was soiled and that only slightly. I warned H to be careful and when in possession of documents to hold them so that this kind of thing could not happen again. However, on the morning of 5 March, I was returning the documents to him in an underground station lavatory. I had tied the package up carefully so that it could not come apart. As I moved towards the door, the package again fell to the floor. Fortunately, there was no-one in the lavatory and the lavatory was clean.'

Blunt had left MI5 at the end of the war to become Surveyor of the King's Pictures, but he continued to have some contact with MI5. He also acted as a go-between for Burgess and later for Philby and Maclean. Cairncross left MI6 in June 1945, returning to the Treasury, but not before giving the Russians details of British agents in Finland, Sweden, Denmark, Spain, Portugal and South America, and plans to monitor Russian radio relay traffic. For three years, he was inactive as a spy. But in mid-1948 he was re-activated by Yuri Modin, who was now based in London, after Burgess reported that Cairncross was working in a Treasury department that dealt with top secret defence estimates and details of Britain's contribution to the fledgling NATO. Now codenamed Karel, Cairncross handed over 'a large quantity of important documents' regarding Britain's defences, his handler said. 'Documents of the highest secrecy pass through his hands.' Cairncross later claimed that very few of the documents he handled during this period were secret and that 'even when one occasionally passed through my hands, I felt no obligation to transmit it to the KGB'. But one of his former Treasury colleagues recalled that Cairncross's role in the Defence Materiel division of the Treasury included overseeing funding for research on atomic, chemical and biological weapons; guided missiles; and radar and submarine detection systems as well as signals intelligence and eavesdropping techniques. 'He therefore had access to some of the most sensitive of all British defence secrets,' the former colleague said. 'He knew what expenditure was planned before it happened and could legitimately ask for as much detail about plans as thought necessary for the Treasury to give its approval.'

Cairncross also appears to have used a meeting with a former colleague at Bletchley Park in an attempt to gather intelligence. 'He invited me to lunch at the Travellers Club in February 1949, when he was back at the Treasury,' Henry Dryden said. 'In the middle of the meal, he disconcertingly asked: "Are we still reading Russian ciphers?" I had no first-hand knowledge of any current work on Russian and the only off-putting response I could think of, on the spur of the moment, was to shake my head and mutter "one-time" [a reference to the theoretically unbreakable one-time pad cipher system]. He did not pursue this.'

But, despite the success of the network, things were about to unravel. In late 1949, Philby was sent to Washington as MI6 liaison officer. Before his departure he was briefed in London on a major American-led counter-espionage operation. A mistake four years earlier by Soviet cipher clerks operating Moscow Centre's communications links with its officers in the field had led to a break into their one-time pad system. In January 1949, American cryptanalysts working on what had become known as the Venona material had succeeded in deciphering a message which showed that in mid-1945 Soviet intelligence had an agent in Washington code named Homer who had access to the secret messages between Truman and Churchill on the fate of the leaders of the Polish Home Army.

Philby's later delight in ridiculing the Western intelligence agencies had a great deal to do with KGB propaganda. But since Harold Macmillan, the British Foreign Secretary, would tell a House of Commons debate on the affair that 'there were 6000 people each of whom might have been the man', Philby's description of the FBI investigation into Homer at the time of his arrival in Washington appears to have been not far off the truth. 'Characteristically, they had put in an immense amount of work, resulting in an immense amount of waste paper,' he said. 'It had so far occurred neither to them nor the British that a diplomat was involved, let alone a fairly senior diplomat. Instead, the investigation had concentrated on non-diplomatic employees of the embassy, and particularly on those locally recruited, the sweepers, cleaners, bottle-washers and the rest. A charlady with a Latvian grandmother, for instance, would rate a 15-page report, crowded with insignificant detail of herself, her family and friends. It was testimony to the enormous resources of the FBI, and to the pitiful extent to which those resources were squandered.'

The Homer investigation led both Maclean and Burgess to lose their nerve. Maclean, who was in the middle of a tour as Head of Chancery in Cairo when Philby learned of Venona, descended into an orgy of drunkenness and homosexuality. This culminated in a rampage through the flat of a secretary at the American Embassy in May 1950 that led to his being recalled to London. The Foreign Office blamed overwork and gave him time off before promoting him to be head of the American Department in the Foreign Office, a post that Harold Macmillan later attempted to play down. 'This department in the Foreign Office principally deals with Latin American affairs,' the then Foreign Secretary told the House of Commons after Maclean's defection. 'The United States questions which are dealt with by the American Department are largely routine.'

In fact the post was an extremely important one, and, in view of the tensions between America and Britain over the Korean War, almost certainly a highly profitable one for Moscow. 'Donald would have had access to almost any kind of information he wanted to see,' said Robert Cecil, Maclean's deputy in the American Department. Among documents known to have crossed Maclean's desk was a detailed briefing-paper on a visit to Washington by Clement Attlee, the British Prime Minister, in order to dissuade the Americans from extending the war into China. 'Assuming that he succeeded even in getting a condensed version to the Russians, and assuming they believed it, it would have been of inestimable value in advising the Chinese and North Koreans on strategy and negotiating positions.'

Perhaps predictably, Burgess was more of a problem for the KGB. McNeil, apparently embarrassed by Burgess's 'insanitary habits', had sought to 'promote' him to a post in the newly formed Information Research Department. Christopher Mayhew, its head, very quickly decided that he was not suitable, although not before a Soviet Bloc newspaper had carried a remarkably accurate article on the secret organisation. Burgess was moved in November 1948 to the Far East department, where, despite a relatively junior position, he provided a large number of key documents at what was a crucial time for Britain in the Far East. India and Pakistan had just gained independence. Burma was about to follow suit. China was in the midst of a civil war between the nationalists and Mao Tse-Tung's communists and the confrontation between the communist-controlled north of Korea and the US-occupied southern zone was about to deteriorate into war. There was concern within the KGB that his position might be too junior to obtain anything of value, but Burgess assured his handlers there was no need to worry. 'It has proved possible to establish excellent personal relations with them, owing not only to my abilities but also to the lucky chance that almost all of them, like myself, have been to Eton. Things of this kind have great importance.'

But by now he was declining into alcoholism, and in autumn 1949 a visit to Gibraltar and Tangiers saw him loudly pointing out British and American intelligence officers in public. Burgess survived only because 'my friends proved to be stronger than my enemies' and was given a last-chance posting to Washington. Two days before leaving for America, on 30 June 1950, Burgess handed over an explosive briefing paper for secret talks between the British and US chiefs of staff on the situation, highlighting the differences between London and Washington. As a result of the setback suffered by US forces in South Korea, the British were about to send in troops, he told his controller. 'Today the decision was taken to send one British armoured tank brigade to Korea. The decision was reached under political and military pressure from the USA. This will have been announced by the time you receive this note, or altered because of further US defeats.' In fact, it was not until four weeks later that Britain announced the decision.

To the dismay of Philby's second wife, Aileen, Burgess lodged with the MI6 officer during his stay in Washington. His role as a second secretary handling the Far East gave him a continued insight into the transatlantic tensions over the Korean War. But he soon fell out with his boss and was moved to deal with Middle Eastern affairs. Then in April 1951, US cryptanalysts working on the Venona material found the vital clue to Homer's identity. For part of 1944 he had regular contacts with his Soviet control in New York, using the fact that his wife was pregnant and staying there as an excuse. The 6,000 names had been narrowed down to one – Donald Maclean.

Philby had no way of warning him. But by chance Burgess had been suspended and ordered home after a series of complaints about his behaviour culminating in his being booked for speeding on three separate occasions in one day. The two decided that when Burgess got to London he should warn Maclean that he must flee to Moscow. If he were interrogated, there was no doubt that the whole network would be exposed. Burgess crossed the Atlantic on the *Queen Mary* with Philby's warning 'Don't you go too' ringing in his ears. He went straight to Blunt, who passed the news on to the KGB. Burgess had dinner with Maclean at the Reform Club and told him that he had no choice but to defect. Maclean was reluctant. But the Centre ordered him to go to Moscow, and, to make sure he did, Burgess was persuaded to go with him.

The MI5 report on the Homer affair was due to be sent to London by Wednesday 23 May, which meant that Maclean's interrogation could be expected to begin the following Monday. Blunt suggested using one of the ships making mini-cruises across the English Channel. They sailed on Fridays, put in at several French ports, and returned on Sunday night or Monday morning. Passenger papers were not checked on the cruises. Maclean could disembark at the first French port and fail to return to the boat, and no one would be any the wiser until the ship returned to England. On Friday 25 May, the two men drove from Maclean's house at Tatsfield, in Kent, then to Southampton and boarded a ship bound for Saint Malo. Once on mainland Europe they were given false documents by Soviet intelligence officers and made their way to Moscow.

The realisation that Burgess was also a Soviet spy came as a shock to British intelligence and, combined with the fact that their defection came just as Maclean was about to be interrogated, threw immediate suspicion on Philby. MI5 was convinced that Philby was the so-called 'Third Man' who was assumed to have tipped Maclean off. He was recalled to London and questioned by Dick White, then head of MI5. Menzies then summoned him to Broadway and told him that the Americans had insisted that he could not return to Washington. The service had no choice but to ask for his resignation – much to the disappointment of some of his fellow officers. A further interrogation by MI5 followed six months later, but with no evidence forthcoming the matter was dropped.

Then in April 1954, Vladimir Petrov, the KGB *Rezident* in Australia, defected, and confirmed that Burgess and Maclean were Soviet spies. The resultant publicity forced the government to issue a White Paper on the affair, and during a subsequent House of Commons debate Sir Marcus Lipton, the MP for Brixton, named Philby as 'the Third Man'. Macmillan was forced into a position where he appeared to exonerate Philby. 'I have no reason to conclude that Mr Philby has at any time betrayed the interests of this country, or to identify him with the so-called "Third Man", if indeed there was one,' he told parliament. Lipton's intervention had backfired, and Nicholas Elliott, a sympathetic former MI6 colleague, was now able to get Philby a post as Beirut correspondent for the *Observer* and *The Economist*. The KGB defector Anatoly Golitsyn confirmed early in 1962 that there was a 'Ring of Five'. But it was not until later that year – when Flora Solomon, who had known Philby since university, told MI5 of his attempts to recruit her – that the evidence against Philby became incontrovertible. Elliott was sent to Beirut in January 1963 to try to get a confession out of him in return for a guarantee of immunity. His remarks summed up the sense of betrayal felt by those MI6 officers who had stood by Philby. 'You took me in for years,' he told him. 'Now I'll get the truth out of you even if I have to drag it out. I once looked up to you. My God how I despise you now.' But Elliott failed to get a confession, and, five days after he left Beirut, Philby boarded a Soviet tramp steamer and sailed for the USSR.

Burgess and Maclean were kept out of view by the Soviet authorities until a 1956 press conference. Burgess fared badly. Although he did acquire a Russian boyfriend, he missed London, never learned Russian, and did not become a Soviet citizen. He drank to excess and was reportedly deeply upset that Philby did not seek him out once he had defected. Six months after Philby arrived in Moscow, Burgess died of heart and liver problems. He is buried in the church-yard at West Meon, Hampshire.

Maclean also drank heavily at first. But in 1953 his wife and children joined him and he built a new life for himself, teaching graduate courses at Moscow's prestigious Institute of World Economics and International Relations and publishing a highly praised study of British foreign policy. His wife and children had left him by 1979, and he died in Moscow in March 1983. His ashes were brought back to England and buried in the family plot in Penn, Buckinghamshire.

Blunt's treachery apparently went unconfirmed until 1963, when Michael Straight, an American whom he had attempted to recruit at Trinity, recounted the incident to the FBI. Blunt, who following the defections of Burgess and Maclean had been used by the Russians only once, as an intermediary to Philby, then made a full confession in return for immunity from prosecution. It was not until 1979 and the publication of a book pointing to him as the Fourth Man that his espionage activities became public. On 15 November 1979, Margaret Thatcher, the then Prime Minister, told the House of Commons that he had been an agent for Soviet intelligence. His knighthood was subsequently annulled, as was his honorary fellowship of Trinity College. He died in 1983.

After the disappearance of Burgess and Maclean, MI5 searched Burgess's flat and, among a collection of classified documents, found one with an accompanying note written in Cairncross's handwriting. He was followed to a meeting with Modin, but the Russian spotted the MI5 watchers and aborted the meeting. 'As soon as I got back to the embassy, I dispatched a report to Moscow, expressing my personal view that the British Secret Service would continue to hound Cairncross in the foreseeable future,' Modin later wrote. 'The answer came back promptly. I was to cease working with him altogether.'

Cairncross was interrogated by MI5, but maintained that, although he had communist sympathies, his relationship with Burgess was entirely innocent and he had no connection with espionage. He admitted innocently passing a secret document to Burgess and, damned as a security risk, resigned from the Civil Service. But in the absence of any convincing evidence against him a prosecution was impossible. He left Britain, initially working for the UN in Italy and later becoming an academic, working at Western Reserve University, Cleveland, Ohio. In 1964, in the wake of the Philby defection, MI5 reopened its mole-hunt and Cairncross was again questioned. This time he made a partial confession and co-operated with the FBI, identifying eight KGB officers and even agreeing to get back in contact with the KGB as a potential double-agent.** But to the FBI's intense irritation, the Immigration and Naturalisation Service insisted that he be expelled from the USA because he had been a communist. His identity as the Fifth Man was only publicly confirmed in 1990, by the Soviet defector Oleg Gordievsky. By this time Cairncross was living in the south of France. He wrote his memoirs and moved back to Britain in 1995, shortly before his death.

None of the five had a more successful 'retirement' than Philby. Apart from a brief period in the late 1960s and early 1970s when the KGB appears to have ignored him, the legend of 'Kim Philby Super-Spy', was used to extol the allegedly superior skills of the KGB at the expense of the reputations of the Western intelligence services, and in particular MI5 and MI6. Philby portrayed himself as a retired KGB general, conducting lone inquiries for his former colleagues into operations that had gone wrong – much in the manner of John le Carré's George Smiley. In reality, by the 1980s his knowledge would have been of only limited use to Moscow Centre and he was never a KGB officer. The legend was simply Philby plying his old trade of black propaganda – this time on behalf of the KGB, which had realised that the high level of public interest in his activities could be harnessed as a continuing, nagging embarrassment to the West.

** Cairncross's decision to work with the Americans is almost certainly why the Russian intelligence service took the unusual step of releasing the KGB files detailing the extent of his treachery.

It is not clear which of the five actually was the super-spy. For all his undoubted value during the war, it was certainly not Blunt. At the end of the Second World War his intelligence-gathering days came to an end, although he continued to play a useful role. He acted as an intermediary for Burgess, Maclean and Philby and his continued contacts with MI5 allowed him to tip the Russians off when Elliot was sent to Beirut to obtain Philby's confession. Cairncross certainly has a claim. As the man who gave the Russians the atomic bomb, his place as one of the KGB's leading agents is secure. He always claimed that he never betrayed atomic secrets, that he did nothing to damage British interests and that once the war ended, he was not in a position to help the Russians. But files released by the Russian intelligence service show all three claims to be lies. The information supplied by both Maclean and Burgess in the immediate post-war years, on Anglo-American relations, the plans for Germany and NATO, and the Korean War, would have been of inestimable value to the Russians. This information was based on irrefutable evidence: high-level classified documents. Maclean also provided vital information on the atomic weapons programme.

Assuming that his product was both trusted and used by Moscow in the formulation of policy – and all the evidence suggests that it was – he must rival Cairncross as the most valuable intelligence-gatherer. Nevertheless, Philby – a Soviet agent who rose to a senior post within MI6, at one point even heading the department tasked with countering Soviet espionage abroad – inevitably attracts the most attention. His main service to Moscow as an intelligence-gatherer was in betraying the countless allied agents sent to certain death behind the Iron Curtain in the early years of the Cold War. Yet it is arguable that in the end the intelligence produced by the Ring of Five was not as useful to Moscow as the damage done to Western intelligence by the loss of trust between the British and the Americans. On the evidence of the intelligence they produced, Cairncross and Maclean appear to have been the real KGB super-spies. But it was Philby in his role as the elusive Third Man and then as the alleged KGB super-spy mocking the allegedly 'inept' Western intelligence services from Moscow who ensured the wounds caused by the Cambridge Spy Ring remained open. It was surely Philby who did the most damage, dominating people's perceptions of British intelligence until long after his death, his ghost exorcised only by the arrest in 1994 of Aldrich Ames, a Soviet agent within the CIA who arguably passed on more intelligence to the Russians than the whole of the Ring of Five.

Thirteen

Payback

Defectors probably play the largest role on the counter-espionage stage. One works hard to procure, persuade, charm and bribe key individuals to defect. Sometimes that hard work succeeds.

John Bruce-Lockhart, former Deputy Chief of SIS, 1987

The existence of yet another KGB mole within MI6 was discovered from information disclosed by Michail Goleniewski, a Polish intelligence officer who defected in 1960 and whose revelations to the CIA also led to the exposure of the Portland spy ring. Goleniewski identified fourteen MI6 files obtained by the KGB. The only common name on the various distribution lists was that of George Blake.

Born in Rotterdam, Blake had inherited British citizenship from his father, who had served with the British Army during the First World War. He made his way to Britain during the Second World War and enlisted in the Royal Navy. He was subsequently seconded to MI6, and in 1947 he was taken on the permanent staff and sent to Cambridge to study Russian. Posted to South Korea, he was captured during the 1950 Communist invasion, and it was during his three years' captivity that he was 'turned' to become a Soviet agent. In the light of Goleniewski's evidence, he was interrogated and eventually confessed. The damage to the service was horrendous. Blake, now stationed in Berlin, had not only worked on both the Vienna and Berlin tunnels, he had access to the file index housing the names of all MI6 contacts in Germany and he had almost certainly been responsible for the deaths of forty agents. On 3 May 1961, at the Old Bailey, he was jailed for forty-two years – the longest sentence ever imposed by a British court.

If the damage caused to internal morale was enormous, the means of repairing it was already in place. Oleg Penkovsky was an ambitious officer in the GRU, Russian military intelligence, who had cultivated influential friends and married a general's daughter to ease his way through the system. But when his career began to hit problems he became disgruntled and began making approaches to the CIA, offering himself as an agent-in-place. All his approaches were rebuffed, vetoed by James Angleton, the agency's head of counter-intelligence, who reasoned that a career officer with a good record and an apparently bright future was an unlikely traitor. Penkovsky was clearly a plant, designed to draw the agency into an elaborate GRU provocation. By November 1960, Penkovsky had become convinced that drastic measures were needed to convince the West that he was genuine. During a routine reception at the Canadian embassy in Moscow, he handed a bundle of top-secret documents to an astonished diplomat. The Canadians passed them on to the MI6 head of station, who decided they were too technical to be evaluated in Moscow: they would have to be sent back to MI6 headquarters in London, Century House. The reaction within R4, the requirements section dealing with military matters, was incredulous. The documents were not just genuine, they were pure gold. Dick White decided that, whatever else Penkovsky was, he was not a plant. The Russians would not have risked handing over such valuable material simply for a provocation.

The CIA was inevitably brought into the operation. Many of the agency's old hands remained highly sceptical. But a combination of John Maury, the CIA's Chief of Soviet Operations, and Maurice Oldfield, head of MI6 liaison in Washington, ensured that wiser counsels held sway. Penkovsky's own knowledge was of minimal use, but he was an incorrigible collector of top-secret documents who seemed to have no fear of being caught. During the eighteen months he was run by MI6, Source Ironbark, as he was known, handed over 110 cassette films, including photographs of thousands of documents taken with a Minox mini-camera supplied by Century House. Among his many revelations was the fact that Soviet military strategy was based on the principle of a massive first strike using tactical surface-to-surface missiles and making extensive use of chemical weapons – a revelation that led to a drastic revamp of NATO war plans.

The key intelligence he provided related to the 1962 Cuban Missile Crisis. One of the Penkovsky documents was a manual entitled *Methods of*

Protecting and Defending Strategic Rocket Sites. Analysis of the information it contained allowed the CIA's photographic interpreters to identify the various 'footprints' of Soviet missile launch sites. It was the comparison of a U-2 photograph of a missile site under construction at San Cristobal, 100 miles west of the Cuban capital of Havana, which confirmed that the Soviet Union was planning to place medium-range ballistic missiles there. This was a direct threat to the United States and broke Khrushchev's pledge to Kennedy that Soviet military aid for Castro would be purely defensive. It was this information that sparked the crisis, leading to a US blockade aimed at preventing the missiles arriving and a stand-off between Kennedy and Khrushchev that arguably brought the world closer to a nuclear holocaust than at any other time. But the most important intelligence Penkovsky had to offer was what ensured that the crisis came to a peaceful end. The hawks in Washington had long argued that there was a missile gap to the Soviet Union's advantage. Their advice to Kennedy as he sought to prevent the Soviet missiles arriving in Cuba was that, if Khrushchev refused to back down, America would have no choice but to launch a pre-emptive nuclear strike. Penkovsky revealed beyond a shadow of a doubt that, while a missile gap existed, it was massively to America's advantage.

On 22 October 1962, with the Cuban Missile Crisis at its height, Penkovsky was arrested. He confessed almost immediately. From then on Khrushchev knew that Kennedy was aware that all the talk of Soviet missiles and their capabilities was just a bluff. A week later the Soviet ships turned around and the world was hauled back from oblivion. Greville Wynne, the British businessman and MI6 courier who had been Penkovsky's go-between, was arrested in Hungary a few weeks later. He and Penkovsky were put on trial. Wynne was sentenced to eight years' imprisonment but was exchanged a year later for Gordon Lonsdale, the Soviet intelligence officer who ran the Portland spy ring. Penkovsky was sentenced to death, and was shot shortly afterwards. Gervase Cowell, the MI6 officer in Moscow who was running Penkovsky, later recalled receiving a telephone call from Penkovsky who gave the pre-arranged code that indicated that the Soviet Union was about to launch an attack on the West. The warning was described by Cowell as 'three blows of breath, repeated in another call one minute later'. But Cowell rightly suspected that

Penkovsky and his codes had been blown and in a remarkable display of stoicism decided not to press the panic button.

At the end of the crisis, White called his staff together in the cinema at Century House. 'I have been asked by the CIA to let you know of the absolutely crucial value of the Penkovsky intelligence we have been passing to them,' he said. 'I am given to understand that this intelligence was largely instrumental in deciding that the United States should not make a pre-emptive nuclear strike against the Soviet Union, as a substantial body of important opinion in the States has been in favour of doing. In making known this appreciation of our contribution, I would stress to all of you that, if proof were needed, this operation has demonstrated beyond all doubt the prime importance of the human intelligence source, handled with professional skill and expertise.'

As British possessions across Africa gained their independence, MI6 took over from MI5, which under the Attlee demarcation directive had responsibility for the colonies. White got rid of the last of the Robber Barons in a 1966 reorganisation that created a new post of Controller (Africa), the other controllers taking charge of the Soviet Bloc, the Middle East, the Western Hemisphere and the Far East. The main reason for the new Africa 'controllerate' was to ward off attempts by France and Russia – or its surrogate, East Germany – to supplant British influence across the continent. Despite the tacit and often open British support for South Africa and Rhodesia, many close relationships were formed with the intelligence services of the newly independent states.

By the late 1960s, with White retiring to be replaced by John Rennie, a career diplomat, and with the likelihood of British military intervention around the world diminishing, MI6 acted increasingly as an arm of the Foreign Office. Notwithstanding a poor performance in Rhodesia, where MI6 failed either to warn of Ian Smith's Unilateral Declaration of Independence or to point out the ease with which sanctions would be broken, good work had been done across Africa throughout the 1960s, cementing Britain's relationships with the new governments. This was particularly so during the Nigerian Civil War – when France backed the wrong side but Britain did not – and in the Belgian Congo, where Daphne Park carried out some 'robust' MI6 operations in tandem with the CIA and Mossad to thwart Moscow's attempts to supplant Western interests. 'Quite frankly, I must have been arrested and condemned to be shot several times,' Baroness Park said of her experiences with MI6. 'It was a hazard that I got used to.'

Rennie's appointment had not been popular within MI6, where it was generally assumed that Maurice Oldfield, White's highly able deputy, would get the job. It was seen as the result of a misapprehension within Whitehall that 'putting an outside man in charge of the Secret Services will bring them under better control and curb the "wild men",' George Kennedy Young said. 'In fact, the opposite happens. The outsider knows neither the qualities of the individuals in the Service nor how in their daily routine work the events arise which determine their decisions. There was general relief when Maurice Oldfield took over as C in 1973.' But as one of the 'wild men' who were the target of the Rennie appointment, Young had an interest in making such a claim. Rennie had a difficult time. For three months, Oldfield ensured that any important operations by-passed him completely. But he eventually won the respect of many if not all of his officers and oversaw a number of key operations, not least the creation of the 'backchannel' to the Provisional IRA that was to lead to the Northern Ireland peace process.

By the time he was succeeded by Oldfield, the reputation of MI6 had improved considerably. Widely seen as the inspiration for John le Carré's George Smiley, Oldfield – known within the service as 'Moulders' – had made his reputation in south-east Asia in the 1950s at the height of Britain's problems with its Far East colonies. He was subsequently posted to Washington, where he succeeded in re-establishing the service's good name with the Americans, despite Philby's flight to Moscow. 'He and Young were the service's two great brains,' one former MI6 officer said. 'With them you always felt you had to be on your toes, whereas with other people you felt quite relaxed. I think George Smiley is as good a caricature of Oldfield as you could get. He was very bookish, devoted to work, had a flat very near to the office and, one always imagined, took work home with him every night.'

It was also under Oldfield that the service acquired a second senior agent inside Soviet intelligence. Oleg Gordievsky was brought up within the intelligence establishment, his father having been a member of the NKVD, and in the early 1960s he joined the KGB. The decisive moment in his career apparently came with the 1968 invasion of Czechoslovakia. Posted to Copenhagen in 1972, he began looking for Western intelligence contacts, and by 1974 he was working for MI6. As a unique high-level source within the KGB, working first in Denmark, then at Moscow Centre, and finally in London, Gordievsky provided the British with a great deal of valuable information. He tipped them off about Michael Bettaney's attempts at treachery, provided an assessment of the damage caused by Geoffrey Prime, a Soviet agent inside GCHQ, and confirmed that Roger Hollis was not, as repeatedly alleged, a KGB mole. But the most important intelligence he provided concerned the Soviet leadership's paranoia over Western intentions and Operation Ryan, set up to provide advance warning of the Nato first strike, which the Russians had become convinced was a distinct possibility. This had been sparked by the development of the MX and Cruise missiles and by American anti-Soviet rhetoric, particularly Ronald Reagan's denunciation of Russia as 'the Evil Empire'. The most dangerous period came in late 1983, in the wake of the shooting down by Soviet MiG fighters of a Korean airliner over the Russian Far East. Amid an increase in international tension, Nato forces conducted a command-post exercise, Able Archer, involving widespread troop movements inside West Germany. The Russians had used such exercises as cover for preparations for the 1956 invasion of Hungary, the 1968 attack on Czechoslovakia, and a similar operation against Poland in 1981 which in the end was not given the go-ahead. When the Nato units changed their procedures halfway through the exercise in a simple communications security measure, Soviet signals intelligence temporarily lost track of what was going on, sparking panic in Moscow. Gordievsky told MI6 that Warsaw Pact commanders had been concerned that the West might be about to launch a nuclear attack under the guise of Able Archer and that Operation Ryan derived from very real fears within the Soviet leadership. As a result, both Reagan and Margaret Thatcher began to scale down their anti-Communist rhetoric, leading to their wooing of Mikhail Gorbachev – who was seen as the coming man of Soviet politics – and the successful arms-reductions talks of the 1980s.

In January 1985, Gordievsky was summoned to Moscow to be told he was to be the next KGB *Rezident* in London. It was a stunning success for both him and his MI6 handlers, promising untold intelligence riches. But by May, while he was still only acting *Rezident*, he had been recalled to Moscow in disgrace, his role as a British agent apparently blown. His escape was the stuff of fiction. Avoiding his KGB watchers, he followed instructions hidden inside the cover of a book to warn MI6 that he needed to be 'exfiltrated'. The signal was to stand on a designated street corner, holding a Safeway carrier bag. Once this had been acknowledged by someone 'chewing something as he passed' – in this case a man with a Harrods bag eating a Mars bar – he was to follow the pre-set instructions and make his way to a rendezvous (RV) on the Finnish border. Here he met up with the MI6 team that was to smuggle him across to the West in the boot of a car. Gordievsky, who had never asked for money from MI6, had spent eleven years as an agent-in-place, risking his life to pass intelligence to the West. Nigel Clive, who retired while Gordievsky was still in place, has described him as 'the most successful British agent'. This is a claim that might just as easily be made of agents from the first half of the 20th century such as TR16 and Jonny de Graaf and others who were yet to come. But Lord Armstrong, who was Cabinet Secretary during much of Gordievsky's period as a British agent, was surely right when he described him as 'one of the most important sources we ever had'. The handling of Penkovsky and Gordievsky did more to restore the reputation of MI6 than all its other operations put together. The service came under fire over the apparent lack of any warning of either the Falklands conflict or the Gulf War. But insiders said there was no lack of such intelligence – merely poor use of it by government.

In early 1982, the British government was in the process of negotiating the Falkland Islands away, MI6, whose only station in Latin America was in Buenos Aires, warned that there were clear signs of the Argentinians' willingness to invade. The fact that this was ignored was attributed by Young to the dislike within Whitehall of 'hard facts which would conflict with its preference for soothing description'. He said, 'The Falklands War is an example of where the latter prevailed at a high price. We had a very good assessment of the situation before it happened. Even our embassy was getting reports of the Argentinians' plans. But Carrington [the British Foreign Secretary] played them down.' Once the conflict had begun, the service played a key role in stopping Argentina's supply of the Exocet air-to-surface missiles that were proving so effective against the British warships. Anthony Divall, a former Royal Marine who had done a number of jobs for the service, persuaded Captain Alfredo Corti, the head of an Argentinian arms-procurement team, that he was in a position to provide thirty Exocets, at a cost of £1 million each, from Iraq and Libya. By committing Corti to the sale and then stringing it out, Divall ensured that the Argentinian air force's supply of Exocets dried up and undoubtedly saved the lives of numerous British servicemen.

Despite the lessons of the Falklands conflict, the Scott Inquiry into the Matrix-Churchill affair – during which MI6 used the Iraqi-owned firm's British managing director, Paul Henderson, as an agent to discover details of Baghdad's weapons development – heard how the service's reports were still frequently ignored by other government departments. The 1990 Iraqi invasion of Kuwait saw MI6 attempting to replicate the type of operations it had conducted during the Soviet occupation of Afghanistan over the previous decade. These were similar to the operations carried out alongside the underground movements in Nazi-occupied Europe by the wartime Special Operations Executive. One of the Afghan operations, carried out on MI6's behalf by 'contract labourers', was the retrieval of a Soviet Hind helicopter gunship which had been brought down by Afghan rebels. A team of rebels led by three contract men brought it back across the border into Pakistan. The men were apparently paid a basic wage with bonuses for retrieving particular items – the Hind's control panel and the lightweight armour-plating on its underbody being among the most highly priced. 'The Hind helicopter went down in Afghanistan, and of course the collectors of Soviet equipment and methodology were grasping for different ways of getting a recovery team into the country to retrieve the helicopter,' said Ed Juchniewicz, former CIA Assistant Deputy Director, Operations. 'And of course the Soviets, I believe, suspected that many of these services were out there trying to retrieve their equipment. So they were sending teams to try and retrieve their own helicopter and take it back to their own lines. My understanding is that a British team – and I don't know what the composition of the British team was – succeeded in getting in and retrieving and bringing the Hind out in pieces.'

MI6 sent an annual mission into Afghanistan to liaise with Ahmed Shah Massoud, who as leader of the Northern Alliance was to be assassinated by al-Qa'eda terrorists shortly before the 11 September attacks. Massoud was regarded as the most reliable of the Mujahideen commanders. He was supplied by MI6 with missiles and communications receivers. These were usually delivered by MI6 officers and contract labourers, some of whom were serving SAS or SBS members who, in order to make the operation deniable, were 'retired' for the duration of the operation and then taken back on with no loss of pay or pension once it was finished. They also gave the Mujahideen training in how to use the equipment and collected captured Soviet weaponry. Baroness Park said the Afghanistan War was 'the most wonderful opportunity for acquiring knowledge of, and in some cases possession of, a large range of the most up-to-date Soviet equipment, including helicopters. And when our forces came to fight the Iraqis in the Gulf War, the Iraqis were of course armed with those very Soviet weapons, and because of that activity in Afghanistan – which is one of the arguments for being global: you never know when things are going to turn up that are going to be very useful – they knew roughly what they were up against. In fact they knew in great detail what they were up against'. The Gulf War operations were on a much smaller scale but reinforced a template that has been used on a number of occasions since, most notably in Afghanistan in the wake of the 11 September attacks. An MI6 officer was posted to Riyadh to help to set up a Kuwaiti resistance organisation. The Kuwaitis were trained in camps inside Saudi Arabia by members of the SAS but were eventually deemed unusable. Nevertheless, the template of MI6 mounting disruptive operations behind enemy lines using internal resistance and members of the SAS and SBS was now in place.

In the wake of the Cold War, Sir Colin McColl, the Chief of MI6, ordered a review of the agency's operations. The result was a reorganisation designed to leave it more flexible and more able to cope with a less predictable world where the main dangers would come from maverick states; nuclear, biological and chemical proliferation; terrorism; and the growth in international crime. But the former Soviet Union – an area which, apart from the two world wars, has been regarded as a major threat ever since the Great Game was first played out in central Asia in the early part of the nineteenth century – remains a key target. Baroness Park, who served in Moscow as a young officer, said: 'We are looking at a country which still has the largest army in Europe, which has got a lot of new research and development, and which, although it is destroying obsolete weapons, is replacing them by new ones all the time. What we have to find out are the intentions of the Russians. They have still got all those missiles pointing straight at this country. That hasn't been changed yet.'

One of the service's most important areas of interest in the former Soviet Union is nuclear, biological and chemical weaponry. MI6 was able to provide crucial evidence of Russia's biological-weapons programme in 1989 when a Soviet 'walk-in' turned up at Britain's Paris embassy. Vladimir Pasechnik claimed to be the director of the Leningrad institute of Biopreparat – the agency which ran Russia's programme for 'weaponry of special designation' – on a research trip to the West. He told MI6 that, although Biopreparat was allegedly a medical research organisation, this was only a cover for its real role. 'Officially we had been told that 85 per cent of the resources of the institute should be directly connected with biological warfare problems and 15 per cent towards concealing our activity,' Pasechnik said. 'There was zero support for real scientific and technological projects on behalf of the National Health. Being the director of one of the institutes, I was involved in all sorts of discussions and was able to see top-secret classified documents which described the aims of these developments. I came eventually to the conclusion that it would be most advantageous if I brought this information to the attention of the West.' His description of Biopreparat's operations included details of a strain of bubonic plague resistant to twenty-six different types of antibiotic. He also revealed that Biopreparat had at least twenty separate research facilities capable of producing large quantities of biological weapons – only five of which were disclosed by President Yeltsin in a 1993 declaration on Russia's biological and chemical weapons.

In July 1992, MI6 had another major success. Col Viktor Oshchenko, the 52-year-old head of Russian intelligence in Paris, was spirited out of France and into Britain. Like Gordievsky, he had been recalled to Moscow where, according to the Russian foreign intelligence service, the *Sluzhba Vneshnei Razvedki* (SVR), 'certain aspects of his work had given cause for suspicion'. He had 'decided to defect to the West, fearing that his "double game" might be exposed,' the Russians said. Oshchenko told his colleagues at the Russian embassy, where he operated under cover as an economics counsellor, that he was spending the weekend travelling in the Loire valley with his wife and 14-year-old daughter Olga. Staff at the embassy first suspected that the weekend away might not be all it seemed when Oshchenko's elder daughter rang to ask what she was supposed to do with a new car her father had had delivered to her St Petersburg home. The next day when he did not return to work, a search was set in place. Oshchenko's car was found abandoned at Orly airport in Paris. The British Home Office announced that he was in Britain where he had asked for political asylum. Oshchenko's defection led to the expulsion from France of four of his former colleagues, including his deputy Sergei Smirov, who controlled a ring of spies at the heart of the French nuclear weapons programme. Oschenko was also responsible for the tip-off that led to the arrest of Michael Smith, a British electronics engineer who had passed military secrets to the Russians, after being recruited by Oshchenko in the early 1970s.

The former Soviet Union's economic difficulties during the early 1990s were to bring a series of Russian 'walk-ins'. The best was undoubtedly Vasili Mitrokhin. His story began in the early 1970s when Mitrokhin, a disenchanted officer in the KGB's foreign intelligence service, the First Chief Directorate, was working as an archivist. His task was to supervise the transfer of several hundred thousand files from the Lubyanka, the old KGB headquarters in central Moscow to its new base at Yasenovo on the Moscow ring-road. For more than a decade he carefully copied out details from the files, compiling a secret archive of names and covernames of Soviet spies in the west and the operations they had taken part in. He made detailed notes on pieces of paper, which he crumpled up and threw into his waste-paper basket. Then at the end of each day, he would retrieve his notes and smuggle them out of Yasenovo hidden in his shoes. Once back in his Moscow flat, he hid the notes under his mattress. Every weekend, he took them to a dacha 20 miles outside Moscow where he typed them up and hid them in a milk churn under the floorboards. By the time he retired in 1984, he had also filled a tin clothes boiler, two tin trunks and two aluminium cases. His intention in compiling the archive, he would later say, was 'to inflict as much damage as possible to the old KGB and party *nomenklatura*.'

It was to be nearly 20 years after he began to compile the secret records before he had his first real opportunity to pass them safely to the West. In March 1992, with Soviet-style communism sidelined by the fall of the Berlin Wall and the failure of the coup against Gorbachev, Mitrokhin travelled to one of the Baltic republics where he went to the US embassy and offered his archive to the CIA head of station. To his astonishment, he was rebuffed; possibly the CIA man believed the information was too good to be true and was forged. So Mitrokhin went to the British embassy, where the MI6 head of station offered him tea and listened to his story. Mitrokhin had brought some samples of his notes with him. The MI6 officer examined them and told him that he had better come back again next month with some more.

Mitrokhin returned on 9 April, this time with around a dozen envelopes, containing over 2,000 closely typed pages of details from the KGB records. One of the envelopes listed hundreds of KGB agents and confidential contacts in America. There was a similar but shorter list of agents and confidential contacts in the UK. An SIS team had flown to the Baltic republics specifically to test Mitrokhin's credentials. He agreed to return in June with still more documents. At this third meeting he was persuaded to go to Britain secretly to help MI6 and MI5 officers examining his archive to understand it better. For the last three weeks of September 1992 and the early part of October, he was debriefed at a series of safe house in London and the countryside. During this time, he made the final decision to defect. On 13 October he was infiltrated back into Russia and three weeks later, he and his family arrived in the same Baltic republic where he had originally made contact with MI6 and were taken to a new life in the UK.

Meanwhile, British and US intelligence officers were trawling through the Mitrokhin archive looking for KGB agents and ways of turning their new knowledge to the best possible advantage. One FBI officer described it as 'the most complete and extensive intelligence ever received from one source. Attention in Britain focussed on Melita Norwood, who during the Second World War had passed the KGB information related to the production of the first atomic bomb, and whether MI5 which had known about her long before Mitrokhin defected, had been right not to have her arrested. But given the scale of the information Mitrokhin produced this was almost an irrelevance.

According to Professor Christopher Andrew, who co-authored a book on Mitrokhin's archive with its original compiler, 'no-one who spied for the Soviet Union at any period between the October Revolution and the eve of the Gorbachev era can now be confident that his or her secrets are still secure'. More importantly perhaps, the SVR had no way of telling which of its agents dating back before 1984 agents was blown. It would have had to assume that it must abandon them all. The disruption caused to Russian intelligence operations abroad was incalculable. It was a major coup for British intelligence, and represented a final payback for the damage done by the Cambridge Five.

Fourteen

The Great Game Continues

Smiley scoffed at the idea that spying was a dying profession now that the Cold War had ended.

John le Carré, *The Secret Pilgrim*

Despite the end of the Cold War, Russia and Britain still regularly report the discovery of each other's spies. When one MI6 agent was arrested by Russia's Federal Counter-Espionage Service, the FSK, at the beginning of 1994, his Lubyanka interrogation was shown on Russian television. Vadim Sintsov, an export manager for a Russian weapons company specialising in armour and artillery systems, admitted having taken £8,000 from MI6 in return for two computer disks and 18 films containing details of the latest Russian weapons technology and arms sales to the Middle East and former Soviet republics. Sintsov claimed that MI6 had discovered he was taking bribes and blackmailed him into working for them. He was recruited at an arms fair in London in 1993 and had eleven subsequent meetings with British intelligence agents in Singapore, Paris, London and Budapest, he said. 'I started working with a certain Mr James Self and after a while he introduced me to his successor, a liaison officer. We met at first in other countries, that is outside Russia. But last autumn they made arrangements for me to communicate with them here. They were interested mainly in two areas where I could offer information because of my job. The first was Russian arms deliveries to Middle Eastern countries and the second was general details about how we conduct weapons sales.' Sintsov was sentenced to ten years hard labour. The FSK claimed that John Scarlett, the MI6 head of station, was expelled as a result of Sintsov's arrest. In fact, his visa was withdrawn in retaliation for the British refusal to allow a senior SVR officer to come to London. 'It was all handled in a gentlemanly fashion,' the FSK said.

The defence links between the former Soviet republics are a major intelligence priority for the West, as is the fate of the Soviet military-industrial complex. Are weapons factories really being converted to civilian uses or are their products still being produced for export to potential world trouble spots like the Middle East? Concern over Russian sales of nuclear materials and technology to the region led MI6 to use another defector from the KGB in a sting operation designed to disrupt Iranian attempts to buy equipment for its nuclear weapons programme. Like Gordievsky, Mikhail Butkov, a former KGB major, had been an MI6 agent-in-place. He defected in May 1991 while stationed in Oslo under cover as a journalist, providing detailed intelligence on KGB operations in Scandinavia, Ireland and Australia. Eight Russian 'diplomats' based in Oslo were subsequently expelled as a result of the information he provided. Butkov was paid £100,000 when he arrived in Britain, and he and his girlfriend were set up under false names in the small Berkshire town of Purley. For a while he continued to assist MI6, most notably in the sting against the Iranians, which took place in Geneva during 1993 and 1994. But as his knowledge became dated, he was of far less use and with plenty of time on his hands he supplemented his £15,000-a-year pension with his own sting operation. The £1.5m fraud, in which a host of Russian companies and organisations were duped into parting with large sums of money in the false hope of receiving business advice from the world's best financial brains, led to Butkov being jailed for three years.

By the start of the 21st century, the lure of Western money had persuaded more than 50 Russians to offer their services to Western intelligence agencies, with varying degrees of success. Among the saddest cases was that of Viktor Makarov, a KGB signals intelligence expert who during the early 1980s had passed MI6 detailed intelligence on Russian operations against the diplomatic communications of a number of western countries, and the reassuring information that the KGB had failed to penetrate Britain's diplomatic ciphers. But he was caught and sent to the gulag. On his release in 1992 he defected to Britain but his knowledge was so outdated that he was granted only a small pension and tried to petition the Queen for more.

A similarly sad case was that of Platon Obukhov, a young Russian diplomat who offered his services to MI6. In May 1996, the Russian security service, or FSB, as it was now known, announced that it had arrested Obukhov for attempting to supply MI6 with information on 'the internal situation, disarmament and the behaviour of Russian leaders'. Under interrogation, Obukhov admitted contacting the British secret service while working at the Foreign Ministry, but claimed he was only gathering material for his novels, the titles of which included *The Sex Demon, Dicing with Death* and *In the Embrace of the Spider*. MI6 had said 'they would pay me $2,000 a month and give me $1,000 extra for really good information,' he claimed. The affair developed into a full-scale diplomatic row, with the FSB, clearly anxious to make its mark under its new name, announcing that nine British diplomats were to be expelled from Moscow because there was 'irrefutable evidence of activities incompatible with their diplomatic status'. After lengthy negotiations, that figure was reduced to four and, in a tit-for-tat reaction, four Russian diplomats were expelled from London. Obukhov was sentenced to 11 years in prison but was later placed in a psychiatric hospital.

By the time the service moved into its new £300 million Vauxhall Cross headquarters in 1994, its role was very different from that first envisaged for it in 1909. Some traditions remain. Those who work for MI6 still call it the Firm, while the Foreign Office refers to it 'politely, but not very sincerely', as the Friends. C still sees the Prime Minister each Tuesday. The service's reports still carry a CX serial number and are known colloquially within the service simply as CX. But the discussions and reports cover areas that would never have been targets for MI6 in the old world.

The 1994 Intelligence Services Act made it clear that, as well as the traditional role of collecting foreign political, economic and military intelligence – particularly in the area of nuclear proliferation – the service had an additional task: 'the prevention or detection of serious crime'. This was an official mandate for operations that had already been going on for some time against terrorism, drug-smuggling and money-laundering aimed at Britain but carried out overseas, where the police, HM Customs and the Security Service MI5 would not normally be able to operate.

'Individual law-enforcement agencies can sometimes benefit from the wider look and the further reach that a foreign intelligence service has when it comes to uncovering illegal networks which operate across frontiers,' Sir Colin McColl said. 'There is a tendency, I think, for bad men to operate where they think they are safe, and if we can help to reach out into some of those places, we can help the law-enforcement agencies in not only this country, but in other countries as well.'

The growth in organised crime in the old Soviet Bloc, primarily in Russia itself, Poland and the Czech Republic, and its operations involving Britain, led by trafficking in drugs and illegal immigrants, are a major concern. Even before the Berlin Wall came down, MI6 was helping the British customs and police prevent drugs coming into Britain via Poland and Czechoslovakia, concentrating its efforts on infiltrating the smugglers at the very start of the drugs supply chain in order to disrupt their operations as extensively as possible.

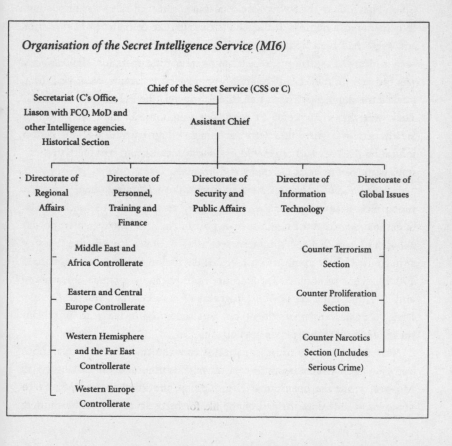

Organisation of the Secret Intelligence Service (MI6)

As early as 1988, MI6 had begun to help the police to uncover attempts to smuggle drugs into Britain via eastern Europe. One such operation began after detectives in London arrested two Czechs, Miroslav Vrana and his son Roman, with five kilograms of cocaine. The detectives found they had stumbled across a drugs route leading from Colombia to Britain, via Poland, Czechoslovakia, Germany and the Netherlands. Working with members of the old Czech secret service, the StB, a member of the Colombian Cali drugs cartel had set up a front company in Prague and was using it to smuggle 500 kilograms of cocaine to Europe a month.

Alonso Delgado Martinez had studied in Prague in the 1960s and around twenty years later set up the Yaros Trading Company, ostensibly to import Colombian food to the Soviet Bloc. But that was not all Yaros was importing. In every cargo, a number of the pallets carrying the containers of beans, rice and sugar had been hollowed out to provide space for plastic bags full of cocaine. In what turned out to be a major smuggling operation, the company was bringing in millions of pounds worth of pure cocaine every year. MI6 tracked the shipments. They came into Europe via the Polish port of Gdynia. They were then transported by road to a warehouse in the Czech town of Hradec Králové, where they were recontainered, given fresh documentation indicating that they had originated in Czechoslovakia, and sent on to destinations in the Netherlands, Germany and Britain.

In 1991, a joint operation was put in place to track a shipment along the route, picking up each member of the gang as the containers passed. The operation faltered at the Czech border post in Nachod, where an alert border guard, unaware that the shipment was already under surveillance, became suspicious. A closer examination revealed the hollowed out pallets containing 100 kilograms of cocaine. Delgado and two Czech associates were arrested and a second shipment of 116 kilograms of cocaine was seized in Gdynia. Delgado denied any involvement but was sentenced to ten years imprisonment, increased to thirteen on appeal.

Nevertheless 'serious crime' constitutes only a small part of MI6 operations with the main targets being terrorism, proliferation and the old enemy in Moscow. While the operational effort against the Russians has reduced by about two-thirds since the end of the Cold War, the core element working in the former Soviet Bloc controllerate, now known as Eastern and Central Europe, is broadly the same as it was before the collapse of communism. The reduction in effort reflects the dramatic decline in Moscow's influence and interference elsewhere in the world. But the political stability of all the other former members of the Soviet Union – particularly those in central Asia and the Transcaucasus – remains a major concern.

Other more traditional targets, such as monitoring potential enemies and world flashpoints, remain – with lack of stability making the Middle East and the former Yugoslavia clear priorities. South Africa is perhaps a less obvious problem in this regard, but, given the country's strategic importance, there is a great deal of interest in internal ANC politics and in the activities of groups from both the extreme right and the extreme left. China unsurprisingly dominates intelligence priorities in the Far East, but Vietnam, North Korea and Cambodia are also important targets. Elsewhere in Asia the key targets are Afghanistan and Pakistan, the latter not just because of its connections with al-Qa'eda, but also because of its dispute with India over Kashmir. In Latin America, Argentina and its attitude towards the Falkland Islands are still among the main areas of interest, although no longer as important as the smuggling of drugs to Britain from Colombia, the Caribbean and the Andean region of South America. Brazil, as one of the world's major weapons producers, is also high on the list of priorities. The economic fragility of many Latin American countries is another key area of interest. But, potential flash points aside, the main concerns are weapons proliferation, trans-national crime and terrorism. Apart from successful operations against Osama bin Laden and al-Qa'eda, MI6 played a key role in the arrest of three members of the Provisional IRA, including the Sinn Fein representative in Cuba, over assistance allegedly provided to FARC guerrillas in Colombia. Intelligence gathered by the stations in Havana and Bogota led to the arrests of the three men.

The service contracted in the immediate wake of the Cold War, a result of the cuts made across the intelligence community as a whole as the politicians demanded their 'peace dividend'. But by introducing information technology and cutting bureaucracy both in London and abroad it has succeeded in maintaining the overseas stations at the 'sharp end' of its operations. One innovation introduced by McColl was the creation of 'shoe box' stations with one officer deploying for six months at a time to trouble spots, such as the various former Yugoslav republics.

But the basic structure of MI6 has not been radically changed. The service still maintains around 2,500 staff, of whom around 400 are Intelligence Branch (IB) officers, the main intelligence production officers, 800 General Service (GS) officers, largely desk officers, and the remainder support staff. There are a total of five directors in charge of the directorates of Personnel, Training and Finance; Security and Public Affairs; Information Technology; Regional Affairs; and Global Issues. The Regional Affairs directorate contains four 'controllerates' headed by 'controllers' and covering various geographical areas of the world: the Middle East and Africa; Eastern and Central Europe; Western Hemisphere and the Far East; and Western Europe. The Global Issues directorate is split into three sections: Counter-Terrorism; Counter-Proliferation and Counter-Narcotics, the last including all 'serious crime'. The sections and regional controllerates are still split into a number of P and R sections, the P or production section providing the intelligence while the R or requirements section liaises with the customers and disseminates the product. A secretariat attached to C's office includes a number of liaison departments from other agencies to ensure smooth co-ordination of joint operations.

The new world order has also brought new links to other intelligence agencies. There had always been good liaison with the CIA and the other secret services of the UKUSA countries – in particular the Australian Secret Intelligence Service. ASIS was set up in 1952 as a direct result of the British need for a covert-operations organisation that could cover the Far East. Its charter was based on that of its British counterpart, and the two services had shared stations and training facilities. Indeed the link was so close that until 1994, when there was a great deal of adverse publicity over its relationship with MI6, ASIS still referred to its senior partner as 'Head Office'. But MI6 links with its foreign counterparts are not limited to the services of the UKUSA countries, as indicated by the Intelligence Services Act, which authorises 'liaison with a wide range of foreign intelligence and security services'. Even before the European Union, there were close although not altogether productive relations with the German *Bundesnachrichtendienst* and the French SDECE, now known as the *Direction Générale de la Sécurité Extérieure* (DGSE).

Neither organisation could hope to come anywhere near the usefulness to MI6 of its close relationship with the CIA and links to France are better with the highly respected French security service, the *Direction de la Surveillance du Territoire* (DST). Links with Mossad and the South African intelligence service have always transcended the occasional difficulties in Britain's formal relations with Tel Aviv and Pretoria, although neither service is what it once was and Mossad's credibility is tainted by its willingness to use disinformation in order to assist Israel's political aims. New partnerships have been formed with old enemies in the former Soviet Bloc, in particular the Czechs, the Poles and the Hungarians, bringing a number of successes but also the occasional problem.

Specific MI6 operations have to be cleared officially by the Foreign Office, or in the most 'politically sensitive' cases by the Foreign Secretary himself. A written proposal is prepared within the service outlining the planned operation and what it is intended to achieve together with an assessment of the risks involved. There is also a detailed internal rulebook laying down what officers may and may not do. Sir Gerry Warner, a former MI6 officer who as Intelligence Co-ordinator in the early 1990s had responsibility for determining how Britain's post-Cold War intelligence requirements were met, claimed that SIS officers did not carry arms. It would be 'unthinkable' for them to be authorised to use violence in peacetime, he said. But given the nature of the people they are operating against, both in the serious-crime role and in the more traditional espionage role, this would seem to put individual officers at unacceptable personal risk. This is particularly so in the wake of the McColl reorganisation, which cut posts abroad with the intention of inserting officers into various areas as and when intelligence requirements developed. These operations, and the exfiltration of agents or defectors, have traditionally been carried out with the assistance of the armed forces – usually members of the British special forces, the Special Air Service and its Royal Navy counterpart, the Special Boat Service, which specialises in the classic spy-thriller-style insertion and exfiltration of agents by inflatable dinghy launched from a submarine waiting offshore. MI6 has worked extremely closely with the SAS and SBS during drugs-busting operations in Colombia and in the allied involvement in conflicts in the Balkans, Afghanistan and Iraq.

The decision to use the SAS in such operations appears to have been made during the late 1960s, following a confidential report by Colonel John Waddy, then Colonel of the SAS, which called for closer co-operation between the SAS and both MI6 and MI5 in 'tasks of a more delicate nature'. These would involve members of the regiment in covert operations abroad, some of them anti-terrorist, others Cold War-related. David Stirling, the founder of the SAS, later wrote, 'Certain delicate operational roles require the Secret Service to invest in the SAS command highly classified intelligence necessary for the effective planning of these operations and, just as importantly, for special training'. To co-ordinate such operations, an SAS officer acts as permanent liaison with MI6 as MoD Advisor Special Operations. Servicemen employed on such jobs are temporarily transferred to the reserves to ensure that where necessary the regiment's active involvement can be denied. The SBS provides a smaller number of its members to assist in operations, most notably in the infiltration and exfiltration of agents or officers by sea using a small submarine approximately 20 feet long and capable of carrying four passengers. The RAF also provides 'the S&D Flight', a small unit of around a dozen pilots capable of dropping people in by fixed-wing aircraft or helicopter. Field communications are provided by 602 Troop, Royal Signals, based at Banbury, Oxfordshire.

For operations where there is a real risk of compromise, such as the Gordievsky exfiltration, MI6 has a select list of specialists, mostly former SAS/SBS members who are taken on for specific contracts. Some of these contract officers are still on 'the Circuit' as it is called, working as bodyguards for Middle Eastern diplomats and businessmen, providing training for foreign governments in anything from basic security to special operations, and sometimes carrying out specific mercenary operations abroad. Others, having left the services, have made new careers for themselves, totally unrelated to the security world, and only become involved 'when someone from Six goes through the list and calls them up'. 'Teams' are put together as and when they are required. Each member is allocated a cover name and told not to reveal his true identity to any other members of the team, which, given the exclusivity of 'the Circuit', frequently makes for strange situations with close friends working alongside each other as if they have never met. The need-to-know principle is strictly adhered to, and individual contract officers will not be briefed on anything other than their own role in the affair.

The old Afghan operations and a few new ones put MI6 in good stead when the allies attacked Afghanistan in the wake of the 11 September attacks. The service reactivated old agents who had been in place during the Soviet occupation and reassigned agents who had been taking part in longstanding efforts to stop the heroin trade inside Afghanistan. But the foundations for its operations against Osama Bin Laden's al-Qaʿeda terrorist network and the Taliban were agents already in place for just that purpose and already providing extremely good information on the terrorist leader. It was only bin Laden's very strict security procedures and continued mobility that had prevented the information these agents provided from being used to attack and kill him. Suggestions by some CIA officers that it had no agents inside Afghanistan ahead of the attacks are simply not true, one MI6 officer said. Both the CIA and MI6 had a number of agents there, although for a number of reasons the CIA had difficulties operating in Afghanistan and the majority there were British agents targeting both al-Qaʿeda and the drugs smugglers. These agents were used in 'highly imaginative ways', said one oficer, during the negotiations that brought about the rapid collapse of the Taliban across the north of Afghanistan, one officer said. Many of the agents were later redirected back to the drugs trade as MI6 officers, assisted by those SAS and SBS members still on the ground, were used to persuade farmers away from poppy production, to destroy drugs stockpiles and to disrupt the reconstruction of the drugs routes. This led to a significant cut in the amount of heroin leaving the country. But a lack of both funds and US interest led to these operations being curtailed by the end of 2002.

In the wake of the 11 September attacks, the service has launched a recruitment drive as it seeks to expand its counter-terrorism and counter-proliferation units. The number of officers working in the counter-terrorism section alone will double to around 100. The number of IB officers recruited annually is expected to double from around 20 to 40, with a commensurate increase in the number of support staff. Even before the 11 September attacks its main focus was al-Qaʿeda. Counter-proliferation was also already a key area with a large proportion of its operational effort dedicated to investigating attempts by groups like al-Qaʿeda and a number of countries, not so-called 'rogue nations', to acquire nuclear, biological or chemical weapons. It is generally regarded as having had 'a good Balkans' and despite allegedly being caught short when Saddam Hussein invaded Kuwait, the parliamentary Intelligence and Security Committee reported in 1999 that the service's efforts 'in obtaining sources to gather intelligence from Saddam Hussein's inner circle continued to be very important.'

MI6 had been running an agent in place inside the *Da'irat al-Mukhabarat al-Amah*, the Iraqi intelligence service. Jabir Salim, the head of *Mukhabarat* operations in Eastern Europe, whose cover was as Iraqi consul in Prague, provided detailed information on Saddam Hussein's attempt to obtain nuclear, chemical and biological weapons technology and on its infiltration of the Iraqi émigré movements. But at the end of 1998, he was forced to defect amid suggestions that his collaboration with the British had been blown by the members of the Czech security service. Salim reportedly took suitcases full of secret documents with him. Earlier that year, MI6 had enjoyed further success against Iraq when it persuaded Sami Salih, a millionaire businessman who was in charge of an Iraqi operation to bypass UN sanctions, to defect to the West. Salih used a network of front companies to smuggle oil to the West via Jordan, Syria and Turkey. The hard currency earnings, as much as £600,000 a day, were deposited in banks in Jordan and used to buy arms and fund the Iraqi leader's lifestyle. But Salih fell from favour with Saddam, was accused of spying, jailed and tortured. He escaped after his wife bribed a security official to take him to Kurdistan, where he was freed. He reached Jordan, walked into the British embassy in Amman and was interviewed by the MI6 head of station. He was a major catch and was flown to a safe house in Cyprus before being debriefed in Britain. Salih and other Iraqi defectors gave the British a wealth of intelligence, including details of Saddam's security and the layout of the presidential complex and the whereabouts of missiles that were being hidden from United Nations arms inspectors. Abbas al-Janabi, a senior aide to Saddam's eldest son Uday, who fled Iraq in 1998, is known to have been among the defectors recruited by MI6. Al-Janabi provided a great deal of intelligence on the working of the Iraqi dictator's inner circle. His evidence also confirmed that Saddam not only saw weapons of mass destruction as being vital to Iraq's status as a Middle East power but also to his own ability to continue to wield power within Iraq.

Given the difficulties of operating in such a brutal regime, MI6 had a surprising number of agents in Iraq, including long-term penetration agents. Human intelligence played a key role throughout the 2003 war on Iraq, beginning with the opening air strike in the early hours of 20 March in which 30 cruise missiles and smart bombs dropped by two F-117A Nighthawk stealth strike aircraft slammed into the Dora Farm Complex belonging to Saddam's youngest daughter Hala. The intelligence came from a 'very good' CIA source, described by President George W Bush as 'a guy on the ground' who 'was convinced that not only Saddam Hussein would be in the complex, but Uday and Qusay, his two sons, would be there as well.' For the first time in any war, human intelligence was received by the commanders in 'real time'. This was partly the result of the increased use by the military of the Internet, but was also due to a remarkable transformation in the way intelligence was sent to the front line.

This was the culmination of a determined policy of closer liaison between MI6 and the military that had begun in the Balkans and continued in Sierra Leone and Afghanistan. Determined to ensure that in Iraq the military received the intelligence it was collecting in 'real time', MI6 had flooded the region with members of its 'Camel Corps' and placed one of its officers inside the British headquarters to ensure that British frontline commanders not only had access to the best possible intelligence in 'real time' but that someone was there to explain to them precisely what level of reliability they could place on it. MI6 had long-term penetration agents in Baghdad who were reporting back to London via the Internet. But its main responsibility, as with the British forces, was for the south and Iraq's second city of Basra. In the months before the war, it developed a number of agents inside the city. These agents were supplied with highly secure short-range communications equipment to pass on the intelligence they collected. At previously agreed times, they went to the outskirts of the city to send their reports to MI6 agent handlers receiving the messages only a few hundred yards away. But throughout the siege, the MI6 officers, wearing local dress and accompanied by SBS minders, also moved in and out of the city, running the agents in the same way their predecessors had on the streets of Cold War Prague or Budapest. The intelligence provided by the MI6 agents inside Basra kept the British informed of everything that was going on in the city and was crucial to the operation to take it.

MI6 has been anxious to distance itself from its old reputation for covert operations reminiscent of Ian Fleming's 007. But as a result of the support it has provided for British military operations in Kurdistan, the Balkans, Sierra Leone, Afghanistan and Iraq, the old covert special operations of the early Cold War years have enjoyed a comeback. Under Colin McColl and his successors David Spedding and Richard Dearlove, the younger IB officers have shown an increasing tendency to model themselves on what one contract officer described as 'a cross between James Bond and the SAS'. Under the 1994 Intelligence Services Act, the Secret Intelligence Service is allowed 'to obtain and provide information relating to the actions or intentions of persons outside the British Isles; and to perform *other tasks* relating to the actions or intentions of such persons'. That of course is a direct reference to covert action, which is why MI6 officers are granted immunity under the Act from prosecution for criminal activities undertaken abroad if the Foreign Secretary deems them to be necessary for the proper discharge of their activities.

The reality is that most major countries have some form of organisation to carry out human intelligence and covert operations abroad. It does not cause the same level of public concern as for example the anti-subversion activities of MI5 did during the early 1980s. The attempt to play down the MI6 covert-action role seems little more than a legacy of the previous position – discarded only in 1993 with the introduction of the Intelligence Services Bill – that Britain had no such organisation except in times of war. Sir Gerry Warner's suggestion that MI6 officers do not carry arms seems to be just another part of the attempts to draw a discreet veil over the service's operations. MI6 officers certainly do not routinely carry weapons. But there is a difference between for instance an officer working under diplomatic cover, who would not be armed, and one employed on a particular operation which may or may not involve an element of risk. 'Just because you were taking part in an operation you wouldn't necessarily say, "Oh, I must go to the safe and get out a gat",' one officer said. 'But where there is some likelihood of weapons being needed, given the proper authorisation, they can be carried.'

Despite the public's general acceptance of the need for an intelligence service, at the beginning of the 21st century the reputation of MI6 came under attack from both David Shayler and its own renegade officer Richard

Tomlinson. Shayler, who at one point worked in MI5's Libyan section, claimed that his MI6 counterpart told him that the service had funded an attempt by an anti-Gaddafi group to assassinate the Libyan leader. This was dismissed by the then Foreign Secretary Robin Cook as 'pure fantasy'. A leaked MI6 document posted on the Internet did not, as Shayler suggested, back up his claims that MI6 wanted Gaddafi assassinated. It merely showed that the service had links with the group in question, knew that it wanted to overthrow the Libyan leader, either killing him or arresting him in the process, and had informed the permanent under-secretary, the top civil servant, at the Foreign Office.

Tomlinson was an exceptionally bright officer who was dismissed after being accused of maverick behaviour while operating in Bosnia under the cover of 'civil adviser' to the commander of the UN Protection Force (UNPROFOR). He was unable to accept his dismissal and, after having his attempts to take MI6 to an industrial tribunal blocked, set about making a series of systematic leaks to the media. Some of the things he said were true. Some were not. But all were designed to keep his name, and what he saw as his fight for justice, in the public eye. He eventually succeeded in publishing a book on his time in MI6, stressing that he was not trying to betray secrets that might help Britain's enemies. 'Under no circumstances would I ever cooperate with a foreign intelligence service,' Tomlinson said. 'Accordingly my book does not tell them anything they did not know already.'

But regardless of whether that was true or not, as far as MI6 was concerned, it scarcely mattered. The fact that a former officer was talking about its operations in an unregulated way was bound to damage a service that lives by its reputation to protect its sources. At the start of the campaign of increased openness about Britain's intelligence services, Sir Colin McColl, the then Chief of MI6, told a 1993 press conference in Whitehall that MI6 could not allow its secrets to be told. 'Secrecy is our absolute stock in trade, our most precious asset,' he said, explaining his refusal to give all but the barest details of his organisation. 'People risk their lives, often their jobs, because they believe SIS is a secret service. I am very anxious that I should be able to send some sort of signal to these people that we're not going to be undressed in public.'

GCHQ Signals Intelligence

Prologue

One dark moonless night in early 1994, a Royal Navy patrol boat pulled out of Hong Kong Harbour and into the East Lama Strait. It was part of the colony's recently formed Anti-Smuggling Task Force, tracking the *dai feis*, the boats that were custom-built for the smugglers who brought immigrants or drugs into the British colony from China's neighbouring Guangdong province before returning with stolen prestige cars to sell to the Chinese party elite.

The *dai fei*, Chinese for 'big flyer', looked like a cross between a military landing craft and a large power boat. But looks were deceptive. Made out of glass-fibre to keep its weight to a bare minimum, and with an open hold just large enough to carry one luxury car back to Guangdong, the *dai feis* had five 225bhp outboard motors capable of pushing them to speeds of up to 70 mph. They were easily fast enough and light enough to outmanoeuvre anything the task force could muster. It had been forced to buy five *dai feis* itself just to keep up with them. But even so, stopping the smugglers was a risky business. Royal Navy patrols had resorted to getting a couple of men on board the vessels to try to cut the fuel lines before they outaccelerated them into the strait. But with the smugglers armed with machetes and AK-47s, the dangers were obvious.

Now the Anti-Smuggling Task Force was trying something different. On board the patrol boat were two signals intelligence operators, soldiers from among the several thousand members of the armed forces who work for GCHQ, the British signals intelligence centre at Cheltenham. The two GCHQ operators had the latest in radio monitoring devices. Their frequency-scanning radio receivers raced up and down the air waves looking for the *dai fei* skippers as they chattered to the members of the Triads waiting on shore, trying to up the pitiful sums they were paid for doing the smugglers' dirty work.

In the Royal Navy patrol boat's communications centre, a scanner locked onto an active frequency. From the radio conversation, it was clear that a *dai fei* was moving out into the delta with a hold full of heroin from the Golden Triangle to the West, via China and Hong Kong. The drugs were to be quietly unloaded at a quiet quayside and replaced by a stolen Mercedes or BMW, the increasing wealth of China's *nouveau riche* and 150 per cent import tarifs on luxury cars providing a profitable return for the smugglers.

But not this time. By listening in to the radio conversation between the *dai fei* crew and the Triads' man on the quayside, the GCHQ operators were able to tell the Hong Kong police precisely where the exchange would take place. The smugglers were arrested with about 45lb of pure heroin with a street value of about £7million and a brand new BMW 728i, stolen to order just 40 minutes earlier.

Fifteen

The Government Code
and Cypher School

*The deciphered telegrams of foreign governments are without doubt the most
valuable source of our secret information respecting their policy and actions.'*
Lord Curzon, Foreign Secretary, on the creation of the Government Code
and Cypher School, 1919

The closure of Bode's Secret Department in the Post Office and the Willes
family codebreaking operation brought Britain's interception of foreign
communications to an abrupt end. It was not resumed until shortly before the
First World War. Military intelligence set up a department to 'censor' foreign
telegraph cables on 2 August 1914. The results were enhanced by the Royal
Navy's success in cutting Germany's submarine cables, forcing it to use those
controlled by the British. An army codebreaking unit was set up to decipher
German military wireless messages with a good deal of success. 'Nobody
could desire more admirable opponents than the Germans for this class of
work,' said E W B Gill, one of the academics employed to unravel the German
codes and ciphers. 'The orderly Teutonic mind was especially suited for
devising schemes which any child could unravel.' The army had a number of
intercept sites in the Middle East and one of the more notable successes for
the military cryptographers came in December 1916, when the commander of
the German Middle East signals organisation sent a drunken Christmas
greeting to all his operators. During the Christmas inactivity, the same
isolated and clearly identical message went out in six different codes, only one
of which, up until that point, the British had managed to break. Under a 1916
reorganisation of military intelligence, the codebreaking section became

MI1b and moved to 5 Cork Street, in London's West End. With the assistance of Major Malcolm Hay, a noted historian, a large number of academics were drafted in to help and, by the Armistice, there were forty-five codebreakers, supported by forty 'ancillary ladies'.

The Royal Navy also set up its own codebreaking unit, called Room 40 after its offices in the old Admiralty buildings and only in 1917 integrated into the naval intelligence organisation as NID25. It had intercept stations at Hunstanton, Aberdeen, Stockton on Tees and Cambridge. Perhaps the best known of its many achievements was the breaking of the Zimmerman Telegram, broken by the brilliant Dilly Knox and Nigel de Grey. The enciphered message from Arthur Zimmermann, the German Foreign Minister, to the German ambassador in Mexico City suggested an alliance with Mexico against the United States. In return it offered 'generous financial support and an undertaking on our part that Mexico is to reconquer the lost territory in Texas, New Mexico and Arizona'. Its publication in March 1917 brought the United States into the war, ending American isolationism and ensuring Germany's defeat. Soon afterwards de Grey was sent to Italy to set up an outstation at Otranto, later moving to Rome.

The Army and Navy codebreaking units rarely spoke to each other, engaging in a turf war apparently fuelled by the Army's resentment of the greater influence of the upstart in the Admiralty. Alastair Denniston, who led Room 40 for much of the war, later complained of 'the loss of efficiency to both departments caused originally by mere official jealousy.' They finally began to exchange results in 1917, but there remained little love lost and the situation came to a head a year after the Armistice when the question of whether or not there should be a peacetime codebreaking organisation was under consideration.

Although there were inevitably some within government who were keen to axe the codebreakers as part of a peace dividend, there were many more who were just as eager to continue to receive the intelligence they were providing. It was decided to amalgamate the two organisations and a conference was held at the Admiralty in August 1919 to consider who should be in charge of the new body. The War Office wanted their man, Major Hay, now head of MI1b, while the Navy was equally determined that Denniston was the worthier candidate. Hay appears to have overplayed his hand, refusing to work under Denniston, while the latter expressed a willingness to do whatever was asked of him. Denniston was given charge of what was to be known as the Government Code and Cypher School, with a staff of just over 50 employees of whom only half were codebreakers. 'The public function was "to advise as to the security of codes and ciphers used by all Government departments and to assist in their provision", Denniston recalled. 'The secret directive was "to study the methods of cipher communications used by foreign powers".'

GC&CS came under the control of the Director of Naval Intelligence Admiral Hugh 'Quex' Sinclair, a noted bon-viveur who installed it in London's fashionable Strand, close to the Savoy Grill, his favourite restaurant. Its material was almost entirely diplomatic traffic. The censoring of telegrams had stopped at the end of the war even though 'every government department was strongly opposed to this because they all wished still to get the information derived from the censorship'. But the cable companies were secretly told to continue handing over their traffic to GC&CS, which copied it and returned it to them. 'Secrecy is essential,' wrote Lord Curzon, the then Foreign Secretary. 'It must be remembered that the companies who still supply the original messages to us regard the intervention of the Government with much suspicion and some ill will. It is important to leave this part of our activity to the deepest possible obscurity.'

The main targets for the fledgling GC&CS were America, France, Japan and Russia, the latter providing what Denniston said was the only real operational intelligence. 'The Revolutionary Government in 1919 had no codes and did not risk using the Tsarist codes, which they must have inherited,' he added. 'They began with simple transposition of plain Russian and gradually developed systems of increasing difficulty.' One of the reasons that the Bolsheviks were unwilling to use the old Tsarist codes was the presence among the British codebreakers of the man responsible for devising a number of them. Ernst Fetterlein had once been the Tsar's leading codebreaker, solving not just German and Austrian codes but also those of the British. He wore a large ruby ring given to him by Tsar Nicholas in thanks for his many achievements. Fetterlein fled from Russia during the October Revolution and was recruited by Denniston. One former codebreaker who was a member of Fetterlein's

Russian team recalled that he was a 'brilliant' codebreaker. 'Fetty, as we addressed him, would arrive precisely at 9.30 and read his *Times* until 10 when he would adjust a pair of thick-lensed glasses and look to us expecting work to be given to him. On book cipher and anything where insight was vital he was quite the best. He was a fine linguist and he would usually get an answer no matter the language. When he deposited his first cheque at a London bank he was asked for his references, to which he replied: "Pardon me? It is my money. Where are your references?"'

As a result of the efforts of Fetterlein and his small team, the British government was kept fully aware of the machinations of various elements of the Russian Trade Delegation, led by the Bolshevik Commissar for Foreign Trade which arrived in London in May 1920. Lev Kamenev, the head of the Moscow Communist Party, was sent to London to take charge of the delegation. Very soon the decrypts showed that he was setting up 'Councils of Action' across Britain that mirrored the Soviets, the committees which the Bolsheviks had used to co-ordinate the Russian revolution. To many of those in authority, it appeared that Britain was perilously close to its own communist insurrection. Field Marshal Sir Henry Wilson, the Chief of the Imperial General Staff, wrote a furious memorandum to Lloyd George. The telegrams showed 'beyond all possibility of doubt' that the delegation 'while enjoying the hospitality of England, are engaged, with the Soviet Government, in a plot to create red revolution and ruin this country'. He received support from Admiral Sinclair, who surprisingly urged the Government to publish the decrypted telegrams, known as BJs from the blue-jacketed files in which they were distributed. 'Even if the publication of the telegrams was to result in not another message being decoded, then the present situation would fully justify it,' Sinclair said. Lloyd George sanctioned publication of eight of the telegrams as long as it was said that they had been obtained from 'a neutral country'. But *The Times* ignored official requests to keep the true source secret, starting its report with the words: 'The following telegrams have been intercepted by the British Government.' Perhaps surprisingly the Russian ciphers were not changed until three months later, when Mikhail Frunze, Commander-in-Chief of the Bolshevik forces fighting the White Russians in the Crimea, reported that 'absolutely all our ciphers are being deciphered by the enemy in consequence of their simplicity'. He singled out the British as one of the main perpetrators. 'All our enemies, particularly England, have all this time been entirely in the know about our internal military operational and diplomatic work,' he added. A week later, the trade delegation was ordered to send correspondence by courier until they received new ciphers.

Within four months of the new ciphers being sent, Fetterlein and his team had broken them.

But despite the codebreakers' successes, the Admiralty saw no reason why it should pay for an organisation that was largely producing diplomatic codes and ciphers and, in 1922, the Foreign Office took charge of GC&CS, moving it to 178 Queen's Gate. A year later it was again put under the control of Admiral Sinclair, who was now the Chief of SIS. The government appeared to have learned nothing from the 1921 leaks that led to the change in Soviet ciphers. When the codebreakers uncovered further evidence of the Russian attempts to subvert the empire in 1923, Curzon used the deciphered telegrams to draft a protest note to the Soviet Government. The 'Curzon Ultimatum' not only quoted the telegrams verbatim, but made absolutely clear that they were intercepts, most of them passing between Moscow and its envoy in Kabul.

These had probably been intercepted and deciphered in India where there was a well-established signals intelligence operation. The leading cryptographer in India at the time was Captain John Tiltman, who was undoubtedly one of the best codebreakers in Britain if not the world. A brilliant man, Tiltman was offered a place at Oxford at the age of 13, but was unable to accept. He subsequently served with the King's Own Scottish Borderers in France during the First World War, where he won the Military Cross. Tiltman joined GC&CS in 1920 and a year later was posted to the small codebreaking section at the Indian Army headquarters at Simla. Composed of at most five people, it not only deciphered the messages, but also garnered intelligence from the locations of the transmitters – which were determined by direction-finding, from the way they operated, and from the routine communications, a process still known today as traffic analysis. 'We were employed almost entirely on one task, to read as currently as possible the Russian diplomatic cipher traffic between Moscow, Kabul in Afghanistan and Tashkent in

Turkestan.' The Indian signals intelligence operation, which was regarded as part of Sinclair's overall organisation and took any Russian traffic it could, including the communications of the OGPU, an early predecessor of the KGB, achieved 'very considerable cryptographic success', according to one military official. The Russian messages were intercepted by outstations at Pishin on the Baluchistan–Afghan border, at Quetta and at Cherat on the North-West Frontier. There were also British Army signals intelligence sites at Baghdad and Sarafand in Palestine which sent their intercepted messages back to GC&CS in London to be deciphered. The number of messages grew to such an extent that more Russian linguists had to be recruited. They included J. E. S. 'Josh' Cooper, who was told that GC&CS was looking for people who spoke Russian through the family of a friend, the novelist Charles Morgan.

'I joined as a Junior Assistant in October 1925. Like many other recruits, I had heard of the job through a personal introduction – advertisement of posts was, at that time, unthinkable. I was one year down from University of London King's College with a first in Russian and had nothing better to do than teach at a preparatory school at Margate. My father was bewailing this at tea with the Morgans one day, and one of Charles's sisters said she had a friend who worked at a place in Queen's Gate where Russian linguists were wanted.' Cooper already knew Fetterlein, having been introduced to him by one of the teaching staff at King's College. 'His experience and reputation were both great, and I was fortunate to find myself assigned to work with him on Soviet diplomatic, which at that time consisted of book ciphers, mostly one part, re-ciphered with a 1,000-group additive key. He took very little notice of me and left it to an army officer who had been attached to GC&CS, Captain [A G] Stuart Smith, to explain the problem and set me to recover some Russian additive key. It took me some time to realise that almost every group had two meanings. After about six weeks work, during which I rubbed holes in the paper with endless corrections, at last I read my first message which was from Moscow to the Soviet representative in Washington and was concerned with repudiation of debts by American states.'

Despite Cooper's problems with the cipher he was put to work on, the amount of Soviet messages continued to increase with the opening of a new Royal Navy intercept site at Flowerdown, near Winchester, and an army site at

Chatham. Sinclair moved both the codebreakers and his SIS staff to a new joint headquarters at 54 Broadway, closer to Whitehall, in 1925. He also added to the intercept facilities by co-opting the resources of a small Metropolitan Police intercept operation, which was run by Harold Kenworthy, an employee of Marconi who was on indefinite loan to the police. Originally set up by Sir Basil Thomson as part of his Directorate of Intelligence, it operated out of the attic at Scotland Yard, employing a number of ex-Naval telegraphists to intercept illicit radio stations.

The Metropolitan Police unit first showed its capabilities during the 1926 General Strike. Although the strike broke out largely for socio-economic reasons, the diplomatic intercepts had shown the Soviet government keen to provoke industrial action and subsidising the striking miners to the tune of two million pounds. The evidence of the BJs and MI5 reports of Soviet espionage centred on the All-Russian Cooperative Society (ARCOS) based in Moorgate, ostensibly set up to facilitate trade between Britain and Russia, infuriated Conservative politicians. Sir William Joynson-Hicks, Home Secretary, put pressure on the more pragmatic Foreign Secretary Sir Austen Chamberlain to back action against Russia. It was the start of a process that would soon lead to a complete diplomatic break with Moscow and disaster for the codebreakers. In 1927, Fetterlein's team, now augmented by Knox, managed to break a crucial set of messages. Over the following weeks, more examples of Soviet espionage were detected and on 12 May the police raided the ARCOS headquarters. The Russians had been warned of the impending raid and removed any real evidence of spying. But the government was now determined to break off all relations with Moscow. In order to justify the move, the Prime Minister Stanley Baldwin and Chamberlain resorted to reading out the deciphered messages in parliament. The Russians immediately changed their ciphers, switching to the one-time pad system (OTP), which if used properly was impossible to break. The codebreakers were horrified. 'HMG found it necessary to compromise our work beyond any question,' recalled Denniston. 'From that time, the Soviet Government introduced OTP for their diplomatic and commercial traffic to all capitals where they had diplomatic representatives.'

But despite the loss of Russian diplomatic material, GC&CS enjoyed success against the communications of the Comintern, the organisation set up in 1919 to promote communism and revolution around the world. It controlled all of the various Communist Parties around the world, each of which formed a so-called 'Section' of the Comintern and was bound to follow its direction. They were also required to set up parallel underground teams controlled by the Comintern to prepare for revolution and carry out espionage. The first sign of illicit transmissions linking the Communist Party of Great Britain to Moscow came in early 1930, when the various intercept units began picking up a large number of unauthorised wireless transmissions between London and Moscow. 'Peacetime GC&CS did · have one experience of successful work on clandestine traffic,' Denniston recalled. 'This, unlike the diplomatic, necessitated close cooperation between interception, T/A [traffic analysis] and cryptography before the final results were made available only to a small select intelligence section of SIS.'

The operation, codenamed Mask, was run by Tiltman, who had returned from India in 1929 with a detailed knowledge of Soviet wireless and cipher practice. 'The analysis of this traffic was studied closely and from it emerged a world-wide network of clandestine stations controlled by a station near Moscow,' Denniston recalled. 'It turned out to be the Comintern network.' The attack on the Comintern ciphers 'met with complete success'. The 'small select' SIS section was Section V, led by Major Valentine Vivian, a former Indian police officer. The Comintern BJs were also discussed with B Branch of MI5, which at the time was responsible for Soviet subversion and espionage. J. C. 'Jack' Curry, who was in charge of MI5 operations against subversion for part of the 1930s, recalled that the messages dealt with a variety of subjects. 'The London/Moscow transmissions were part of a large network with a number of stations in different parts of the world and the material dealt with a variety of the affairs of the Comintern and its sections in different countries. Those from Moscow included directions and instructions regarding the line to be taken in propaganda and in party policy generally. They gave, among other things, details regarding subsidies to be paid by Moscow, a large part being allocated to the *Daily Worker*.' The operation ran until 1937. The bulk of the messages were obscure but nevertheless Vivian managed to extract a great deal of useful intelligence on Comintern finance and organisation, which allowed SIS to recruit agents inside the Comintern in a number of countries. Despite clear friction between SIS and MI5, Curry was full of praise for the 'close and fruitful collaboration' between the two on the Comintern.

Very little attention was given to military or naval communications during the early years of GC&CS, although a naval section was set up in 1925. The Royal Navy had intercept sites at Irton Moor, near Scarborough, and Flowerdown. It also used operators on board Royal Navy ships, who monitored Russian, German and Japanese naval communications. Lieutenant Eric Nave, a Royal Australian Navy officer who had done particularly well on an interpretership course run at the British embassy in Tokyo, was appointed to the China Squadron in 1924 to break Japanese naval codes and ciphers. The Army opened an intercept site at Fort Bridgewoods, Chatham, in 1926 and Tiltman set up a military section in GC&CS in 1930 with five staff based at Broadway Buildings and three in Sarafand. The RAF did not begin intercepting communications until 1927 when a site was set up at Waddington, Lincolnshire, and it was not until 1936 that an air codebreaking section was created in GC&CS with Cooper in charge. Two years later, the RAF intercept site moved from Waddington to Cheadle, in Staffordshire. By now, the codebreakers had their first live target in the shape of the Japanese occupation of China. A Royal Navy intercept station was set up in Hong Kong in 1934 as the threat from Japan to the British empire became more evident. Around the same time, Italian preparations for the 1935 invasion of Abyssinia provided a second live target for the codebreakers.

But by now, they were beginning to realise that the greatest threat to Britain lay in Germany and its new Nazi government. The publicity given to the success of the British codebreakers during the First World War had led Germany and a number of other nations to start using cipher machines, which were seen as more difficult to break. The most famous of these was the Enigma machine. Ironically, during the 1920s, the British army considered buying it. Hugh Foss, a GC&CS machine cipher specialist, was asked to test a commercially available machine, which had been bought by Dilly Knox during a visit to Vienna.

The Enigma machine resembled a small typewriter encased in a wooden box. It had a typewriter-style keyboard, set out in the continental

QWERTZU manner, which differed slightly from the standard British QWERTY keyboard. Above the keyboard, on top of the box, was a lampboard with a series of lights, one for each letter of the alphabet. The operator typed each letter of the plain-text message into the machine. The action of depressing the key sent an electrical current through the machine, which lit up the enciphered letter on the lampboard. There were two crucial features to the machine. A letter could not be enciphered as itself (so the only letter that would not light up on the lampboard if the operator pressed 'A', for example, would be 'A' itself), and the machine was reciprocal, ie if 'A' was enciphered as 'X', 'X' would encipher as 'A'. The encipherment mechanism consisted of three, or on some later models, four wheels or rotors, each having 26 different electrical contacts, one for every letter of the alphabet, on each side. Each contact, or letter, was connected to another on the other side of the rotor. These connections were different for each of the three rotors. The rotors could be set at different positions to allow any one of the 26 contacts to form part of a complete circuit and could also be placed in different orders within the machine to add further difficulties for anyone attempting to break the cipher. The action of depressing each key turned the first rotor one position. When that rotor had moved a set number of times, the second rotor moved round one position, and when the second rotor had turned a certain number of times, the third rotor moved round one position.

The number of different possible settings for the machine was put at several million, giving it what Foss described as a 'high degree of security'. But radio operators use highly predictable formats and phrases in order to ensure that messages can be easily heard even when conditions are bad. Foss said that if bits of the original text, or 'cribs', could be accurately predicted, then the commercial Enigma machine was relatively easy to break. 'If the wiring was known, a crib of fifteen letters would give away the identity and setting of the right-hand wheel,' Foss said. 'If the wiring was unknown, a crib of 180 letters would give away the wiring of the right-hand and middle wheels.' Based on Foss's investigation the British decided not to buy the machine. But the German navy had introduced it in 1926 and two years later the German army began to use it. Within two years, they had introduced a refinement that greatly increased its security. The *Stecker*-board was an old-fashioned telephone-style plugboard, which allowed the operator to introduce an additional encipherment, using cables and jack-plugs to connect pairs of letters: 'A' to 'Y', 'K' to 'T', etc. This made the machine very much more secure, increasing the number of possible settings to 159 million million million and blocking British attempts to read the German systems for around eight years. The Spanish Civil War brought a flood of operational Enigma messages and on 24 April 1937, Dilly Knox managed to break the basic machine supplied by Germany to its Italian and Spanish allies, which did not have the plugboard. Shortly afterwards, assisted by another codebreaker, Tony Kendrick, he began working on the machine with the plugboard which was being used by the Wehrmacht for high-grade communications between Spain and Germany. Two mathematicians, Alan Turing and Peter Twinn, were brought in to help and the British codebreakers managed to make some progress. They had wheel and plug settings for certain days with enciphered messages to go with them. But without a machine in front of them, they were unable to work out the order in which the keys were attached to the machine's various electrical circuits. 'Dilly, who had a taste for inventing fanciful jargon, called this the QWERTZU,' Twinn recalled. 'We had no idea what the order was. We had tried QWERTZU. That didn't work. There are 26 letters in the alphabet. Our ordinary alphabet has them in a certain order but the Germans weren't idiots. When they had the perfect opportunity to introduce a safeguard to their machine by jumbling it up that would be the sensible thing to. After all there were millions of different ways of doing it.'

It was then that the French, and more importantly, the Poles, lent a hand. The British had exchanged information on Russian ciphers with the French *Deuxième Bureau* since 1933. But it was not until 1938 that the two sides began to discuss the Enigma machine in any detail. Given that the exchange on Russian material had been somewhat one-sided, with the British providing far more than they received in return, the French had a surprisingly large amount of material on the Enigma machine. Since the French Enigma reports were sent via the SIS station in Paris and passed on to the codebreakers in the same red-jacketed files the British secret service used for all its reports, they were nicknamed 'Scarlet Pimpernels'. But they were not produced by the

French codebreakers. They came from a *Deuxième Bureau* agent codenamed Asché. Hans Thilo Schmidt worked in the German Defence Ministry's cipher centre. Schmidt's reasons for betraying his country conformed to the time-honoured traditions of the spy. 'He was a playboy,' said Captain Gustav Bertrand, the head of the French codebreaking operation. 'He was fond of money which he needed because he was fonder still of women.' For seven years, the *Deuxième Bureau* provided Schmidt with money and a succession of beautiful women in a number of European capitals. In return, he handed over more than 300 secret documents including instructions for using the Enigma machine, photographs of the plugboard system and a description of how it worked, and a long piece of text in both its original and enciphered forms together with the settings used to encipher it. The Scarlet Pimpernels also suggested that the French were not working alone, Cooper recalled. 'They had not disclosed that they had other SIGINT partners,' he said. 'But a Scarlet Pimpernel on the German Air Force Safety Service traffic had obviously been produced from material intercepted not in France but on the far side of the Reich. It gave data on stations in eastern Germany that were inaudible from Cheadle, but was weak on stations in the north-west that we knew well. Eventually, the French disclosed that they had a liaison with the Poles, and three-sided Anglo-Franco-Polish discussions began on the Enigma problem.'

The first meeting took place in Paris in January 1939 and was attended by Denniston, Knox and Foss. The British codebreakers had high hopes that the meeting with the Polish and French codebreakers would produce the answer. But it was to be a major disappointment. The French codebreakers described their own method of breaking Enigma, which were not even as useful as the system used by Foss to break the basic commercial model. Knox described the latest British system, which was a refinement of the Foss system known as rodding. The Poles, under orders to disclose as little as possible, merely described how lazy operators set the machines in ways that produced pronounceable settings, such as swear words or the names of their girlfriends. Tiltman had long since worked this out and the British were frustrated by the lack of any new information that might help them to progress, Foss recalled. 'Knox kept muttering to Denniston, "But this is what Tiltman did", while Denniston hushed him and told him to listen politely. Knox went and looked out of the window.' But at their next meeting, at the Polish codebreaking headquarters just outside Warsaw, in July 1939, the Poles described how they had completely reconstructed the German Army Enigma machine fitted with the plugboard.

The Polish codebreaking organisation, the *Bureau Szyfrow*, had broken a number of German codes during the early 1920s, but the introduction of Enigma had left it unable to read the Wehrmacht's messages. Like the British, the Polish codebreakers realised that they needed mathematicians to help them break the machine ciphers. They recruited a number of mathematics students and put them through a codebreaking course. Only three passed. Their names were Jerzy Rozycki, Henryk Zygalski and Marian Rejewski. Initially, they were only taken on part-time and it was not until September 1932 that Rejewski, the most brilliant of the codebreakers, was asked to solve the German Army Enigma machine fitted with the plugboard. A few months later, using Enigma key lists given to the French by Asché, he had managed to work out the wiring. The German failure to change their settings on a regular basis during the 1930s meant that by the beginning of 1938, the Polish codebreakers could read 75 per cent of the Poles' intercepts of German Army Enigma messages. In the autumn of 1938, the Poles began to use an electro-mechanical rapid analytical processing machine, known as the *Bomba*, or bomb, because of the ticking noise it made when operating, to help to break messages by identifying repetition of particular features. But in December 1938, the Germans changed the system again, introducing two new rotors. Rejewski managed to reconstruct the wiring of the two new rotors but there were not enough *Bomba* machines to run through the much greater number of possible settings. The Poles desperately needed assistance and believed the British with their long experience of codebreaking dating back to the successes of the First World War could provide it, said Colonel Stefan Mayer, the officer in charge of the *Bureau Szyfrow*. 'As the danger of war became tangibly near we decided to share our achievements regarding Enigma, even not yet complete, with the French and British sides, in the hope that working in three groups would facilitate and accelerate the final conquest of Enigma.'

At a conference held at the headquarters of the *Bureau Szyfrow* , in the Pyry Forest, just outside Warsaw, in July 1939, the Poles explained to the British how they had used the *Bomba* machines and an alternative manual process, the *Netzverfahren*, a system invented by Zygalski, which used lettered sheets of paper with holes punched in them to help to break the keys. Knox was initially furious to discover that the Poles had got there first, sitting in 'stony silence' throughout. But his mood changed completely when the Polish codebreakers told him that the keys were wired up to the encipherment mechanism in alphabetical order, A to A, B to B, etc. Although one female codebreaker at GC&CS had suggested this as a possibility, her proposal was dismissed and never put to the test. 'It was such an obvious thing to do, really a silly thing to do, that nobody, not Dilly Knox or Tony Kendrick or Alan Turing, ever thought it worthwhile trying it,' said Twinn. 'I know in retrospect it looks daft. I can only say that's how it struck all of us and none of the others were idiots. Assuming our stolen message was genuine, what the Poles had told us was quite sufficient for us to start reading the messages. I'm told that after the meeting, Dilly returned to his hotel in a taxi with his French colleague, chanting, "*Nous avons le QWERTZU, nous marchons ensemble.*" I can quite believe it. I wish I had been there.'

A few weeks later, the Poles presented Bertrand with two replicas of Enigma machines they had built, one for the French and one for the British. Bertrand would later describe taking the British copy to London. Having got off of the Golden Arrow London-to-Paris train at Victoria Station, he handed it over on the platform to Colonel Stewart Menzies, then still the Vice-Chief of SIS. Menzies appeared out of a swathe of smoke wearing black tie with the rosette of the Legion d'Honneur in his buttonhole. It was, said Bertrand, a triumphant welcome, '*Accueil Triomphal*'.

Sixteen

The Codebreakers of Bletchley Park

That vast and successful body whose full story will perhaps never be told.
Alastair Denniston, Operational head of the Government Code and Cypher
School, describing Bletchley Park

Britain's codebreakers had made no progress against the main German diplomatic ciphers during the years leading up to the Second World War. But fortunately they were able to read the Japanese Red diplomatic machine cipher, which gave them vital intelligence on German thinking and plans via the dispatches of the Japanese ambassador in Berlin, General Oshima Hiroshi. The messages were sent back to Tokyo on the commercial telex system via the Cable and Wireless relay station on Malta from where copies were passed back to London, 'ostensibly for accounting purposes' but in fact to be handed over to GC&CS.

Shortly before the Munich crisis of September 1938, some of the codebreakers and a number of MI6 sections moved to a newly purchased war station at Bletchley Park, near what is now Milton Keynes in Buckinghamshire. Admiral Sinclair had bought Bletchley Park in the spring of 1938 as a 'War Station' for both MI6 and GC&CS, acting entirely on his own initiative. Having realised that, if it came to war, he would need to protect his staff from the inevitable air raids, he had asked the Foreign Office to pay for the new station. Its response was that the War Office was responsible for war, the generals should pay. The generals told Sinclair that as a former director of naval intelligence he should go to the admirals, who told him he was part of the Foreign Office and the mandarins should pay. Frustrated by his inability to get anyone to pay the £7,500 asking price, Sinclair dipped into his own pocket to buy it. 'We know he paid for it,' said one former MI6 officer. 'We're not sure if he was ever repaid. He died soon afterwards so he probably wasn't.' The park itself was given the covername 'Station X', not, as might be assumed, a symbol of mystery but simply the tenth of a large number of sites eventually acquired by MI6 for its various wartime operations and designated using Roman numerals. Sinclair put a Captain Ridley RN, one of the MI6 officers, in charge of the move to Bletchley and those involved were dubbed Captain Ridley's Shooting Party. 'MI6 provided some cars for transport, but many people used their own cars and gave lifts to others,' Josh Cooper recalled. 'It fell to my lot to be driven in by Knox who had a remarkable theory that the best way to avoid accidents was to take every cross-road at maximum speed.' The Broadway tradition of living well was to be maintained during the rehearsal. Sinclair called in his favourite chef from the Savoy Grill and the staff ate haute cuisine. Shortly afterwards, Chamberlain returned from his meeting in Munich with Hitler proclaiming 'peace in our time', Cooper recalled. 'We all trooped back to London with mixed feelings of shame and relief.'

Denniston, who realised that the elderly classicists who made up the bulk of his codebreakers would not on their own cope with the new tasks, spent the months before the war touring the universities looking for mathematicians and linguists needed to break the German Enigma cipher. 'He dined at several High Tables in Oxford and Cambridge and came home with promises from a number of dons to attend a "territorial training course", Cooper recalled. 'It would be hard to exaggerate the importance of this course for the future development of GC&CS. Not only had Denniston brought in scholars of the humanities, of the type of many of his own permanent staff, but he had also invited mathematicians of a somewhat different type who were specially attracted by the Enigma problem. I have heard some cynics on the permanent staff scoffing at this. They did not realise that Denniston, for all his diminutive stature, was a bigger man than they.'

The academics who attended the course were made to sign the Official Secrets Act and told that on receipt of a telegram they should report to Bletchley Park, where they would be paid £600 a year with the remainder of their former salaries being made up by their colleges. On 23 August 1939, Russia signed a non-aggression pact with Germany and it became clear that war was inevitable. Telegrams were sent out calling the dons to Bletchley Park to help to solve 'the Enigma problem'. Nigel de Grey later recalled how in the first few weeks of the war, the academics recruited by Denniston 'began to drop in with the slightly unexpected effect of carrier pigeons'. They found the staff of GC&CS completely unruffled by the commencement of hostilities. At lunchtime, most of the codebreakers would troop out onto the lawn in front of the house to play rounders. 'We had a tennis ball and somebody managed to commandeer an old broom handle, drilled a hole in it and put a leather strap in it,' recalled Barbara Eachus, one of the GC&CS support staff. 'It was all we had, things were getting a bit tough to get. If it was a fine day, we'd all say rounders at 1 o'clock; we'd all go out and play, just to sort of let off steam. Everybody argued about the rules and the dons just laid them down, in Latin sometimes. We used trees as bases. "He got past the deciduous," one would say. "No he didn't," another would argue. "He was still between the conifer and the deciduous." That was the way they were.'

Initially, all the codebreakers were crowded into the mansion, with the exception of Knox and his small team of mathematicians, Turing, Twinn and John Jeffreys, who were working on the Enigma traffic in an adjoining cottage. But a number of wooden pre-fabricated huts were erected in the grounds and a neighbouring school was taken over to house the commercial and diplomatic sections. Soon the various sections began to move out of the mansion into the newly constructed buildings, adopting the name of the hut they were in as their section title.

Bletchley Park's first break into Enigma traffic occurred in December 1939 when Turing managed to break five days of pre-war German Navy Enigma. But despite the Polish assistance, the codebreakers were unable to break any wartime Enigma. So in January 1940, Turing was sent to see the Poles – who had now moved to the French Army codebreaking base at the Château de Vignolles, in Gretz-Armainvillers, near Paris – to find out what they were doing wrong. He discovered that there had been a mix-up in the detail of the wiring on the rotors. Turing took with him a large number of newly made Zygalski perforated sheets, which allowed the Poles to make the first break into wartime Enigma traffic on 17 January 1940, when they read the cipher used for communications between the *Wehrmacht*'s military districts or *Wehrkreise* inside Germany.

The operation at Bletchley Park to break Enigma was now undergoing a major reorganisation. Gordon Welchman, one of the new mathematicians brought in by Denniston, had realised that the codebreakers would be in a unique position to produce intelligence on the German order of battle but would need a much better structured organisation if they were to do so efficiently. They would also need far more contact with the armed forces' wireless operators intercepting the messages. This represented a major revolution in the British signals intelligence operation. 'GC&CS had always tended to take too little interest in the radio by which they lived,' Cooper recalled. Similarly the three services had been dismissive of the work of the codebreakers. They believed their intercept operations, known as Y Services, produced sufficient intelligence simply by analysing the activities of the radio networks they were monitoring – indeed the new RAF site at Cheadle was completely ignoring the Enigma traffic. When Cooper suggested that it should begin taking Enigma, the head of the RAF intercept operation replied: 'My Y Service exists to produce intelligence, not to provide stuff for people at Bletchley to fool about with.' Welchman was given the go-ahead to set up the new system and began his own recruitment drive. He brought in a number of leading mathematicians to work in his new codebreaking section, which was to be housed in one of the new pre-fabricated buildings, Hut 6. Stuart Milner-Barry, the chess correspondent of *The Times* and a fellow student of Welchman's at Trinity College, Cambridge, was one of the first to join Hut 6. When war broke out, he had been in Argentina, playing chess for Britain, along with his friends Hugh Alexander and Harry Golombek. They too were recruited as codebreakers, as were Dennis Babbage, from Magdalene College, Cambridge; John Herivel, a former student of Welchman's; and Howard Smith, like Welchman from Sydney Sussex College, Cambridge, and later the head of MI5.

The organisation of Hut 6 reflected Welchman's vision of a totally integrated interception organisation. At one end of what would eventually become something of a production line was Bletchley Park Control, which was manned 24 hours a day and in constant touch with the intercept sites to ensure that their coverage of radio frequencies and networks was co-ordinated and that as little as possible was missed. Where an important station was difficult to hear, it was to be 'double-banked', taken by two different operators, normally at different stations, so that the chances of picking up a false letter that might throw a spanner into the works were cut down. There were two main intercept sites abroad: the Far East Combined Bureau, which moved from Hong Kong to Singapore on the same day that GC&CS moved to Bletchley Park, and the Combined Bureau Middle East, set up in Cairo in the summer of 1939. Both carried out traffic analysis, codebreaking and intelligence reporting, sending any messages they could not break to Bletchley. The main pre-war intercept sites in the UK were the two Royal Navy sites at Scarborough and Winchester; the Army site at Fort Bridgewoods, Chatham; the new RAF site at Cheadle; and the Metropolitan Police site at Denmark Hill, south London. In the months leading up to the war, the Post Office built a number of other intercept sites for diplomatic traffic to allow the armed forces to concentrate on military and naval traffic. One of these, at Sandridge, near St Albans, was already in place working directly under the control of Bletchley Park. The messages arrived from these British outstations by motorcycle courier. But 'Traffic Registers' giving the preambles and first six groups of the messages intercepted by the outstations were sent by teleprinter to the Hut 6 Registration Room. Here a number of female graduates recruited from Newnham College, Cambridge, where Milner-Barry's sister had been vice-principal, tried to establish the specific Enigma cipher in use from the preambles, carefully examining them to see if there was any intelligence that could be garnered before the codebreakers got to work. A description of each message, containing the frequency and callsigns, the message number, whether or not it was urgent, and the first two groups, was carefully logged on so-called B-Lists, a contraction of Banister Lists, named after Michael Banister, the codebreaker who designed them. These became known colloquially as Blists and the female graduates were dubbed 'Blisters'.

Early Hut 6 attempts to break into the keys for the Army and Air Force Enigma ciphers centred on the sheet-stacking room, where codebreakers used Zygalski grid sheets to try to break the key in the same way as the Poles. Once a key was broken, the messages were passed to the Machine Room, which contained a number of British Typex cipher machines, modified to act like Enigma machines. Here they were deciphered. 'When the codebreakers had broken the code they wouldn't sit down themselves and painstakingly decode 500 messages,' said Peter Twinn. 'I've never myself personally decoded a message from start to finish. By the time you've done the first 20 letters and it was obviously speaking perfectly sensible German, for people like me that was the end of our interest.' Diana Russell Clarke was one of a group of young women in the Hut 6 Machine Room, deciphering the messages. 'The cryptographers would work out the actual settings for the machines for the day,' she said. 'We had these Typex machines, like typewriters but much bigger. They had three wheels, I think on the left-hand side, all of which had different positions on them. When they got the setting, we were to set them up on our machines. We would have a piece of paper in front of us with what had come over the wireless. We would type it into the machine and hopefully what we typed would come out in German.'

Once the message had been deciphered it had to be passed on to someone who could make use of it. Since there had been no deciphered Enigma messages to pass on, no system was in place to do this. So a team of what was initially four intelligence officers was set up in Hut 3, an L-shaped building which nestled behind Hut 6. Their task was to use their knowledge of German to work out what should have been in the numerous gaps in the messages. They then had to translate them, transform them into a disguised format, that of a typical agent report in order to hide the fact that the British were breaking Enigma, and send them on to MI6 for distribution. The original Hut 3 was made up of one officer from each of the three services and F L Lucas, a Fellow of King's College, Cambridge, and author of *The Decline and Fall of the Romantic Ideal*.

When Turing returned from France, he used the correct data about the rotor wiring to lead a successful attack on a recent day's *Wehrkreise* Enigma, known in Hut 6 as the Green. The Enigma ciphers were initially named after colours from the different coloured crayons used to distinquish between them. But the deciphered messages contained little intelligence for Hut 3 to report. 'On a snowy January morning in 1940, in a small bleak wooden room with nothing but a table and three chairs, the first bundle of Enigma decodes appeared,' Lucas said. 'The four of us who then constituted Hut 3 had no idea what they were about to disclose. Something fairly straightforward like

German Police, or something more like diplomatic – neat and explicit documents straight from the office-tables of the Führer and the *Wehrmacht* that would simply need translating and forwarding to ministries? They were neither. In after-years, even the *Führer*'s orders were duly to appear. But meanwhile here lay a pile of dull, disjointed, and enigmatic scraps. All about the weather, or the petty affairs of a *Luftwaffe* headquarters no-one had heard of, or trifles of *Wehrkreis* business; the whole sprinkled with terms no dictionary knew, and abbreviations of which our only guide, a small War Office list, proved often completely innocent. Very small beer, in fact, and full of foreign bodies.'

Shortly afterwards, Hut 6 broke a second Enigma cipher, the Red, a *Luftwaffe* cipher used for liaison with the German Army. This would prove to be an important break. The Red was to become the most productive of the Enigma ciphers and Hut 6's staple diet throughout the war. But in the first few months of 1940, with little activity taking place, it could be broken only sporadically. The easiest Enigma cipher to break was the so-called Yellow cipher used for the invasion of Denmark and Norway, largely because of the sheer amount of traffic produced by the invading German forces. Although there was little that Bletchley could do to help the British and Norwegian troops, this provided a useful test of the codebreakers' new organisation. The four-man Hut 3 was totally overwhelmed by the amount of material and rapidly expanded. Until now, all the reports had been bagged up at the end of the day and sent by van to MI6 headquarters in Broadway, from where they were passed on to the War Office, Air Ministry and the Admiralty. This was clearly no longer sufficient and teleprinters were put into Hut 3 allowing direct contact with MI6. Each Hut 3 watch consisted of four intelligence officers, a Watch No 1 and three others, together with a number of typists and clerical assistants. 'Hut 3 and Hut 6 were side by side,' said Ralph Bennett, one of the watch intelligence reporters. 'They were linked by a small square wooden tunnel through which a pile of currently available decodes were pushed, as I remember by a broom handle, in a cardboard box, so primitive were things in those days.'

But on 1 May 1940, a major change in the way the settings were produced left Hut 6 unable to break the Red, which was already seen as the most productive of the different types of Enigma. It was used by countless *Luftwaffe* units and, because they needed to liaise closely with the army in order to provide them with air support, gave a good overall picture of all major German plans and operations. It was vital that the codebreakers managed to read it. John Herivel came up with an answer. By imagining how the cipher clerks operating the Enigma machines might work, he realised that they would probably be too lazy or too pushed for time and too confident in the machine's security to change the rotor settings properly at the beginning of a new message. So at the start of the day, it was likely that they would be close to the day's settings, Herivel said. 'By analysing all the different stations' first messages of the day we might be able to narrow down the 17,576 possible ring settings to a manageable number, say twenty or thirty, and simply test these one after the other in the hope of hitting on the right answer.' By the end of May, the Herivel tip had worked and Hut 6 never lost the Red again. 'From this point on it was broken daily, usually on the day in question and early in the day,' recalled Peter Calvocoressi, one of the new members of Hut 3. 'Later in the war, I remember that we in Hut 3 used to get a bit tetchy if Hut 6 had not broken Red by breakfast time.'

The codebreakers ability to break Enigma ciphers was enhanced immeasurably by the introduction of the bombe. This was a fast-running electrical machine invented in the second half of 1939 by Alan Turing to use 'cribs' to break Enigma messages. Despite the similarity in names, the British machine bore little resemblance to the Polish *Bomba* and was much more capable of breaking the Enigma settings. It was built to Turing's specification by Harold 'Doc' Keen, the chief engineer of the British Tabulating Machine Company in Letchworth. The bombe was encased in a bronze cabinet the size of a large wardrobe. It initially contained a series of 30 rotating drums equating to the wheels of ten Enigma machines, although later versions simulated the action of 12 machines. The bombe was designed to run through all the various possibilities of rotor settings at high speed in order to see if a 'crib', a likely piece of plain text, appeared in the message. The codebreakers provided the operators, mostly Wrens, with a 'menu' suggesting possible matches of clear letters to enciphered letters, which was fed into the bombe. Each time the machine found a possible match, it was quickly tested on a replica Enigma machine to see if it produced German text. If it did, it was passed back for decryption. The first bombe, christened Victory, was installed in March 1940 in part of Hut 1, the other end of the hut being the station sick bay. For five months, it was effectively on trial, attempting to break Naval Enigma. In early August, a second more sophisticated bombe, known as Agnus Dei, commonly corrupted to Agnes, was added providing assistance to both Hut 6 and a small Enigma research section set up in the Naval Section Hut 4. Initially comprising just Turing and Twinn, this research section would become Hut 8, the naval equivalent of Hut 6.

Despite his early intervention into army Enigma, Turing had concentrated on the much more difficult naval Enigma from the start 'because I could have it to myself'. Naval Enigma had a much more complicated system of settings or keys and the lack of vital continuity made breaking the daily settings even more difficult. But in mid-1940, thanks to the capture, or 'pinch' as it was known among the codebreakers, of two of the new rotors, Turing managed to solve six days of Dolphin, the German Navy Home Waters Enigma, from April 1940. In November, after another pinch had given the codebreakers a full set of naval rotors, Hugh Foss managed to break the keys for 8 May and the keys for 7 May followed shortly afterwards. The newly created Hut 8 enjoyed sporadic breakthroughs over the next six months. It was helped substantially by further 'pinches' and the discovery that some Dolphin messages were also being sent using an easily read hand cipher. The various pinches and the messages sent in both ciphers gave them the continuity they needed and, with the assistance of the bombes they managed from August 1941 to continue to break Dolphin until the end of the war.

Hut 8 passed the deciphered messages on to Hut 4's Z Watch, the naval equivalent of Hut 3, which sent them to the Admiralty's Operational Intelligence Centre (OIC) by teleprinter. The breaking of Dolphin allowed the OIC to re-route the convoys bringing supplies across the Atlantic away from the German U-boats. The results were dramatic, although they cannot all be put down to the work of the codebreakers. Between March and June 1941, the U-Boats had sunk 282,000 tons of shipping a month. From July, the figure dropped to 120,000 tons a month and by November, when the wolf packs were temporarily withdrawn from the Atlantic, to 62,000 tons.

The first campaign which showed the potential of the Red Enigma to provide a comprehensive intelligence picture of what the Germans were doing was the occupation of the Balkans in the spring of 1941. This was a moment of particular triumph for Knox and the small team of female codebreakers who worked alongside him in the Enigma research section. Alerted by the codebreakers, the Royal Navy's Mediterranean Fleet, under Admiral Andrew Cunningham, crushed its Italian counterpart, sinking three heavy cruisers and two destroyers at the Battle of Matapan, off the southern tip of Greece, in March 1941. Mavis Batey was one of Knox's assistants. 'The first Matapan message was very dramatic stuff: "Today's the day minus three", just that and nothing else,' she said. 'So of course we knew the Italian Navy was going to do something in three days' time. Why they had to say that I can't imagine. It seems rather daft but they did. So we worked for three days. It was all the nail-biting stuff of keeping up all night working. One kept thinking: "Well would one be better at it if one had a little sleep or shall we just go on," and it did take nearly all of three days. Then a very, very large message came in, which was practically the battle orders for what turned into the Battle of Matapan. How many cruisers there were, and how many submarines were to be there and where they were to be at such and such a time, absolutely incredible that they should spell it all out. It was rushed out to Cunningham. It was very exciting stuff. There was a great deal of jubilation in the cottage and then Cunningham himself came to visit us. The first thing he wanted to do when he came was to see the actual message that had been broken. I think we had a drink and we were in this little cottage and the walls had just been whitewashed. Now this just shows how silly and young and giggly we were. We thought it would be jolly funny if we could talk to Admiral Cunningham and get him to lean against the wet whitewash and go away with a white stern. So that's what we did. It's rather terrible isn't it. On the one hand, everything was so very organised and on the other these silly young things are trying to snare the admiral.'

A direct 'Special Signals Link' was set up between Bletchley Park and Cairo in early 1941 to feed the Most Secret Source intelligence to the British forces in the Middle East and it was extended to the British headquarters in Athens shortly before the German invasion of the Balkans. The Red *Luftwaffe* key provided comprehensive details of the discussions of the German

Fliegerverbindungsoffiziere or *Flivos*, the air liaison officers who co-ordinated air and ground operations, and although this had to be passed on in a highly sanitised fashion, it ensured that the British could make an orderly retreat. It also gave early warning that German airborne forces were about to attack Crete. A series of messages beginning in late March provided the British with every detail of the operation, from the preparations to the complete plan of the airborne assault, and the day, 20 May 1941, on which it was to be launched. The problem was to find a plausible way of camouflaging the source of all this intelligence so as to ensure the Germans did not realise that Enigma had been broken.

On Churchill's orders, Josh Cooper's Air Section produced a detailed report purporting to be a complete dossier of the German plans obtained by an MI6 agent inside the German GHQ in Athens. This was sent to General Bernard Freyburg, the New Zealand Commander in Crete. Although he did not have the resources to fight off a sustained attack, the knowledge garnered from the 'German documents' robbed the Germans of any element of surprise – Freyburg allegedly looked at his watch when the German paradrop began and said: 'Right on time'. Alerted by the codebreakers, his men were able to pick off the enemy paratroopers at will, causing carnage and considerably delaying, although not preventing, the defeat. 'Crete was an example of how knowing a great deal, through the Red, didn't necessarily lead to the correct results,' said John Herivel. 'All the German plans, the details for the invasion of Crete were known through Hut 6 decodes on the Red and therefore we felt very confident that we would defeat it. But in fact we didn't. What did happen was that they had such enormous difficulty in taking Crete and suffered such enormous losses that Hitler decided he wouldn't try a parachute descent in that strength again.'

Throughout the Balkan campaign, railway Enigma had been indicating a series of troop movements heading north and east towards Poland. Hut 3 began reporting that Hitler appeared to be ready to attack the Soviet Union. But it was not until 10 June, when the Japanese diplomatic section translated a message to Tokyo from the Japanese ambassador in Berlin confirming that the invasion was imminent, that Whitehall finally accepted the codebreakers had got it right. Twelve days later, Hitler launched Operation Barbarossa, the invasion of the Soviet Union. It was to bring some of the most distressing decrypts the codebreakers had to handle.

Some of the messages of the SS and the *Ordnungspolizei*, the German police who were mopping up behind the German lines during Operation Barbarossa, made chilling reading, providing details of the systematic murder by the advancing German forces of thousands of Jews. On 18 July 1941 Erich von dem Bach-Zelewski, commander of the SS and police troops in the Soviet republic of Belorussia, informed Kurt Daluege, head of the *Ordnungspolizei* and Heinrich Himmler, the *Reichsführer-SS*, that 'in yesterday's mopping-up operations in Slonim, carried out by Police Regiment Centre, 1,153 Jewish plunderers were shot.' Three weeks later, he reported that his men had already killed 30,000 'partisans and Jewish bolsheviks'.

On the same day, the SS Cavalry Brigade based in the Minsk area of Belorussia reported having carried out 7,819 executions to date. Friederich Jeckeln, commander of the SS and police troops in the Ukraine, told Daluege and Himmler that on 27 August 27 'the Special Action Staff with *Ordnungspolizei* Battalion 320 shot 4,200 Jews near the town of Kamenets-Podolsk'. In the last week of August alone, 12,361 Ukrainian Jews were murdered, most of them by the police rather than the SS. On 1 September Jeckeln reported that the same battalion had executed a further 2,200 Jews. A month later, he said his men had 'disposed of 1,255 Jews, according to the usage of war' near the town of Ovruch.

The messages left little doubt as to what was going on. The killings that followed the invasion of the Soviet Union are now recognised as the beginning of the Holocaust. By August 1941, Churchill had become so enraged over the evidence of systematic extermination provided by the police hand cipher that he issued an angry warning to the Germans. The British Prime Minister publicly denounced the 'scores of thousands of executions in cold blood' committed by the German police and SS forces. 'Since the Mongol invasions of Europe in the 16th century, there has never been methodical, merciless butchery on such a scale, or approaching such a scale,' he said. 'We are in the presence of a crime without a name.'

He was taking a gamble that the Germans would assume that their hand cipher was broken rather than the Orange Enigma, which the British had also broken. It was a high-risk decision, which put the Bletchley secret at threat and disproves claims of a British cover-up. Churchill's speech could have completely cut off access to his Most Secret Source, almost certainly lengthening the course of the war. A few weeks after Churchill's speech, Daluege warned his commanders that the British might be listening and told them to send details of all future 'executions' to Berlin by courier. Far from covering the massacres up, the British appointed two officials, one inside Bletchley Park and one in the Foreign Office, to collect evidence of the German atrocities for Commission for the Investigation of War Crimes.

By the autumn of 1941, so many messages were being intercepted and deciphered that the intelligence they produced was given a special codename Ultra, which followed the Most Secret classification at the top and bottom of each message. This not only helped to improve the recipients' confidence in the material they were receiving, it ensured that they knew that the intelligence they had in their hands had to be protected at all costs. Bletchley Park was at the centre of a wide network of intercept stations. Two more post office sites had opened at Cupar and Brora in Scotland and Whitchurch in Shropshire to relieve the military sites of the job of intercepting commercial and diplomatic messages. Another two RAF intercept sites were operating at Chicksands Priory, near Bedford, and West Kingsdown in Kent, the latter having played a key role during the Battle of Britain in warning of approaching German bombers. The military intercept site at Fort Bridgewoods, Chatham, had been badly damaged by bombing during the winter. The army operators moved initially to Chicksands to form a joint RAF and military station before opening up a new station, under the title Special Y Group, at Beaumanor, south of Loughborough, Leicestershire, in October 1941. The bombe section had expanded, moving to Hut 11 and setting up outstations at Wavendon Manor, and Adstock. Three more bombe outstations would be established during the war at Gayhurst, Stanmore and Eastcote. But the codebreakers were frustrated by their inability to obtain the resources they needed, particularly in terms of manpower. With very few people aware of what was going on at Bletchley, the services were reluctant to release valuable new recruits to work there. On 21 October 1941, four of the leading codebreakers, Turing, Welchman, Milner-Barry, and Hugh Alexander, wrote to Churchill, who had recently visited Bletchley, pleading with him to help them obtain more staff. They were careful to emphasise that the problem lay with the civil servants in Whitehall. 'They seem not to understand the importance of what is being done here or the urgent necessity of dealing promptly with requests,' they wrote. 'If we are to do our job as well as it could and should be done, it is absolutely vital that our wants, small as they are, should be promptly attended to.' Churchill famously sent a memo to General Hastings Ismay, his Chief of Staff, saying: 'Make sure they have all they want extreme priority and report to me that this has been done.' At the top of the memo were the words 'Action this day'.

A few months later, Denniston was moved sideways to take charge of diplomatic and commercial codebreaking, all of which now moved to Berkeley Street, London, and Commander Edward Travis was placed in charge of military codebreaking, which remained at Bletchley. The codebreakers played a major role in the North African campaign from July 1941 onwards due to the breaking, by Hut 4, of an Italian navy machine cipher, the Hagelin C38m. This carried details of the convoys taking supplies to General Erwin Rommel's Afrika Korps, which together with German messages sent in an Enigma cipher broken in Hut 6, provided all the information the Royal Navy need to attack and destroy the convoys, crippling Rommel's supply lines. Hut 6 was able to read a number of Enigma keys used by the German forces in north Africa and mobile SIGINT units also provided valuable assistance to the British commanders. By July 1942, with Ultra now totally in the ascendant, Churchill decided to replace the British Commander-in-Chief Middle-East, Claude Auchinleck, with General Harold Alexander and bring in General Bernard Montgomery as commander of the Eighth Army.

Within days of his arrival, Montgomery was the beneficiary of a major piece of Ultra intelligence that was to change the military's view of the codebreakers. On 15 August Rommel explained to Hitler what he planned to do next. They were carried on part of their route back to Berlin via the Red cipher, which Hut 6 had no problems reading. Two days earlier, Montgomery had outlined what he believed the Desert Fox would do. It matched the signal sent to Hitler almost to the letter. Rommel intended to attack around the time of the full moon due towards the end of August, swinging south around the end of the British lines before striking north to come up behind the Eighth Army, cutting it off from Cairo. But to do so he would have to cross a major obstacle, the Alam Halfa ridge. Two other new developments at Bletchley Park also helped Montgomery. Hut 3 had just started receiving reports deciphered from the Chaffinch cipher, giving a complete breakdown of the fighting strengths of the Afrika Korps and comprehensive returns on the availability of tanks.

Throughout the second half of August, the RAF and the Royal Navy redoubled their attacks on the Axis convoys. Meanwhile, the codebreakers were able to monitor a series of high-level exchanges between the German commanders, revealing that Rommel and his immediate superior Field Marshal Albrecht Kesselring were barely on speaking terms. They also revealed that the Desert Fox was unwell. Then came the approval, first by Hitler and later by Mussolini, of Rommel's plans. Bletchley and Cairo were also able to chart the regrouping of the German forces in readiness for the attempt to outflank the Eighth Army as well the problems caused by the non-arrival of supply ships. Montgomery had briefed his troops on what Rommel was about to do. Everything happened according to plan, boosting the morale of his men and paving the way for victory. After finding his way through the Alam Halfa ridge blocked, Rommel was forced to retreat for lack of fuel. From then on, Ultra played a major part in Montgomery's plans. It did not play a direct part in the Battle of El Alamein. But its indirect contribution was immense. Montgomery knew from the Bletchley and Cairo decodes exactly how many troops and tanks he faced, while the sinking of the supply ships, 50,000 tons in October alone, nearly half of the cargo which left Italy for north Africa, had a crucial influence on the Afrika Korps' ability to resist. So tight were its margins of supply that the sinking of an Axis convoy during the battle itself had a direct influence on the fighting. On the afternoon of 2 November, with Montgomery having punched two holes in the Panzer Army's defences and about to force his way through, Bletchley deciphered a message from Rommel to Hitler asking permission to withdraw. '*Panzerarmee ist erschopft,*' he said. The Panzer Army was 'exhausted' and had precious little fuel left. The response from Hitler was that Rommel should stand his ground at all costs. He was to 'show no other road to his troops than the road leading to death or victory.' But in the face of far superior troops, and with only 11 tanks left, he was forced to retreat. It was the turning point for the generals' recognition of the usefulness of Ultra.

The Navy was already relying on its interception of Dolphin and the U-boat Enigma, codenamed Shark, to redirect the Atlantic convoys around the wolf packs. But in February 1942, the U-boats began using a new four-rotor Enigma system. It began a ten-month period known at Bletchley as 'the Shark Blackout'. For the first half of 1942, the wolf packs concentrated on sinking undefended merchant ships off the US eastern seaboard. But when they returned to the Atlantic in August 1942 they ran riot, sinking 43 ships in August and September alone. October and November brought no relief and the Admiralty began to step up the pressure on Hut 8. In a tersely written memorandum, it urged Hut 8 to pay 'a little more attention' to the U-boat cipher and complained that the Battle of the Atlantic was the only area of the war in which the codebreakers were having no influence. But the solution to the problem was almost in place. Two days after the Admiralty memorandum, a pinch of two German 'short signal' codebooks arrived at Bletchley, providing new cribs for the U-boat messages. The books had been recovered from the U-559, which had been attacked by the British destroyer HMS *Petard* off the Egyptian coast. Lieutenant Anthony Fasson and Able Seaman Colin Grazier swam to the submarine before it sank and managed to recover its signal documents. They were joined by the 16-year-old Naafi-boy Tommy Brown. He succeeded in getting out with the codebooks. But Fasson and Grazier went down with the submarine. They were both awarded the George Cross posthumously. Brown received the George Medal. The honours were well deserved. The short weather messages were to provide the way into Shark. In order to allow the U-boats to receive messages from the weather ships, which only had the three-rotor machine, the four-rotor machine also had the capacity to operate like a three-rotor machine. This gave Hut 8 a way in and on 12 December 1942, using the short weather signals as cribs, they broke Shark. Within hours, the Atlantic convoys were being re-routed around the Wolf Packs. It was still far from easy but any remaining problems were solved by the introduction into service of superior US bombes in September 1943.

By now Hut 6 was already preparing for D-Day. It had broken a large number of army and air force Enigma systems that had provided vital intelligence during the campaigns in north Africa, in the Balkans and on the Italian and Eastern Fronts. But its staple diet remained the Red *Luftwaffe* air liaison system. This was so rich in detail on Air Force operations that it shaped the direction of Bletchley Park's attacks on the German teleprinter ciphers, known collectively by the codename Fish. The easy availability of intelligence about *Luftwaffe* operations culled from Enigma led to the decision to concentrate on Tunny, the German Army's SZ40 Lorenz teleprinter cipher machine, at the expense of Sturgeon, the Siemens and Halske T52 machines that were mostly used by the German air force. Tunny provided details of the high-level German discussions in the run-up to D-Day but it also had a highly significant side-effect in the construction of the Colossus computer that was used to break the Tunny messages. Colossus, which was built by Tommy Flowers, a Post Office engineer, on principles laid down by Turing and Max Newman, was the world's first semi-programmable electronic digital computer.

Although Bletchley Park provided a running commentary on German intentions and activities during the allied invasion of Europe and the advance towards Berlin, its biggest contribution, possibly of the whole war and certainly to the D-Day operations was the Double Cross system. The messages being passed on the German intelligence networks confirmed that the Germans believed every detail of the Allied deception plan. Without it, the Allies would almost certainly have been thrown back into the sea. The key codebreaking role in this regard was the breaking of the German military intelligence or *Abwehr* Enigma in December 1941 by Dilly Knox, who was then already terminally ill from cancer. He died just over a year later in February 1943.

Bletchley Park did not just break German and Italian codes and ciphers. It also worked on those of a large number of other states, including Romania, Spain, Vichy France, Bulgaria, Yugoslavia, China, and of course Japan. Britain's contribution here is greater than sometimes imagined. The main Japanese naval code JN25, introduced in June 1939, was broken by John Tiltman within weeks of its appearance. Details were sent to the Far East Combined Bureau, which by May 1940 had enough codegroups recovered to read simple messages. From early 1941, months before the Japanese attack on Pearl Harbor, the British and Americans began sharing their progress on a range of Axis codes and ciphers, including JN25 and other Japanese codes and ciphers. Although the British were further ahead on JN25 and Japanese army codes at this time, the US Army had broken the new Japanese diplomatic machine cipher, codenamed Purple and supplied the British with a Purple machine which allowed them to continue to read Oshima's informative dispatches from Berlin. When Malaya was attacked, the FECB's Royal Navy codebreakers moved first to Colombo and later to Mombasa in Kenya before returning to Colombo as the fortunes of war fluctuated. The army and RAF codebreakers went to Delhi, with outstations in Abbottabad, Calcutta, Comilla, and Bangalore. The Japanese codes and ciphers were also broken at Bletchley Park, where Tiltman made the initial breaks into the Japanese Military Attaché cipher and the Army Air Force General Code. The British codebreakers made the first breaks of all the main wartime Japanese codes and ciphers with the exception of Purple, the Japanese Naval Attaché cipher, which was a joint effort between Hugh Alexander and the US naval codebreaker Frank Raven, and the Army Water Transport Code, which was broken simultaneously in Delhi and at a US Army unit in Brisbane, Australia. Co-operation with the US Army, which also worked on the Japanese military codes at its main headquarters at Arlington Hall, Virginia, was exceptionally good. But the relationship with the US Navy, whose main sites were in Washington, Melbourne and Pearl Harbor, was not such a happy one. The Americans may not have made many initial break-ins to the Japanese codes but they were much better at using tabulating punched card machinery to exploit them. A combination of a lack of British expertise in this area, repeated changes in the JN25 codebook, and co-operation problems, caused largely by the personalities in Washington, and Melbourne, threatened to stop all exchanges on the Japanese naval side and put back the British attacks on JN25. But fortunately the conflict was resolved by early 1944.

Although the first part of the Battle of the Atlantic and the war in north Africa are clear examples of how Ultra had a tangible effect on the war, it is difficult to quantify the overall difference it made. But Sir Harry Hinsley, who was not only a leading naval intelligence analyst at Bletchley Park but was also the main author of the history of British wartime intelligence, believed that it cut the length of the war by about three years. It would, for instance, have been impossible without Ultra to launch the D-Day landings in 1944, he said. 'Operation Overlord would certainly not have been launched at that time without Ultra. Or at least, if it had been launched, it would probably not have been successful.' It was still possible that the Russians might have gone on to capture Berlin in 1945 or that Britain might have been so badly hit by Hitler's V-bombs that the Allies responded by using the atomic bomb, he added. 'But my own belief is that the war, instead of finishing in 1945, would have ended in 1948 had GC&CS not been able to read the Enigma ciphers and produce the Ultra intelligence.'

Seventeen

Signals Intelligence
and the early Cold War

We all have our prejudices and radio men are one of mine.
George Smiley in John le Carré's *Tinker, Tailor, Soldier, Spy*

At the start of the Second World War, the British were intercepting a great deal of enciphered or encoded Soviet military messages. This was bolstered by relationships between GC&CS and its Finnish, Estonian and French counterparts. The French had their own links with the Lithuanians and the Latvians and passed material obtained from them onto the British. Tiltman was in charge of the anti-Soviet operations and a Russian military codebreaking unit was set up at Wavendon Manor, another country house close to Bletchley. There was also a Russian section covering the southern Soviet Union at the Sarafand outstation in Palestine.

But the crucial breakthrough on Russian armed forces material came in the north during the Russo-Finnish War in late 1939 and early 1940. The large amount of traffic created by the Russian army's invasion of Finland, and the Finns' determined defence of their territory, gave the codebreakers enough depth to solve at least one five-figure high-grade Soviet military cipher. They also broke a number of Soviet navy codes, fully reconstructing the codebooks in at least two of these cases. It was during this period that Tiltman negotiated an extremely useful co-operation deal with the Finnish codebreaking unit under which the British provided equipment in return for the highly advanced results obtained by the Finns. Unfortunately, there were immediate complications. No sooner had Tiltman returned to England than the Russo-Finnish War came to an end. Nevertheless, the Finns remained determined to expand their SIGINT operations against the Russians and provided GC&CS with a large amount of Russian military and KGB traffic, two Russian Army codebooks and the codebooks used by both the Baltic and Black Sea Fleets.

Royal Navy intercept sites at Scarborough and Flowerdown monitored Russian Navy frequencies, as did those in Singapore, Malta, and Alexandria and Ismailia in Egypt. The army sites in India also monitored Russian and the RAF set up an experimental intercept site in Baghdad to target Russian army and air circuits in the Caucasus. It also monitored Russian navy wireless traffic from Cairo. Meanwhile, French naval codebreakers who had been moved to GC&CS began working on high-grade Baltic and Black Sea Fleet ciphers. The flow of material from Estonia dried up in June 1940 when Russia occupied the Baltic states. But the fall of France brought willing replacements in the form of Polish wireless operators and codebreakers, who having escaped Poland to work with Bertrand had now been forced to flee the German Blitzkrieg for a second time. Based at Stanmore in west London, they found they were able to monitor Russian material from the Ukraine and were co-opted to provide more material for the Russian section. But there was a major rethink of operations against the Soviet Union in June 1941 when Germany invaded the Soviet Union.

According to popular mythology, all intelligence operations against the Soviet Union now came to an abrupt halt on Churchill's orders. The reality was nowhere near as clear-cut. There was a long drawn-out debate over whether or not to drop Soviet traffic. It was not until the beginning of 1942 that the order was given to stop all work on Soviet material. Even then the Poles were told to continue intercepting Soviet military communications and trying to break it at Stanmore, while the British kept two sets monitoring known Russian frequencies at the Scarborough Royal Navy site and the RAF station in Cheadle. Although interception of Soviet military and naval traffic was cut to the bare minimum, within weeks, the Metropolitan Police intercept site at Denmark Hill and the Radio Security Service had begun to pick up messages between Moscow and its agents in Britain. By January 1943, little more than a year after it had closed its Russian Section, ostensibly for the duration of the war, the British codebreakers were again trying to break Soviet codes and ciphers to read the messages of the Comintern agents operating in Britain and across the globe.

By September 1944, with senior intelligence officials preparing for the next war, in which the Soviet Union would be the target, Menzies set up a committee 'to study and set out a plan for the post-war organisation of GC&CS'. Travis, Hinsley, Tiltman and Welchman were all heavily involved in the discussions. Their conclusion that the codebreakers needed to be 'closely fused with SIS under the Director-General [Menzies] as the one and only intelligence-producing service' flies in the face of suggestions that they resented the fact that the head of MI6 was in overall control of their work. Welchman identified a need to coordinate the work of GC&CS closely with the services and the certainty that machine ciphers would become even more difficult to break. In an attempt to make use of German codebreaking successes against the Russian codes and ciphers, teams from a top secret Anglo-American mission known as TICOM, the Target Intelligence Committee, were sent into Germany. One team, including Selmer Norland, a US officer based at Bletchley, and Major Edward Rushworth, one of the senior British officers in Hut 3, found a number of German codebreakers who showed them a cache of cryptographic machinery specifically designed to decipher the Red Army's most secret radio communications. Soviet technicians had devised a system of encrypting teleprinter communications which split each message into nine different elements, each of which was sent on a separate radio channel. The message was then reassembled by the receiving station. The German codebreakers had developed a technique to intercept and decipher these transmissions and were hoping that the Allies might allow them to remain free to set up their equipment to continue monitoring the Russians on their behalf.

Rushworth and Norland were ordered to take the equipment and its operators back to England. 'I'll never forget leaving Rosenheim fairly early one morning,' said Norland. 'Major Rushworth was riding up in the front of the convoy of five lorries and I had the dubious honour of riding in the fifth lorry. That turned out to be slower than all the others. So with a very sinking feeling, I saw the other four lorries disappear out of sight. I felt very much alone because the four ahead had all of the equipment and all of the German personnel were riding in my lorry. I was surrounded. I had a German driver and assistant driver in the cab with me and all of the other German personnel, I don't remember how many, 15 or 20, in the back of the lorry. I didn't realise then, I only discovered later, that neither hell nor high water would have kept them from following their equipment, they were so devoted to it. But I did have some very uneasy moments. Most of the overpasses on the Autobahn had been blown up. So there was a detour every time you came to an intersection and that would run down through German villages and as soon as the population, mostly women of course, saw there were German prisoners on the back of this truck, they came rushing out with food and coffee and things of that sort. So I felt very much alone and very insecure I can tell you.'

The top secret equipment was taken, together with its operators, to Wavendon Manor where it was set up and tested against real Soviet transmissions. GC&CS had recommenced work on internal Soviet military and civilian teleprinter material in late 1944 and in January 1945 a 'covert party' was set up under Richard Pritchard in Sloane Square to deal with the material. Large numbers of the codebreakers were already being trained in Russian. 'At the end of the war, you were given a choice,' said Jean Faraday Davies, who worked in Hut 3. 'You could go and work on Russian intercepts, which most of us didn't want to do, or you could leave.' A similar process was going on at the overseas outstations, particularly in the Indian sub-continent, a major centre for British attempts to monitor Soviet communications in the inter-war period. 'I spent almost a year at a tiny outpost at Abbottabad, in North-West Frontier Province, after a one-man crash course in that elegant language Farsi,' wrote Alan Stripp, an Intelligence Corps officer who was monitoring Iranian diplomatic traffic. The Indian Intelligence Branch had been using the Abbottabad station to monitor Russian diplomatic and military traffic since before the First World War. Having dropped Soviet coverage in 1941, it was now back in business. 'By October 1946, I was in Singapore halfway through yet another crash course, in Russian,' Stripp said. 'The Cold War was already beginning to concentrate everybody's minds.'

It is still unclear how much Russian military and naval wireless traffic was monitored between the time the USSR became a British ally against Germany and the end of the war, but it was certainly more than is generally believed. The Polish 'Wireless Research Unit' remained operational throughout the war, with its decrypts being translated by a team of 30 White Russians who worked for MI6 in Paris in the 1930s and were brought over to Britain before the fall of France. Sometime during 1944, the Polish codebreakers supplied the British with 29,510 intelligence reports, almost certainly mainly based on intercepts of Russian material. Bletchley Park had also been able to read the cipher of the *Luftwaffe* signals intelligence organisation, which was listening to Soviet communications and passing them back to Berlin, since early 1943. This material was used by the JIC to build up a picture of Soviet capabilities. Captured German signals intelligence documents also provided valuable assistance, as did German and Italian signals intelligence operators who were employed by the British and used on Russian intercept tasks. But the crown jewels of the assistance obtained by the British codebreakers in building up their knowledge on Russian codes and ciphers came from Operation Stella Polaris. This was the codename given by the Finnish codebreakers for their escape from what they suspected was the impending Soviet annexation of their country. In a remarkable operation in September 1944 they fled en masse with their families and equipment to Sweden where to make ends meet they were reduced to auctioning off their cryptographic successes among the diplomatic community in Stockholm. The Finns had spent the past 17 years attacking Soviet codes and ciphers. They not only provided assistance to the Swedish codebreaking operation, *Försvarets Radioanstalt*, but also sold reconstructed Soviet codebooks and cipher systems to MI6, the US Office of Strategic Services (OSS) and the Japanese military attaché in Stockholm, who promptly turned them over to the Germans. The Finns also tried to sell the same codebooks to the Germans direct and offered both the Germans and the Japanese details of British and US codes and ciphers they had broken. They even cheekily sold the Americans material on British codes and ciphers as well as details of how they had solved the US State Department's strip cipher system. Then in late 1945, in a joint British–French operation, four of the Finnish codebreakers were taken to France, under the pretence that they were joining the Foreign Legion, even travelling via the Foreign Legion's training base at Sidi bel Abbès in Algeria. They were housed in the Château de Belloy just outside Paris, producing detailed reports from their archives on Soviet order of battle, which were passed on to the British codebreakers via the MI6 station in Paris. Curiously, the American Strategic Services Unit, the predecessor of the CIA, mounted a large-scale operation to infiltrate Stella Polaris to find out what the Finns were doing, apparently unaware that the British were passing it all on to the US Army codebreaking organisation, the Army Security Agency.

But the Soviet Union was not the only new target for the British codebreakers, recalled Jimmy Thirsk, a Bletchley Park intelligence analyst. 'I remember there being almost a mutiny at the end of the war with Germany because we started working on French intercepts. Quite a lot of us objected to this and a delegation of 15 or 20 of us went to one of the officers in charge and made our complaint and said we didn't want to do it. Someone else was called in and we were given a lecture and told: "Well, if you don't want to do it, you're redundant." But there was a definite revulsion about spying on our former allies.' The bombes were put back into action almost immediately after the end of the war, according to the official history of the bombe sections. Some countries continued to use Enigma machines, including East German paramilitary units, which were still using them in 1950. This suggests that the Russians did not tell them that Enigma had been broken during the war, almost certainly so they too could keep a watch on the activities of their supposed allies. 'Some of these machines were to be stored away,' the official history of the bombe sections said. 'But others were required to run new jobs and 16 machines were kept comparatively busy on menus. It is interesting to note that most of the jobs came up, and the operating, checking and other times maintained were, faster than the best times during the war periods.'

Thirsk and his friends were not the only ones made redundant. The number of people at Bletchley Park had reached a wartime peak of around 10,000 people in early 1945 but by the spring of 1946 GC&CS had around 2,000 employees, including the former Radio Security Service and the department producing codes and ciphers for government departments. This had spent the war at Mansfield College, Oxford, in order to be close to the Oxford University Press, which produced the official codebooks. But despite the recommendations of the leading codebreakers, there was to be no joint organisation with MI6. In fact the reverse happened; the link between the two in the shape of C's control of both organisations was completely severed. In

April 1946; the codebreakers moved to Eastcote, in north London, the site of one of the bombe sections, where they briefly operated under the title of the London Signals Intelligence Centre before adopting the current title Government Communications Headquarters (GCHQ) in June 1946. This was one of at least two similar covernames used before and during the war, the other being the Government Communications Bureau.

The British codebreakers continued the success they had enjoyed against German systems in the early days of the Cold War, agreeing in June 1945 to co-operate fully with the Americans on the breaking of Soviet codes and ciphers in a programme codenamed Rattan. By September, they were sending the Americans material produced from a Russian enciphered teleprinter system known as Caviar, which was almost certainly the result of the Norland–Rushworth TICOM mission. The most important success against Soviet armed forces machine ciphers of the early Cold War came at the beginning of 1946 when GCHQ broke the first of several mainline Soviet armed forces machine ciphers which it dubbed the 'Poets Systems'. The initial break came with a system codenamed Coleridge, which was used on the Soviet army, navy and air force mainline circuits inside the Soviet Union. Broken by the British codebreakers in early 1946 and exploited from at least March of that year, it was similar in type to the Swedish commercially produced Hagelin machine. The Coleridge operation was led by Hugh Alexander. The Soviet circuits using the machine were largely concerned with administrative matters but this nevertheless produced a great deal of intelligence on the Soviet armed forces, order of battle and peacetime activities. The ability to read Coleridge was a very important success. Soviet military strengths, capabilities and locations were second only to the extent of Soviet atomic capabilities in the wish-list handed out to Britain's intelligence agencies by the post-war JIC. GCHQ also broke another Soviet cipher machine, Albatross, a name that suggests that it may have been associated in some way with Coleridge.

The superior British ability to make the initial breaks into new systems, which had been one of the key foundations of the wartime alliance, was also an important factor in forcing a hesitant US signals intelligence establishment to realise how much it needed to maintain the relationship with the British.

The US Navy liaison officer at Eastcote reported back to Washington in April 1947 that Coleridge was 'the most important, high-level system from which current intelligence may be produced and is so in fact regarded here'. There was a further break into a Poets system in February 1947, when GCHQ cryptanalysts led by Major G W 'Gerry' Morgan, working in tandem with a team of US Navy codebreakers led by Commander Howard H Campaigne, solved and began to exploit a system which they codenamed Longfellow.

Despite their ability to read the traffic produced using the Poets systems and a number of other successes against lower-grade Soviet machine ciphers, both the British or their US counterparts struggled to break the Soviet high-grade additive systems, which were enciphered using so-called one-time pads. In 1951, the American codebreaker in charge of Russian material wrote that no Russian armed forces high-level additive traffic had been read since early 1940 when the British were breaking it. But the Americans had begun to make progress against KGB one-time pad traffic after the discovery of a partially burned codebook in Finland and duplication of pads. Operation Venona was set up by the US Army codebreakers during the war in an attempt to break messages passed between the KGB's Moscow Centre and its stations in the West. It took several years to make real headway with the messages but the resultant intelligence was passed to the British, who in 1947 joined the programme themselves. One of the most important decrypts proved that Donald Maclean was a spy and led to the unravelling of the Cambridge spy ring. Other Venona transcripts revealed the identities of the British atom spy Klaus Fuchs and his American counterparts, Ted Hall and Julius Rosenberg, who were working within the US–British Manhattan project to produce the atomic bomb. Similar Soviet naval intelligence one-time pad systems, attacked as part of the Venona programme, resisted all efforts to break them until 1957 when GCHQ managed to find a way in.

As well as the successes against Soviet codes and ciphers, GCHQ's codebreakers and their US counterparts made significant progress against those used by Moscow's East European satellites, including Bulgarian, Hungarian and Czechoslovakian systems as well as the East German Enigma systems. But on 29 October 1948, subsequently known as 'Black Friday', there was a complete change of Soviet codes, ciphers, and communications procedures as a result of information provided by William W Weisband, a Soviet agent inside the US Army codebreaking organisation. Nevertheless, some of the East Bloc systems do not appear to have changed and traffic analysis continued to provide useful details of Soviet order of battle as well as a continued watch on major changes in readiness. The US and British codebreakers also continued to make progress against some Soviet cipher systems and by the mid-1950s a number of machine ciphers had been broken with the assistance of computers.

The thinking behind GCHQ's initial move to Eastcote appears to have been predicated on the assumption that the codebreakers should be based in London. But it was soon apparent that, in the event of the widely expected 'next war' with the Soviet Union, GCHQ would be better off outside London. The large amount of special machinery in use, which still included a number of Colossus computers and bombes, would make a swift mobilisation to another 'war station' like Bletchley Park impossible. As a result, within a year of moving to Eastcote, GCHQ was looking for a new home far enough from London to be safe in the event of a nuclear attack on the capital but close enough to have good communications. A return to Bletchley Park was contemplated but eventually two separate sites at Cheltenham, one of them a former US Army base with a large number of specially prepared communications cables, were selected. In 1952, the codebreakers moved to the Oakley Farm site in Cheltenham while the Knockholt experimental radio station and GCHQ's other research departments moved to nearby Benhall. Two of the Colossus computers were among the deciphering equipment taken to Cheltenham and at least one was still working into the 1960s.

Britain's post-war signals interception was carried out by all three services and by civilians working initially under cover of the Admiralty Civilian Shore Wireless Service, the Government Civilian Radio Organisation and the Air Ministry and War Office wireless services. The four civilian intercept services would later be absorbed into the GCHQ-controlled Composite Signals Organisation. The main UK intercept sites were at the wartime bases of Cheadle, Winchester, Beaumanor, Scarborough and Chicksands, the last of which was taken over by the Americans in 1948, and at Gilnahirk, on the outskirts of Belfast. Overseas bases were in Germany, the Middle East, the

Ceylon, Singapore and Hong Kong, from where Soviet and Chinese radio transmissions were intercepted. Soviet military activity in eastern Europe was most easily monitored from the British zones of Germany and Berlin, where the War Office Y sections also intercepted telephone communications, watching for evidence of subversion by both communists and former Nazis. The main Army Y organisation in Europe ended the war at Minden, where it was given the title of No 1 Special Wireless Regiment. A year later it moved to Glückstadt near Hamburg. It was renamed 1 Wireless Regiment in 1947 and in 1950 moved to Münster. Soviet military communications were also monitored from the Middle East, by No 2 Special Wireless Regiment based at Sarafand in Palestine with a detachment based in Habbaniya in Iraq, at least in part as a result of the concern over Soviet interference in Iran. The Army, Navy and RAF outposts sent high-grade cipher traffic back to GCHQ but traffic analysis of mainline systems and *en clair* transmissions on lower-level communications provided a wealth of detail on Soviet armed forces capabilities and tactics. JIC reports on Soviet intentions in the Middle East for the immediate post-war years show detailed knowledge of military dispositions and troop levels in southern Europe, almost certainly gathered from Sarafand. With the 1947 decision to withdraw from Palestine, plans were put in place to build a new intercept site for No 2 Special Wireless Regiment at Ayios Nikolaos, near Famagusta in Cyprus.

It is still unclear whether the mobile Y units were completely disbanded at the end of the war. Since the first of the Army's many post-war confrontations was in Palestine, which was also the location of the main Middle East intercept site, it may not initially have seen any grounds for retaining the units. In the short term at least, the main priority – establishing Soviet atomic and military capabilities – was best pursued from static sites. The reaction to the various emergencies and counter-insurgency campaigns in which British troops became involved appears to have been similar to the response to the 1946 Azerbaijan Crisis in which Stripp was involved: the dispatch of a small static detachment following a crash course in the local language.

Nevertheless, in the immediate post-war period, GCHQ expressed interest in the RAF's mobile monitoring vehicles, which had facilities both for intercepting VHF and HF voice transmissions and for direction-finding.

Considerable research was undertaken into the use of aerial interception platforms, or 'ferrets', for gathering both communications and electronic intelligence. The first RAF electronic warfare flights had been flown during the Second World War, using specially equipped Anson aircraft to jam the Knickebein beam navigation system that guided German bombers to their targets. Attempts to intercept communications from aircraft were also made with a radio receiver fitted into a Hudson aircraft, during the 1944 Italian campaign, to intercept E-boat communications in the Ligurian Sea. By 1947, RAF Lancaster and Lincoln bombers modified to include radios and radar monitoring equipment and with on-board photo-reconnaissance cameras were patrolling the border between the Soviet and British zones of Germany. The flights triggered the Soviet air defences, allowing operators on board the aircraft and on the ground at RAF Gatow in the western sector of Berlin to record reaction times and build up a picture of the Soviet air defence locations and capabilities. Similar operations took place elsewhere on the borders with the Soviet Union with signals intelligence operations mounted from the UK carried out by 192 Squadron based at RAF Watton in Norfolk. In September 1948, a Lancaster and a Lincoln equipped with both photo-reconnaissance and signals intelligence equipment flew to Habbaniya, from where they undertook a number of eight-hour missions, almost certainly along the Iraqi–Soviet border. Further experimental sorties were flown using Lincoln, Washington and Canberra aircraft. At the end of 1951, a dedicated communications intelligence Lincoln was 'urgently required for useful work', most likely related to the decision to beef up the intelligence operation in Malaya following the assassination in October 1951 of the British high commissioner. But there were also problems in Egypt and a continual need for more intelligence from the Soviet Bloc countries. US electronic and signals intelligence aircraft also operated out of Britain. But there were considerable dangers for the allied airmen. US operations were suspended for six months in mid-1950 after a US Navy Privateer electronic intelligence aircraft based in Britain was shot down over the Baltic while monitoring Soviet coastal radar installations. In March 1953, amid confusion and infighting in Moscow over who would succeed the recently deceased Stalin, an RAF Lincoln flying in the corridor from Hamburg to Berlin was shot down by three Soviet MiG-15 fighter aircraft with the loss of all seven crew. The Lincoln was a trials aircraft flying out of RAF Leconfield and according to the station log was taking part in 'a regular exercise testing reactions to simulated fighter attacks'. The Russians said the Lincoln had strayed outside the corridor and that it opened fire on the MiG-15s first and was shot down as a result. The RAF board of inquiry said the aircraft was unarmed but the Russians managed to produce a number of spent cannon rounds alleged to have been fired by the Lincoln. A few hours before the Lincoln was shot down, a BEA airliner was buzzed by Soviet MiG fighters after briefly straying out of the southern air corridor. Given the degree of co-operation between the British government-owned airlines and intelligence services at that time, this may well have been a deliberate attempt to test the Soviet air defences and trigger off radar and communications links. RAF signals intelligence operations were also carried out by ground stations at Gatow in West Berlin and the old wartime base at Cheadle. In the summer of 1955, the RAF inter-cept operators based at Cheadle, by then known as 399 Signals Unit, moved to the former fighter base at Digby in Lincolnshire, where they were joined by an RAF communications security (Comsec) unit, 591 Signals Unit. GCHQ's civilian Composite Signals Organisation took over the Cheadle base as one of its main intercept sites. The priority target for 399 Signals Unit was high-frequency Warsaw Pact air force activity in Eastern Europe and the western USSR. There was close collaboration with the US 6950th Electronic Security Group based at the other wartime RAF interception site at Chicksands, including exchanges of personnel and information.

The 1948 UKUSA agreement carving up signals intelligence coverage of the world between Britain and America left the US Armed Forces Security Agency and the US army, navy and air force tactical signals intelligence operations covering the Far East, albeit with the assistance of the GCHQ outstation in Hong Kong. It was the failure of the US agencies to detect North Korean preparations in June 1950 for the Korean War and the poor standard of communications intelligence provided during the war that led to the creation of the National Security Agency (NSA). This was an amalgamation of the US Army, Air Force and Navy tactical signals intelligence organisations and the umbrella organisation the Armed Forces Security Agency, which had responsibility for strategic signals intelligence. The NSA mirrored GCHQ's mix of a civilian-dominated headquarters codebreaking and analysis operation with the three services providing the main collection stations abroad. It is important to qualify the word 'failure' in respect of the US signals intelligence operations immediately before the North Korean invasion. The US codebreakers certainly failed to pick up on the North Korean preparations, largely due to a shortage of Korean experts and the fact that all the US sites in the region were concentrating on Soviet communications. But they had detected significant movements of Chinese forces towards the Korean border. Even more importantly an indication of the reason behind the Chinese troop movements had been intercepted in the form of a message from the Chinese armed forces commander saying that China was about to intervene in Korea. But these appear to have been ignored by the decision-makers in Washington. The response to the signals intelligence indicators prior to the 1956 Soviet invasion of Hungary was apparently significantly better. NSA and GCHQ, and their military outposts in Germany and Austria, were able to follow the progress of Russian troops from the surrounding East Bloc countries moving towards the Hungarian border in readiness to quash any opposition.

In the late 1950s, the group of Baltic émigrés originally employed in a house overlooking Regent's Park to process MI6's Berlin-tunnel material were transferred to GCHQ's control, working from a building in the City of London as the London Processing Group and transcribing Russian language intercepts. But by the late 1960s many were reaching retirement age and their replacements were mainly language graduates or former servicemen who had carried out similar work with the armed forces. The group, which became known as the Joint Technical Language Service, was moved to Cheltenham in the mid-1970s.

The British signals intelligence operations in support of the 1956 Suez invasion were impressive. Washington aircraft of 192 Squadron were deployed to Cyprus to map out the Egyptian air defence system, detecting the curious but extremely useful habit of the Egyptian operators of shutting down the radar systems shortly after midday for a siesta. The army's Arabic-speaking intercept operators and intelligence analysts at what was now known simply as 2 Wireless Regiment in Cyprus also played a major role in the invasion, with a small tactical signals intelligence team accompanying the invasion force. There were also Royal Navy intercept operators on board some of the ships. In London, thanks to a joint operation with MI5 codenamed Engulf, GCHQ was able to read the Egyptian high-grade cipher. Messages between the Russians and the Egyptians, intercepted by GCHQ and indicating that Moscow was prepared to deploy military aircraft in support of Nasser, were probably as crucial as US influence in forcing a British withdrawal. The Egyptians also used a number of Enigma machines, which had been sold to them by Norway in the early 1950s and were easy for GCHQ to solve. After the crisis was over, Selwyn Lloyd, the then Foreign Secretary, sent a congratulatory message to Eric Jones, who had been head of Hut 3 during the D-Day invasion and was now Director of GCHQ. 'I have observed the volume of material which has been produced by GCHQ, relating to all the countries of the Middle East,' he said, a form of words which strongly suggests that Britain was monitoring the communications of its Israeli ally as well as those of Egypt and Syria. 'I am writing to let you know how valuable we have found this material and how much I appreciate the hard work and skills involved in its production.' The message was passed on to the navy, army and air force operators and intelligence analysts involved in the operation.

The joint MI5–GCHQ Engulf operation, run on the MI5 side by Peter Wright, had important implications for GCHQ. Wright and Tony Sale, his assistant, realised that radio waves were given off by unscreened circuits between the keyboard of a cipher machine and the encipherment mechanism that would transmit up to a distance of around 1,000 feet. By setting up special receiving equipment close to foreign embassies, they would be able to pick up the diplomatic cables before they were enciphered, enabling GCHQ to break the ciphers in use. In an operation codenamed Stockade, this technique was used to monitor high-grade messages between the French embassy in London and Paris during the abortive British negotiations to join the Common Market. The French messages were intercepted for three years from an operations room in the Hyde Park Hotel, directly opposite the embassy. But in 1963, the French discovered a Russian bug and screened all their cables, ending Operation Stockade. Nevertheless, similar operations were mounted against other embassies in London, some on the ground using specially built vans with non-metal bodies to make reception easier and some using RAF Ferret aircraft flying over London. Similar operations were mounted abroad by MI6. The operations came under the control of the Radiations Operations Committee. Those operations designed to break foreign ciphers that would produce straightforward intelligence were given the overall codename Clan, with those aimed at detecting spies codenamed Counterclan. Other ciphers read in the Clan operations included those of the Greek embassy during the 1963 fighting in Cyprus and the Indonesian embassy during the 1963–66 confrontation with the newly formed Federation of Malaysia.

Eighteen

GCHQ and the New World

GCHQ has been by far the most valuable source of intelligence for the British Government ever since it began operating.

Denis Healey, House of Commons debate on the GCHQ unions, 1984

Throughout the Cold War, GCHQ relied very largely on the three services for the collection of material on the Warsaw Pact countries. The Royal Navy had continued the practice of placing intercept operators and intelligence analysts on board ships that was originally instigated by the GC&CS Navy Section in the 1920s. During the Second World War, a number of Royal Navy warships were fitted out to intercept radio communications, but only in support of particular operations, such as the amphibious landings at Anzio and Salerno. But during the Cold War, intercept operators and signals intelligence analysts routinely worked on Royal Navy ships. The cruiser HMS *Superb* spent a month in the Arctic Ocean in late 1949 gathering electronic intelligence on the Murmansk headquarters of the Soviet navy's Northern Fleet. The Royal Navy had been using submarines to collect signals intelligence and was so since 1943 and was now so at it that when the US Navy decided to send some of its own submarines into Arctic waters to listen in on Soviet naval communications, they were fitted out in Portsmouth by British technicians.

The main UK base and training establishment for Royal Navy signals intelligence operations was the Special Communications Unit at HMS *Mercury*, on the South Downs just south of Petersfield. British submarine-based signals intelligence operations were briefly suspended after the Crabb affair but had resumed by the early 1960s when the Porpoise-class diesel submarines were regularly carrying out spying operations against Soviet ships exercising in the Barents Sea. The Soviet response was now much more aggressive, almost certainly more a sign of improved anti-submarine detection systems than a change in attitude.

One officer involved said some of the Soviet submarine captains were 'absolutely mad and behaved in an astonishing manner'. Royal Navy submarines on these trips, known for understandable reasons as 'dodgies', were frequently depth-charged by the Soviet warships on which they were spying. The charges used were small 1lb 'scare charges', but under the water the effect was still chilling for the Royal Navy submariners. The charges were easily capable of lifting the hatches, which were routinely welded down before the submarine left port. There were also a couple of collisions, although none that disabled the Royal Navy submarines involved. The Royal Navy also placed intercept operators on board deep-sea trawlers that fished in the Barents Sea. The use of trawlers had originally been part of an MI6-controlled operation in which trawlermen were issued with cameras and asked to take photographs of Soviet shipping. The Soviet reaction was extremely aggressive and the policy led to the controversy surrounding the sinking in November 1974 of the *Gaul*, a Hull-based trawler that, under a previous name, had been warned off by the Russians over its involvement in the spying operations. The MoD's response to the suggestions that it was on a spying mission was initially to claim that no such operations had ever taken place. When too many of those involved came forward to refute this, the MoD made the improbable claim that it had carried out the trawler missions but had discontinued them in the summer of 1974, at the height of the Cold War but shortly before the *Gaul* set sail from Hull. As a result the controversy continued into the late 1990s when the wreck of the trawler was found and an inquiry ruled that it had been swamped by high seas after leaving its hatches open, a conclusion that singularly failed to dispel the suspicions of spying.

The most aggressive incident thus far admitted by the MoD involved the British nuclear-powered attack submarine HMS *Sceptre*, which collided with a Soviet submarine. The British boat was one of the Swiftsure-class boats, all specifically built to monitor Soviet ICBM-equipped nuclear submarines. They were fitted with signals intelligence equipment capable of jamming the soviet missile command and control systems and the latest sonar sensors, towed behind the boats in what is known as a towed array. As a result of their specific covert intelligence-gathering role, carried out in tandem with US submarines in an operation known as Operation Holystone, they were known as 'sneaky boats'. The collision between *Sceptre* and her Soviet target, which despite the Soviet aggression is believed to have been accidental, occurred in the Barents Sea on a

Saturday night in the late summer of 1981. *Sceptre* had lost the Soviet submarine for about 30 minutes, said one of the officers on board. Then suddenly the whole boat began to shake. 'There was a huge noise. It started very far forward, sort of at the tip of the submarine, and it trailed back. It sounded like a scrawling. We were hitting something. That noise lasted for what seemed like a lifetime. It was probably only a couple of seconds or so. Everybody went white.' The British boat was subsequently pursued for two days by a Soviet attack submarine, which chased it into the North Sea. Once they had shaken off the pursuing Soviet submarine, *Sceptre* surfaced to survey the damage. There was a long tear along the outer hull and the conning tower and traces of the phosphor bronze from which propellers are made. The mangled metal indicated that the much larger Soviet submarine had driven across *Sceptre*'s bow, with its propeller ripping into the submarine. 'The tear started about three inches from the forward escape hatch,' the officer said. 'If that hatch had been hit or damaged – it's about 2ft 6in diameter – if that had been ruptured, then the fore ends would have shipped water which would have made the boat very heavy. We would probably have sunk.' The submarine returned to Plymouth for repairs with the crew ordered to tell anyone who asked what had happened that they had hit an iceberg. On another occasion, one of *Sceptre*'s sister boats lost the towed array of sonar sensors that the submarines used to track their Soviet counterparts. It was initially believed to have been caught up on a Soviet submarine and ripped off, but astonishingly it turned up some time later in the stomach of a migrating whale caught off South Africa.

RAF electronic reconnaissance flights continued through the 1950s with 192 Squadron being renamed as 51 Squadron in August 1958. It initially flew modified Canberras, but later acquired Comet R2 dedicated aircraft, carrying up to twenty signals operators. Leonard Hooper, GCHQ Director, said that while the 'Radio Proving Flights', as they were known, were expensive compared to ground-based operations 'some of the results are unique'. Despite the shooting down of a U-2 aircraft over the Soviet Union, which brought a temporary end to such operations by US aircraft, British flights continued, Hooper said. 'A carefully controlled programme of Radio Proving Flights continues to be national policy, each operation being approved by ministers.' Aircraft from 51 Squadron frequently overflew the Middle East, staging out of Akrotiri in Cyprus. The squadron moved from Watton to Wyton, Cambridgeshire, in 1963 and in

1971 received the first of the three Nimrod R1 aircraft which flew 'ferret' missions over the Baltic, Mediterranean and Barents Seas, the Persian Gulf and the Balkans. They subsequently moved to RAF Waddington, in Lincolnshire.

In 1955, 1 Wireless Regiment moved to Birgelen, close to the Dutch border town of Roermond. It was renamed 13 Signal Regiment in 1959. It had outstations in Berlin and on the border with East Germany. Its primary task was monitoring the static Morse and enciphered teleprinter links between the units of the Group Soviet Forces Germany base in East Germany. Basic traffic analysis of these links laid down a template against which any changes reflecting major deployments or moves could be checked. The rigid nature of such static links meant that preparations for any major deployments either for an attack on the West, or indeed moves to subjugate Warsaw Pact members who became too independent as in Hungary in 1956, Czechoslovakia in 1968 and potentially Poland in 1981, could be swiftly picked up. But equally an over reliance on this trip wire system would have made Nato vulnerable to a relatively simple communications deception operation, where levels of activity on the main static nets were kept at normal routine levels while all communications relating to the deployment were sent by other means. The other main Cold War role of the signals intelligence personnel based in Germany was the monitoring of exercise traffic, largely from VHF and microwave voice transmissions. The army had mobile signals and electronics intelligence squadrons comprising both Royal Signals and Intelligence Corps personnel at Scharfoldendorf, Langeleben and Wesendorf on the border with East Germany. In July 1977, the two remaining mobile units, 225 Signal Squadron, at Langeleben, a mobile communications intelligence unit, and 226 Signal Squadron, at Wesendorf, which specialised in electronic intelligence, amalgamated to form 14 Signal Regiment, retaining their forward bases with a regimental headquarters initially at Hildesheim and then at Celle. The regiment had a range of mobile and static electronic intelligence, communications intelligence and communications security roles.

The Cyprus-based No 2 Special Wireless Regiment also changed its name, becoming first 2 Wireless Regiment and then 9 Signal Regiment, GCHQ's main Middle East outstation. It had a remote site at Troodos, 1,800 feet up on Mount Olympus in the centre of the island, and was manned by members of all three armed services together with 'a large civilian contingent'. It monitored a wide range of communications and electronic transmissions throughout the Middle East and the southern Soviet Union – a brief that appeared to have changed very little from that allocated to Sarafand in the period between the wars.

The extent of GCHQ's success against the codes and ciphers of Warsaw Pact during the 1960s is not clear, although there certainly were some. During the mid-1960s, MI6 obtained a number of codes and ciphers of Warsaw Pact countries from Adam Kaczmarzyk, a Polish cipher clerk. But he was swiftly compromised, arrested and executed. But there were other successes. During the London negotiations aimed at ending the Vietnam War, GCHQ was able to intercept the telephone conversations between Soviet Prime Minister Alexei Kosygin in London and Soviet leader Leonid Brezhnev in Moscow. Nevertheless, during the mid-1970s GCHQ and NSA went through a period where they were having extreme difficulty breaking Warsaw Pact ciphers, which implies that until then they had managed to break at least some.

The period between the mid-1970s and the end of the century was one of major changes for GCHQ and its armed-forces outstations. The first came as a result of the increasing importance of spy satellites and widespread computerisation. In the mid-1960s, Goonhilly Downs near Falmouth, in Cornwall, one of the first satellite earth stations, became an important staging post for the new Intelsat international satellite communications system. Both GCHQ and NSA were anxious to ensure they could tap into the new systems. The close ties with the Americans forged during the Second World War and formalised under the UKUSA Accord had allowed GCHQ to punch above its weight. But if Britain did not get into satellite monitoring from the start its contribution to the alliance would drop dramatically, raising questions on the other side of the Atlantic as to whether it should continue to receive the fruits of the massive American effort. Leonard Hooper, the then GCHQ Director and a veteran of Bletchley Park, was determined to prevent this happening, and later admitted to having 'shamelessly exploited' the need to keep the UKUSA relationship intact in the battle for funds for the move into satellite monitoring. In early 1967, GCHQ announced plans to set up its own satellite station at Morwenstow near Bude, sixty miles north of Goonhilly. Officially, the two satellite dishes were to be used to provide a secure communications link between Britain's embassies abroad and London. GCHQ officials even visited the GPO site at Goonhilly 'to study the methods used there for handling telephone traffic'. In reality, the dishes were designed to scoop up all the communications passing through the Intelsat system. Around the same time as GCHQ was setting up the Morwenstow site, the NSA took over the RAF base at Menwith Hill, near Harrogate, North Yorkshire, installing a number of satellite dishes. The Menwith Hill site, now the largest signals intelligence site in Europe, acts as a ground station for signals intelligence 'ferret' satellites targeting Europe and the former Soviet Union. The first US signals intelligence satellites, code-named Heavy Ferret or Grab, were launched in the early 1960s. The first really effective such satellites were the Rhyolites, which were launched in the early 1970s. These collected a wealth of intelligence, most notably from the microwave telephone systems used by the Soviet Union and its Warsaw Pact allies for government, party and high-level military conversations. The microwave signals travelled in straight lines, bouncing around networks of relay stations, and therefore travelled on straight out into space where they could be collected by the US satellites. There have been a number of different US signals intelligence satellites since the Rhyolite, with the most recent models codenamed Mercury and Trumpet. Despite their distance from the earth – they orbit at more than 20,000 miles above the earth's surface – the US satellites have a remarkable ability to pick up communications across the frequency range. During the 1988 Chernobyl nuclear disaster, a US Vortex satellite stationed above Africa was able to monitor all the communications of the various Soviet organisations involved, from the short-range VHF radios of the police, to the military's command links back to Moscow and the telephone conversations of party officials.

By the early 1980s, with satellites reducing the need for the bases around the world that had made the UKUSA deal with Britain so attractive to the Americans, it became clear that the special relationship was waning. One GCHQ official noted that the Americans were taking a tougher stance on exchanges of information under the UKUSA Accord. 'This hard-nosed attitude was becoming apparent during the mid-70s as overseas bases became less and less efficient and useful because of technical advances,' he said. 'In the past, allied operational policy was based upon close ties with, and a begrudging respect for and reliance on, GCHQ. Time alone has severed many of the close personal ties as Hot and Cold War colleagues retired, died or otherwise passed on.' There were also tensions caused by two other factors. The first was the discovery in 1982 that Geoffrey Prime, a former RAF and GCHQ linguist, had been a KGB spy and was largely responsible for changes, in the mid-1970s, to high-level Soviet ciphers systems that GCHQ and NSA had previously been able to read. The second was the increasing use of industrial action by GCHQ staff, which led in 1984 to a blanket ban on trade unions.

The Falklands conflict showed that the transatlantic signals intelligence alliance was vital to Britain. GCHQ provided the first serious warnings of the Argentinian invasion of the Falkland Islands. On 26 March 1982, from information provided by the NSA, it reported that Admiral Jorge Anaya, the head of the Argentinian navy had ordered two frigates to pull out of a joint exercise with the Uruguayan navy and head south. Five days later, it reported the Argentinian submarine *Santa Fe* was to land a reconnaissance team on Mullett Creek, three miles south of Port Stanley. By now the invasion force was at sea. GCHQ's station on Ascension, the American sites in Panama and Chile, and a Royal New Zealand Navy site at Irirangi, in the Kaimanawa Mountains of North Island, began to pick up a large number of ship-to-ship and ship-to-shore communications.

Although the official US stance was that of a neutral intermediary, this did not affect the close links between GCHQ and NSA, which continued to pass 'raw take' on to Cheltenham throughout the conflict. Nevertheless, the Thatcher government believed that Britain had become too dependent on US satellite intelligence. It authorised a 'Top Secret' project to place Britain's own signals intelligence satellite above the Indian Ocean under cover of Britain's Skynet military satellite system. The £500 million project, code named Zircon, caused a major row in 1987 when its existence was revealed in the *New Statesman* journal. It was subsequently abandoned. Instead, the British agreed to pay towards the cost of NSA's three new Magnum satellites, now codenamed Mercury, in return for the ability to task the satellites.

The deal with the Americans on the use of their satellites and the end of the Cold War brought further changes in the deployment of the British armed forces' intercept operations. In late 1994, following the end of the Cold War and the unification of Germany, 13 Signal Regiment was disbanded and its staff were dispersed to other units. Most of them went to a new joint NSA/GCHQ monitoring site set up under conditions of great secrecy at RAF Digby. The British elements, initially 399 Signals Unit and the bulk of 13 Signal Regiment, were formed into the Joint Service Signal Unit (Digby). This unit was augmented in 1996 by Royal Navy signals intelligence personnel from HMS *Mercury* and in

1998 by some of the staff from 9 Signal Regiment in Cyprus. It has its own Pusher antenna system as well as remote-controlled receivers located in Europe, Cyprus and the Persian Gulf. The British units were joined in 1994 by a USAF signals intelligence detachment, which moved to Digby with the closure of the US base at Chicksands. This was followed in 1995 by a US Army Intelligence and Security Command detachment from Menwith Hill in Yorkshire, and in 1996 by a 30-man US Navy detachment from the Naval Security Group Command. The US Navy and Royal Navy personnel man a Combined Cryptologic Shore Support Activity (CCSSA) providing intelligence for US and Royal Navy ships operating in the Atlantic, Mediterranean and Persian Gulf. Despite the loss of some of its personnel, the signals intelligence operation at 9 Signal Regiment in Cyprus remained in place. It continued to monitor traffic around the Middle East and from the southern former Soviet Union and in 1999 amalgamated with an RAF intercept unit, 33 Signals Unit, to become the Joint Service Signal Unit (Ayios Nikolaos). It provides a forward signals intelligence operations base in the Middle East as well as operating and maintaining remote receivers for Digby. The final part of the reorganisation of British armed forces signals intelligence operations during the mid-1990s saw the move of 14 Signal Regiment to a former US submarine-monitoring base at Brawdy in South Wales from where it has sent detachments to the Balkans, Sierra Leone and Afghanistan. Mobile Y Service-style deployments accompanying British military deployments abroad continued throughout the Cold War and into the 'Hot Peace' that followed. Signals intelligence operators had been deployed in Oman during the early- to mid-1970s, when the SAS, under the cover of British Army Training Team (BATT), and locally recruited forces fought a guerrilla war against communist rebel tribesmen sent into Oman by the People's Democratic Republic of Yemen. Signals intelligence operators were subsequently sent to Rhodesia as part of Operation Agila, the mobile Commonwealth force monitoring the ceasefire between Rhodesian government forces and the rebel Patriotic Front in the run-up to the 1980 elections. Similarly, a detachment from Communications and Security Group (UK) – a signals intelligence unit then based at the old Beaumanor site in Leicestershire – went to the Falklands with the Task Force together with elements of 14 Signal Regiment. A number of Royal Navy vessels that joined the deployment also had intercept facilities. GCHQ's attempts to break the Argentinian codes and ciphers were supplemented by material provided by the Americans and the Germans. The results were impressive, one British officer said. 'We are evidently able to intercept much if not all the enemy's signals traffic. Without it we would never have achieved what we have.' A signals intelligence unit, Joint Service Signal Unit (Falklands), was set up on the islands following the British victory. A similar unit was located in British Honduras/Belize from 1972 to 1994, helping to ensure a secure transition to independence which had been threatened by Guatemalan territorial claims. Signals intelligence operators played an important part in the Gulf War, elements from 9 Signal Regiment continued to serve in Jordan and Kuwait into the mid-1990s and it is reasonable to assume that at least some of Digby's remote receivers and probably personnel remained in those countries monitoring Iraqi military communications, including missile-firing exercises in advance of the 2003 Gulf War. GCHQ provided the Arabic linguists, almost certainly from what was then 9 Signal Regiment, for an operation to monitor the communications of the Special Security Organisation and the Special Republican Guard who were responsible for the security of both the weapons programme and Saddam Hussein and his family. The operation, initially codenamed Code Red and later Shake the Tree, began in February 1996. It involved the creation by NSA and CIA technicians of a covert communications intercept system inside the Baghdad headquarters of the UN weapons inspectors UNSCOM, who also agreed to carry sophisticated automated frequency-scanning radio receivers concealed inside their rucksacks when they were on inspections. GCHQ left the operation in April 1998, possibly as the result of a comprehensive government review of British intelligence operations.

There were also elements of 14 Signal Regiment and the Royal Marines' own dedicated signals intelligence unit, Y Troop, 3 Commando Brigade, operating during the Balkans operations in Bosnia, Kosovo and Macedonia and in Iraq. These units now use the Odette advanced tactical electronic warfare system, which was first deployed in Kosovo in August 2000 and subsequently in Afghanistan and Iraq. There are three separate operational squadrons in 14 Signal regiment each with the appearance of an independent squadron, plus a headquarters squadron, which contains the Electronic Warfare Coordination Center (EWCC) and a separate air mobile rapid deployment unit, 640 Troop. The operational squadrons are 226 Signal Squadron, a so-called 'Depth Electronic Warfare' unit equipped with the Ince electronic intelligence system. This has three separate receiving stations with rotating dish antennas and a control station fitted aboard Pinzgauer 4x4 vehicles. It can locate, identify and where necessary jam battlefield surveillance, artillery, early-warning and air-defence radars. A much faster system, codenamed Soothsayer and capable of operating against both communications and electronic emissions like radar, is due to enter service in 2006. There are also two dedicated communications intelligence squadrons equipped with Odette, which provide tactical SIGINT and electronic warfare for the British army's combat divisions – 237 and 245 Signal Squadrons – the latter is an armoured unit to allow it to operate as part of an armoured battlegroup. The SAS also now has its own small signals intelligence unit and a further innovation is the Transportable Cryptologic Support Group, a mobile codebreaking unit. This deployed to Afghanistan with the International Security and Assistance Force that kept the peace in the Afghan capital, Kabul, after the creation of the interim government.

The Royal Navy's signals intelligence capability was expanded in the early 1980s, when six Type-22 Frigates were fitted with the joint US-UK Outboard intercept system. This included direction-finding equipment with a capability ranging from low frequency to ultra-high frequency and automated signals acquisition systems capable of tracking frequency-hopping radio nets. It was used extensively in operations against the Soviet navy's Northern Fleet. During major Northern Fleet exercises, specially trained RN SIGINT detachments deployed from the Royal Navy's Special Communications Unit at HMS *Mercury* to the Barents Sea to carry out extensive intercept operations. But Outboard was designed for use against the Soviet navy rather than for the amphibious support operations in support of ground forces which are now the Royal Navy's main role and was unable to keep pace with technology, in particular the increasing use of cellular telephone systems. In a joint procurement project with the US Navy, the Royal Navy installed a revamped Outboard system with greatly improved capabilities on each of its four Type-22 frigates. In addition, eight UK submarines will be fitted out with a new system capable of recognising radio transmitters, tracking them across the HF, VHF and UHF frequencies and pinpointing their locations. The system, to be installed on five Trafalgar-class submarines and all three of the new Astute-class submarines, will be able to intercept mobile telephone conversations.

The Nimrod R1s of 51 Squadron took part in the majority of operations carried out by the British armed forces from the Falklands to Afghanistan. This included over flying Iraq as part of the monitoring of the no-fly zones imposed in the wake of the allied victory in the Gulf War. By the mid-1990s, they were equipped with the computerised Star Window system. This had two high-speed-search radio sets to locate active frequencies, twenty-two intercept receivers to which those frequencies can then be transferred – allowing further search operations – and a wide-band digital direction-finding system to locate target transmitters. The ground analysis station could access the data directly via satellite. This system appears to have been updated in 1998 with the addition of a £4m mobile-telephone intercept facility provided by the US company Applied Signal Technology. The capabilities remain classified but those of AST's standard product are not. The Model 1235 Multi-Channel Digital Receiving System is fully computerised and has 60 independent digital receivers, each of which can switch between the various mobile telephone modes as required. They are also said to be 'adept' at tracking the communications of the mobile telephone under attack and its base station as they switch frequency. The Nimrod R1 is expected to remain in service until 2008. The aircraft itself is an extremely robust platform ideal for signals intelligence operations and may simply be re-fitted with new equipment. Alternatively it could be replaced by a modified civilian executive jet or a high-altitude unmanned aerial vehicle (UAV) such as the US Global Hawk fitted with a remote signals intelligence payload.

The R1 is not the British armed forces' only airborne signals intelligence platform. The Army Air Corps's No 1Flight, based at Aldergrove in Northern Ireland has five Britten-Norman Islander aircraft equipped with DF locating systems and mobile telephone monitoring capability to gather intelligence on terrorist groups. These aircraft have also been used over London and other British cities as part of the war on terror.

British military, naval and air force signals operations now share a home training base at Chicksands. The US intercept site closed in 1994 and the camp was taken over by the armed forces as a joint headquarters for military, naval and air force intelligence training. The Defence Intelligence and Security Centre includes the Defence Special Signals School formed from the Army signals intelligence training unit Communications and Security Group (UK), its RAF counterpart the Communications Analysis Training School and the training elements of the Royal Navy's Special Communications Unit. The 100-strong rapid deployment SIGINT elements of the Special Communications Unit, known as the Fleet Electronic Warfare Support Group, moved from HMS *Mercury* to HMS *Collingwood* at Fareham, Hampshire, in early 2002.

GCHQ's civilian intercept organisation, the Composite Signals Organisation, still exists, although advances in satellite monitoring and computer automation have left it bearing the brunt of the cuts in staffing levels. For similar reasons many of the post-war monitoring sites have gone. GCHQ maintains a London liason office: at 9–10 Palmer Street, only yards from New Scotland Yard, the headquarters of the Metropolitan Police. Cheadle was closed following the end of the Cold War. But Irton Moor, the site near Scarborough, is still in existence, as is the satellite-monitoring station at Morwenstow. The foreign monitoring stations at Colombo and Singapore all went in the retreat from empire. Hong Kong went in 1997 with the hand-over of the colony to China, leaving bases on Ascension Island, Gibraltar and Cyprus, together with a number of small detachments at embassies and High Commissions around the world.

GCHQ is still based at its two sites in Cheltenham, although the main emphasis moved from Oakley to Benhall in 2003 with the construction of new premises, known locally as 'the Doughnut' because of the circular shape. GCHQ's stated role is to monitor all forms of radio, electronic and acoustic transmissions to gain political, military and economic intelligence. It also provides advice on the security of communications and computer systems for government departments, the armed forces and the police, through its Communications Electronics Security Group. It is required by law to act 'in the interests of national security, with particular reference to the defence and foreign policies of Her Majesty's Government in the United Kingdom; or in the interests of the economic well-being of the United Kingdom in relation to the actions or intentions of persons outside the British Islands; or in support of the prevention or detection of serious crime'. The most noteworthy point of this brief is that only in respect of 'economic well-being' does the act specify that the monitored activity must be taking place abroad.

GCHQ is divided into a number of directorates, the most important of which is the Directorate of SIGINT Operations and Requirements. This has been the main area of reorganisation since the Cold War, when its eight divisions included:

Z: Requirements and Liaison – the department that co-ordinated coverage according to the requirements of the domestic customers, of which the foremost are now likely to be the Foreign Office, the Ministry of Defence, the Department of Trade and Industry, the Treasury, the Bank of England, and GCHQ's sister organisations MI5 and MI6, as well as the police – in particular the National Criminal Intelligence Service. It also performed the same role with similar foreign organisations with which exchange deals existed or could be negotiated, not just those from the main UKUSA countries but also including Germany's *Bundesnachrichtendienst*, which began exchanging signals intelligence with Britain and America in 1973.

X: Computer Services – in charge of the agency's highly developed supercomputers that are capable of deciphering some of the most sophisticated of encryption systems, picking out keywords from a mass of transmissions or detecting suspicious financial transactions passing through the international banking system.

H: Cryptanalysis – during the Cold War this was one of Britain's most important bargaining chips in terms of the UKUSA Accord. One GCHQ official, speaking in 1982, described H Division's contribution as 'the major factor in GCHQ's case'. At that time it was estimated that the division constituted 75 per cent of GCHQ's practical worth to the Americans. US officials frequently based their foreign policy on reports derived from signals intelligence collected by both the British and the Americans, which only the British had been able to decipher. 'The time difference alone means that material can be on desks first thing in the morning.'

J and K: SIGINT Production. These are almost certainly the main areas of reorganisation. J Division was formerly Special SIGINT, the analysis and reporting of signals intelligence from the Soviet Bloc. K was General SIGINT, covering the rest of the world and economic intelligence. Clearly J's role has changed, with total signals intelligence effort against the former Soviet Union more than halved since the end of the Cold War. But the former Soviet Union remains an important target area, as does the Middle East, which traditionally fell within K Division's ambit. As with the other intelligence agencies, the so-called 'new' targets such as nuclear proliferation, terrorism, organised crime and economic intelligence all have their own specific sections. The old divisional responsibilities have been modified to allow more flexible specialist teams with a mix of cryptanalytical, linguistic and research skills to be set up as different targets emerge.

The capabilities of GCHQ and NSA are by turns overstated or underestimated. Their interception systems, often wrongly described as Echelon,* cannot scoop up and process every message that is sent. There are so-called Dictionary computers that can pick out keywords in printed text, something that should come as no surprise to anyone who has ever used an Internet search engine. Newer more discriminating systems can be programmed to look for subject matter rather than just key words, 'fingerprint' voices, and recognise spoken words. The advent of widespread computerised cryptography has inevitably caused problems. But the fact that one of the most significant advances in computer cryptography, Public Key Cryptography, was invented and developed by three GCHQ employees, James Ellis, Clifford Cocks, and Malcolm Williamson, during the early 1970s, several years ahead of its subsequent, and separate, invention by US academics, suggests that GCHQ has not, as is often suggested, failed completely in its efforts to keep track of computer technology. Since Cocks went on in 1999 to create Identifier Based Encryption, a much more reliable and efficient form of Public Key Cryptography, it also seems likely that GCHQ's current 'boffins' are better placed than most to make the mathematical advances needed to find ways around such systems. The other key problem for GCHQ and NSA has been the massive increase in fibre-optic cables, thin glass cables surrounded by plastic along which data is transmitted as pulses of light rather than electrical pulses. Contrary to popular belief, these can be tapped relatively easily. But this cannot be achieved without an agent on the ground. Nevertheless, NSA and or GCHQ appear to have found ways around this particular problem. Terry Thompson, NSA Deputy Director for Services, said in September 1999 that the agency, and by extension GCHQ, was 'much further ahead now in terms of being able to access and collect fibre-optics,

---

* Echelon is the software programme that allows the UKUSA first parties, Britain and America, and second parties, Australia, Canada and New Zealand, to pool their resources using a network of interconnected computers known as Platform.

cellular data, all the different modalities of communications that we are targeting. And that results in a lot of output for our analysts.'

The cellular data referred to by Thompson is communications intelligence collected by the interception of mobile telephones which are not just intercepted from the air but increasingly by tactical ground signals intelligence operations. The ease with which mobile telephones can be obtained and operated has led to their increased use by the type of people the intelligence services want to monitor, not just criminals and terrorists but also the military. Despite the encryption processes used in modern digital mobile telephones a well-equipped intercept station will have little problem monitoring calls made on a target telephone. A typical mobile telephone system is made up of a series of base stations controlled by a mobile telephone switching office (MTSO). Once a mobile telephone is turned on, its transceiver automatically searches for the local base station with the strongest signal and sets up a communication link along which it transmits information about its identity to allow incoming calls to be directed to the base station to which it is linked. In a process known as 'meaconing', the intercept system takes control of the mobile telephone. It first jams the link, forcing the mobile telephone to look for another base station. It then sets up a new counterfeit base station with a much stronger signal, which attracts the mobile telephone. Any incoming or outgoing calls are now redirected through the counterfeit station and since it is the base station that controls encryption, the counterfeit station simply denies encryption, allowing the operator to listen into the call unimpeded by encryption and without either party being aware of what is happening.

It is the very success described by Thompson in expanding 'output' which is the key problem facing both GCHQ and NSA. Although there is material that they cannot decipher, there is too much that they can read for their linguists and intelligence analysts to process. This is likely to be less of a problem for GCHQ, which with limited resources compared to its US partner and firm directives from the JIC has always had to prioritise its targets much more carefully. But so closely intertwined are the two agencies that any problem for one is a problem for the other, a situation demonstrated most vividly in January 2000 when the NSA's main computer system crashed. 'NSA headquarters was brain dead,' said General Michael Hayden, the NSA Director. 'We had some residual ability at our locations around the world, but I don't want to trivialise this. This was really bad.' For three days, GCHQ provided all signals intelligence reporting to both British and US policy-makers. GCHQ has played a key role in the surveillance operations against Osama bin Laden and his al-Qaʻeda terrorist network. This is in part due to the way in which the world is split up between NSA and GCHQ, and the fact that Morwenstow is the main UKUSA ground station monitoring satellite communications from the Middle East and downloading the intercepted 'take' from a Mercury satellite positioned in geosynchronous orbit above the Indian Ocean. As a result, GCHQ has much greater expertise in the key languages used by al-Qaʻeda – Arabic, Pashto, and Urdu. When bin Laden moved to Afghanistan from Sudan in 1996, one of his known associates based in London made the mistake of buying an Inmarsat satellite telephone with his credit card. For two years, GCHQ monitored the telephone, transcribing thousands of conversations and building up a detailed picture of bin Laden, his key associates, and how al-Qaʻeda operated. It was the GCHQ transcripts that provided the first 'compelling evidence' that bin Laden was financing a 'holy war' against America. The line went dead in 1998, after the success was revealed in the US media. But GCHQ was still able to monitor key al-Qaʻeda conversations and according to Francis Richards, GCHQ Director, by 2000, bin Laden had become 'a major preoccupation'.

It was GCHQ, and not as reported NSA, which monitored two key telephone conversations that took place on the eve of the 11 Septemebr attacks. With hindsight, the messages appeared to refer to 11 September as the start of an al-Qaʻeda operation. Speaking in Arabic, one participant said: 'The match begins tomorrow,' A second said: 'Tomorrow is zero [hour]' GCHQ and NSA monitor a large number of telephone numbers and email addresses associated with al-Qaʻeda. It took only two days to find and transcribe these two particular conversations from among the very large number of conversations and messages sent by telephone and email addresses on the UKUSA watch list. This is in fact an indication that the particular telephones used were given a high priority, although not the highest priority. This appears to have been a correct assessment since, although the telephones were believed to be linked to al-Qaʻeda, it was not clear who was using them. The British Intelligence and Security Committee (ISC) investigation into the intelligence services' response to the attacks found that there had been no forewarning of the attack. Sir Stephen Lander, the then Director of MI5, said that a subsequent re-examination of material across the intelligence community, which included the two messages monitored by GCHQ, 'did not find any that, with the wisdom of hindsight, could have given warning of the attacks'.

In the immediate aftermath of the attacks, between thirty and forty per cent of GCHQ's efforts was concentrated on al-Qa'eda and Afghanistan. During the operations against Afghanistan, the RAF's Nimrod R1 signals intelligence platforms were in constant use. The NSA satellite above the Indian Ocean and the remote radio sets linked to the Joint Service Signal Units at Ayios Nikolaos and Digby are also likely to have provided good coverage. This will have been augmented by the remarkably well-placed German intercept operation in China's Pamir mountains overlooking Afghanistan. The *Bundesnachrichtendienst* site, codenamed *Lanze* (Lance), has been in existence since the mid-1980s and is known to have provided good intelligence on al-Qa'eda and in particular its support for Chechen terrorists long before the 11 September attacks. Once allied troops were on the ground, they were immediately joined by signals intelligence operators from 14 Signal Regiment and later by Y Troop, 3 Commando Brigade. GCHQ has also doubled its counter-terrorism effort and begun 'significantly improving its capability' to monitor terrorist communications, an indication that coverage of al-Qa'eda could have been better. It is not clear where the improvements have been made but bin Laden is known to have pumped large sums of money into acquiring the latest communications technology. This includes equipment that allows messages to be pre-recorded and then sent as a very short burst transmission as well as sophisticated computerised encryption systems.

Signals intelligence operations during the 2003 war in Iraq were preceded by the leaking of a memorandum showing that GCHQ had been involved in operations to intercept the communications of the various UN Security Council members to discover their positions with regard to a resolution backing the war. While this was a matter of routine, the curious US decision to compromise the interception of high-level Iraqi communications in an attempt to secure such a resolution was not. Colin Powell, the US Secretary of State, played the Security Council recordings of Iraqi officers discussing a cover-up of Iraq's chemical and biological weapons programme on what appeared to be microwave telephone links. The move failed to persuade the UN to back the war and probably ensured that a valuable source of intelligence dried up just as it was needed most. Nevertheless, signals intelligence played an important part in the war with every possible asset brought into use. GCHQ took a key role through the satellite 'take' downloaded at Morwenstow and Joint Service Signal Units at Digby in the UK and Ayios Nikolaos on Cyprus. Two US satellites collected signals intelligence from Iraq - the Mercury satellite in geosynchronous orbit above the Indian Ocean in which Britain has a part share, and a Trumpet satellite in a high elliptical orbit used for the monitoring of mobile telephone conversations. These were reinforced by more than a dozen allied signals intelligence aircraft including at least one RAF R1 Nimrod from 51 Sqn.

Mobile signals intelligence units from 14 Signal Regiment and Y Troop, 3 Commando Brigade, equipped with the new Scarus man-portable electronic warfare system, as did the small team attached to the SAS and the Royal Navy's Fleet Electronic Warfare Support Group. Signals intelligence is known to have been extremely important in the operations to destroy the Republican Guard formations defending Baghdad. In the first week of the war it revealed that they were using heavy sandstorms to re-deploy to new positions, allowing allied air power to destroy scores of the Iraqi T72 tanks. It was also crucial in determining the timing of the American assault on the Iraqi capital. This was planned for 30 March but when the allies intercepted radio communications ordering the Republican Guard divisions based south of the capital to pull back they decided to wait. As the Iraqi troops pulled out of their dug-in positions into the open they came under heavy bombardment from a mass of allied aircraft which effectively took all but a few remnants of the Republican Guard out of the battle for Baghdad. Signals intelligence also told coalition commanders about the sorry state of Iraqi command and control. By early April, intercepted high-level communications were revealing that Saddam's younger son Qusay was still alive and controlling the Iraqi resistance. But so terrified were Iraqi officers of what he might do to them that they repeatedly spoke of having defeated the US troops in battle and claimed to have inflicted high levels of casualties on coalition forces.

Communications intercepts are also believed to have been instrumental in the second allied attempt to assassinate the Iraqi leadership. An intercepted conversation confirmed intelligence from agents on the ground that the Iraqi leadership, including Qusay and, if he had survived the first strike of the war, Saddam Hussein would be meeting in the Mansur district of north-west Baghdad on the afternoon of 7 April. As a result the building was reduced to rubble by an allied air strike, although subsequent intelligence suggested Saddam was not inside the building when the bombs hit.

Military Intelligence

Prologue

The cluster of camouflaged green military vehicles parked amid the junipers and scrubby oaks of a forest clearing, 8,000 feet up on the slopes of Mount Ljuboten on the border between Macedonia and Kosovo, appeared relatively innocuous, even harmless. It was shortly after 4am on the morning of Saturday, 12 June 1999, but already the sun was moving up in the sky and it was turning into a typically warm June day in the Balkans. Nato troops were about to pour into Kosovo to replace the withdrawing soldiers of the JNA, the Yugoslav National Army, following the decision by President Slobodan Milosevic to give up the fight. These apparently unarmed Hagglund BV206 all-terrain vehicles and Land Rovers could scarcely have any important role to play in the Nato advance.

Inside the Hagglunds, Royal Marine Commando electronic warfare operators were scanning the radio frequencies tracking the military communications nets of the JNA. The intercept operators from Y Troop, 3 Commando Brigade, had been rapidly trained up on the new Odette communications electronic warfare system, which had been rushed into service to allow its involvement in the Kosovo campaign. The Odette intercept equipment, capable of tracking sophisticated frequency-hopping radio stations across the HF, VHF and UHF frequency bands and locating individual stations through direction-finding, was not due to be operational for another year. But it was enjoying the most realistic of trials. Odette's capabilities, and the perfect direct line of sight from Mount Ljuboten down the Lepenac and Sitnica valleys to the Kosovan capital Pristina, were providing the commando intercept operators with an intelligence bonanza. Not only had they tied down every one of the main JNA radio nets, the commandos' specialist Serbo-Croat linguists were able to listen in to the mobile telephone calls of Yugoslav commanders as they talked to Belgrade during the negotiations with Nato over the JNA's hurried withdrawal.

Now they were about to carry out one more vital task to help the Nato advance into Kosovo. Down below to the east, at the Macedonian end of the Kacanik Gorge, British Challenger 2 tanks were preparing to lead the 50,000 Nato forces into Kosovo, waiting for the order from Lieutenant-General Sir Mike Jackson, commander of Nato's Kosovo Force (K-For), that would set them on their way. As the order came, British and Gurkha paratroopers from the 1st Battalion, the Parachute Regiment, swept into Kosovo in a fleet of Chinook helicopters to secure the high ground overlooking the gorge. On the road below, the tanks and armoured personnel carriers of the British 4th Armoured Brigade began to move slowly into Kosovo, their progress impeded by a massive traffic jam of military vehicles, returning refugees and journalists. High above the melee, on the rugged slopes of Mount Ljuboten, the commando electronic warfare operators activated Odette's jamming system and each of the carefully tracked JNA radio nets became instantly unworkable. JNA signals operators in the remaining Serb forces scattered across the north of the province ripped off their headsets as a continuous burst of noise removed their transceivers' abilities to talk to each other, ensuring there was no possibility of Milosevic reneging on the peace deal.

Nineteen

A Contradiction in Terms

Military intelligence is a contradiction in terms.

Old army adage

David Henderson, the head of British intelligence in the Boer War, had a lasting influence on British military intelligence, repeatedly lobbying the War Office to set up an Intelligence Corps 'to enable the General Staff to deal with the large and varied staff of subordinates required for Field Intelligence work'. In response to Henderson's sustained offensive, Colonel George M W Macdonogh, who in 1910 had succeeded James Edmonds as head of MO5, began to compile a list of likely members. Henderson outlined the requirements. 'The successful intelligence officer must be cool, courageous and adroit, patient and imperturbable, discreet and trustworthy,' he wrote. 'He must have resolution to continue unceasingly his search for information, even in the most disheartening circumstances and after repeated failures. He must have endurance to submit silently to criticism, much of which may be based on ignorance or jealousy, and he must be able to deal with men, to approach his source of information with tact and skill, whether such source be a patriotic gentleman or an abandoned traitor.' Macdonagh selected his candidates on the basis that they would need a mixture of intellect, linguistic ability and an unorthodox approach. On the outbreak of war, an odd assortment of academics, businessmen, artists, schoolteachers, musicians and adventurers were surprised to receive a telegram inviting them to join the new Intelligence Corps. They were to report to Southampton, where they were graded as Second Lieutenants (Interpreters) or Agents (1st Class).

The commandant of the new corps was Major T. G. J. Torrie of the Indian Army – appointed because he was back on leave when war broke out and, not wanting to miss the action, badgered Macdonogh into giving him a posting to France. But within weeks of arriving in France Torrie had moved on, having found himself a posting to an infantry regiment where he was assured of front-line action. He was replaced by Major A. P., later Field Marshal Lord, Wavell, who had been working as a Russian linguist in the Directorate of Military Operations but was also eager for action. Wavell was unimpressed by his subordinates – 'an odd crowd of thirty to forty officers with a smattering of languages' – and, like Torrie, had no commitment to intelligence work. 'Once I had got a grip on the purpose of the Intelligence Corps, got it organised, cleared up one or two minor scandals and dismissed one or two unsuitable types, I found there was only one or two hours work a day.' After three and a half weeks as corps commandant – even less time than Torrie – Wavell had found himself a more active post.

Most regular officers took a somewhat dim view of their new colleagues. 'The green-tabbed official of the Intelligence Corps was at first regarded with the utmost suspicion,' one officer wrote. 'His reserve was very marked and he had an insatiable curiosity, a combination of characteristics which the average Britisher resents, and this rather led the soldier to imagine that his efforts were not so much directed towards gleaning information about the enemy as about the state of the unit that he visited, and he was consequently looked upon at first as suspect.' The corps had not got off to a good start and, given the hostility of many of the Army's senior officers, might have completely fallen apart were it not for the presence in France of two of its main architects within the Directorate of Military Operations, Major Walter Kirke and Colonel Macdonogh, who had been posted to the British Expeditionary Force's GHQ as Head of Intelligence. While working in MO5 with Macdonogh, Kirke had laid down the role of the Intelligence Corps as being to provide linguists, to carry out secret service work and to form the nucleus of a counter-espionage network.

Henderson had stressed that counter-espionage was just as important as intelligence-gathering, and his recommendations had been fully reflected in the regulations. 'Preventing the enemy from obtaining information is, in European warfare, almost as of great importance as securing information for one's own side,' he wrote in *Field Intelligence, Its Principles and Practices*. 'With civilian inhabitants, foreign military attachés and newspaper correspondents about, it will be impossible to obtain complete concealment, but measures must be taken to secure that they see as little as possible and hear nothing.' But it was inevitably the secret service work – which was to play a minimal role in military intelligence – that captivated the minds of those recruited into the corps. Sigismund Payne-Best, who was later to become better known for his role as a member of the Secret Intelligence Service in the Venlo incident, recalled how he and a number of other potential 'I' Corps officers had been recruited. Best, who was not on Macdonogh's original list, was told to report to the War Office: 'Men were being ushered in, one by one to this room. Some of them came out very promptly, others stayed there some time, and gradually it was rumoured that it was intelligence. They were recruiting men for intelligence work in France. A lot of talk then went on about intelligence service. Spying. You get shot if you get caught spying in France. When the last man had been interviewed, we were told to follow a sergeant and he led us out and we marched, or rather we straggled, behind the sergeant to Burlington House. Well, the sergeant walked in front. I think if he'd walked at the back, perhaps more of us would have reached Burlington House, for I certainly noticed that quite a number of people seemed to disappear. I think they had got cold feet. They'd got the idea that we were to spy and that spying was a dangerous job.'

Best was one of the few corps officers who did find themselves involved in secret service work. Two separate sections were set up – one based in London, the other in Folkestone – to collect intelligence from refugees coming into Britain from the Lowlands. Best, working under Major Ernest Wallinger, from a headquarters in Basil Street, Kensington, was successful not only in obtaining information from the refugees but in setting up networks of agents and train-watchers in Belgium to report on German troop movements. The train-watchers included housewives living in houses overlooking railway lines who knitted encoded reports of the German movements: a plain stitch for a carriage containing men, purl for those carrying horses. Wallinger controlled agents throughout Belgium, Holland, Switzerland and Germany, competing with MI6 operations – much to Cumming's chagrin. Intelligence Corps officers were also sent behind enemy lines, usually parachuted in at night, and dressed in French peasant clothing or occasionally even German military uniform, collected intelligence needed quickly for operational reasons, or liaised with agents.

But spying was to play only a peripheral part in the new corps's work. Intelligence was being transformed by new technology in the shape of the radio and the aircraft. Aerial reconnaissance and the interception of wireless signals were to be two of the three main methods of intelligence collection employed by the new corps. The other, with the scope for forward reconnaissance limited by trench warfare, was the interrogation of enemy prisoners and deserters. Henderson had advocated the classic 'nice guy, nasty guy' method of interrogation. 'Skill in eliciting information grows rapidly with practice,' he wrote. 'Sympathy with inhabitants, camaraderie with prisoners, affected suspicion of deserters, is often successful. Gentleness will sometimes melt reserve, harshness may break it down. A bottle of brandy is a powerful weapon against a physically exhausted man. A method frequently found effective in important cases is to bring an unwilling witness first before an officer who will question him harshly and threaten him, and then hand him over to the care of a sympathetic underling.'

Aerial reconnaissance had begun with a balloon flown by the French forces over the positions of their Austrian enemy at the Battle of Fleurus in July 1794. During the American Civil War, Union troops used a balloon to take photographs of Confederate positions at Richmond. Similar methods were used in the Franco-Prussian War, and in 1884 the British Army set up its own balloon reconnaissance unit. By the turn of the century the War Office was being urged to carry out 'special and early experiments in connection with a dirigible balloon, man-lifting kite and photographic equipment for the balloon sections'. As a result, the main military advantage of the fixed-wing aircraft was at first seen in its use as a vehicle for aerial reconnaissance. The first recorded use of an aircraft for such purposes was by Captain Piazza of the Italian Army in October 1911, during the Italo-Turkish war. He was also the first to take aerial pictures, photographing Turkish positions on 24 and 25 February 1912. David Henderson – who had been appointed to head the newly formed Royal Flying Corps – set up a photo-reconnaissance unit, No 3 Squadron, RFC. Lack of funds led the officers involved to buy their own cameras, which were not very efficient. Nevertheless, they were used in the first operational success for No 3 Squadron, the photographing of brick stacks close to the Bassée Canal, which uncovered a new German trench thereby assisting a subsequent allied attack. Henderson created an experimental photographic section, which devised a new camera specially designed for use from aircraft and capable of being fitted on to the fuselage. During the 1916 Battle of the Somme alone, the RFC took more than 19,000 air photographs. Intelligence sections were attached to any squadron carrying out aerial reconnaissance. A school of photography, mapping and reconnaissance was set up at Farnborough, Hampshire, in September 1916, and a few months later the first manual on photo-interpretation was published. Aerial photography could disclose camouflaged positions and installations that were missed by human observers and the amount of intelligence provided was beyond the belief of many officers. By the end of the war, around six million aerial photographs had been produced.

Interception of the ground telephone wires linking the German trenches was carried out using copper rods attached to an amplifier designed to pick up the faint signals going to earth from the wires. The British were very slow to recognise the military potential of the wireless but the British Expeditionary Force did have some wagon-mounted wirelesses intended for the use of the cavalry. By the end of 1914 they were being used almost exclusively to intercept German radio communications – 'a task that was carried out with considerable success'. Traffic analysis rather than code-breaking was the main method of producing intelligence from the German messages. All of these Intelligence Corps operations were mirrored in other theatres, in particular the Middle East, where one Intelligence Corps officer, Colonel Richard Meinertzhagen, carried out one of the most famous deception operations of all time. Shortly before the Second Battle of Gaza, Meinertzhagen rode out in front of Turkish troops pretending to be wounded by their shots and dropped a haversack, previously soaked in blood and containing false plans, in order to plant misleading information about the British plans.

At the end of the war, the Intelligence Corps continued in operation in occupied Germany, monitoring German compliance with the Armistice and carrying out counter-espionage. But there were few who saw any need for military intelligence in peacetime and by December 1929 the corps had disappeared. This created predictable difficulties in 1939, with the corps being hurriedly pulled together now under cover of the Corps of Military Police. Yet again the Army targeted intellectuals, who, while undoubtedly suited to the work, were unlikely to have the respect of the professional soldier. Malcolm Muggeridge, one of those arriving at the training centre at Mytchett in Surrey, recalled, 'The Red Caps looked with ill-concealed distaste and disdain at we Field Security men, mostly schoolmasters, journalists, encyclopaedia salesmen, unfrocked clergymen and other displaced *New Statesman* readers.' As in 1914, they had similar problems getting field commanders to take their work, and perhaps more importantly their product, seriously. Under persistent lobbying from Major W F Jeffries, the officer responsible for military intelligence personnel, the War Office finally agreed to the creation of an independent Intelligence Corps, approved by King George VI on 15 July 1940. Jeffries was appointed as its first commandant.

'Intelligence, with all its ramifications and duties, became so vast and grew up so rapidly that I felt it was impossible to control properly or obtain that esprit de corps which was essential,' he said. 'I had numerous talks with the late Brigadier Martin (the DDMI) and with General Beaumont-Nesbitt (the DMI) pleading for a Corps. Both agreed on the necessity, but masses of difficulties arose, chiefly as to where a proper and large enough building and training ground could be obtained. I asked for Holloway College, Virginia Water, which would have been ideal, but was told that the education of women could not be interfered with!'

Nevertheless, using private connections, Jeffries succeeded in acquiring two Oxford colleges, Oriel and Pembroke, as a corps headquarters and officer training centre, while other ranks were trained at King Alfred's College, Winchester, where their experiences were similar to those of Muggeridge. 'Having been brought up on Buchan's Richard Hannay novels, there was a certain romance in answering an advertisement in the personal column of the *Daily Telegraph* in 1940 inviting one to apply to a box number if one spoke foreign languages and wished to serve one's country,' recalled David Engleheart, one of those joining the new corps. 'Spice was added on discovering that the address for the subsequent assignation was the legendary shop at the Trafalgar Square end of Northumberland Avenue. Upstairs to a door opened by a bespectacled corporal and into an untidy room presided over by an unmistakably schoolmasterly captain, who, without ceremony, proceeded to give a few chaps and me a French dictée which was taken away to be corrected by the corporal. He then told us to confess to any pink, red or other political rashes into which we might have broken out during adolescence ("We will find out anyway"), said that we had volunteered for the Intelligence Corps and would be inducted at an undisclosed date.'

Engleheart, who was transferring from the Royal Signals, was told to report to Winchester: 'Having slept for weeks on a palliasse on the floor of a shoddy mill in a rundown Yorkshire town called Ossett, I thought there was little new King Alfred's could teach me. This was a mistake. Instead of the heterogeneous intake up north from every walk of life, welded together by homesickness, compulsory fitness, a better diet than most civilians, and Vera Lynn, I found a sophisticated mixture of intellectuals, world travellers, artists, journalists, film directors, jockeys, MPs – you name it they were there.'

The Directorate of Military Intelligence had expanded with the start of the war and a number of new sections had been created, including MI8, controlling signals intelligence; MI9, prisoner-of-war intelligence; and MI14, a special section concentrating on building up a complete picture of German military formations from all available sources. The main roles of the new Intelligence Corps were the collection of strategic intelligence from aerial photography and signals intelligence; the assimilation of tactical intelligence from a variety of sources – including both of the above plus forward reconnaissance, captured documents and the interrogation or debriefing of prisoners of war, agents and refugees – and counter-intelligence and security, of everything from documents to military bases, airfields, ports and even brothels. Debriefing one soldier who had reported information being freely circulated in a Middle East 'knocking shop', Maurice Oldfield, then just an Intelligence Corps lieutenant, but later to become the Chief of MI6, asked: 'Couldn't you have stayed with the girl just a bit longer, until breakfast time, say? I'm sure she could have told you a lot more.'

Interrogation of enemy prisoners was controlled initially by MI9, as part of a general PoW intelligence organisation covering both British servicemen in enemy hands and captured prisoners. But at the beginning of 1942 intelligence from enemy PoWs was split off and placed under the control of MI19. The intelligence was collected both in Britain and in theatre by the Combined Services Detailed Interrogation Centres. The headquarters organisation and main interrogation centre for PoWs brought to Britain was based initially at Cockfosters Barracks, Trent Park, north-east London, before moving to new purpose-built interrogation centres at Latimer and Wilton Park, Beaconsfield. A number of German prisoners cooperated with their British captors. Others were infiltrated by 'stool pigeons' or bugged in so-called Source X operations. There were 30 purpose-built 'miked' rooms in each of the two camps and prisoners expected to produce valuable intelligence were held in pairs with nothing to do apart from sleep or talk to each other while teams of German-speaking operators, working in shifts of six per room to ensure nothing was missed, listened in.

The Second World War established signals intelligence and air photography as the two most valuable methods of gathering information on enemy military activity. Before the war, the RAF's reluctance to undertake aerial intelligence missions over Europe had led the Air section of MI6 to create its own photo-reconnaissance organisation. Sidney Cotton, an Australian pilot, carried out a number of missions, some in co-operation with the French, to photograph border areas of Germany and Italian-occupied territory in the Mediterranean and East Africa. The first flight over Germany came in March 1939, when using a Leica camera Cotton photographed Mannheim. During July and August 1939 Cotton flew his Lockheed 12A deep into German territory, under cover as a businessman and amateur pilot, photographing a number of locations of interest to British intelligence, including Berlin and the German naval base at Wilhelmshafen. John Weaver, a member of Cotton's unit, described how shortly before the outbreak of war, Cotton flew to Berlin's Tempelhof airport. 'Goering and his lieutenants were there. Seeing the aircraft, they made enquiries as to whom it belonged. On finding out, they approached Cotton for a flight and asked where he would take them. Cotton said: "I have a dear old aunt who lives in such an area and if you have no objections we could fly over there." It was agreed and off they set. But what they did not know was that dear old Sydney was pressing the tit the whole time, taking photographs.'

Cotton offered his services to the RAF in August 1939 but was turned down, the RAF being 'unsympathetic to irregular operations in general, and Cotton in particular'. But within weeks the RAF had realised that Cotton was providing MI6 with valuable intelligence and insisted on taking over his operation. Cotton was commissioned as a wing commander in charge of the Photographic Development Unit at Heston, just west of London. Initially the RAF tried to use Blenheim and Lysander aircraft, but they could not fly high or fast enough to evade the German fighters and eventually 'Cottonised' Spitfires were used. Cotton himself continued to rub the RAF top brass up the wrong way. 'He obtained what he wanted where he could get it; he was impatient of "the usual channels"; he applied business methods to government officials and, instead of filling in forms, put them in the waste-paper basket,' one officer said. 'Nor did he hesitate to tell senior air officers who obstructed him precisely what he thought of them. The air staff loathed him. Their opinion was that he was "a line-shooter, racketeer and salesman who does not deliver the goods".' But the other services had an entirely different view of him. Admiral John Godfrey, the Director of Naval Intelligence, said: 'He has delivered the goods most loyally as far as we are concerned and has been the driving force in the development of air intelligence from photography.' By mid-1940, demand for aerial photography had grown to such an extent that the services of 'Cotton's Crooks' were no longer sufficient. The RAF gratefully used this as an excuse to dispense with his services. The unit was re-christened 1 Photographic Reconnaissance Unit and a separate Photographic Interpretation Unit was set up in the north-London suburb of Wembley.

Within a year the success of aerial reconnaissance – which was in marked contrast to the early difficulties in the acquisition of human intelligence and the collection and dissemination of signals intelligence – led all three services to clamour for more, and the number of photo-reconnaissance aircraft was more than doubled, from 33 to 78. The introduction of Mosquitoes at the end of 1941 allowed vast areas of eastern Germany and the Baltic ports to be photographed and the development of more powerful cameras led to details of U-boat construction being studied for the first time. By 1944, no enemy-controlled area in Europe was beyond the RAF's range, making photographic intelligence one of the widest used and most important sources of intelligence. 'Intelligence information from other sources has proved most difficult to obtain on account of the stringent German security precautions and other reasons,' one JIC report said. 'Moreover, we have practical proof of the value of air photographs as they enabled the front of the German attack on 10 May 1940 to be predicted with accuracy more than one month before the attack took place.' Shortly afterwards, the Wembley PIU moved to Danesfield House on the banks of the Thames at Medmenham in Buckinghamshire, where it was renamed the Central Interpretation Unit to reflect the fact that Intelligence Corps and Royal Navy photographic interpreters had joined the original RAF contingent. From then on Medmenham was involved in the planning stages of virtually every wartime operation.

At the end of the First World War, naval intelligence rested on the laurels earned by Room 40 – with disastrous results. For most of the inter-war period it virtually ignored the signals intelligence produced by the GC&CS naval section, relying largely on the pre-war naval agreements for its knowledge of enemy shipping. As a result, the Naval Intelligence Division took a far too optimistic view of German intentions and it was not until Godfrey took over as Director of Naval Intelligence, in January 1939, that it began seriously to prepare for war.

The central focus of naval intelligence during the Second World War was NID8, the Operational Intelligence Centre, which tracked the passage of enemy shipping and in particular the U-boats. Its sources were initially limited. Attempts to place intelligence officers on merchant ships to gather evidence from ports and passing ships were largely unproductive. Godfrey recalled how one officer sent to the Black Sea, apparently to observe Russian naval movements, 'ended up in a Braila nightclub defying the Romanian Gestapo with a pistol in each hand. It was only by the personal intervention of the British minister that he was smuggled out'. At one point the NID even devised a scheme to predict what Hitler might do next by having astrological charts drawn up for him, since 'it had been known for some time that Hitler attached importance to astrological advice'. But by mid-1941 the breaking of the German navy's Enigma ciphers at Bletchley and the use of direction-finding and radio-fingerprinting co-ordinated from the Admiralty Y station at Scarborough were providing more reliable methods of charting the movement of enemy shipping. Signals intelligence was supplemented by human intelligence from MI6 agents and coastal watchers in Scandinavia and France, but by the latter stages of the war nearly 90 per cent of the intelligence handled by NID8 was signals intelligence, with human intelligence used in the main for confirmation.

At the end of the war the Intelligence Corps was run down but not disbanded, playing an important security role in the occupied zones of Germany and Austria and in the areas liberated from Japanese control. One of its primary roles in Germany was tracking down war criminals and prominent members of the Nazi Party. Intelligence Corps field security sections captured Heinrich Himmler, the SS leader, Joachim von Ribbentrop, the Nazi foreign minister, and the entire government of Hitler's successor, Admiral Dönitz. Norval Rogers, a member of 93 Field Security Section, serving in the town of Lüneburg in April 1945, recalled interrogating four German police officers. 'They were all in proper German civil police uniform and at first sight looked as though they might all be genuine. I questioned the two senior officers as to who they were, where they were going and why. In reply there followed a long-winded account of how there was a shortage of German police in what was to become the American zone and at the Americans request the Hamburg police were posting these four south to act as reinforcements. I began to address myself more and more to the one who seemed to be the most senior (he was certainly the fattest). Eventually the second officer, who I shall call the thin one) began to appear restive and he interrupted to ask why I did not address him, as he was the senior officer. The plump one did not dispute this and it came out that they were both of the same rank but one was of higher seniority. This was hardly surprising but there seemed to be a certain element of competition between the two who began to argue between themselves. In the course of this I heard the word *Standartenführer*, which was the SS rank equivalent to a full colonel in the army. In formal tones, I addressed the thin one as *Herr Standartenführer* and surprisingly he gave himself away by responding. This was an unexpected stroke of luck. The fat one now abandoned his police role and confessed to being a *Standartenführer* likewise. Further interrogation elicited that all of them had been members of

Himmler's personal staff. I was surprised to learn that these officers still had a strong sense of loyalty to Himmler. When I pointed out that he had been responsible for inhuman cruelty to multitudes of innocent people, they replied simply that he took no pleasure in cruelty, he was merely impervious to it when he considered it necessary. The real reason for the journey of these Germans now gradually came to light. They had hoped to make their way to Bavaria where they thought there might still be a possibility of organising a resistance movement centred on Hitler's mountain resort at Berchtesgaten, known as the Eagle's Nest.' Rodgers passed the four on to an internment camp for further interrogation.

With anxiety over Russian intentions increasing, demands for both signals and photographic intelligence was very high. For much of the war the Medmenham photographic intelligence centre had effectively been a joint British/US organisation, known as Allied Central Interpretation Unit, and approaches were made to Washington as early as August 1944 to continue these close links in peacetime. The Americans were very keen – not least because Britain provided an ideal location for photo-reconnaissance flights across eastern Europe and the Soviet Union, as well as a number of strategic airfields elsewhere, in the Middle East, the Indian subcontinent and south-east Asia.

The allies made a good start in their efforts to obtain aerial photography of the Soviet Union thanks to the Germans, who had accumulated large stocks of pictures taken by Heinkel photo-reconnaissance aircraft during the campaign on the Eastern Front. In an operation codenamed Dick Tracy, large numbers of aerial photographs were rescued by allied airmen sent in to Germany specifically to collect them. One particularly valuable haul was collected at Berchtesgaten only hours before a Russian team, which knew it was there, arrived to try unsuccessfully to prevent it falling into allied hands. Other operations collected similar material from Oslo, Vienna, and Berlin, taking up to a million photographs back to Medmenham. German wartime aerial photography of the Soviet Union continued to turn up for a number of years. As late as 1954, photographs of areas not covered by the allies' archives were purchased from 'two gentlemen' in Vienna for an undisclosed sum.

The German photographs filled a large gap in the allies' photographic intelligence archives. At the end of 1945 the RAF had begun a large-scale aerial reconnaissance operation, taking stock photographs first of the whole of western Europe, then of the Middle East, and later of North Africa. The USAF meanwhile was covering south-east Asia and the Americas. Neither side was prepared to overfly eastern Europe or the Soviet Union, for fear of offending the Russians. But in August 1946, four years before the US even began flying photographic reconnaissance flights over the Soviet Union, the RAF started making a limited number of flights over Russian-occupied Europe, 'in order that the present shortage of factual intelligence should, in some measure, be remedied'. The risk of detection was slight, the JIC was told. The Russians had only a few captured German radar installations, and the British aircraft – camouflaged pale blue – were invisible from the ground. Even if they were spotted, there was no Soviet aircraft capable of intercepting them. The RAF formed two photo-reconnaissance units at RAF Benson, in Oxfordshire; No 540 was equipped with Mosquitoes and No 541 with Spitfires. Flights over the southern Soviet Union were flown from bases in Crete, Cyprus and Iraq. British photographic interpretation operations moved from Medmenham to Nuneham Park, just outside Huntingdon in Cambridgeshire, in mid-1947, becoming known as the Joint Air Reconnaissance Intelligence Centre (JARIC).

The end of the war saw renewed efforts to improve the coordination of intelligence between the Royal Navy, the Army and the RAF. Pre-war attempts using the 1936 Inter-Service Intelligence Committee and its successor the JIC, which initially was a relatively limited body, were not a great success. There was a marked tendency for each service intelligence department to go its own way without consulting the others, epitomised by the Royal Navy's refusal to accept the inevitability of war with Hitler until shortly before it began. As VE Day approached, the JIC worked on ways to improve the situation. 'Intelligence before the war was starved of resources, especially in trained personnel,' it said in a report on the Post-War Organisation of Intelligence. 'It was not then realised that the less money we have to spend on preparations for war, the more important it is to have a first-class intelligence system in peacetime. An equally important shortcoming was the lack of a sufficiently authoritative means of putting forward considered views based upon the results of the intelligence produced. This failure to maintain an adequate intelligence organisation in peacetime led to the need for rapid and largely improvised expansion under the imminent threat of war and to the development of a complicated and uneconomical organisation. We now have an opportunity to set our house in order.'

The solution was to be the creation of the Joint Intelligence Bureau, a tri-service organisation that would 'collect, assess and, where appropriate, appreciate intelligence material of inter-departmental significance'. Although the JIB was headed by the influential General Sir Kenneth Strong, formerly Eisenhower's chief intelligence officer, it never quite fulfilled these lofty ambitions. 'The Bureau had a considerable battle for existence,' Strong wrote later. 'The armed services never really liked it and many of their senior men regarded it as a threat to the traditional forms of service intelligence.' The bureau was a relatively large body, with 220 staff. It had four separate divisions: one General division – which acted as a link with the service intelligence bodies and MI6 – and three geographical divisions: Western, covering western Europe; Central, covering the Soviet Union, eastern Europe, the Balkans and the Middle East; and Eastern, for Asia, the Pacific and the Americas. It never acted as the co-ordinating body that the JIC had envisaged but was primarily concerned with the collation of topographical, logistical, scientific, technical and economic intelligence. This last task, taken over from the Ministry of Economic Warfare, was seen as an important indicator of potential trouble spots. 'The economic contribution in assessing the strength of potential enemies is bound to be considerably more important than in wartime,' the JIC noted. 'Since in peace a country's capacity for war-making must chiefly lie in its war potential which is predominantly an economic factor.'

Military intelligence officers continued to play a key role on the ground in Germany and Austria in particular throughout the late 1940s and into the 1950s. They also worked alongside their colleagues from MI5 and MI6, many of whom wore the corps uniform as cover, preventing the spread of communist influence to the British zones and ensuring the return of a democratic political system. This was the early period of the Cold War when communist sleeper agents were sent into the West among the floods of displaced persons trying to return to their homes. Bob Steers, another member of the

Intelligence Corps, was part of the City Detachment of Field Security Vienna in 1953, interviewing the illegal frontier crossers (IFCs). 'As so often in life, one stubs one's toe against a situation totally by accident. One of the IFCs was a woman in her late fifties. The description of her escape across the Austro-Hungarian border just did not add up. Of one thing I was certain, she was no penetration agent. But why was she lying about the escape route. For the next two or three hours, I gently but persistently questioned her. Most interrogation is about persuasion and convincing. Eventually she related the true facts. Several times a week a train would travel from Budapest to Wiener Neustadt carrying Soviet staff officers from Hungary to their HQ in Austria. There was no document check or halt at the frontier. One of the drivers was the nephew of the woman sat before me. All she had to do was to go to the station in Budapest, walk on to the platform, where there were no security checks, step into the driver's cab and stand in the hanging curtained space for his coat. On arriving at Wiener Neustadt, where again there was no security check, all she had to do was to take the next train to Vienna, some 25 miles away. From an intelligence point of view, it was the Holy Grail. We had quite a traffic to and from Hungary. When our people had to return to Vienna it was a simple matter for them to make contact with the lady's nephew and "persuade" him to accommodate them in the space provided for coats.'

Twenty

Setting the House in Order

He who knows his adversary as well as he knows himself will never suffer defeat.
Sun Tzu, Chinese military tactician in *The Art of War*, 6th century BC

The RAF flew almost continuous aerial reconnaissance flights along the border between the Soviet and British zones of Germany during the late 1940s and early 1950s. No 541 Squadron was re-equipped with the Gloster Meteor PR10 in early 1951 and moved to Buckeburg in Germany. When President Truman banned US aerial reconnaissance flights over Warsaw Pact airspace in May 1950, following the shooting down of a US Navy Privateer caught in Latvian airspace, the RAF took over. US RB-45 aircraft, repainted with RAF insignia, flew a number of missions over eastern Europe and the Soviet Union.

There were three routes,' said Wing Commander Rex Sanders, the navigator on one of the flights. 'One was through Germany to the Baltic states. The second was south of that, through Germany towards Moscow, and the third was south of that, going down through the centre of Russia and then arcing down south on the way out. There was a fear, of course, that they might think this was something more serious than just reconnaissance. It did cross our minds that the Soviets might think we were attacking.'

An RAF Canberra – a new aircraft capable of flying higher than the Soviet fighters – flew an aerial reconnaissance mission over a new Soviet missile test site for the Americans in late 1953, overpassing the Volgograd site and then landing in Iran. The Canberras made a number of such flights over the Soviet Union and were so effective that the latest variant was still the main RAF photo-reconnaissance aircraft in 2003. Meanwhile, the Nuneham Park inter-pretation unit had undergone a further name change, to the Joint Air

Reconnaissance Intelligence Centre (JARIC), and in July 1957 it moved to Brampton, just outside Huntingdon.

The close links with the Americans fostered in the early years of the Cold War paid dividends even at the most unlikely of times. During the Suez Crisis, with America violently opposed to the Anglo-French/Israeli invasion, a USAF U-2 on a routine reconnaissance flight over the Mediterranean flew over an Egyptian military airport the RAF was about to bomb. Normal procedure was to make one overpass, turn, and make a second overpass before continuing on the mission. Between the two overpasses, the attack had taken place. The CIA, with the trans-Atlantic intelligence links unfazed by the inter-governmental friction, wired the 'before and after' photographs to the British, receiving the response: 'Warm thanks for the pix. It's the quickest bomb damage assessment we ever had.'

During the Cold War, the British and the Russians set up official missions to each other's zones of occupation, ostensibly as a liaison and confidence-building measure, although in fact they were little more than de-facto human intelligence organisations. The British mission, Brixmis, was formed in mid-1946 with a staff of around thirty, including interpreters, drivers, radio operators and 'four fairly high-ranking intelligence officers representing all three services plus a technical expert to collect technical intelligence, scientific intelligence and economic intelligence'. The missions were given qualified freedom of travel. There were a number of permanent restricted areas, and on occasions temporary restricted areas were imposed, to cover an exercise or a secret deployment. Brixmis spent much of its time making covert expeditions into the restricted areas to gather intelligence on military installations and equipment or to monitor military exercises. As a result, its members were frequently attacked by the Russians or the East Germans. Their vehicles were forced off the road, they were beaten up, and on occasion they were even shot at. But they produced endless photographs of new pieces of Soviet equipment that had never been seen before. Brixmis produced some of its best intelligence by tapping into Soviet landline terminals to intercept high-level communications. It also came back from some of its missions with extremely useful Soviet or East German documents. In 1986, Tim Spacey, then an army captain, was leading a Brixmis team parked up alongside railway sidings in the East German town of Magdeburg when a military train stopped close to their car. 'It was full of T-80s and other new kit. I couldn't believe my eyes. I woke up the others. Two of us got out. We knew that Russian guards were at the front of the train. My companion, an RAF flight lieutenant, kept watch while I cut through the camouflage net covering the nearest tank. Then I climbed up to the turret. I tried to open the hatch and it moved. It wasn't locked. I got inside with a camera and using flash shot an entire film. It was a senior captain's tank. He had left his briefcase inside. It contained a lot of useful stuff about the exercise his regiment had just completed. I took that back to Berlin. Our people were particularly interested in details of a wire-guided missile fired through the 125mm tank gun.'

One aspect of the Brixmis mission which has received little attention was the RAF's use of a small Chipmunk light aircraft to take photographs of Russian and East German military equipment in the airspace over Berlin. The Berlin Controlled Zone (BCZ), as it was known, was very much like the air corridors, in that it was open to Nato military aircraft albeit only if they were operating from West Germany and 'solely for the reinforcement of the Garrison'. The two Chipmunk aircraft based at RAF Gatow in the British sector of West Berlin were used for continuation training of RAF pilots. But for five days in each fortnight, they were used by Brixmis to take photographs of Soviet and East German bases and equipment located inside the BCZ, and occasionally, on even riskier missions inside German air space. The photographer occupied the front seat of the two-seater aircraft, using standard camera bodies with either a 55mm or 80mm lens for normal shots, and a 500mm lens for close-up photography. Roy Marsden, one of the RAF officers involved in the operations recalled how on one occasion, this time inside the BCZ, two Soviet Hind attack helicopters flew straight at one of the Chipmunks in an attempt to force it down. 'The aircraft only escaped by putting on 90 degrees bank and flying between the approaching Hinds,' Marsden said. Because the flights did not originate in West Germany, the Soviet liaison officers clearing the flights always stamped 'Safety of Flight Not Guaranteed' on the flight request card. 'Then came the daunting and dangerous task of flying a single-engined aircraft within the 1,200 square miles of the BCZ over many Soviet and East German installations. That on its own would have been bad enough, but we were at the same time photographing equipment of intelligence value that the Soviets and East Germans would have preferred to keep secret. The sorties were normally between one hour forty-five minutes and two hours fifteen minutes but we were given a great deal of latitude in which installations we photographed in the BCZ. The installations that lay within the zone included several major divisional headquarters, several ground ranges, a Soviet reconnaissance base equipped with MiG-25 Foxbat aircraft, two helicopter bases and many other important but less prestigious targets.'

The 1964 reforms of Britain's armed forces, which dissolved the Admiralty, War Office and Air Ministry to form a single Ministry of Defence, led to an amalgamation of the three service intelligence organisations with the JIB to form the Defence Intelligence Staff. The role of DIS was 'to provide objective all-source integrated intelligence assessments of defence matters in peace, crisis and war'. Its intelligence came from a number of sources, GCHQ and the services signals intelligence operations; JARIC; MI5; MI6; Brixmis; and defence attachés in Britain's embassies abroad. The practice of appointing military attachés to embassies abroad to collect intelligence was started by the French in the early part of the nineteenth century. But it was not until 1854 that Britain took up the practice, appointing 'commissars of the Queen' to Britain's allies in Paris, Turin and Constantinople and to the French headquarters in the Crimea. The intelligence role of the attaché is often played down but remains important, both in gauging intentions and in the collection of overt and covert intelligence.

In the retreat from empire that marked the decades following the Second World War, the British Army found itself involved in a series of conflicts in which intelligence was to play a major role. The most influential of these was the Malayan Emergency of 1948–60, which saw the first use of the 'hearts and minds' policy that lay at the heart of the British post-war counter-insurgency successes. It was linked to an intensive intelligence campaign, closely integrating military intelligence (both the Intelligence Corps and the Special Air Service) with MI5, the Malayan Security Service (an inferior local equivalent of MI5) and the Malay Police Special Branch. The 'hearts and minds' policy – known early on as political pacification – was devised by General Sir Harold Briggs. The intelligence plan was implemented by General Gerald

Templer. Formerly the post-war Director of Military Intelligence, Templer was dispatched to the colony in early 1952, following the assassination by Chin Peng's communist insurgents of Sir Henry Gurney, the British High Commissioner. He brought with him MI5 officers intended to revitalise the inefficient Malayan Security Service. 'Fleetingly, Whitehall became alarmed, sending Gerald Templer to devise new anti-terrorist methods,' recalled one of the Intelligence Corps soldiers sent to Malaya on national service. 'Intelligence was the key to the Templer method. Intelligence Corps involvement expanded into more conventional army intelligence activities and secondment to the Special Branch of the police. The political pacification role the SAS played, directed by this police/army intelligence unit, had much to do with wrenching the initiative from the rebels and putting it firmly in the hands of the post-independence government.'

The SAS, formed in 1941 to fight in North Africa, had been disbanded at the end of the Second World War. But senior officers fought a rearguard action to keep it alive, and in 1947 a territorial regiment was created. One of its squadrons was subsequently sent to Malaya and merged with the Malayan Scouts – a special forces unit set up by Mike Calvert, a veteran SAS officer. The result was a regular British Army unit, 22 SAS – known simply to insiders as 'the Regiment'.

Templer laid out the plan to win the 'hearts and minds' of the population from the very start. 'Any idea that the business of normal civil government and the business of the Emergency are two separate entities must be killed for good and all,' he said shortly after arriving in the colony. 'The shooting side of this business is only 25 per cent of the trouble and the other 75 per cent is getting the people of this country behind us.' The SAS set about denying local support for the communist guerrillas, identifying and eliminating causes for discontent with the British to win over the 'hearts and minds' of the local population. In a carefully staggered operation, more than 400 villages were moved to specially constructed *kampongs*, or new villages, away from the insurgents, as area after area was declared 'white' – clean of communist influence – and emergency restrictions were lifted, thereby providing more incentive for other areas to co-operate and become 'white'. The intelligence contribution, in a context where British troops had problems simply identifying the enemy, was to build up a comprehensive picture of communist activity and support in each area – a job that had to be started practically from scratch.

'What was lacking was information about the terrorist organisation and order of battle and their supplies,' one officer said. 'Our main task was to track them down by means of every kind of intelligence – informers from the towns and villages where supplies were obtained, captured documents from camps overrun by our patrols, prisoners and aerial photographs. At the start of the year, we knew where Chin Peng had been four months before and when I left we knew where he had been six weeks before. Eventually, some time later, they got so close on his tail that he fled over the border into Thailand.'

The combination of extensive highly integrated intelligence and a minimum-force 'hearts and minds' operation was to work throughout the retreat from empire in Borneo, Aden, Kenya, Cyprus and Oman where between 1970 and 1976, the SAS honed the policy to perfection. Under the guise of a British Army Training Team (BATT), based in the Dhofari capital Salalah, they fought a guerrilla war against communist rebel tribesmen from the so-called People's Front for the Liberation of Oman (PFLO) sent in by the Marxist government in the neighbouring People's Democratic Republic of Yemen. Meanwhile, Sultan Qaboos, who replaced his unpopular father in a bloodless coup at the start of the campaign, put in place a large number of reforms. Assisted by the SAS, he provided water, electricity, medical facilities and communications, including television to improve the lot of the local population on the Dhofari *Jebel* and to undermine any support for the rebels. The main fighting force was the *Firqat*, small teams of former rebels, turned by the SAS to fight against their former colleagues under SAS leadership. The SAS received support from a number of other British forces, including an armoured reconnaissance squadron, a field-engineer squadron, military intelligence units, and RAF pilots who flew the Omani Air Force Jaguar ground attack aircraft, as well as from Omani and Iranian troops.

The 1982 Falklands conflict was a more conventional war and one in which the intelligence services were initially caught napping. But teams of SAS and SBS were landed on the islands by helicopter or from submarine from early May, a month after the Argentinian invasion, to survey potential landing-sites and to collect information on enemy positions, strengths and morale. General Julian Thompson, then commander of 3 Commando Brigade, complained that early on in the campaign there was no imagery intelligence at all, making the intelligence gathered by the British special forces invaluable. 'Not until the very end of the campaign were there any air photographs showing enemy dispositions, defence positions, strong positions, gun positions and so forth,' he said. 'Even they arrived late and were so poor that they had no influence on planning. Detailed intelligence would have to be gleaned by the "mark one eyeball". So important was the acquisition of intelligence that Special Forces, and particularly the assets to insert them, could be spared for only one direct-action raid in the run-up to D-Day.'

But by the time the British troops landed on the Falklands, considerable intelligence had been collected. Much of this would have been provided from signals intelligence, which is believed to have produced the complete order of battle of the Argentinian forces. The British had a number of signals intelligence collection methods available. Apart from the GCHQ station on Ascension Island, there were US stations in Chile and Panama and the New Zealand navy intercept site at Irirangi. Army signals intelligence detachments from Communications and Security Group (UK) and 14 Signal Regiment sailed with the task force, and a number of the Royal Navy vessels, including HMS *Endurance*, had electronic-warfare operators on board. As the task force assembled, one GCHQ official noted that a number of Royal Navy surface vessels had recently been fitted with Outboard signals intelligence equipment that would 'provide a major contribution to NATO's tactical planning'. RAF Nimrod R1s signals-intelligence ferrets also overflew the area from Ascension, monitoring Argentinian communications. 'We are evidently able to intercept much if not all of the enemy's signal traffic,' wrote one British officer. The intelligence available from military radio and even international radio-telephone communications was 'impressive indeed', he said. 'Without it, we would never have achieved what we have.' An American SR-71 Blackbird, which overflew the Falklands at the request of the British was probably used in both the imagery and signals-intelligence roles. But, as with Ultra during the Second World War, the battle tended to have moved on before the process of interception, decryption, analysis and reporting could be concluded. The

DIS subsequently ordered that in some circumstances raw intelligence could be passed direct to commanders.

The shortage of imagery intelligence was also supplemented by access to the product of a US Keyhole satellite over the south Atlantic. Other information was collected by an Intelligence Corps unit, that debriefed the Royal Marine detachment repatriated from Port Stanley and interrogated Argentinian soldiers captured in South Georgia. Once the land battle was in place, joint forward interrogation teams obtained considerable intelligence from the large numbers of Argentinian prisoners. All operational intelligence was collated by the intelligence cells of 5 Infantry Brigade and 3 Commando Brigade and the intelligence section of Major-General Jeremy Moore's headquarters organisation Land Forces Falkland Islands. There was also a nine-man reporting team with analytical back-up at the Joint Services HQ in Northwood, north-west London. Despite his complaints over the early lack of useable imagery, Thompson later said he had been impressed by 'the quality of the intelligence assessments that were produced from quite early on and right through the campaign by the intelligence staffs in my own headquarters. The "pièce de résistance" was the identification of positions occupied by the Argentine regiments, before we landed, which proved to be amazingly accurate.'

The end of the Cold War has produced more rather than less work for Britain's military intelligence analysts as they track the locations of old Soviet units, particularly those equipped with nuclear weaponry, and build up fresh pictures of potential enemies around the world. The Russians have complained that, although there has been some let-up in the number of reconnaissance aircraft breaching their airspace, there are still thousands of such incursions each year, most of them carried out by Nato aircraft. The modern successor to Cotton's Crooks – 39 (1 PRU) Photographic Reconnaissance Unit, based at Marham in Norfolk, is equipped with three Canberra PR9 aircraft, an ageing air-frame that is due for replacement in 2005, possibly by a high-altitude long-endurance UAV like the US Global Hawk. There are also two Tornado reconnaissance squadrons, also based at Marham, and a Jaguar squadron at RAF Coltishall. These aircraft have been used extensively over the period since the end of the Cold War collecting intelligence over Iraq, as part of the patrols of the iraqi no-fly zones, the Balkans, Sierra Leone, Angola, Rwanda, Afghanistan and Sudan. Until its retirement, the SR-71 flew out of British bases in the UK and Cyprus. USAF U-2R spy aircraft continue this tradition. The quid pro quo appears to have been access to photographic, infra-red and radar imagery from the American Keyhole and Lacrosse satellites, which can see in the dark, through poor weather conditions and through camouflage. This is an important asset. The Keyhole satellites will be replaced in 2008 by a new £15bn chain of 24 smaller more mobile US satellites so secret that they are referred to only as the Future Imagery Architecture. There will be four times as many satellites positioned further out in space allowing the system to take pictures or video of a much larger expanse of the world. Advances in communications and computer technology have transformed aerial reconnaissance. Imagery can now be 'remotely sensed' and transmitted direct to JARIC's computers, which can produce enhanced three-dimensional pictures of the target area and even identify standard pieces of equipment.

The Defence Intelligence Staff is headed by the Chief of Defence Intelligence, a three-star general, admiral or air marshal, who also acts as Deputy Chairman of the JIC. His deputy, a civilian who is also a member of the JIC, is responsible for the Defence Intelligence Analysis Staff (DIAS), the DIS analytical wing and its assessments. A two-star officer controls intelligence collection and is responsible for defence attachés, and the Defence Geographic and Imagery Intelligence Agency, which includes JARIC. DIAS is the direct successor to Strong's JIB and the largest group of all source analysts anywhere in the United Kingdom. Its analysts – a mixture of members of all three services and civilians – examine traditional military intelligence topics such as the tactics, orders of battle, weapons, capabilities, personalities, loyalty and morale of the armed forces of around 100 countries around the world. But this provides only a part of the defence intelligence picture. Other areas of interest include economic, political and scientific information relevant to defence capabilities or intentions; defence industries; technology transfer; and arms sales. The DIS is responsible for collating the information needed to verify arms control, working with the teams of inspectors who check weapons stockpiles, and, as with MI6 and GCHQ, one of its biggest areas of interest is the proliferation of nuclear, chemical and biological weapons.

'It is self-evident that when there was a Warsaw Pact, there was a huge concentration on the Warsaw Pact,' one senior defence intelligence official said. 'As the world has developed, our organisation changed to reflect the fact that we no longer expect Russia to invade the UK in the immediate future. The analytical wing has three main branches. One looks at the world geographically, another covers functional areas – things like proliferation – and there is a third very important branch which looks after science and technology. Now within that third element you have a distinction between technologies and, if you like, technologies incorporating weapons systems. So we have some people who are looking at tanks but we'll have other people who look at the technology that we reckon in years to come could be critical on the battlefield.'

DIS intelligence assessments are disseminated in a variety of forms: in contributions to JIC and MOD papers, in separate DIS reports and minutes, and in various briefings, including a weekly closed-circuit television briefing for MOD customers that can be extended to include other government departments in times of crisis. The Defence Intelligence and Security Centre, a tri-service intelligence organisation based at Chicksands, Bedfordshire, includes the Defence Intelligence and Security School – which also provides training in psychological operations – and the Joint Services Intelligence Organisation. This trains military interrogators and those who may need to resist interrogation measures, including members of MI6, the SAS and its naval equivalent, the Special Boat Service. It also supports the Defence Debriefing Team, which gathers intelligence by interviewing people returning from war zones, typically mercenaries like those who fought in Bosnia during the early 1990s. The Chicksands base also includes the Intelligence Corps training depot, previously based at Ashford, Kent; the Defence Special Signals School and the Joint School of Photographic Interpretation.

The long run-up to the Gulf War allowed the allies to collect a great deal of intelligence from strategic assets. A comprehensive knowledge of the Iraqi order of battle, weaponry and tactics was already on file, built up during the Iran–Iraq War, largely from signals and imagery intelligence but also because the US Defence Intelligence Agency had provided Saddam Hussein with a team of more than 60 officers to provide detailed secret intelligence assessments of Iranian forces and capabilities. By the time the air war began, intelligence reports available to divisional commanders were providing extensive details of the dispositions of Iraqi forces in Kuwait and southern Iraq, although a number of enemy formations remained unidentified or on the move. A great deal of this information could also be ascertained from signals and imagery intelligence collected by satellites, static monitoring stations in the region – among them the Cyprus-based 9 Signal Regiment – and aerial platforms like the American RC-135 Rivet Joint aircraft, the high-altitude U-2Rs and the E-8A Joint-STARS aircraft. Air activity was monitored and controlled by the E-3 Sentry AWACS aircraft, which can identify and track enemy aircraft, and dispatch fighters to destroy them. The E-8A's Joint-STARS stand-off battlefield surveillance radar, still in the development stage, reported direct to the allied headquarters in Riyadh, providing invaluable 'real time' intelligence throughout the war. Patrolling along the Saudi side of the border and tied in to the Navstar satellite global positioning system, it was able to produce detailed imagery of the situation deep inside Iraq, pinpointing the position of a vehicle the size of a small jeep and even determining whether it was tracked or wheeled. A British version known as ASTOR is due to come into service in 2004.

The most forward elements of the intelligence machine were the special forces from the SAS and the SBS; the US Army Rangers; the Green Berets; Delta Force; the US Marines; and the SEALs, the American equivalent of the SBS, operating behind Iraqi lines. Although the location of the Iraqi Scud missiles was their highest priority, they also carried out a number of missions. One British-led operation involved 20 members of the SAS and the SBS together with four members of the US special forces, who were dropped by helicopter just south-west of Baghdad on 23 January 1991 to destroy a buried fibre optic cable thought to be used for Scud missile command and control. They dug into the ground, cutting a number of cables and, unable to identify the fibre optic cable, placed 800lb of explosive into the holes and destroyed it all before being safely extracted by helicopter. The SAS also relayed back intelligence on the positions of Iraqi troops in central and western Iraq and a wide variety of information vital to divisional commanders. This did not just include the location and strengths of enemy defences. Major-General Rupert Smith, commander of the British 1 Armoured Division, required details of any artillery in a position to bring down fire on the division, and of all enemy armoured and mechanised infantry formations within twenty-four hours of divisional positions. He needed to know the types of terrain and obstacles, both natural and man-made, his troops would have to face; details of any roads capable of supporting heavy, wheeled fuel tankers and the locations of alternative sources of fuel; the predicted weather conditions; the times of sunrise and sunset; and the likely extent of any civilian resistance.

Once the ground war began, information started coming into the divisional intelligence cell from a variety of tactical intelligence assets. At the forward edge of the battle area, army advanced posts (APs) and observation posts (OPs) scanned the skyline for enemy activity, reporting back to their units. Infantry and armoured reconnaissance patrols probed the enemy defences to obtain information about the numbers of troops and the types of equipment. Artillery- and mortar-locating units acted as self-contained intelligence for the artillery, bringing down fire on any enemy guns or mortars they detect, but also constantly feeding information back to the divisional headquarters.

Forward interrogation teams questioned PoWs, deserters and refugees to determine enemy dispositions, the state of morale, and how supply lines were affected by the air war. Mobile signals intelligence units located and identified enemy positions ahead of the advance, gathering a wealth of information from low-level encoded traffic. Communications security would have been an early casualty as enemy units came under pressure from the advancing allies, providing easy pickings from 'clear' radio messages that ought to have been enciphered. Tactical imagery intelligence (Imint) was provided by 'drones' – remote-controlled aircraft – or unmanned aerial vehicles (UAVs), equipped with electro-optical sensors, which flew over Iraqi positions providing the analysts with real-time imagery via a video terminal.

The remarkable combination of strategic and tactical intelligence assets available to the Gulf War allies should have produced a comprehensive picture of the battlefield. Yet so much information was being collected that dissemination became a major problem. General Norman Schwarzkopf, the allied commander, later complained of receiving inadequate intelligence while Brigadier Christopher Hammerbeck, commander of Britain's 4 Armoured Brigade, said he crossed into Iraq 'intelligence blind'. Satellite intelligence in particular rarely reached the war zone in anything like real time. The Pentagon's official history pointed a finger at the CIA and NSA, and by implication MI6 and GCHQ, who were simply unable to cope with the pace of the allied advance: 'During the Second World War, signals intelligence from Bletchley Park reached North Africa at best within three hours but on average in around six hours. Fifty years later, what the US military calls 'sensor-to-shooter' time was if anything even worse.'

Defence intelligence units were used in a variety of situations during the 1990s, including Kuwait and Jordan, where the target was obviously Iraq, Angola, Sierra Leone and Rwanda. The four-man Intelligence Corps detachment sent to Rwanda was tasked with gathering information on anything that might affect the UN relief operation, including movement of refugees, the orders of battle of the warring factions, details of any atrocities, and assessments of the political or military intentions and capabilities of the new and previous governments. But the area which dominated the 1990s for Britain's defence intelligence units was the Balkans. There were a number of initial difficulties in Bosnia where, according to one officer, UNPROFOR 'lost ownership of the picture of the battlefield to the point where it was irrecoverable'. The UN has traditionally had a poor reputation in the intelligence field, preferring to use the term 'military information', which is seen as avoiding the subterfuge and secrecy inherent in intelligence-gathering operations. The DIS set up a dedicated Yugoslav Crisis Cell very early on. The SAS and SBS were brought in to act as Joint Commission Observers (JCOs), carrying out liaison between the various national force commanders in order to ensure that they understood the divisional commanders' orders and intentions. At the same time they were carrying out reconnaissance and intelligence operations, providing UK Eyes Only intelligence as part of the British intelligence-collection operations. The British special forces operated as part of the Combined Joint Special Operations Task Force, which was initially commanded by a British officer. During Operation Deliberate Force, between April 1993 and December 1995, the SAS carried out laser designation of Bosnian Serb targets and called down artillery fire on Bosnian Serb positions. Intelligence Corps personnel working with the UN in Bosnia were grouped together in a single Force Military Information Unit which not only monitored the military situation but also collected intelligence on political, economic and humanitarian issues. But the creation of IFOR, following the 1995 Dayton Peace Agreement, brought more military structures with an Allied Military Intelligence Battalion made up mainly of British Intelligence Corps personnel and including a Joint Services Interrogation Organisation which doubled as the Defence Debriefing Team. Aerial reconnaissance was conducted by RAF Nimrod R1, Jaguar and E3 Sentry AWACS aircraft. Ground-based signals intelligence was provided by a small tactical unit set up in late 1992 and staffed from 14 Signal Regiment, 9 Signals Regiment and later from JSSU (Digby). British military signals intelligence units not only monitored tactical military communications but also the Yugoslav government's internal microwave telephone network. This allowed them to intercept the telephone conversations of many of the key players, including Slobodan Milosevic, the Serb leader, General Ratko Mladic, the Bosnian Serb military commander, and the Bosnian Serb leader Radovan Karadzic. It is alleged that some of these conversations showed the complicity of Milosevic in atrocities but that the British vetoed their use in evidence against him for security reasons.

The focus on the Balkans, and in particular the existence of the Yugoslav crisis cell, meant that the Kosovo crisis was predicted and good intelligence was available before the campaign. But as in the Gulf War, the same problem in trying to get intelligence collected by strategic assets to commanders in the field in real time resurfaced. Despite significant contributions from GCHQ, including 14 Signal Regiment and Y Troop, 3 Commando Brigade, and MI6, which had a large number of agents in the former Yugoslavia, the commanders of both the air and ground wars were still not getting the intelligence they needed in real time. An MoD report on the lessons learned from the intelligence war in Kosovo found the problem was aggravated by the armed forces' communications difficulties. These affected both satellite communications between Nato and force commanders and those between commanders on the ground. At times during the allied occupation of Kosovo, the inadequacy of British communications equipment forced commanders to resort to using the

Yugoslav mobile telephone network to communicate, making the passage of intelligence difficult if not impossible. The production of good imagery intelligence was also hampered by orders to switch targets from the monitoring of the Yugoslav forces moving into Kosovo to focus on tracking refugees, evidence of ethnic cleansing and the identification of mass graves, to provide information to the International Court for the Former Yugoslavia. When the imagery interpreters came back to focus on the Yugoslav military equipment inside Kosovo in preparation for the bombing campaign, they discovered they had completely lost track of it.

But the key problem remained the failure to get intelligence to commanders in real time. Admiral Sir Alan West, the then Chief of Defence Intelligence, said this was the major lesson learned from Kosovo, or as he admitted 'relearned' since the problem has existed since signals intelligence began to be collected en masse during the Second World War. 'What we need to get better at is what the Americans call sensor-to-shooter,' he said. 'Being able to use your sensors, ranging from strategic right through operational tactical sensors, to pull all that data together to actually be able to identify targets very quickly and then link that through to the thing you are shooting at it with. Sensor-to-shooter is extremely important. I believe we have got to get to grips with that.'

The war in Afghanistan may well have been a key turning point for the British defence intelligence system. The natural instincts of the US Army to use its overwhelming power were repressed in favour of a scheme using the Northern Alliance as a proxy force. It was pushed hard by British military planners who believed that the combination of a local proxy force led by special forces and a 'hearts and minds' policy that had been so successful in Oman could be repeated in Afghanistan. Like the US Army, the State Department were initially nervous of the plans, in part because the Northern Alliance and its warlord allies were neither representative of the whole of the population nor entirely respectable. The alliance included very few members of the mainly Pashto population which dominated the south of the country, it had led a massacre of communist supporters in the wake of the Soviet withdrawal, and its funds largely came from the heroin trade. On the plus side, there were still contacts between the alliance and MI6, which had worked closely with it during the Soviet occupation. The policy of using the alliance as a proxy force, with liaison carried out by the SAS and US special forces, worked very swiftly in the north. This was in great part because MI6 was able to use its existing agents, and others reactivated from the time of the Soviet occupation, to pull the strings behind the scenes to obtain sensible surrenders by Taliban and al-Qaʻeda forces. During the campaign itself, intelligence worked spectacularly well. This success was marred later by human intelligence blunders in the south caused by the US forces' reliance on untested local Afghan sources. A US Army lessons-learned report noted that where operations relied on information from such sources, it should be confirmed by special forces teams. But the overriding feature of the intelligence campaign was the startling effectiveness of what were in reality a very few American UAVs. Their use changed the face of military intelligence. Generals in the Pentagon were able to watch as a Predator UAV fitted with Hellfire anti-tank missiles attacked a convoy of Taliban forces. The US Air Force set up a video-link between their Predators that allowed its remote-control pilot and sensor-operator to communicate with both the Combined Air Operations Centre at Prince Sultan air base in Saudi Arabia and the US ground-attack aircraft themselves. US AC-130 aerial gunships were fed real-time video from UAVs circling over their targets. What until then had appeared to be the dream of 'network-centric capability', the jargon for linking different levels of command – from the Prime Minister right down to the commander of the smallest army unit – into a network of real-time intelligence, was shown to be a real possibility.

The 2003 war in Iraq was to prove a landmark in terms of improving the 'sensor-to-shooter' time that had been so poor during the 1991 Gulf War. All the changes put in place initially in the Balkans and later in Sierra Leone and Afghanistan began to bear fruit. The key to the intelligence problem was much closer coordination. One of a number of MI6 officers handling the agents inside Basra was embedded in the 1 (UK) Armoured Division HQ to ensure that Maj-Gen Robin Brims, the British military commander, had access to the best possible intelligence in 'real time' and that someone was on hand to explain precisely what level of reliability he could place on it.

Nowhere was it more useful than in the British assault on Basra, which was a classic 'Hearts and Minds' operation that in many ways mirrored the first such operation in Malaya. Just as Gen Templer had divided Malaya into sectors and proceeded gradually to turn them 'white', free of the communist guerrillas, the British troops took Basra piece by piece. Once again, intelligence and the judicious use of special forces were the key. While some American commentators criticised the 'Brits' for their slow progress and their failure to take out important regime targets like the city's Ba'ath Party headquarters at the start of the battle, the British plan ultimately proved highly successful. The key moment, justifying the decision not to bomb the party HQ earlier, came on 28 March when one of a number of MI6 agents inside the city reported that around 200 Ba'ath Party loyalists, including Saddam Fedayeen and Special Security Organisation fighters, were meeting there. The information was passed swiftly back to the MI6 officer advising Gen Brims. The British commander immediately ordered up an aerial attack by two US Air Force F15E Strike Eagle aircraft, with the British special forces inside the city using laser designators to guide the bombs onto their target. A similar operation failed to kill Ali Hassan al-Majid, the governor of southern Iraq, better known as Chemical Ali for his role in the 1988 chemical attack on the Kurdish village of Halabja, but persuaded him to flee.

The SAS and SBS played an important role in the war. Two full sabre squadrons, a total of 120 men, plus more than 100 members of the SBS and support troops took part in the operations. Coalition special forces were formed into two separate Joint Special Operations Task Forces (JSOTFs), one for Kurdish-controlled northern Iraq and one for the rest of the country. The special forces operating in the north worked with the Kurdish guerrillas, the *Peshmerga*, training and coordinating their operations, an important role given that in the absence of a substantial northern front they would form the main fighting force to take the northern cities of Kabul and Mosul. The allied special forces in southern and western Iraq operated from forward bases in Jordan, Saudia Arabia and Kuwait. Their pre-war roles included reconnaissance of the Iraqi command and control system and Iraqi military positions to check that potential targets spotted using satellite intelligence were not dummy targets, which had been widely used in the 1991 war.

Eight hours before the war began, allied special forces flew into southern and western Iraq to destroy Iraqi command posts, in particular those that

Oleg Gordievsky, MI6's best agent-in-place in the KGB.

MI6 headquarters at Vauxhall Cross in London.

The first codebreakers from the Government Code and Cypher School arrive at its wartime headquarters at Bletchley Park under the cover of Captain Ridley's Shooting Party.

John Tiltman, arguably Britain's best ever codebreaker (right, in uniform) with Alistair Denniston (left), the first head of the Government Code and Cipher School, and Professor E.R.P. Vincent, who specialised in Italian and later Japanese codes and ciphers. (Barbara Eachus)

The new Government Communications Headquarters (GCHQ) building at Cheltenham, known locally as 'the Doughnut'.

GCHQ's main satellite intelligence collection site at Morwenstow in Cornwall.

(Marc Hill/Apex Photo Agency)

An Intelligence Corps analyst and a Royal Signals intercept operator using the British Army's Odette military signals intelligence system.

RAF Nimrod R1 signals intelligence aircraft.

Iraqi SA6 surface-to-air missiles at Mosul railway yard photographed in 2002 by an RAF Jaguar GR3 flying so low that some of the Iraqis are running for cover, others covering their ears against the aircraft noise and others simply looking up at the aircraft. (RAF, via Tim Ripley)

Sir Alfred 'Andy' Cope (seated, second from left), the British official who initiated the 1920 talks between the British government and the IRA, pictured with other members of the British administration in front of Dublin Castle. Seated on his left are John Anderson and Mark Sturgis.

Frank Steele, the MI6 officer who made the first British contacts with the Provisional IRA in what became known as 'the Backchannel'.

Michael Oatley, the MI6 officer known to the Provisional IRA as Mountain Climber who was the main exponent of 'the Backchannel'.

Y Troop, Royal Marine Commando, using the Odette signals intelligence system on the border between Kosovo and Macedonia during the Kosovo conflict.

were to be used to launch chemical and biological weapons. They also blew up key junctions in the fibre-optic communications links in order to disrupt the Iraqis' command and control system and force their communications up onto the airwaves where they could be monitored by the allies. The SBS, which specialised in protecting the North Sea oilfields from terrorist attack, secured oil wells to prevent the Iraqis from setting them on fire. It also carried out reconnaissance for the amphibious assault on the Faw peninsula. The SAS searched for weapons of mass destruction and repeated their main operations during the 1991 Gulf War, ensuring Saddam could not launch Scud missiles at Israel in order to bring it into the war. This would have complicated coalition strategy and caused problems for those Arab countries that were allowing the allies to base troops or command posts on their territory.

The military intelligence picture was not entirely one of success. Most notably, the DIS played down the danger from the Saddam Fedayeen militia who provided the bulk of the resistance to the allied invasion. A top secret DIS assessment dismissed the threat from the Fedayeen as largely based on Iraqi propaganda adding that 'while they may be capable of a lucky strike they probably lack any real capability to conduct significant attacks'. But there were important successes for imagery intelligence. The full-range of allied assets were again in use including the imagery reconnaissance aircraft like the U2s, the E-8C Joint-STARS, the RAF's Canberra PR9, and the American Global Hawk and Predator UAVs. The Global Hawks played an extremely important role in spotting the targets for the allied aircraft, particularly in the destruction of the Republican Guard around Baghdad, while Predators were used to fire Hellfire missiles on at least a dozen occasions. Perhaps the most stunning coup for imagery intelligence was in an investigation of Iraqi television footage of Saddam Hussein. The Iraqi leader was shown greeting supporters on a walkabout in the Mansur district of north-west Baghdad. The footage was broadcast on 4 April, after coalition troops had entered the capital. Given that there was evidence that Saddam had been killed in the 'decapitation' attack that started the war, allied intelligence was extremely keen to work out when the walkabout took place. Using the mass of satellite imagery taken of the capital during and preceding the war, the analysts went back through the footage taken by the spy satellites, building up a computer-generated three-dimensional picture of the area in which Saddam's walkabout took place. They compared the state of the buildings, the light, the weather and the presence of the crowds and vehicles shown in the television broadcast to the imagery on every day of the previous month. It was not until they got back to early March that they found the precise moment when everything on the imagery matched the television broadcast proving that the footage was recorded a fortnight before the war began.

But the most important success of the war remains the revolutionary way in which the 'sensor-to-shooter' time for intelligence from the CIA, NSA, MI6 and GCHQ was cut if not to 'real time' to something very close to it. Nothing demonstrated this more than the 7 April strike on the complex in which members of the Iraqi leadership, possibly including Saddam, were meeting. The time between the receipt of the intelligence indicating that they would be in the building and the time the first bomb dropped – the so-called sensor-to-shooter time – was just 45 minutes. Whether or not Saddam was there, the cutting of the 'kill chain' from the six hours of the Second World War to a matter of minutes was a defining moment in the use of intelligence on the battlefield.

Parallel Diplomacy

Prologue

The twin-engined Piper Chieftain aircraft carrying Richard Edis, Britain's ambassador to Mozambique, came into land at the small airstrip in the middle of the bush less than an hour after take-off from Maputo. As the plane taxied to a halt, a Honda 200 trials bike roared down the strip towards it. The motorcyclist wore fashionable sunglasses and the uniform of a four-star general. He was Afonso Dhlakama, leader of the Mozambique National Resistance, Renamo. It was October 1994. Two years earlier, Dhlakama had signed a peace deal with President Joachim Chissano that was about to produce the country's first free elections. But now the Renamo leader was having second thoughts and there were serious fears of a return to the guerrilla war that had ravaged Mozambique since the 1970s, leaving countless thousands dead.

There were those within Maputo's diplomatic community who expressed surprise that the British ambassador was prepared to venture out into the bush alone. Dhlakama may have spent his early teens studying to be a priest, but he was a dangerous and volatile man who had fought a 16-year civil war most notable for its senseless brutality. Yet Edis had made a number of hazardous journeys to Renamo's headquarters at Maringue in his efforts to coax Dhlakama through the peace process. A degree of trust had grown up between the two men. At any event, the British ambassador was not alone. His pilot and chief adviser in the negotiations was riding pillion on another motorcycle, and he had made many more trips into the bush to see Dhlakama. He had a great deal of experience in dealing with people like Renamo. He was an MI6 officer with a particular expertise in parallel diplomacy – negotiations with terrorists and others that the government might want kept secret, and if necessary deniable.

Edis was an astute and experienced negotiator himself, having spent the early 1980s on secondment in Northern Ireland, where he worked alongside

MI6 talking to 'the street communities' – a euphemism for the terrorists on both sides of the political divide. Posted to Maputo at the start of the peace process, he immediately realised it would need careful nurturing if it were to succeed. It was a situation that was made for the kind of secret talks practised by Britain's Secret Intelligence Service. Edis persuaded the Foreign Office to buy the Piper Chieftain and to send him an MI6 officer with a pilot's licence who could fly it on what were to become regular trips into the bush to keep Dhlakama on side.

The flying visits to Maringue managed to keep the peace process on track until just six hours before the elections, when the Renamo leader pulled out claiming they were rigged. It took a lot of work by Edis and his MI6 colleague to coax him back on board. But within 24 hours, with Chissano expected to win a slender majority and Dhlakama's ego badly bruised by the election defeat, there was yet again a real danger the peace process would collapse. Closeted with Dhlakama in the colonnaded 19th century embassy building in Maputo, Edis and his MI6 colleague worked into the early hours drafting an agreement in English and Portuguese that would bring him back into the fold. They told him how he had shown the world that Renamo was not just the 'bunch of bandits' Chissano had claimed. They pointed out that with fresh elections due in two years, and the government's majority wafer-thin, he had everything to play for in sticking with the ballot box as opposed to returning to the gun. It was a close-run thing, but they managed to bring Dhlakama back on side, leading Aldo Ajello, the UN official overseeing the elections, to describe Edis as 'the principal architect of a real miracle'.

Twenty One

Talking to Terrorists

No stone should be left unturned to advance the cause of peace.

Sir James Craig, Ulster Unionist leader,
justifying secret meetings with IRA leaders in 1921

One of the least discussed uses of the intelligence services is in 'parallel diplomacy' – establishing channels of communication with the enemy that would be too dangerous, both physically and politically, for ministers or ordinary civil servants to contemplate. Such links have the advantage of being totally deniable and in the early 1990s they were used to bring a number of long-running conflicts to an end. Both the CIA and Mossad had secret back-channels to the PLO which were used to set up the Oslo peace talks while the peaceful transition to black rule in South Africa was set up by that country's National Intelligence Service (NIS).

The NIS began holding talks with Nelson Mandela in Pollsmoor Prison in 1988. 'We started to realise we have to turn our attention to Mr Mandela and other members of the Rivonia Group,' said Niel Barnard, the former NIS head. 'The question was asked whether we could reach a political solution while these persons were incarcerated. We were thus sanctioned by the government to try to establish from Mr Mandela whether he was able to play a role in finding a political solution.' Talks with Mandela were followed by secret meetings with the ANC leadership, the first of which took place in Lucerne in September 1989. 'For the NIS to meet the ANC in Europe was no easy matter,' Barnard said. 'These were not chaps who could meet openly in some hotel. We knew that when we travelled abroad, we were being openly watched, and the same applied to the particular ANC persons. We had to use quite interesting methods to evade observation by other intelligence agencies.' Mike Louw, one of the NIS officers involved, has described waiting in the hotel corridor for the first tense meeting with the ANC delegation, led by Thabo Mbeki. 'Then they came round the corner and they see us standing there. Thabo walked in and said: "Well here we are, bloody terrorists and for all you know fucking communists as well." That broke the ice and we all laughed and I must say that from that moment there was no tension.'

The British Secret Intelligence Service MI6 has made a particular speciality of parallel diplomacy. Its involvement in the Northern Ireland peace process has been widely reported. But it has also taken part in secret negotiations that resulted in the end of long drawn-out conflicts in a number of countries, including Mozambique, Angola, and the former Yugoslavia. At the beginning of 2003, MI6 officers were involved in secret talks aimed at resolving conflict in half a dozen parts of the world.

One obvious advantage of using the secret services to hold secret talks is that they are more experienced at getting into the difficult situations in which such talks must take place, and know better how to extricate themselves should things become too difficult. But the most important advantage of such talks is their very deniability, one former officer said.

'If you have an undeclared back-channel, which carries with it the kind of trust which a front channel of politicians meeting openly in order to move one step forward in negotiations can't possibly carry. Because each knows the other has his own agenda, it is easy to develop that to the point where you can have some basis for trusting what the other person's telling you, because they're not completely committed to it. If they say, "Look, this is the way it's going to be as far as our party's concerned. I'm telling you this off the record. There is no comeback on me if it doesn't turn out as well," then it's much easier to develop a concept of both sides going a little further than it is possible to go in an open negotiation.'

Although the intelligence officer gives the appearance of negotiating, he or she is actually simply positing ideas which, if they produce forward movement, can either be taken up by his or her political masters or dismissed as they see fit. The end result tends to drive the talks forward in a way that could never be the case were they taking place in the full gaze of the media with politicians seeking to protect their own positions from the opposition and indeed rivals within their own parties.

The other advantage is that such talks can provide useful intelligence, the former MI6 officer said. 'You can verify what is being said because you have got the intelligence. So when you are in quasi-negotiation with the other side in fact you are also running intelligence sources into them and penetrating them, and when they say, "This is the situation," you also have some means of judging whether or not they're telling you something that isn't a lie. It makes it a little more solid foundation to help to resolve conflicts.'

Despite their public refusal to talk to the IRA, British governments have made use of parallel diplomacy to do just that from the time of Lloyd George right up to the present day. During the early part of the twentieth century, intelligence operations in Ireland were dominated by the assumption that first the French and then the Germans would seek to foment rebellion there as a means of attacking Britain. There were a number of organisations collecting intelligence on the militant advocates of independence, though none of these organisations was particularly efficient and all of them were caught off guard by the growth in support for the republican movement that followed the First World War. 'Our Secret Service is simply non-existent,' complained Field Marshal Sir John French, the Lord Lieutenant of Ireland, in 1920. 'What masquerades for such a service is nothing but delusion and a snare.'

Police intelligence was split between the Dublin Metropolitan Police Detective Department's G Division and the Royal Irish Constabulary Special Branch, most information being collected by sending officers to public meetings, reading the newspapers or by 'discreet inquiry'. It suffered badly from lack of funds, and what intelligence it did produce was 'meagre and patchy'. A 1916 report on intelligence operations in Ireland, compiled by Basil Thomson, the head of Scotland Yard's Special Branch, noted that the budget for paying informers was so small that 'it cannot be said that any system of secret information has been developed'.

The British Army had an Intelligence Branch with an intelligence officer in each of the military districts to supply reports of what was going on. This and the 'meagre' intelligence gleaned from the police was passed on to MI5, which in turn provided information derived from the interception of mail and communications, and reports from mainland police and the Naval Intelligence Division.

In Thomson's view there was 'much overlapping' and not enough liaison. 'Although all the material reports may reach the Irish executive,' he noted, 'there is certainly a danger that from lack of co-ordination, the Irish Government may be the last Department to receive information of grave moment to the peace of Ireland.'

The lack of funds left police intelligence overstretched and its officers underpaid. Both the civil administration and the police were riddled with republican sympathisers. A rare British informant code named Chalk estimated that 'the Sinn Feiners obtain a considerable amount of official information and that as far as can be ascertained it comes from the Chief Secretary's Office'. A number of the British secret agents, fearing that they might be betrayed at any minute to the IRA, 'refused to work under the police' and offered their services to the Army. An urgent inquiry into the state of police intelligence operations remained written in hand because the committee could not be sure that whoever was tasked to type it was not an IRA informer. To add to the low morale, Sinn Fein swiftly realised that it could seriously disrupt the British intelligence system by assassinating the more efficient officers. 'The compilation of complete and up-to-date records was very difficult owing to the inadequate staffs available and as time went on, and the Sinn Fein movement spread, it became impossible,' an internal Army history of the conflict noted. 'Each crimes special sergeant or man was compelled to rely more and more on his memory and less and less on records. Sinn Fein were not long in recognising that these men and the best and most energetic of the RIC who had accurate local knowledge were the most dangerous of their opponents. From 1919 they carried out a systematic murder campaign, with the result that many of the best of the RIC were killed. Consequently the police source of information, at the time the only one on which the authorities could rely, dried up and the intelligence service paralysed.'

The IRA, which had previously been easy for British intelligence to infiltrate, developed a very effective method of deterring informants. 'Contacts with my so-called agents had to be personal and this could be an extremely dangerous undertaking for the informant,' one intelligence officer recalled. 'A few shots in the night and next morning a corpse and pinned to it a label "Traitor. Shot by orders of the IRA".' The army history noted that 'Secret Service was on the whole a failure in Ireland. For many reasons it was practically impossible to place a man in any inner circle. Consistent, regular and unsuspected informers, such as had been employed on other occasions were almost unobtainable at any price.' The inquiry into police intelligence concurred with that view. 'Owing to the terrorism of Sinn Fein and kindred organisations, even respectable and loyal people are afraid of speaking to a policeman.' It was scathing about the ineffectiveness of the RIC Special Branch, and its view was shared by the Army. When the authorities decided to deport several hundred leading Sinn Feiners in the hope that this would break the back of the movement, the Army was dismayed to discover that 'the local RIC could give little reliable information about such persons beyond a statement that so and so was "a bad boy" or "a bad article".'

The inability of the Dublin administration to deal effectively with 'the Troubles' and the recommendations of a highly critical report by Sir Warren Fisher, the head of the Civil Service, led in May 1920 to a drastic re-organisation. Within weeks, a new administration was in place headed by Sir Hamar Greenwood as Chief Secretary and Sir John Anderson as under-secretary. From the start, the new government's public brief was to instigate a tough crackdown on Sinn Fein. This was epitomised by the activities of police reinforcements and auxiliaries – the so-called Black and Tans – who committed a series of outrages that served only to increase support for the republican cause. But its secret brief – a result of Fisher's call for 'an exploration or settlement of problems' that acknowledged the fact that the majority of Irishmen now supported Sinn Fein – was completely different.

Alfred 'Andy' Cope, a member of Fisher's inquiry team, was given a key role within the new regime 'ostensibly as assistant under-secretary but actually as the Prime Minister's personal and secret envoy for the purpose of establishing contact with the Sinn Fein leaders with a view to negotiating peace'. Cope, a 43-year-old former customs officer, had spent ten years investigating the smugglers and illicit distillers of London's Dockland – 'a calling which taught him the intricacies of undercover work and the technique of dealing on terms of intimacy with gunmen and lawbreakers'. He was sent 'on Special Service in Northern Ireland' and was told by Lloyd George to find someone in Sinn Fein who could 'deliver the goods'.

One of the most vital prerequisites for both the public and secret briefs was to improve intelligence. 'The police forces were in a critical condition,' Anderson wrote later. 'The all important matter of intelligence and secret service had been entirely neglected.' A short-lived attempt to take civilian intelligence out of the hands of the DMP and the RIC, placing it under Thomson's control, had enjoyed little success. So the authorities appointed an intelligence co-ordinator based in Dublin Castle, the headquarters of the British administration, 'to collate information and form by degrees a secret service or detective branch for the police force in Ireland, which is non-existent'. The man chosen, the bemonocled Brigadier-General Ormonde de l'Epée Winter, or 'O', was described by one member of the administration as 'a most amazing individual. He looks like a wicked little white snake, is clever as paint, probably entirely non-moral, a first-class horseman, a card genius, knows several languages'.

Distrustful of the police, the Army formed its own Special Branch in Dublin and, with the assistance of MI5, set up a 'spy school' in the relative safety of London. One of those recruited into the Cairo Gang, so called because most of its members had served with military intelligence in Egypt during the First World War, was Captain R. D. Jeune. 'After a short course of instruction at Hounslow, we were sent over to Dublin in the early summer of 1920,' he recalled. 'The first batch were instructed to pose, initially, as Royal Engineer officers, but this rather futile procedure was soon dropped and the work consisted of getting to know the town thoroughly, tailing "Shinners" and carrying out small raids.' Much of the Cairo Gang's material came from informers, the interrogation of suspects, and captured documents. Women made the best informants, 'but their employment sometimes involved relations that were more than friendly. This was occasionally inconvenient.' If the authorities hoped that Winter's appointment would improve the flow of intelligence, they were to be disappointed. 'The double system of police and military intelligence continued to involve loss of efficiency, duplication of work and complications in almost every way,' the Army history concluded. If all the intelligence had been controlled from one office, 'better results might have been achieved and a great deal of friction and irritation would certainly have been avoided.' When Sir John Anderson complained about the poor supply of intelligence, General Nevil Macready, the Army commander, testily blamed Winter. 'Everything seems to point to the view that he has not got the right method, and we here very much doubt whether he will ever get it,' Macready wrote. 'He is, I fancy, a "born sleuth", but I doubt his organising power, and that, so far as I can see, is what is holding up the machine.'

But the military's opinion of the police was as nothing to its view of those within the administration who appeared to be willing to 'conspire' with the enemy. Cope made contact with Eamonn Duggan, a Dublin solicitor who was the IRA's Director of Intelligence, and 'at considerable danger to himself' began a series of exploratory talks with the IRA. 'Taking his career in his hands, he abandoned the traditional methods of the Castle peace parleyings and got into direct and personal contact with the leaders of the Irish people,' one contemporary recorded. 'He had first to convince the powers of Sinn Fein that he meant to play straight with them, and then to persuade the powers residing in Dublin Castle and elsewhere that the leaders of "the murder gang" desired an honourable settlement.' In a letter to Fisher, a few weeks after arrving in Dublin, Cope wrote: 'I have met quite a number of prominent Sinn Feiners – two were sentenced to death in the rebellion and reprieved – and I feel that I have the temper of the present position.' Cope's activities were so secret that very few people knew about them, and he soon came under suspicion of being an IRA informer. 'In September 1920, it was decided to raid several houses in Drumcondra,' Jeune wrote. 'Particular attention was attached to the house of a man called O'Connor, known to us as an active Sinn Feiner.' During the search, the soldiers found a letter from Cope, Jeune said: 'It was on official Dublin Castle paper and was in these words:

Dear Mr O'Connor,
   I am having the papers you require sent up to you.
   Yours sincerely
   A. W. Cope

This was distinctly interesting. Here was the assistant under-secretary writing to a notorious Sinn Feiner with whom he had obviously already been in contact. After this, I made a point of trying to find out more about this individual's doings and found that he had done some rather strange things, such as arranging for some electricians of known Sinn Fein views to come into the Castle at unusual times. Also he was one of the very few Castle officials who could safely walk about the streets of Dublin. But it was decided that no drastic action could be taken against him, as it turned out that he was a protégé of Lloyd George who had picked him out . . . and sent him over to Ireland in order to get a foot in the Sinn Fein camp.'

Cope's years in the East End of London meant that he was used to 'irregular negotiations, unavowable activities and unconventional approaches', one colleague said. He was also 'a very unorthodox character, extremely persistent, as brave as he was quick witted,' and willing to try anything to secure peace, one colleague wrote. 'He faced considerable opposition from the military. GHQ regard Andy as a complete "shinner" and believe him no more or less than they would believe Michael Collins, so anything he says they regard as *ipso facto* something to be resisted.' There were several false starts, but eventually Cope managed to build up a relationship of trust with the rebels. The military clampdown was having its effect on them, creating 'divided counsels' among the republican leadership. Although many were quite prepared to fight the British to a standstill to create a united, independent Ireland, a growing minority was willing to contemplate negotiations. On 26 September 1920 Arthur Griffith and Sir John Anderson met in a solicitor's offices in St Andrew's Street, Dublin, for preliminary talks. It is not clear how far these went, and leading members of Anderson's administration were later divided over whether the two men even sat down in the same room. But by early November optimism in Dublin and London over the potential of the peace feelers was such that Lloyd George declared, 'We have murder by the throat.' Less than two weeks later, on Sunday 21 November 1920 – the original 'Bloody Sunday' – the IRA shot dead thirteen men and wounded a number of others, some of them dragged out of their beds in their pyjamas and killed in front of their wives and families. 'The object of this exercise on the part of the IRA was to eliminate Intelligence and Courts Martial officers because the gunmen felt that the net was closing round them,' Jeune wrote. 'Men were brought up to Dublin from other parts of the country, particularly Tipperary, in order to catch as many as possible of us unawares on a Sunday morning when most people slept late.' The cream of the army's intelligence officers were killed in the attacks. 'It has been a day of black murder,' Mark Sturgis, Cope's fellow under-secretary, wrote in his diary that night. 'What they hope to gain by it, God alone knows.'

Following the killings and spurred on by the resentment within the military over Cope's dealings with the enemy, the Cabinet's Irish committee ruled that 'no person serving in the Irish government should in any circumstances be permitted to hold communication with Sinn Fein'. But Cope kept his lines of communication to the IRA leadership open, constantly probing for a possibility of peace. 'Again and again all Mr Cope's laboriously worked-out schemes must have seemed to everybody but himself completely wrecked,' a contemporary wrote. 'But besides inexhaustible optimism and belief in himself, he had extraordinary powers of work and during the Terror would frequently sandwich an all-night excursion into the country between two long days at his desk.' A few weeks after Bloody Sunday, the Most Revd Dr Patrick Joseph Clune, Roman Catholic Archbishop of Perth in Australia, stepped in as a mediator, arriving in Dublin in early December with proposals from Lloyd George for an armistice and a peace conference. At the same time the British Prime Minister increased the military pressure, imposing martial law on Cork, Kerry, Tipperary and Limerick and hinting that it could be extended to the whole of Ireland.

With Cope's assistance, Clune saw Griffith, who had been interned in the wake of Bloody Sunday, and Michael Collins, the IRA leader, even though he was still on the run from British troops. They agreed a cease-fire, but it was vetoed by the military. 'They have convinced themselves that they have the boys in the hills beaten and they want no talk of truce to interfere with them now,' Cope said. The Cabinet, a coalition of the Liberals and the staunchly unionist Conservative Party, insisted that the IRA must surrender its arms as a pre-condition of any truce. Anderson, Cope and Sturgis all warned that this would wreck the talks, but to no avail. 'There is no evidence of sincerity on the other side,' Eamon de Valera, the Sinn Fein president, told the volunteers.

'The British Premier was but manoeuvring for an opportunity to put the attitude of the representatives of this nation in a false light.'

Cope was living on his nerves by now – 'a victim alike to ebullient optimism and devastating despair' – and the failure of the Clune talks left him despondent. But by the spring of 1921 pressure on both sides for some form of agreement was intense. Lloyd George's coalition government had lost public confidence, with the failure to resolve the Irish situation one of the most frequent criticisms, while the military campaign had brought the IRA close to defeat. Slowly, Cope's efforts began to bear fruit. Lord Derby, a former ambassador to France, went to Ireland in April for secret talks with the IRA, wearing horn-rimmed glasses in an attempt at disguise and booking into a Dublin hotel under an assumed name. On 21 April 1921, Lloyd George went public with an offer of peace talks, telling the House of Commons that he was ready to meet representatives of the Irish people 'for the purpose of discussing any proposals, which offer the prospect of reconciliation and settlement'. Cope persuaded Sir James Craig, the leader of the Ulster Unionists, to meet de Valera at a secret location just outside Dublin. Since Cope had brought the two together by telling each of them that it was the other who wanted the meeting, it broke up without any tangible results, but the mere fact that they had met was enough to give the peace process fresh impetus in London.

One of Cope's colleagues said, 'He had the power of bending people to his will. He cared not how or where he had to seek his information provided that it led him a step nearer to his goal.' He had contacts at the highest levels within the IRA, with volunteers swapping stories of how after one boozy night Collins had 'carried him to bed'. When Cope asked a Sinn Fein intermediary to put him in touch with de Valera, she asked: 'Do you not want to meet Michael Collins?' Cope replied: 'No, I meet Michael every night.'

The military, having got the IRA on the run, saw little need for peace talks and regarded Cope as very close to a traitor. 'By the early summer, the IRA were driven into the south-west corner of Ireland and would have been quickly finished,' wrote Captain Jeune. 'But certain influences were to save them as I learned in London later from Jeffries, who had been in our show in Dublin and had set up, from London, a proper secret service in Ireland.' On 22 June an Army search party arrested a suspected member of Sinn Fein at a house in Mount Merrion, just outside Dublin. A few days earlier one of their officers had been ambushed by the IRA, taken from his car, and shot dead in front of his three female companions. The soldiers were therefore understandably cock-a-hoop when they realised that the 'Shinner' they had arrested was de Valera. Their elation turned to bewilderment when Cope ordered his release. 'Army GHQ at Kilmainham wired to London: "De Valera captured. Cope suggests release",' Jeune wrote. 'Jeffries took it to Lloyd George who rubbed his hands together and said: "Well done the military. He must on no account be released." Taking this as read, Jeffries left. But as soon as he had gone Lloyd George sent orders for de Valera to be released, which was done.'

The incident has been portrayed as a simple case of lack of communication between the Army and the civilian authorities. But the raid produced invaluable intelligence on the rebels' negotiating stance and may well have been deliberately engineered for that purpose. Two days after the raid the British made a formal offer of a truce. The Troubles were effectively over. The bitterness of many in the military and the Conservative Party over what was seen as a betrayal orchestrated by Cope continued well after the creation of the Irish Free State. 'Negotiations with the murder organisation began long before the Army or the Police knew that a truce was being arranged,' the Conservative newspaper the *Morning Post* complained. 'While they were still fighting in the illusion that the Government was behind them, Mr Cope was establishing friendly relations with their would-be murderers.'

Twenty Two

The Backchannel

A line of contact has existed between Sinn Fein and London for over twenty years.
Gerry Adams, *Free Ireland: Towards a Lasting Peace,* 1995

When the conflict resurfaced in Northern Ireland in the late 1960s, the Army was again horrified at the dearth of police intelligence. 'Financial constraints and lack of foresight led, in Ulster, to insufficient attention being paid to the activities of the Special Branch and other intelligence-gathering agencies,' one senior Army officer recalled. The Royal Ulster Constabulary was totally dominated by Protestants, and the Special Branch suspect files included no one but Catholics. With the help of Metropolitan Police Special Branch officers and a small team of MI5 officers, the Army and the RUC began to build up the intelligence picture. Local censuses were carried out to create a street-by-street record of the local population, Army patrols reported whatever information they could, and details of suspected terrorists were placed in a card index which recorded their families, friends, known contacts and lifestyles. Although the principle of police primacy remained paramount, the paucity of RUC intelligence led to pressure from above to obtain information through other means, and Brigadier Frank Kitson, the Army's counter-insurgency expert, set up a covert intelligence operation based on his Kenyan 'counter-gangs', groups of Mau Mau terrorists who were turned and used against their former colleagues. A small group of IRA terrorists were rounded up and told they had two options: either face the prospect of very long terms of imprisonment or work under cover for the Army. They all opted for the latter, and under the command of a British Army officer became known unofficially as 'the Freds', or more formally as the Special Detachment of the Mobile Reconnaissance Force.

The military sought to obtain covert information by virtually any means it could, but it remained distrustful of the RUC and there was little intelligence co-ordination. The politicians talked tough, backing the role of the Army in public, but behind the scenes looking for a political solution. The post of UK Representative in Northern Ireland was created in August 1969 with a brief to build up contacts with all sections of the community and to encourage moderate Catholic political activity. The formation, a year later, of the Social Democratic and Labour Party (SDLP) provided representatives of nationalist opinion with whom the government could talk without giving the impression of bowing to terrorist pressure.

The problems with intelligence in the province were demonstrated most vividly by the government's decision – against the advice of some, although not all, of the experts – that internment of all known IRA suspects would end the violence. The only intelligence on which a round-up could be based was that of the RUC, which varied across the province from weak to practically non-existent and still did not include details of Protestant extremists. The Army set up a joint internment working party with the RUC and MI5 in an attempt to improve the picture, but to no avail. Operation Demetrius, implemented in the early hours of 10 August 1971, was a shambles. On the basis of the largely inadequate RUC list (some of those apparently seen as a threat to law and order were already long dead), the Army picked up 342 men across the province. As interrogations got under way, it became clear that the numbers of active terrorists did not reach beyond double figures. Within forty-eight hours the security forces had been forced to release 115 of the detainees. They included middle-class civil-rights activists, trade unionists and a drunk arrested as he waited for a bus.

The débâcle of internment forced the generals and the politicians to realise that things had to change. 'The Army's frustration led to gradual and increasing pressure that it should rely less on Special Branch and do more to obtain its own intelligence,' wrote General Sir Michael Carver, the then Chief of the General Staff. 'It was a tendency which I was initially reluctant to accept, all experience in colonial fields having been against this and in favour of the total integration of police and military intelligence. However, the inefficiency of the RUC Special Branch, its reluctance to burn its fingers again, and the suspicion, more than once proved, that some of its members had close links with Protestant extremists, led me finally to the conclusion that there was no alternative.'

The intelligence picture had to be improved. In early 1971, Edward Heath, the British Prime Minister, decided to send in MI6. Within weeks, the UK Representative in Northern Ireland had a new deputy. Frank Steele was a large man, rarely seen without his pipe, who, according to his entry in *Who's Who*, had held a number of diplomatic posts, mainly in the Middle East. He was also a senior MI6 officer. MI6 began its own covert operations in the province while Steele used the UK Representative's office at Laneside, a large surburban house on the shores of Belfast Lough, as a base for contact with the 'street communities' – a euphemism that allowed contact between a senior government official and extremists on both sides of the political divide. The dangers involved in operating in the no-go areas of Belfast and Londonderry were obvious. At one point Steele had to warn his contacts, 'If the IRA were to shoot me now there would be rather a row.'

Just as the Army had been opposed to Cope's 1920 negotiations with Michael Collins, so it was now opposed to any MI6 involvement. It saw Northern Ireland as a classic counter-insurgency situation. Collecting intelligence was its role and, in Kitson's words, 'We beat the terrorists before we negotiate with them.' But William Whitelaw, Secretary of State for Northern Ireland, overruled the objections. At the same time, the SDLP was making its own contacts with PIRA/Sinn Fein, through Austin Currie, Paddy Devlin and John Hume, who had links with David O'Connell, one of the IRA's most senior leaders, that dated back to his involvement in the Irish Credit Union movement.

Then on Sunday 30 January 1972, members of the Parachute Regiment shot dead 13 unarmed civilians after trouble flared during a march in Londonderry – an event that was to become known as Bloody Sunday. Within days, Steele had made contact with Frank Morris, the Provisional IRA's adjutant in the area covering Derry, Donegal, Tyrone and Fermanagh. The aim was to ascertain what it would take to gain the IRA's tacit support for a round-table conference of all sides in Northern Ireland. Steele reported that Morris demanded a return to direct rule and a guarantee that internment would be phased out. 'The Provisionals would not expect, nor insist, that reunification should be on the agenda initially but they would, nevertheless, keep the issue to the forefront and propose its early introduction into any negotiations,' Steele added.

His report gave an indication of the type of intelligence that could be gained in such talks. 'The Provisional contact admitted that in Belfast since internment between three-quarters and seven-eighths of their command structure in the Falls and the Ardoyne had been destroyed, but claimed that the position in the other Catholic enclaves, notably Andersonstown, was largely unimpaired. He added that the deterioration in Belfast had been off-set by a substantial and rapid improvement in Donegal, where Provisional organisation had previously been poor, and that from this base Derry was now under Provisional control. The contact's final comment was that the Provisionals would continue to struggle for a long time and while they accepted that they could not defeat the British Army they were confident the British Army could not defeat them.'

Steele proposed that the contacts should be allowed to continue on the basis that they were providing useful intelligence. But the nervousness within Whitehall at the idea of any officially sanctioned talks with terrorists led to the proposal being turned down. The contacts were 'too close to negotiations as opposed to gathering intelligence', one official said. But despite the nervousness in London the imperative for talking peace was strong. Northern Ireland appeared to be on the verge of civil war. With the death toll mounting rapidly and the eyes of the world focused on the province, the government was anxious to find some way of defusing the situation. MI6 covert intelligence indicated that there was potential for splits within the IRA, with some volunteers becoming disillusioned with its lack of success.

In June 1972 Martin McGuinness, commander of the Derry Brigade, suggested to Sean MacStiofain, the IRA Chief of Staff, that they offer Whitelaw a cease-fire if he agreed to meet them. MacStiofain saw it as a clever idea that would put the British on the defensive. 'If Whitelaw made a public refusal, Britain's stock would go down,' he said. 'The onus of rejecting a reasonable offer would be on London and we would be none the worse off.' Publicly, Whitelaw rejected the IRA offer. But behind the scenes his advisers persuaded him that the time was right for secret talks with the IRA. 'Within hours of publicly refusing to treat with terrorists, the British were secretly agreeing to discuss a truce with us,' MacStiofain said. Working through Hume and Devlin, the two sides agreed to talks with the IRA laying down a number of pre-conditions: IRA prisoners should be granted political status. There should be no arrests of IRA members during the cease-fire and Gerry Adams, a leading member of the IRA's Belfast Brigade, should be released from internment in Long Kesh prison to take part in the talks. The first preliminary meeting – between Steele and Phillip Woodfield, a deputy secretary in the Northern Ireland Office, and O'Connell and Adams – took place at Ballyarnett, a farmhouse across the border from Derry in County Donegal. Woodfield and Steele agreed beforehand that they would keep the discussions as informal as possible 'with the object of drawing out the IRA representatives and helping each other if the discussions reached awkward corners.' During the three-and-a-half-hour meeting both sides were at pains to stress that they had no authority to negotiate any deals, only to put points forward and report back. Nevertheless, effectively negotiations had begun. In his official report on the meeting, Woodfield noted later that the atmosphere was relaxed and informal:

There is no doubt that these two at least genuinely want a cease-fire and a permanent end to violence. Whatever pressures in Northern Ireland have brought them to this frame of mind there is also little doubt that now that the prospect of peace is there they have a strong personal incentive to try and get it. They let drop several remarks showing that the life of the Provisional IRA man is not a pleasant one. Their appearance and manner were respectable and respectful. Their response to every argument put to them was reasonable and moderate. Their behaviour and attitude appeared to bear no relation to the indiscriminate campaigns of bombing and shooting in which they have both been prominent leaders.

A series of meetings followed, mainly held in IRA safe houses in Derry. Despite the enmity of their two sides, a cautious relationship grew up between them. Steele was pleasantly surprised to find that, instead of the aggressive young tough the briefings had led him to expect, Adams was 'a very person-able, likeable, intelligent, articulate and persuasive young man'.

On 26 June PIRA announced that it was suspending 'offensive operations'.

The talks were fixed for London on 7 July 1972. The IRA representatives met up with Steele at a prearranged location in the Derry countryside and were taken by helicopter to Belfast's Aldergrove airport, a nervous flight in which McGuinness was somewhat concerned that they might prove to be too tempting a target for some of his unsuspecting colleagues on the ground. From there they were flown by RAF Andover to RAF Benson in Oxfordshire, and two cars driven by Special Branch officers then took them to London, to the Chelsea home of Whitelaw's junior minister Paul Channon. The IRA delegation comprised O'Connell; MacStiofain; McGuinness; Adams; Ivor Bell, the commander of the Belfast Brigade; and Seamus Twomey, the hard man and firmest opponent of any deal with the British. He was there to keep an eye on O'Connell, a realist who was the most committed to the talks. On the British side were Whitelaw, Channon, Woodfield and Steele. The meeting was, in Whitelaw's words, 'a non-event'. He attempted to dispense bonhomie. They were distrustful – anxious to ensure that the British were treating them seriously. MacStiofain demanded the British withdrawal from Northern Ireland by 1 January 1975, a general amnesty for political prisoners, and an end to internment. London's interest in talks appears to have 'misled the IRA into believing that it was close to achieving its objectives. Why else would the British want to negotiate unless they were defeated? But it had badly misjudged the situation. Whitelaw's view of the talks shows how far apart the two sides remained. 'The IRA's leaders simply made impossible demands, which I told them the British government would never concede,' he said. 'They were in fact still in a mood of defiance and determination to carry on until their absurd ultimatums were met.'

Despite the failure of the talks, the two sides agreed to keep up the unoffi-cial channel of communication via Steele. On the flight back to Belfast, the MI6 man tried to impress the realities of the political situation on the Provisional leaders. As he began to talk, MacStiofain whispered to Twomey, 'Listen very carefully to this guy. What we are getting off the cuff is as valuable as anything at the meeting.' They were listening but they did not hear. 'I hope you're not going to start your bloody stupid campaign of violence again,' Steele said. If the IRA really wanted a united Ireland, it was wasting its time shooting British soldiers and bombing Northern Ireland into an industrial and social slum, he said. It would be better employed persuading the Protestants that they could have a good life in some sort of union with the South. They dismissed his arguments. There was only one way to get a united Ireland – by forcing the Brits out – and the only way to do that was through 'physical force' which included 'economic warfare'.

To the IRA, the British appeared to be engaging in 'doublespeak and jargon'. The hard men took control. Two weeks later, on Friday 21 July, the campaign resumed. More than twenty bombs exploded across Belfast in the worst violence the city had seen. Nine civilians died. More than 100 were injured. Designed to teach the British a lesson, Bloody Friday backfired badly. Whitelaw's political initiatives had caused problems for the Army's intelligence effort, by cutting back on patrols and interrogations. Now the Army was given the go-ahead to move into the 'no-go areas' of Free Derry. Ten days after Bloody Friday, armoured cars and bulldozers moved into the Creggan and the Bogside. Operation Motorman brought a wealth of intelligence from ordinary Catholics sickened by the resumption of the killings. The failure of the old leadership's tactics, both during the talks and in the bloody response, led to the establishment of a younger, more political, leadership able to develop the policy of 'the Armalite and the ballot box', boosting the role of Sinn Fein and ensuring a more sophisticated approach to any future dealings with the British.

The inability of the various agencies to get on with each other, the Littlejohn fiasco (in which a Dublin bank was allegedly robbed on behalf of MI6) and the spread of IRA violence to the mainland led in 1973 to an increase in MI5 activities at the expense of MI6. The Security Service was seen as being better able to liaise with both the Army and the RUC than MI6. The senior MI5 officer was given the title of Director and Co-ordinator of Intelligence. But the MI6 political role continued. The Whitelaw talks had established the principle of a secret channel of communication to the IRA. When Merlyn Rees became Northern Ireland Secretary in March 1974, he authorised Woodfield's and Steele's successors, James Allan, a Foreign Office man, and Michael Oatley, an MI6 officer, to continue with what he described as 'explanatory talks'.

The back-channel was kept open via a go-between, Denis Bradley, a former priest who had been a witness to the Bloody Sunday killings and was determined to see the violence come to an end. Sometimes Oatley would meet IRA representatives on his own, sometimes with Allan. Sometimes messages would be passed through Bradley. Following the Birmingham pub bombings, which killed nineteen people in November 1974, concerted attempts were made to bring an end to the violence. Within weeks, a group of Protestant clergy met O'Connell and Twomey in the Republic with the full backing of the British government. The IRA declared a temporary cease-fire and asked for 'an indication of the British government's attitude' towards their calls for withdrawal and an amnesty for all political prisoners. Encouraged by a clear sign that the IRA leadership wanted to talk, attempts were again made to raise the status of the behind-the-scenes talks, Rees said. 'I laid down the basis for meetings between staff and Provisional Sinn Fein which I now decided to put on a more formal basis than the sort of explanatory meeting I had already sanctioned.' Meanwhile Bradley was called to a meeting of the IRA's ruling Provisional Army Council and told them that Oatley wanted to meet Billy McKee, Officer Commanding the IRA's Belfast Brigade. The meeting took place, witnessed by a senior member of the Derry Brigade. According to McKee, Oatley said a British withdrawal was on the agenda.

This was not something that Rees could possibly have even hinted at. But he was unaware of the fine detail of what was being said. Oatley would have known that without the suggestion that withdrawal could be talked about, and that was all he had committed himself to, the IRA would not have even considered talking to him. But one of the fundamental advantages of secret talks such as these is that things can be said that could never be said by a politician. 'You can produce a much more flexible interpretation of what your government is happy to concede,' one MI6 officer said. But in mid-January 1975 the talks broke down and the cease-fire came to an end. 'It was evident that despite all our efforts the Provisional IRA had not understood what we were saying,' Rees commented. 'We were convinced that our basic problem lay with the Provisional Sinn Fein representatives in Belfast, who were inexperienced and not up to their task. I authorised that in future contact with the Provisional Sinn Fein should be at a higher level and away from Belfast and its incestuous gossip.' Allan and Oatley met McKee and Ruairí Ó'Brádaigh, Sinn Fein president. The first meeting was difficult but led to further talks and eventually to a new cease-fire in return for the phasing out of detention without trial. Numerous meetings with the IRA took place at 'incident centres' set up across the province, at Laneside, and through the 'backchannel' run by Oatley who was known to the Provisionals' leadership as Mountain Climber.

The political moves caused widespread disquiet within military intelligence and MI5. General Sir Frank King, the Army commander in Northern Ireland, openly attacked the Northern Ireland Office 'interference', claiming it was merely giving the IRA time to re-group. 'The Army was making such good progress that in another two or three months we would have brought the IRA to the point where they would have had enough,' he said. The phasing out of detention without trial was giving the IRA back its best men. 'About 200 have been freed from detention and nearly all the remainder – perhaps another 300 or 400 – will probably be out by October. Then they will be in a position to start all over again.' The Army began to engage in 'dirty tricks' in an attempt to discredit Rees. 'On one occasion, I spent three weeks discussing with senior soldiers how we could carry out an operation that would put no one's life at risk,' Rees said. 'The following day in the newspapers, briefed by the Army Department, was a report that I had put the lives of soldiers at risk – a deliberate policy of double briefing.' The IRA also felt it gained nothing from the cease-fire, and by the end of 1975 this had petered out amid widespread internal feuding. Meaningful discussions on the 'backchannel' ended around the same time, after Oatley was posted to MI6's Hong Kong station. He was replaced by another MI6 officer and both the IRA and Bradley lost confidence in the back-channel.

The turf battles between the various agencies continued, and the decision, in January 1977, to put the RUC in charge of intelligence collection did nothing to help. The Army still marked many of its documents 'UK Eyes Only: Not for RUC' – particularly when they referred to future operations. In October 1979, following the murder of Lord Mountbatten and the

Warrenpoint massacre of eighteen members of the Parachute Regiment, Sir Maurice Oldfield, the former chief of MI6 was sent to Belfast as Security Co-ordinator with a brief to end the rivalries. The Army's early covert intelligence activities had been regarded as amateurish by MI5 and MI6. The operations run by the Mobile Reconnaissance Force included the Four Square Laundry, which collected dirty clothes and tested them for traces of explosives or blood before washing; a massage parlour that provided ample opportunity for blackmail; and door-to-door cosmetics sales run by female soldiers. But in October 1972 they were blown when the IRA succeeded in turning one of the Freds. The IRA ambushed a Four Square van in West Belfast, killing the driver. A few months later the MRF was disbanded. Within a year, the Army was mounting new covert operations. This time they were developed with the aid of the SAS and were a great deal more professional. Like the Cairo Gang before them, the soldiers involved were recruited from a variety of units and originally operated under cover as Royal Engineers. A variety of cover names followed – most famously 14 Int – but within the limited circle of soldiers familiar with the unit's activities it became known as 'the Det', short for the Detachment because it had a number of detachments across the province. It also recruited a number of women soldiers as well as men on the basis that women often found it easier to infiltrate places where men were seen as a threat and courting couples usually look less out of place than someone on their own.

The Det's role was Close Target Reconnaissance (CTR): undercover work in among the civilians, observing the terrorist at close quarters, carrying out covert searches of offices and houses for information and weapons. These were left where they were found but were 'jarked' with tiny transmitters placed inside them that would provide warning should they be moved. The unit had a UK Det at Hullavington, in Wiltshire, and three sub-units in Northern Ireland – one in Derry, one in Belfast and one in Newry. In the words of one former member, its operations were 'invariably hairy'. The role of 14 Int is purely surveillance and as such a principal aim is not to get involved in any shooting. But sometimes that is inevitable. On 28 May 1981, the officer in charge of the 'North Det', having completed a job earlier than expected, decided to carry out a recce for the next. It was a foolish thing to do without back-up, and a clear breach of standard operating procedures. He was driving an unmarked Opel Ascona car but was spotted by four members of an IRA active service unit who followed him and then drove their car in front of him, blocking his path. Two of the terrorists, each carrying an Armalite rifle, approached his Opel – one of them standing at the front, one at the rear. The 14 Int officer was in serious difficulty. But the man at the front made the mistake of turning to signal to the two men left in the car. The British officer took his chance, firing a series of pistol shots into the IRA man's back, followed by an over-the-shoulder shot at the man at the rear. The two other terrorists fled, firing at the Opel but missing the British officer, who returned to the North Det HQ to be given a thorough dressing-down by the duty ops officer – a lowly corporal – for venturing into a republican area without backup. By 2002, the unit's name had been changed to C14 amid reports that it had operated in Bosnia, carrying out close target surveillance of alleged war criminals ahead of SAS snatch operations.

The SAS was deployed officially to Northern Ireland in 1976. Although it was heavily involved in the Det in the early stages and small teams had been sent to the province for special jobs on a number of earlier occasions, it was not until 1976 that it could deploy there in strength. It had two main roles: covert reconnaissance, often spending weeks in hides dug into the ground in the South Armagh 'bandit country' to report on IRA activity, and ambushing terrorists. This latter role caused controversy, with allegations that the SAS carries out 'assassinations'. If an SAS team mounts a successful ambush, any terrorists will be lucky to come out of it alive. But, while many of the wilder claims about SAS assassinations can be discounted as IRA propaganda or conspiracy theory, there is no doubt that in the early days a number of killings did take place – at least one of them in the Irish Republic. In addition, a number of wanted IRA men were lifted from across the border and brought into Northern Ireland where they could be arrested by the security forces.

The RUC Special Branch, which co-ordinated all intelligence and covert operations through the Tasking and Co-ordinating Groups, was split into a number of sections, of which the most important were E3, Intelligence, and E4, Operations. The latter had its own surveillance unit, similar to the Det, known as E4A. The RUC Special Support Unit and Headquarters Mobile

Support Units had a back-up role similar to that of the SAS. Members of these units were involved in the Lurgan hayshed killings that led to the Shoot-to-Kill inquiry. The units were taken over by the Police Service of Northern Ireland (PSNI) but disbanded in September 2002, six months after a raid on their Castlereagh headquarters, allegedly carried out by members of the Provisional IRA, that caused immense damage not just to the police but also to the British Army, MI5 and Garda intelligence operations. Computer disks taken from Castlereagh included the names and addresses of more than 250 serving and former members of Special Branch; the codenames of informers; and the intelligence they provided, with the possibility that in some cases real names can be put to the codenames. But not only did it tell the IRA Army Council what the intelligence services knew about their organisation, in many cases they will be able to work out how they knew, allowing them to change their practices to thwart future intelligence operations. Just as importantly, it told the IRA what the intelligence and security services did not know and it will act as a major barrier to the recruitment of future agents. The raid may not have totally crippled the intelligence and security services' operations but it did them and the PSNI, in particular, untold harm.

So damaging was it to the PSNI Special Branch that it forced changes that led to a downgrading of the branch's previously dominant role, with the Security Service MI5 taking over the lead role on intelligence operations against Northern Ireland terrorists inside the province. MI5 has always had the lead role in countering Irish terrorist activities outside of Britain, primarily in preventing groups from both sides of the divide from acquiring weapons and supplies. It had taken over the lead role on the mainland from the Metropolitan Police Special Branch in October 1992 in an operation known as Ascribe. MI5's operations in Northern Ireland are controlled by the Director and Co-ordinator of Intelligence. The MI5 section responsible for countering Irish terrorism is now known as T Branch.

The reputation of military intelligence was severely damaged by the findings of the Stevens Inquiries into allegations of collusion in a number of murders carried out by terrorists. It now comes under the control of 12 Military Intelligence Company (Force Intelligence Unit), which includes a counter-intelligence section and the Special Military Intelligence Unit, which liaises with the police. There is also an Intelligence Database Management Company, which operates the intelligence computer systems, including the Vengeful system, which is linked to the Northern Ireland vehicle licensing office and to cameras capable of reading vehicle number plates, and Caister, which contains personal information about every known terrorist or suspect. The Reconnaissance and Geographic Intelligence Centre interprets air imagery, looking for bombs, arms caches and evidence of IRA activity. The Incident Investigation Company attends the scene of every bombing, shooting or weapons find, to help establish terrorist *modi operandi* and forensically to identify the weapons and to try to pinpoint the terrorists involved.

Signals intelligence has played a key role in the British response to IRA terror campaigns. There were army communications intelligence units on the ground throughout the Troubles and more recently the monitoring of mobile telephones, not just to intercept conversations but to track the locations of key players, has had an important role witht the Islander SIGINT aircraft playing a full part. There has also been an important and less obvious role for army electronic intelligence operators from 14 Signal Regiment, and its elint predecessor, 226 Signal Squadron, in preventing bomb attacks. Early IRA bombs were very primitive devices, which led to a number of inadvertent premature detonations. As PIRA developed its technical abilities, it began using more sophisticated detonation systems, initially based on a model-aircraft radio-guidance system. In an operation known as MacCounter, the army electronic intercept operators began monitoring the frequencies and detonating the bombs before the bombers could plant them. In what one source described as 'useful detonations' a number of bombers were killed and the IRA began to improve its technology. By the mid-1970s, it was using sophisticated electronic switches as detonators to try to prevent premature detonation of the bombs by the Army signal operators jamming the airwaves. During the early 1980s, an IRA cell based in Boston, Massachusetts, was designing, developing and procuring sophisticated rocket-guidance systems and laser- and radar-controlled detonators. Among the systems they introduced was one using a police radar gun as the remote detonation device and a radar-gun detector, designed to help motorists evade speed traps, as the detonator trigger. The Defence Experimental and Research Establishment at Farnborough, Hampshire, produced electronic scanning equipment that allowed the army operators to sweep the airwaves for the emissions given off when the bombers tested their equipment and then duplicate them to detonate the bombs prematurely.

The MI6 back-channel to the IRA resurfaced during the 1980-81 hunger strikes, when the PIRA leadership contacted Bradley. He in turn contacted Oatley, who was back in London, and an attempt was made to negotiate an end to the protests. The backchannel remained in abeyance throughout the rest of the period during which Mrs Thatcher was in power. But Bradley remained in occasional contact with Oatley and with Martin McGuinness, whose wedding he had conducted as a priest. In October 1990, after a long period of silence, Oatley got in touch with McGuinness via Bradley to tell him that he was about to retire and would like to see him. Intelligence from inside the PIRA/Sinn Fein leadership indicated that some members were looking for ways to end the violence.

'The meeting was in a quiet residential area somewhere in the north of Ireland,' McGuinness said. 'I arrived by car; he arrived by car. There was absolutely no security whatsoever and everybody was at ease. He intimated to me that after his retirement a new British Government Representative would be appointed and there would be an effort to reactivate the line of communication.' Peter Brooke, the then Northern Ireland Secretary, confirmed that he had authorised the reactivation of the backchannel in 1990. 'There was somebody in place who had been involved for quite some time and he had the advantage of retaining the confidence of both sides,' Brooke said. 'It was not negotiation. I was not sanctioning a whole series of things. It was the opportunity to carry on conversation.'

There was then a break in communication until April 1991, when Oatley again got in touch, to tell McGuinness that the loyalist paramilitaries were about to call a cease-fire. Two months later, the new British Government Representative (BGR), an MI5 officer, introduced himself, with a letter of confirmation from Brooke. According to Gerry Adams, Oatley's meeting with McGuinness and a subsequent statement a few weeks later by Brooke that the British government had 'no selfish strategic or economic interest in Northern Ireland' led to a period of 'protracted dialogue' between the two sides. 'Over three years, outlines of Sinn Fein and British Government policies were exchanged and discussed.' There are differences between the two sides over the precise chronology and extent of the talks, with the British government – anxious to keep the Unionists on board – denying that individual contacts occurred or describing them as 'unauthorised'. While not every meeting may have been authorised beforehand, the overall policy was, and it should be remembered that part of the value of parallel diplomacy is its deniability. Confirmation that Oatley's reactivation of the backchannel was not unauthorised was given to parliament by Douglas Hurd, the former Foreign Secretary, when asked by David Trimble, the Ulster Unionist leader, about claims that the MI6 (SIS) talks were unauthorised. 'The SIS and GCHQ do not work to their own agenda, invent their own requirements for information or act independently without the prior knowledge and clearance of ministers,' he said. 'They do not invent adventures of their own; they carry out tasks in support of specific policies.'

The British government later claimed that the first official contacts followed an unsolicited oral message from the Provisionals in February 1993 which allegedly said, 'The conflict is over but we need your advice on how to bring it to a close. We wish to have an unannounced cease-fire in order to hold dialogue leading to peace.' The IRA subsequently denied that this message was ever sent and it was never likely that McGuinness, a known hardliner, would have used precisely that form of words. But, with their need to keep the hardliners on board, those within the PIRA/Sinn Fein leadership who were looking for peace had as much reason to deny such conciliatory messages as did the British government in claiming that this was the first contact. It was not of course. The new British Government Representative, codenamed Fred, had exchanged a series of messages with PIRA/Sinn Fein via Bradley. The phrase 'the conflict is over' was coined by Bradley as a representation of what PIRA/Sinn Fein had said. A senior intelligence officer confirmed that the backchannel was occasionally 'noisy' and that not every exchange was reported back entirely accurately. Bradley has since described how he and two other intermediaries put together the phrase, which he believes was further embellished by the British Government Representative. 'We all spoke about it, talked about it, threw out sentences and so forth. We didn't use those words "The war is over" but we put them in – I put them in – a vague, vague way that this conflict was coming to an end. We sent it, we gave it to Fred.' The suggestion that PIRA/Sinn Fein needed the British government's advice on how to get out of the conflict was added, he believes by Fred. 'I think Fred knew that with those words, he could turn the rest of the people in the room round to engage with each other – and Fred was doing what we were doing and adding on to it to make sure that it happened.'

Whatever the truth of who said what, it was the key breakthrough, sparking concessions from the British government, which indicated that in exchange for a cease-fire, it was prepared to engage in 'dialogue' with nothing, neither a united Ireland nor a continuation of partition, ruled out. The reply from PIRA/Sinn Fein was positive, although this time it was not prepared to take any chances on anybody 'improving' the message. 'Martin McGuinness arrived at the meeting and he began to read out, dictate his statement,' Bradley said. 'I was given the task of writing it down on a piece of paper to be printed up to be given to the British with a very strong warning that not one single word of this was to be changed.' According to McGuinness, the BGR subsequently said: 'Eventually the island of Ireland will be one. It is going to happen anyway. Unionists will have to change.'

The talks on the backchannel continued throughout 1993, despite the IRA's Warrington, Bishopsgate and Shankhill bomb attacks, the Loyalist Greysteel massacre, and the death of twenty-five British intelligence officers from Northern Ireland, including John Deverell, in the 1994 Mull of Kintyre helicopter crash. The 'conversations' with PIRA/Sinn Fein were part of a twin-track process that was fronted by the Hume–Adams talks and the Anglo–Irish agreement. Sir Patrick Mayhew, Brooke's successor, emphasised the importance of this process when he finally conceded the existence of the secret backchannel to the IRA. 'There has been a channel of communication open for something like twenty years – a secret channel by which messages have been able to be passed,' he said. 'I think that if you have an established channel of communication which has proved its value it is not only very sensible but it is your duty to maintain its secrecy. If that chain of communication had been destroyed, I think there would be a lot to be answered for.' Without the 'backchannel', and the 'creative ambiguity' that went with it, the Northern

Ireland peace process would never have got off the ground.

The New Threats

Prologue

It was a bitterly cold day in early spring 1995. Antonio, a tall Italian-American with a grey crew cut and an Armani suit, sat at the back of Marco Pierre White's Knightsbridge restaurant savouring braised oxtail en crepinette and listening impassively. Li Chung, a small soft-spoken Chinese man with thinning hair, was leaning across the starched white linen tablecloth to explain the deal.

The restaurant's volatile chef is known for storming in and out of kitchens to berate customers for 'impertinent' requests. It was not something that seemed to worry Antonio or his guest – but then it would have taken more than a hot-tempered chef to make either of them nervous. Antonio had been introduced as the head of a New York Mafia family; Li Chung was a leading member of the Triads. Sitting to Antonio's left was David, a well-built man in his early thirties with close-cropped hair and the sort of straight back that can be acquired only in the British Army. He had not spoken a word since Li arrived. But it was clear from the way he sat scanning the restaurant's frosted swing doors and the other guests that he was Antonio's minder.

The fourth man at the large round table was Frank, who had been introduced as Antonio's 'London associate'. He was in his forties, with an expensive haircut, a black pencil moustache and the look of an East End barrow-boy made good. Frank was the one asking all the questions, probing Li's story for inconsistencies.

The Hong Kong Triads were looking to cut a deal with the Mafia, trying to take their multi-million-pound credit-card operation into the American market. Li was explaining how it worked. A customer went into a Triad-controlled shop in Hong Kong and paid by credit card. The card was taken out to the back – 'to check the credit limit' – and run through a machine that recorded the information on the electronic strip. Blank cards were produced in China and smuggled into Hong Kong, then a British colony, where they were embossed with the stolen customer details and electronically programmed.

The beauty of the fraud, Li explained, was that the customer still had his card. So neither he nor his credit card company was any the wiser until the bills started coming in. Li could give them 10 counterfeit cards now at £300 each. He was prepared to take just £1,500 to cover the cost of five and let them have the others on credit 'as an act of good faith'. Antonio said Frank would be in touch. Li could report back to Hong Kong that the American venture was going well.

But his act of good faith was misplaced. He had been drawn into an elaborate sting that would eventually see him jailed for two years by a British court. Antonio was not from the New York Mafia. He was an FBI agent. David and Frank were members of SO11, Scotland Yard's Directorate of Intelligence, which works against organised crime in London. The meeting in Marco Pierre White's was part of an Anglo-American undercover intelligence operation. Li's extensive explanation of how the fraud worked had been taped and would form the bulk of the evidence against him.

Twenty Three

A Very Dirty Game

The Cold War is over: the most dangerous threat to a nation's security comes
from organised crime. Europe is now one vast criminal space, from the Atlantic
to the Urals. What matters is using intelligence to crack the criminal at source.
Raymond Kendall, British General-Secretary of Interpol, May 1996

The creation of the Secret Service Bureau in October 1909 brought substantial changes to the role of Special Branch. Previously it had never had more than thirty-eight officers and its main targets had been Irish and anarchist bombers. Now it expanded to help the domestic counter-espionage section of the SSB, under Vernon Kell, in the hunt for German spies, with the odd diversion against that other great threat to the empire – the suffragettes.

The greatest increase in its activities came under Basil Thomson, who was appointed Assistant Metropolitan Police Commissioner with responsibility for the Special Branch in June 1913. Thomson was the son of an Archbishop of York and had at various times been the governor of Wormwood Scrubs prison and the Prime Minister of Tonga. He was an inveterate empire-builder, and the First World War gave him ample opportunity. In the summer of 1914 the Branch had just seventy officers. By the time of the Armistice there were 700, and German spies were the least of their concerns. Thomson set them loose on anyone who might disrupt the war effort, from pacifists to trade unionists. He was far more politically adept than Kell, whom he repeatedly outmanoeuvred. It mattered not that MI5, as Kell's section became in 1916, was uncovering the spies and subversives: since the Branch arrested them and he personally interrogated them, Thomson was able to exploit the secrecy of Kell's role to take full credit for any successes himself. But, despite his expertise at political infighting, Thomson's interrogation technique bore all the hallmarks of Inspector Clouseau. He began his questioning of Roger Casement, the Irish nationalist, by asking, 'What is your name?' When a puzzled Casement, replied, 'But you know it', Thomson's response was, 'Ah yes, but I have to guard against impersonators.'

It was Thomson, and not Kell, whom the government chose in March 1919 to head its new civilian Directorate of Intelligence, with a role 'to foresee and prevent political agitators from committing crime in order to terrorise the community into granting them what they want'. Thomson sought to have MI5 brought under his control, but Field Marshal Sir Douglas Haig was reluctant to allow a branch of military intelligence to involve itself in civil matters and Kell was restricted to maintaining internal military security. 'I would not authorise any men being used as spies,' said Haig. 'Officers must act straightforwardly and as Englishmen. "Espionage" among our men was hateful to us Army men.'

Thomson produced a weekly *Report on Revolutionary Organisations in the UK*, which was circulated to Cabinet ministers and senior officials. But by 1921 both the politicians and the new Metropolitan Police Commissioner, Sir William Horwood, had had enough of his reluctance to let them know what was going on. Thomson's obsession with the scourge of Bolshevism had led him to carry out intelligence operations against the Labour Party and had produced only 'misleading and inaccurate' reports, Horwood complained. The Directorate of Intelligence was 'approaching the continental system of domestic espionage' and was offensive to a large proportion of working people.

In what bears all the hallmarks of a sting operation, Thomson was finally forced to resign after being arrested in Hyde Park for indecency with a known prostitute called Thelma de Lava. Special Branch, then reduced to around 120 officers, was absorbed back into Scotland Yard under Sir Wyndham Childs, whose reputation for subservience had earned him the nickname of Fido. Unlike Thomson, Childs could be relied on to do what he was told, although virtually his first act was to refuse the Labour Prime Minister Ramsay MacDonald access to his secret file. The Branch retained control of the fight against Bolshevik subversion and espionage, taking charge of the 1927 raid on the Soviet ARCOS trade mission, but in 1931 that role was handed back to MI5. Special Branch responsibilities were cut and its intelligence staff were absorbed into the Security Service. From then on, Special Branch's role in Britain's security, apart from the threat of Irish republicanism and the protection of VIPs, was strictly as a subordinate of MI5, gathering intelligence on Bolshevik subversion and foreign espionage and making arrests as directed by Kell. The Branch became MI5's link with the judicial process. Security Service officers could not make arrests, nor did they have the expertise needed to gather evidence that would pass muster in the courts. That work was carried out by Special Branch officers. From the mid-1930s the size of Special Branch remained constant at around 200 officers, apart from an increase during the Second World War to cope with the threat of German spies. But in the early 1960s there was another expansion, with the number of officers in the Metropolitan Police Special Branch jumping to 300 and a series of small Branches being set up in provincial forces. There are now around 500 officers in the Metropolitan Police Special Branch and several hundred in the provincial Branches.

The main role of the modern-day Special Branches is to gather and analyse intelligence in relation primarily to terrorism, but also with regard to public order, espionage, proliferation and subversion – the last three in support of MI5. They are directly accountable to their chief constable, and officers have no powers additional to those of any other police officer. Special Branch officers are stationed at each major port and airport in Britain, where their main role is to monitor the entry of 'persons of interest', be they foreign agents or terrorists. Officers based at points of entry to Britain assist in some immigration and child-abduction cases and in the arrest of wanted criminals attempting to flee the country or return surreptitiously. The Branches also gather intelligence on animal-rights extremists, and the Metropolitan Police Special Branch oversees the Animal Rights National Index, a database on all animal-rights activity to which all police forces have access.

The relationship between Scotland Yard's Special Branch (SO12) and its Anti-Terrorist Branch (SO13), is often misunderstood. Essentially, Special Branch mounts intelligence-gathering operations, often covertly, while the Anti-Terrorist Branch is restricted to investigating the circumstances surrounding specific bombings and shootings. Although the two work closely together, under the Director of Intelligence, arrests and compilation of evidence would normally be carried out by anti-terrorist detectives, allowing Special Branch to keep its own role out of the public eye.

A number of officers work in A Squad of the Metropolitan Police Special Branch, providing specialist personal protection for ministers, former ministers, and those thought to be under threat mainly from terrorists – one prime example being Salman Rushdie. Foreign dignitaries are also given Special Branch bodyguards. Heads of foreign missions who are thought to be at particular risk from terrorist attacks, as in the case of the American and Israeli ambassadors, are allocated a team of A Squad officers. B Squad has responsibility for collecting intelligence on Irish terrorism in London. The main covert collection operations are carried out through B Squad's Intelligence Source Unit, which recruits and handles agents. Analysis is undertaken by the Research Unit, which acts as a clearing-house for all incoming intelligence reports. A number of Special Branch officers are routinely attached to MI5, which has its own liaison cell within B Squad. International terrorism is the responsibility of the Counter-Extremist Squad, which also has responsibility for countering subversion and the activities of extremist groups on both the left and the right. Special Branches still retain their responsibility for collecting intelligence on threats to public order, advising chief constables on the likely implications of marches and demonstrations where there is a threat of subversion or politically motivated violence. Under the 1984 guidelines for Special Branches, this was regarded as paramount, reflecting a traditional fear among successive governments from the 1920s onwards that the left wing would seek to use demonstrations and industrial unrest to overthrow or undermine parliamentary democracy. But with the end of the Cold War, and despite the Northern Ireland peace process, the counter-terror role has become the most important single function.

Many Special Branches outside the metropolitan areas are very small, and there tends to be a lot of co-operation within regions, either informally or through the Regional Special Branch Conference, allowing the exchange of information and experience and the sharing of specialist technical resources. Representatives of the various Special Branches man the National Joint Unit at New Scotland Yard, which helps to prevent embarrassing incidents such as the 1991 escape from Brixton prison of two leading IRA terrorists.

Staffordshire Special Branch had conducted 'a long-range operation' inside Brixton, employing an informant to get close to Nessan Quinlivan and Pearse McAuley. The three discussed an escape plan under which Quinlivan and McAuley would smuggle in a gun and shoot their way out of the prison after Sunday mass. Their subsequent escape followed that plan to the letter.

All Special Branch officers are trained by the Metropolitan Police Special Branch and the Security Service. The Met Branch also provides a great deal of technical and operational assistance to the provincial forces and acts as the link on Irish terrorism with MI5. 'The Metropolitan Police Special Branch and the Security Service act in a close partnership to ensure that intelligence is exploited to the maximum to counter terrorist activity,' the 1994 Special Branch guidelines state. 'This also enables the Metropolitan Police Special Branch to add the police perspective and to provide advice for provincial forces on assessed intelligence where police action may be necessary.' The Special Branch responsibilities of terrorism, subversion and espionage are no longer the only areas of policing that require sophisticated intelligence operations. Police officers generally use the term 'intelligence' to mean any information collected from a covert source, such as a 'snout' or informer, which will help in a specific investigation – what might be called tactical intelligence.

Scotland Yard has its own Criminal Intelligence Branch (SO11), which traditionally took on a de facto nationwide criminal intelligence role, although the collection of long-term intelligence was fairly limited. But from the 1970s onwards, the easy-profits, low-risk potential of drug-trafficking brought a new type of criminal to the streets of Britain. Although gangs such as the Krays and the Richardsons had long had an organised structure, they tended to operate only within their own territories and were relatively easy to keep track of. Those criminals involved in drug-related crime acted very much like international corporations: they operated across national borders, developed links with numerous domestic criminal groups in order to market the drugs, and had long-term strategic goals. The need to track the patterns of activity of such groups, and where possible to anticipate their next move, created a requirement for strategic rather than tactical intelligence. But operational police forces rarely had the time or resources to undertake long-term intelligence operations.

A series of reports in the 1970s and early 1980s on Britain's relative lack of any such strategic criminal intelligence capability gave rise first to the Central Drugs and Illegal Immigrants Intelligence Unit. A number of other intelligence units were also set up during this period, among them the National Football Intelligence Unit, to keep track of the central core of hooligans causing soccer violence. But the explosion in organised crime – and in particular drug-related crime – that occurred in the 1980s, and was exacerbated by the relaxation of the strict controls over eastern Europe following the fall of communism, revealed how inadequate this system was, and in 1992 a new National Criminal Intelligence Service (NCIS) was created. It brought together the various national police and customs intelligence units, with a brief 'to develop and assess information and intelligence on serious crime and major criminals and to disseminate that intelligence to the police, other law-enforcement agencies and government departments'.

At the same time, Scotland Yard also re-examined its use of intelligence concluding that the Criminal Intelligence Branch (SO11) should be run as a 'Directorate of Intelligence' on similar lines to a military intelligence operation. A central intelligence unit at Scotland Yard would control a network of intelligence officers at the various stations around London whose main role was to be long-term targeting of organised crime groups. The threat from organised crime was seen as so great that even national security might be at risk. MI5 had recognised this danger as early as 1991, when Stella Rimington flew to Moscow for talks with Russian officials on 'co-operation in the fight against international terrorism and drug trafficking'. The JIC ordered the foreign intelligence services, GCHQ and MI6, to examine the problem, and a role in the fight against 'serious crime' was included in the 1993 Intelligence Services Bill. Senior SIS officers were initially highly sceptical that they had a role to play in this area, but the service's success in a number of major operations against drug-smugglers persuaded them otherwise. The importance of new threats like crime, terrorism and weapons proliferation, has led to the creation of a Global Issues Directorate, in which the Counter-Narcotics section deals with all aspects of serious crime.

The Treasury had been a key player behind the call for the intelligence services to investigate organised crime. With the annual figure for the laundering of drug money alone exceeding £500 billion worldwide, the process of laundering the profits could easily cause considerable damage even to a strong domestic economy. There was particular concern that the transfer of illicit funds out of Asia, South Africa and eastern Europe through 'underground' banking systems operated by organised crime groups could be used to manipulate the currency markets and might destabilise the British economy. The chaos caused in the old Soviet Bloc by the collapse of the Soviet system had led to widespread fears over the threat from trans national organised crime. Even before the collapse of the communist regime, the level of crime in the Soviet Union was rocketing, encouraged by Mikhail Gorbachev's market reforms. By mid-1995 the anti-*Mafiya* department of the Russian interior ministry estimated that there were more than 8,000 criminal gangs in the country, with around 35,000 members. An estimated 80 per cent of Russian businesses were said to pay protection money to the gangs, who controlled close to half the country's turnover in goods and services. Many 'owned' corrupt government officials and operated behind legitimate 'front' companies whose only role was to launder money. The number of gangs that had diversified into overseas operations was growing.

All of Scotland Yard's separate intelligence branches, Covert Operations (SO10), Criminal Intelligence (SO11), and Special Branch (SO12), are now under the control of the Yard's own Director of Intelligence as part of the continuing efforts to apply intelligence techniques to the war against organised crime. 'There has been an astronomical growth of organised crime in eastern Europe as they try and move towards democracy – particularly decentralised banking systems,' said John Grieve, a former Scotland Yard Director of Intelligence. East European organised crime has a relationship with drug-related violence. Both Scotland Yard and NCIS have built up the links with their counterparts in the former Soviet Bloc to track senior crime figures from the Balkans, the Baltic, Russia and Ukraine, he said. 'We have a good working relationship with all those places – some better than others. Some of them we have a very tight working relationship with. They are good people to work with.'

Russian gangs are involved in drug-trafficking, widespread protection rackets, which have forced many of the Western firms that originally bought into Russian companies to withdraw, illegal immigration, organised prostitution, and large-scale car theft, with high-value vehicles being targeted in western Europe for resale within eastern Europe and the former Soviet Union. The former Soviet Union has always been a major drug producer. The economies of the central-Asian republics of Kyrgyzstan, Tajikistan and Uzbekistan depend to a large extent on drugs and are therefore accorded a high priority by British intelligence. Even before the 1917 revolution, Krrgyzstan accounted for a fifth of the world's opium supply. An Uzbek farmer can earn between 15,000 and 20,000 roubles a year from a hectare of fruit orchards. The same area planted with poppy would produce five kilograms of raw opium worth an estimated 2.5 million roubles. The drug routes start out in the southern Tajik town of Khorog, heading either up through Osh in Kirghizstan on the border with Uzbekistan or west through Dushanbe, the Tajik capital. Underpaid police and customs officials are bribed to turn a blind eye to the trade, and once through the borders the drugs are moved on to Europe, mostly via rail. The Russian drug-smugglers are so adept at using these routes that the Colombian cartels are even moving cocaine into western Europe via Moscow, exporting it in containers labelled as food products and repackaging it as Russian exports to the West.

The former Soviet Bloc has also become a major source of synthetic drugs produced in the old state laboratories of Poland, the Czech Republic, Latvia, Lithuania and Estonia. Poland is Europe's largest producer of amphetamine sulphate and is a significant source of heroin, made from poppies grown in the Polish Triangle between the southern towns of Kraków, Miechów and Proszowice. The gangs move the drugs west and easily disposable consumer products such as high-prestige cars east, while the authorities look on helplessly. The growth in Russian and east European organised crime led in 1994 to a joint British intelligence study of the potential threat, under the direction of NCIS, but also including MI5, MI6, GCHQ and Scotland Yard's Directorate of Intelligence. This led to increased operations against Russian criminals, said Albert Pacey, former NCIS Director. 'There is a significant threat posed by gangs organised in, or centred on, that geographic area,' he said. 'Our assessment is that the greatest threat to the UK in the long term is from the money-launderer.'

There is a false perception that Britain has remained relatively untouched by the growth in international organised crime. 'You have to understand that organised crime does not work on the strict hierarchical model of the Mafia and the Triads here in London,' said Grieve. 'It is very attractive to impose a hierarchy on these things, and the Mafia, the Triads, they do have a hierarchy and they are here. But most of what goes on under the heading of organised crime is loosely organised. Yes, it is project crime. Yes, it nets them vast profits. But it is not hierarchical like people want it to be. It is much more like a patchwork quilt. It is like a webwork of old relationships, hatreds, alliances, blood relationships.'

A number of the more recognised organised-crime groupings are active in Britain. There has been a noticeable increase in Italian criminal activities in the UK since 1990, especially in the London area, where the Sicilian Mafia, the Neapolitan Camorra and the Calabrian Ndrangheta are all known to have set up front companies and been mainly involved in money-laundering, drug-trafficking and fraud. Paradoxically, Britain's reputation as a reasonably violence-free country has led some Italian gang members to use it as a safe haven from vendettas at home.

Drugs are imported by a number of groups. The Colombian cartels, which have diversified into growing poppy to produce heroin because of a glut of cocaine on the American market, have been active in the UK, linking up with the Jamaican Yardies and Posses, which dominate the UK drug market. The Jamaican gangs are mainly involved in pushing cannabis and crack cocaine. The hallmark of both Yardies and Posses is an extravagant use of weaponry to enforce territory and status. This is largely responsible for the increasing pressure within the Metropolitan Police Force for officers to be armed. Both Posse members and Yardies base their respect for other gang members on the firepower of their weapons and their willingness to resort to extreme violence. They are largely restricted to the inner-city areas of London, Manchester, Bristol, Birmingham and Leicester, and they tend to rely on loose, often family-based, links between Britain, the Caribbean and the eastern seaboard of the United States and Canada. But the Jamaicans are not the only groups active in the drug market. Indian and Pakistani gangs specialise in heroin, which is reasonably easy to import as a result of the close links between

Britain and the sub-continent, and they have easy opportunities to launder money within the British Asian business community. Turkish and Kurdish immigrant groups have been particularly active in north London in drug trafficking and extortion, and the increasing importance of Nigeria as a trans-shipment point for drugs from the Caribbean and Latin America has led west African gangs based in London to graduate from organised illegal immigration and benefit fraud to drug trafficking. The Hells Angels, with twelve chapters in the United Kingdom, have also become increasingly involved in organised crime, largely trafficking in cannabis, LSD and amphetamines. Triad groups, mainly from Hong Kong and working almost exclusively within the Chinese communities, are involved across a wide spectrum of organised crime, including drug-trafficking, prostitution, illegal immigration from both mainland China and Hong Kong, illegal gambling, extortion and fraud. Murder is frequently used to enforce obedience, with the most favoured 'muscle' being Vietnamese associates, whose willingness to resort to extreme violence makes them an extremely potent threat.

Another group which has had a great deal of publicity is the Japanese *Yakuza*, who have a far stronger influence within Japan itself than the Mafia has in America for instance. As Japanese companies diversified their operations and set up factories abroad, the *Yakuza* followed. They traditionally follow the tenets of *giri*, the obligation to repay favours, and *ninjo*, compassion for the weak. Their main activities in Britain so far have been confined to that of the financial crime specialists, the *Sokaiya*, who have been involved in commodity-futures fraud and money-laundering.

The Home Office Organised Crime Strategy Group, which includes all the British intelligence agencies plus the National Crime Squad and Customs and Excise, sets the overall priorities and strategy based on the NCIS Threat Assessment for Serious Crime. These are currently led by drugs, illegal immigration, revenue fraud, and money-laundering. The main NCIS unit tracking the gangs, known in the jargon as Organised Crime Groupings (OCGs) is the Specialist Intelligence Branch. This is split into a series of units: the Drugs Teams; the Economic Crime Unit, which covers fraud, counterfeiting and money-laundering and has direct links to the major clearing banks; the Organised Immigration Crime Section; the National Hi-Tech

Crime Unit, which investigates criminal abuse of the Internet by hackers employed by the organised crime for fraud and economic espionage; and the Specialist Crimes Unit, which includes teams working on organised vehicle crime, West African organised crime, kidnap and extortion, football violence and serious sex offences. Following the 11 September attacks, a terrorist finance unit was set up to track terrorist funds.

Scotland Yard's Criminal Intelligence Branch is organised around its Drugs and Violence Intelligence Unit. The DRVIU co-ordinates all intelligence-led operations against organised crime in the capital. There are five devolved Force Intelligence Bureaux (FIB) – one in each of the Metropolitan Police areas – and a network of sixty-three intelligence cells – one in every police station in London. 'Each of the sixty-three cells has its own analytical capability, and some to a greater or lesser extent have some surveillance capability – though mostly this is static surveillance as opposed to mobile,' said Grieve. 'You really don't get mobile surveillance until you get to the area force intelligence bureaux, each one of which has a mobile surveillance team and an analytical capability. Our focus is always on London. But on a daily basis, at this very moment, there will be somebody on the phone in some part of both SO11 at the centre and the FIBs and the divisions talking to the rest of the country. There is nothing in London that doesn't touch on something somebody else is doing. Coming the other way, 70 per cent of serious crime has its focus in the South-East, and the bulk of that will be something to do with London, so they're talking to us all the time. It is never-ending, and we probably have the biggest intelligence database – massive.' The directorate's Memex computer is linked to forty different databases from all over the world, including the New York District Attorney's records of all known Jamaican drug-dealers. 'We do a lot of work on what we call thematic crime, of which drug-related violence is probably the most noteworthy – very dangerous people. Sometimes the threat is so great that you have to act before you might want to and just hope that you are going to generate the evidence that you want. We do a lot of strategic analysis, and NCIS do a lot of strategic analysis. We also run some of the most dangerous live sources of information, and we run a lot of technical kit to go with that.'

There is clear demarcation between the roles of Scotland Yard and NCIS, with the former now very much restricted to the London area, while the latter covers the whole of the country. Scotland Yard's boundary is the M25, although it is also tasked with liaising with other criminal intelligence agencies both in Britain and internationally on crime in London. Liaison between the two organisations is very close, Grieve said. 'It is unlikely that we are running a major intelligence development plan and we haven't got NCIS in. It is very unusual not to find NCIS in it. It is very unusual not to find the South-East Regional Crime Squad in it, and not to find some local team in it as well. It is generally a task unit put together from all those people, trying to take out the main quarry.'

The strong co-ordination developed not just because it made sense to pool intelligence but as a result of limitations imposed on NCIS from its conception. Because of fears over lack of accountability, there were severe restrictions both on the extent to which it could collect intelligence and on what it could do with it once it had been collected. It had no operational arm and was not allowed to carry out mobile surveillance. All it could do was produce intelligence packages, which it then attempted to 'sell' to the relevant provincial forces, with no control over how or even whether they would be acted on.

A confidential 1994 Home Office report found that NCIS was 'underfunded, under-used and ineffective'. Although there are regional offices in Manchester, Birmingham, Wakefield, Bristol and Scotland, a lack of officers on the ground and its restrictive mandate were hampering its operations. To rectify the situation, in October 1995, the government announced a national crime squad based on NCIS supplemented by other agencies – mainly the regional crime squads, but also including elements of MI5 and GCHQ. Michael Howard, the then Home Secretary, stressed that it was not intended to be a British FBI: 'We are going to develop the role of our National Criminal Intelligence Service, allowing their staff to undertake mobile surveillance of targets. We are going to build on the work of the regional crime squads to ensure that national problems are met with national solutions. The Security Service has a part to play in support of the law-enforcement agencies. The government will legislate shortly to enable the service itself to work in this area.'

MI5 was already taking part in operations against organised crime led by NCIS and co-ordinated through the Joint Intelligence Committee, as were SIS and GCHQ. The military presence in Afghanistan, the source of most of the heroin reaching Britain, and the Balkans, a key staging post on its route, has also led to contributions from military intelligence, and in particular the use of air reconnaissance and satellite imagery interpreted by the Joint Air Reconnaissance Intelligence Centre, in the fight against organised crime. In the wake of the allied victory in Afghanistan, MI6 took a leading role in co-ordinating the disruption of a resurgent drugs trade, working with both the SAS and military intelligence. Liaison between the various agencies on drugs and crime takes place through the NCIS Special Liaison Unit. One senior NCIS officer said he and his colleagues had been working very closely with MI5 and MI6 for some time: 'I deal with them and work with them on a daily basis, because it's all about sources of intelligence. They've got some fantastic sources of intelligence, and at the end of the day I would be naïve in the extreme if I didn't work with them. But in all our dealings with the Security Service and the Secret Intelligence Service it is made abundantly clear to everyone that it is in support of law enforcement, and in fact we task them in our field.'

The most common source in criminal intelligence operations is the informer, said John Grieve. 'Paying informants is very cost-effective, providing that you manage all the risks – all the moral risks, all the physical risks, and all the legal risks. Economically it is a very, very cost-effective way of doing it if you compare the price of one of my mobile surveillance teams, an eight-hour day for them, and then you compare that with how much you pay informers. With an informer, we have got somebody inside the tent looking out. With a surveillance team, you are outside the tent looking in. There are very few jobs with the category of people that I deal with that two or three days work by a surveillance team will get a result. Very usually you will barely be off first base.' But the handling of informers presents a difficult balance between ensuring that they do enough within their group to gain acceptance without ever crossing the very thin line between being an informant and acting as an *agent provocateur*. The Directorate of Intelligence was widely criticised in 1995 over its recruitment of a member of a Jamaican Posse as the inside man on a major international operation against drug-trafficking. While still working as a Scotland Yard informer, Eaton Green took part in an armed robbery in Nottingham, shooting one man in the leg. He was subsequently jailed for six years. But Nottinghamshire police were irate to discover not only that he was an informer but that his handlers were apparently very anxious that he be allowed to remain free so that he could continue in that role. 'We were involved in an international intelligence operation,' Grieve said. 'We took a view that it is better to know where some of these people are if you have no grounds to bar them from your country at the time.' He conceded that his officers were operating in 'morally difficult territory' but was unrepentant about the fact that Green had continued to sell crack cocaine, carry arms and commit robberies during his time as an informer. 'Criminals involved in some parts of drug-related violence are paranoid, treacherous, violent and unstable. It is an unstructured and chaotic environment. They operate in a culture which is different from other cultures and which is more difficult to penetrate. It's impossible to tackle serious crime of this nature without the use of informants who turn out – surprise, surprise – to be criminals who are still committing crimes. If they didn't have that sort of background, they wouldn't be accepted. Green was an extremely successful informant. He was well worth the investment and it is extremely unfortunate that we no longer have him available to us.'

International co-operation is co-ordinated through the NCIS International Tactical Services Division, which controls links with Interpol and with the overseas liaison officers, police or customs officers who are posted to Britain's embassies abroad and whose role is being expanded to cover all aspects of organised crime. Interpol – set up in 1956 – was until recently little more than an international conduit for police communication. But, following widespread criticism, it has now been revamped with the creation of a European Liaison Bureau to help national forces to mount joint operations and an Analytical Criminal Intelligence Unit to exploit the information stored on the agency's computer database.

Both NCIS and Scotland Yard also liaise with Europol, the European police organisation based in The Hague. First proposed by Germany in 1991 as the European equivalent of the FBI, it was formally set up as part of the Maastricht Treaty but its role was limited to that of a co-ordinating body for the exchange and analysis of criminal intelligence and it had no operational powers. Its responsibilities are being increased on a step-by-step basis, starting with countering drug-trafficking and gradually adding money-laundering; the international trade in stolen cars, illegal immigrants and nuclear materials; enforced prostitution; and finally terrorism. Illegal immigration had jumped to the top of the priorities alongside drugs even before the discovery of 58 dead Chinese migrants in the back of a container lorry entering Dover in June 2000. The number of illegal immigrants caught at UK ports rocketed during the 1990s from just 61 in 1991 to 16,000 in 1999. Tens of thousands more evade the controls. John Abbott, Pacey's successor as NCIS Director, said the high profits and relatively low risk was attracting gangs to switch to the trafficking of illegal immigrants from drug smuggling. An estimated one million illegal migrants are smuggled internationally each year, with the criminal gangs involved earning in excess of £10billion from the trade. There were now dozens of Chinese, Sri Lankan, Turkish and Albanian gangs whose sole business was smuggling immigrants into Britain and links between British-based gangs and their counterparts in Russia, China, Colombia, Brazil and Nigeria. 'Entrants are asked to pay thousands of pounds to be brought into this country invariably in extremely dangerous conditions,' Abbott said. 'Upon arrival, they are often held prisoner until further money is paid or forced into bonded labour to pay off their debts, being forced to work in slave labour conditions in sweatshops or restaurants or being forced into prostitution are common. Whenever debts are not paid, the facilitators often resort to violence. The indications are that despite actions being taken, the market will increase and profits will remain high.' MI5, MI6 and GCHQ all make a contribution to the NCIS operations against illegal immigration, which are controlled by the Organised Immigration Crime Section. One joint operation between MI5 and the Russian FSB, successor to the domestic arm of the KGB, led to the break-up of a gang smuggling immigrants from China through Russia and into Britain. 'We intercepted the communications between the Moscow and London operations of this international gang,' an FSB officer said. 'Through our FSB representative in Britain, we contacted MI5 and our co-operation began. The British side offered us a very useful detailed report about this gang. They have been following its operations for a long time. It's the first example of such fruitful joint work of Russian and British secret services in the field of preventing illegal immigration.'

There are inevitable security worries for any intelligence organisation sharing the product of covert operations with foreign organisations over which it has no control and particularly with police forces that might not apply the same rigour in terms of security. Stella Rimington has pointed to the need for Europe's security services and law-enforcement agencies to be sure that any information they exchange is kept secure: 'They must have confidence in each other's ability to keep the most sensitive information secret. Because there is no doubt at all that those people who risk their lives to give us intelligence from within the hearts of those organisations which threaten our security will not do so unless they are confident that we will not compromise their safety.' This is said to have caused major problems within Europol. But John Grieve said it had not hampered Scotland Yard's links with Europol. 'We have a very close relationship with Europol,' he said. 'Most of the work we do with them is on east-European organised crime and banking systems. I would be surprised if there was a single solitary country in Europe that we haven't run an operation with. Of course there is intelligence that is UK Eyes Only. But you do not want to have a major row running with one of your allies, so there is a need for diplomacy and tact, and on operational issues we share everything. We have no problems with that.'

Chasing drug money through the banking system represents an increasing part of the work of Scotland Yard's Criminal Intelligence Branch. 'Actual activity in this area is skyrocketing,' Grieve said. 'You learn some stuff from it by serendipity. Things come in that are very obviously drug trafficking. Things crop up that are really good intelligence coups, really good sources of intelligence. The problem is that you have to get into the world banking system, and different countries have a very different set of regulations. You need an organised banking structure with its own self-regulation as well as external regulations before you can make that work. There are countries in the world that just don't play that game, and once the money reaches them it is very hard to track it – very, very hard.'

Money-laundering – the process by which illicit funds are given the appearance of legally owned income – can take many forms. The money, which normally begins as cash, will be passed through a series of stages to disguise its origins and make it difficult to trace. In its most basic form, a luxury item like a car or a piece of jewellery is bought and then re-sold. But in more complex cases this will be only the first stage – the so-called 'placement' of the funds. The next stage is 'layering', in which the funds are normally split up and passed through a complex trail of financial transactions. This has become particularly easy for the international criminal since the introduction of electronic payment systems that allow the money to be transferred easily around the world to a variety of different bank accounts. Finally comes 'integration', the point at which the money has all the semblance of legitimate funds and is regarded as safe to use. Frequently, 'shell' companies are used as fronts through which to launder the money. Totally innocent companies become drawn into the web. Investigators in the United States discovered that Colombia's Cali drug cartel had used hundreds of American companies – including General Electric, General Motors, Apple Computer and Microsoft – to launder the money earned from the sale of drugs. One of Scotland Yard's joint operations with the New York District Attorney's office found that the Cali drug cartel was laundering the proceeds of its drug operations by buying and selling pictures in the art galleries of Mayfair and Manhattan.

In Britain, financial organisations are obliged under the 1988 Drug Trafficking Offences Act and the 1993 Criminal Justice Act to report any transactions which they suspect of being part of a money-laundering operation to the police, who have extensive powers to trace the so-called 'money trail' through the banking system and to freeze or confiscate funds acquired through criminal means. 'It is often said that the way to tackle organised crime is through the money trail,' said Albert Pacey. 'If publicity is the oxygen of the terrorist, then money is the oxygen of organised crime. If we can remove the illegally acquired assets from the criminal then we can remove their motivation, their *raison d'être*.' The banks make around 20,000 so-called 'suspicious transaction reports' a year. 'Whilst we do not claim that these disclosures by themselves lead to the conviction of gangsters, it is true to say that they have in many cases supplied the missing piece of the jigsaw that has led to the completion of a fuller picture of criminality.'

One of the biggest problems facing the intelligence services as they tackle organised crime is disclosure. Under the British legal system, the defence must have access to any evidence collected against its client that might help its case. Police reluctance to disclose evidence that will reveal intelligence sources leads to an average of one court case a week being aborted. Disclosing the identity of an informer has to be avoided at all costs, and numerous prosecutions have had to be aborted because the judge backed up demands from the defence for an informer to be identified. Even the act of aborting such a case is risky, said one NCIS officer. 'It tips off the defendants that they had an informer in their midst and they will try to find him by a process of elimination. With the increased use of violence, that could well cost him his life.'

One of the most graphic examples of a criminal case involving intelligence being aborted to protect sources of information began in the early hours of 3 February 1993 when two police officers on patrol in the Thames Valley became suspicious of a Maestro van. When they stopped and searched it they discovered a radio scanner, balaclava helmets, rope ladders and home-made Molotov cocktails. The three men inside the van were members of the Animal Liberation Front who were planning to release animals being delivered to a slaughterhouse and to set fire to the transporter. They exercised their right to silence during questioning by police and were subsequently charged with conspiracy to cause criminal damage. During the trial at Reading Crown Court, defence lawyers asked that files on the three accused held in the Animal Rights National Index be disclosed and, to the dismay of officers working on the case, the judge agreed. 'The information they were requesting would have had the effect of dismantling our intelligence database, exposing our techniques and putting informants at risk,' said one police officer. 'Frankly, if we have to disclose that sort of detail even when it is of little or no relevance to the case, we might as well pack up and go home.' The prosecution was forced to withdraw its case and the three men walked free, stopping on the steps of the court to make a full admission to a waiting television crew. But it is not only informers that need to be protected. Methods of detection can be just as vulnerable. 'The constant see-saw is the counter-intelligence from their side,' said John Grieve. 'They are constantly trying to find out how we did it.' Even where a case proceeds and the defendant is convicted, other members of the gang frequently learn enough about police methods from disclosure of evidence to allow them to develop their own counter-measures and render sources useless.

The German urban terrorist group the Red Army Faction developed into a highly professional organisation, always ensuring that no fingerprints were left behind in safe houses. But the *Bundeskriminalamt* (BKA), the German federal police, discovered the terrorists were neglecting to check the underneath of toilet seats. When fingerprints were produced as evidence in open court, the terrorists' defence lawyers insisted on being told exactly where in a safe house the fingerprints were discovered. Although that prosecution was successful, the BKA never found fingerprints under a toilet seat again. For security reasons, the Red Army Faction would pay the rent and power bills for its safe houses in cash. But since Germany has become a relatively cashless society BKA investigators were able to search through the power company's computers for customers who moved out of addresses close to where attacks took place at roughly the same time and who paid their bills in cash. After the Red Army Faction's lawyers forced disclosure of this technique in open court, the terrorists stopped paying in cash. Defence lawyers constantly mount 'fishing expeditions' to find out what they can about police intelligence techniques, Grieve said. 'The big issue for us is how to do these things without showing all our secret toys,' he said. 'Intelligence is anathema to the lawyers. They want their hands on absolutely everything. They are not just content with the product. They want the process as well, including some of our tricks of generating live sources of information. "Where was the microphone? What was the frequency? Where was it positioned in the room?" All those kind of issues. "Where were the surveillance teams? What technical kit did you use? What colour vehicle were you in? Tell us everything about everything. Or drop the case." If we get a weak judge, we get ordered to disclose all kinds of things, and no lawyer in this day and age will say, "I won't tell my client." So a massive amount of material gets released. It's a big issue for us – a really big issue.'

MI5 has already come across these problems in open court. 'Sometimes this acts as a constraint on our investigations,' Stella Rimington said. 'There is an inherent uncertainty in judging in advance how the courts may view individual operations and methods which we regard as sensitive. Many such sensitive techniques have to be protected at all costs, because they cannot be replaced. This sometimes means that we are unable to use the most effective investigative methods in cases that may result in prosecution. In some cases, rulings by the judge may cause the prosecution to be discontinued because the material information is so sensitive that it is not possible to disclose it in any form.'

While many police officers have expressed disquiet about the use of MI5 to counter organised crime, those who have been involved in criminal intelligence are less dismissive. John Grieve said that during his time as Scotland Yard's Director of Intelligence, the police had very good relations with MI5. 'They have been very supportive. We aren't doing well enough to reject help from anybody quite frankly. We're awash with drugs in London – and violence and everything else. If they want to help, they want to get a bit of the action, fine – come and help us. But be ready for rolling about in the gutter and getting yourself smeared in excrement, because this is a very dirty game out there with the people we're dealing with.'

Twenty Four

Milk and Honey

Commercial intelligence may very largely supplement political intelligence, if it be properly used.

War Office report dated 9 December 1893

As the Cold War came to an end and the intelligence services cast around for new roles, one of the most commonly suggested was economic espionage. Frequently it was put forward as if it was something new that spies had not considered before. Its significance was by turns either overstated or discounted. Depending on who was asked, it was the most important target for the intelligence services in the new world or it was just something the spies were inventing to keep themselves busy and their budgets intact – a straightforward case of jobs for the boys. In fact economic espionage has been carried out since Moses – obeying God's orders to send spies into Canaan – laid down the first list of intelligence priorities. Caleb and his men were to find out 'whether the land is rich or poor' – a directive that was reflected in the main thrust of their report on 'a land flowing with milk and honey'.

But, new role or not, by end of the 20th century, with the old world order falling apart, it had become clear that economic intelligence had to be a high priority. In the short term at least, the new superpower system would be based on economic strength. The new 'geo-economic' power blocs would be the United States, the European Union and a Pacific Rim dominated by Japan but also including other commercially powerful newly industrialised countries (NICs) such as South Korea and Singapore. Economic intelligence has long been a useful tool in evaluating the strategic threat, and has continued to be so with the collapse of communism. The stability of the countries of the former Soviet Union and eastern Europe is heavily dependent on the success of economic reforms, and British intelligence has carefully tracked their progress, looking for signs of industrial unrest and the social problems associated with high unemployment.

For the same reasons, the economies of post-apartheid South Africa and the countries involved in the Middle East peace process are kept under close surveillance for any problems that might bring renewed tensions, while those of the West's main *bêtes noires* – China, North Korea, Libya, Iran and Iraq – are monitored for any sign that sanctions or restrictions on technology imports are being breached and for economic problems that might lead to instability or to the weakening or strengthening of anti-Western policies. The state of trade and economic links between the various countries of the former Soviet Bloc is also a very high priority, as are the financial activities of various Central and South American governments which are monitored closely to determine their ability to repay international debt. Intelligence on Argentinian fishing and oil exploration activities around the Falklands is also a natural priority for the British agencies.

Britain, buoyed by its position as the world's leading trading nation, took what one official described as a '*laissez-faire* approach' to the collection of commercial intelligence until the later part of the nineteenth century, when a 'revival of economic nationalism' and the widespread belief that war in Europe was inevitable led to a growing interest in such matters. Not only would commercial information help Britain's exporters to ward off the increasing competition in trade – particularly from Germany – but an army fighting abroad would need to know where supplies might be found.

By 1893, General E F Chapman, the British Director of Military Intelligence, was pointing out that the ability of a potential enemy to wage war would depend on the strength of its economy, and that its preparations for war could be detected by studying government contracts. 'Commercial intelligence may very largely supplement political intelligence, if it be properly used,' Chapman wrote. 'Whenever warlike operations are about to be undertaken, it is clear that the issue of contracts, and other steps affecting the commercial world must precede the actual start of any expedition,' he explained. 'The subject requires study, but the great advantage we possess over other nations, in possessing the closest commercial relations with every port, and every large town in Europe, should gain us in the matter of obtaining information, which I believe to be one of the main reasons for success in every operation of war.'

Chapman suggested that Britain's commercial attachés abroad be asked to monitor any new contracts for supplies of war *matériel*, food, horses or medicine and to relay the information back to England 'with the utmost expedition, consistent with secrecy'. His ideas were taken up within the Foreign Office, where one official called for 'a separate intelligence organisation' to be set up within the Commercial Department 'for obtaining early information of all contracts made by foreign governments for the supply of such stores as may be required in the active operations for war, and of the collection of such stores in such places, or under such circumstances as may indicate their intended application in premeditated active operations.'

In 1900 the Board of Trade formed a Commercial Intelligence Branch, which collated economic intelligence sent home by British diplomats around the world. But the Foreign Office did not like the idea of another government department having control over what went on in its embassies, and the two sides 'squabbled like kids' over who should control the new branch. By 1917, with the First World War creating a large demand for commercial intelligence, military intelligence was collecting economic information on foreign countries, and in particular 'questions of military policy connected with the economic and financial resources of the enemy'. Meanwhile, the turf battle between the Board of Trade and the Foreign Office over the Commercial Intelligence Branch showed no signs of abating. Eventually, it was agreed that it would be resolved only by creating 'a single department charged with the compilation and distribution of intelligence, from whatever source it is obtained'.

That new ministry was called the Department of Overseas Trade, and by the mid-1930s it was sending out routine reports on Britain's trading partners to exporters and to other government departments. It had also set up a 'Special Register' of companies who, for a nominal fee, received 'some information ... particularly that which is of a confidential character'. The Committee of Imperial Defence had meanwhile set up its own subcommittee specifically to look at the potential of economic intelligence. This was not just a question of detecting preparations for war. Destroying the enemy's means of production would severely limit his ability to wage war, and economic intelligence would be vital in determining which targets would cause most damage. The subcommittee built up its own research staff, known as the Industrial Intelligence Centre and led by Major Desmond Morton, an SIS officer.

The centre, which was initially controlled by the War Office and based at SIS headquarters, became part of the Department of Overseas Trade in 1935. Its role was 'to collate, study and interpret existing industrial and other civilian information in relation to the war potential of foreign countries'. There were six sections, whose main targets were Germany, the Soviet Union, the Americas, the Far East, France, and the Mediterranean and Middle East. Its reports were sent to the War Office, the Treasury, the Foreign Office and the Board of Trade.

The IIC was very successful, warning that Hitler was preparing for war long before the War Office or the Air Ministry. But at the outbreak of the Second World War it was subsumed into the Intelligence Department of the Ministry of Economic Warfare. Its role was 'to collect, collate, appreciate and present to the Service and other departments ... all information about the enemy's economic strength, dispositions and intentions, which may be of use in attacking him'. At the same time, a special commercial circulating section (Section VI) was set up within SIS, which by now was also known by its more familiar name of MI6, to pass on any economic intelligence collected by its agents or by the Government Code and Cypher School.

At the end of the war, when MI6 was re-organised and the circulating sections became the Directorate of Requirements, the commercial section was retained as R6, with a brief to disseminate economic intelligence, which was then seen as one of the main post-war roles. 'The economic contribution in assessing the strength of potential enemies is bound to be considerably more important than in wartime,' a secret Foreign Office report said. 'In peace a country's capacity for war-making must chiefly lie in its war potential, which is predominantly an economic factor.' There was particular interest in acquiring German 'trade secrets' and passing them on to British companies. The JIC decreed that economic intelligence gathered in occupied Germany 'should be pooled between the US and British Governments on the understanding that they were free to make such use of it as they thought fit, including its release to civil industry'.

Ian Fleming, then a naval intelligence officer, told the JIC that the British Overseas Airways Corporation was among a number of companies being given intelligence by the British authorities. Another Admiralty representative said there was no reason why other British companies would not be willing to work with British intelligence on a reciprocal basis. 'Business firms had been keen to co-operate before the war and he saw no reason why the Joint Intelligence Bureau should not have the same co-operation from business firms at the present time.'

The collection of economic data has provided a key role for the British intelligence services ever since – a fact which was tacitly acknowledged when both the 1989 Security Service Act and the 1994 Intelligence Services Act authorised operations in the interests of Britain's 'economic well-being'. Economic intelligence is passed to government departments direct and is also analysed by the JIC's assessments staffs. Their conclusions are overseen by the Economic Current Intelligence Group, a JIC subcommittee which issues intelligence reports to a number of customers, including the Department of Trade and Industry, the Export Credit Guarantee Department, the Treasury and the Bank of England. Although such intelligence is intended for use by government departments, the extent of the informal relationships with British companies was confirmed by Baroness Park, a former MI6 officer who said they might be given useful information in exchange for allowing their executives to be used to collect intelligence. Asked what businessmen and women might expect from MI6 in return for risking their lives on its behalf, Baroness Park said: 'I think that is an entirely individual thing. With some people, it may be money; with others a little bit of help, a little bit of influence, a little bit of knowledge. For instance, if you knew a British company was coming out to try and get the order for helicopters in a particular country and you knew from other sources that the Italians and the French were both bidding, you would certainly tell the man you wanted to help that so that he was forearmed and knew that he had competition.'

A former GCHQ official who worked for the agency in the early 1970s described monitoring what she said were 'random pick-ups' of commercial telexes. But GCHQ's role in collecting economic intelligence was well-entrenched long before that. Its predecessor, GC&CS, set up a specialised section to monitor foreign commercial traffic, mainly on behalf of the Industrial Intelligence Centre, in 1938. Nor was this the first time that it had involved itself in such matters. 'Once or twice perhaps we may have looked out for individuals,' said A. G. Denniston, the then Director of GC&CS, in an internal history of the inter-war years. 'Once most certainly we did investigate the telegrams of certain oil companies.' GCHQ's interest in this area appears to have increased. Recent advertisements for linguists have asked for graduates with a specialist knowledge of Japanese, Portuguese, Dutch, Italian and German – languages more likely to be used by our commercial competitors than by our military or political enemies. Dennis Mitchell, a former GCHQ cryptanalyst, gave evidence to the Scott Inquiry on how the communications of foreign companies were monitored. Sir Robin Butler, the Cabinet Secretary, intervened to ensure that Mitchell's evidence remained secret. But Robin Robison, a former administrative officer for the Joint Intelligence Committee in the 1980s, claimed that the communications of leading British and foreign companies were routinely intercepted. The companies under surveillance included GEC Marconi, Rolls-Royce, Lonrho, and a large number of foreign companies, among them General Motors, he said, adding that 'sackfuls' of commercial information were collected. Lord Mackay, the then Lord Chancellor, told Parliament in 1994 that preserving Britain's role as the world's fifth largest trading nation was essential for its economic well-being and that the intelligence agencies kept 'a particular eye on Britain's access to key commodities like oil or metals'. Justifying this, he pointed out that 'the profits of Britain's myriad of international business interests ... and the jobs of a great many British people are dependent on the ability to plan, to invest, and to trade effectively without worry or danger.'

American Congressional hearings examining what the post-Cold War intelligence targets should be were told that the British were among a number of 'friendly countries' carrying out espionage against US companies. 'The British almost never get caught and they fully exploit the access provided by a long history of colonial alliances,' said Gerard Burke, a former CIA official who now heads one of America's leading commercial security companies.

They would certainly not be alone among America's allies in doing so. Former CIA Director James Woolsey told the Senate that a number of so-called friendly countries – including France, Japan, South Korea, Israel, Sweden and Switzerland – were spying on US companies. 'Not everyone around the world plays the game the way we do,' he said. 'Some of our friends and allies are involved in economic intelligence operations against our corporations.'

Perhaps the most aggressive of America's 'friends' in the search for commercial secrets have been the French. Count Alexandre de Marenches, former head of the SDECE, *Service de Documentation Extérieure et de Contre-Espionage*, the then French equivalent of MI6, revealed in his memoirs that it had an Economic Intelligence Service which gathered 'not only financial and economic intelligence but industrial espionage as well'. De Marenches claimed that in 1971 the SDECE learned in advance of American plans to devalue the dollar, allowing the French treasury to make enormous profits on the currency markets. The coup 'financed the service for years', he claimed. After François Mitterrand came to power in 1981 the SDECE was renamed the *Direction Générale de la Sécurité Extérieure* (DGSE). The new President appointed Pierre Marion, a former head of Air France, to head the agency, ordering him to improve its ability to gather economic, financial, industrial and scientific intelligence. Marion set up a section for global economic intelligence, assigning twenty agents to collect such information from America alone. He later claimed that his men placed bugs in the seats of Air France aircraft to pick up the conversations of foreign businessmen, and that, among other things, the intelligence obtained by the section had secured a billion-dollar sale of French Mirage warplanes to India in the face of stiff competition from the United States and the Soviet Union. 'It would not be normal that we spy on these states. In political or military matters, we are allied,' Marion said. 'But in the economic competition, in the technological competition, we are competitors.'

Despite a 1988 agreement between the DGSE and the CIA not to steal each other's commercial secrets, the French made repeated efforts to recruit employees of IBM and Texas Instruments to acquire technological and marketing information that would help prop up the ailing Bull computer company, which was partly owned by the French government. These operations culminated in a botched attempt at garbology – spy tradecraft in which the contents of rubbish bins are examined in an attempt to find information that might help build up the pieces of the intelligence jigsaw. The incident in question took place in the early hours of 18 February 1991. America and France were ostensibly staunch allies, preparing for the ground offensive against Iraq in the Gulf. But in an affluent suburb of Houston, Texas, a very different relationship between the two countries was being played out. A van stopped outside the executive mansion of a senior official of Texas Instruments. Two men jumped out, rummaged through the refuse bins, and threw some sacks in the back of the van. As it drove off the licence plate number was noted by an off-duty policeman. It was later traced to the French consulate in Houston, and the FBI were called in. The French diplomats claimed they were collecting grass cuttings to fill in an unfinished swimming-pool in the consulate gardens. 'Spy on people's garbage?' said Bernard Guillet, the French Consul-General, when questioned about the affair by FBI agents. 'That's ridiculous.'

Then in April 1993 the CIA obtained a secret 21-page French file listing the types of technologies the DGSE was interested in, together with a total of seventy-three business and financial organisations that had been or were to be the subject of French economic espionage. Most were American, such as aircraft manufacturer Boeing and the computer giants IBM and Texas Instruments. But others were British, including Ferranti, Vickers, Westland and British Aerospace, the subject of a DGSE operation to discover the full specifications and performance details of the European Fighter Aircraft, a direct competitor of the French-produced Rafale. A number of American aerospace companies subsequently pulled out of the Paris Air Show after being warned that the DGSE planned to use it to conduct covert operations against them. Two French agents discovered working at the Bell Helicopter plant in Fort Worth, Texas, and identified as a result of the DGSE file, were recalled to Paris. Amid intense embarrassment, Claude Silberzahn, the new head of the DGSE, was fired after admitting that the organisation now concentrated on economic intelligence and that much of the information it acquired was passed on direct to French companies.

The simmering row between the two countries over French economic espionage erupted into a major diplomatic incident in February 1995, when

France ordered five CIA agents – four of them diplomats – out of the country on the grounds that they had engaged in 'activities incompatible with their status'. Privately, French officials briefed journalists that they had been gathering economic intelligence. The Americans conceded that that was true, but said it was nothing to what the French had done to them. Robert Gates, the CIA's Director, said, 'France is among a certain number of countries who have planted moles inside American firms, stolen American businessmen's briefcases and who carry out classic spying operations to obtain industrial and economic information.' The diplomatic row with America had little if any effect on the amount of economic espionage conducted by France. A few weeks later the French government set up a new body, the Committee for Economic Competitiveness and Security, to 'research, analyse, process and distribute information in order to help industrialists and to carry out prospective and strategic research for the government'.

The only country to rival France in its willingness to spy on its allies' commercial secrets is Japan. A 1987 classified CIA survey estimated that 80 per cent of Tokyo's intelligence assets were directed against America and western Europe. The Ministry of International Trade and Industry (MITI) and the Japanese foreign ministry's Information Analysis, Research and Planning Bureau trawl any publicly available commercial documents, translating and analysing them before passing the resulting data on to Japanese companies. Japanese businessmen and academics travelling abroad routinely collect documents and take photographs or video-recordings of equipment. The bigger Japanese corporations such as Hitachi, Mitsubishi and Mitsui run their own intelligence departments, many of whose employees were trained at the Institute for Industrial Protection, a school for commercial spies set up in 1962 with MITI backing.

But even Japan is not as voracious in its efforts to uncover Western technology as the Chinese. With Beijing's record on human rights severely limiting its access to Western technology, around a half of all illegal technology-transfer cases investigated by the FBI in the Silicon Valley area of California are the result of covert economic intelligence operations by the Chinese intelligence services. One senior FBI official has described China as 'the most active foreign power engaged in illegal acquisition of American technology'. Chinese students and businessmen travelling abroad are routinely briefed to acquire targeted technologies. French military investigators recently spotted members of a Chinese scientific delegation to a Paris trade show discreetly dipping their ties into a new photographic processing fluid developed by the German company Agfa. One British university which introduced photocopier access cards to keep track of the use of its facilities found that the vast bulk of its annual usage was taken up by a visiting Chinese academic who was copying virtually every scientific paper and sending it home. Some restricted technology is purchased direct by Hong Kong-based front companies, and where this is not possible the Chinese have attempted to buy foreign companies with access to the desired technology.

The Soviet intelligence services have stolen Western commercial and technical secrets since the New Economic Policy of the early 1920s. The *Tcheka*, the early predecessor of the KGB , acquired an economic intelligence role in 1920. By the mid-1970s 'Line X', as the operation to acquire Western technology became known, was worth an estimated $50 million a year, leading Leonid Zaitsev, the head of Directorate T, the KGB department responsible for economic espionage, to claim that it was funding the KGB's entire foreign operating costs. The full scale of the Soviet economic espionage effort was revealed to the West in the early 1980s by a French agent-in-place inside the KGB codenamed Farewell. By 1983 Western intelligence was reporting that 'technology procurement' was now the KGB's primary foreign role. Several thousand economic spies, armed with precise shopping lists, were using a variety of different methods to bypass the COCOM regulations, which restricted exports to communist countries, mainly in America, Japan, France, Britain and Germany. As well as straightforward theft of economic secrets, the KGB was setting up phoney front companies to buy Western technology. This activity is reported to have increased during Mikhail Gorbachev's presidency, with a major drive to acquire the latest Western developments in advanced electronics. Oleg Gordievsky, the KGB's former deputy *Rezident* in London, recalls that in a speech to staff at the Soviet Embassy during a 1984 visit to Britain the former Soviet leader singled out the 'Line X' work for special praise. 'It was already clear that he regarded covert acquisition of Western technology as an important part of economic *perestroika.'* Farewell is believed to have been executed by the KGB in 1983, but the French expelled more than fifty Soviet diplomats and journalists as a direct result of the information he supplied. A 1985 Pentagon report based on analysis of the Farewell material said, 'The magnitude of the Soviets' collection effort and their ability to assimilate collected equipment and technology are far greater than was previously believed.' Soviet intelligence obtained 6,000 to 10,000 pieces of equipment and 100,000 documents every year, the report said.

Before the collapse of communism, east-European intelligence agencies, like Hungary's AVH , Czechoslovakia's StB and in particular the East German Stasi, made a major contribution to Soviet accumulation of Western technology. Robbed of their assistance, the Russian foreign intelligence services, the SVR and the military GRU, have increased their espionage activity, with economic intelligence accorded an even higher priority than it already had. 'Of course one of our emphases will shift to the commercial sphere, that is quite natural,' said Yevgeny Primakov, shortly after he was appointed as SVR director. Primakov, who would later become Russian prime minister, added that with numerous restrictions on the export of high-tech equipment still in place, Russia had no choice. 'Many secrets are still kept from us. If this information were openly available then there would be no need to engage in such intelligence.'

In America, the post-Cold War debate was dominated by calls, particularly from Congress, for the intelligence agencies to use some of the resources previously aimed at the Soviet Bloc in order to collect economic intelligence that would help America compete with the other 'geo-economic' superpowers. William Webster, CIA Director at the time of the collapse of eastern Europe – anxious to keep the agency's resources and show that it was still relevant to the new world – formed an Office of Resources, Trade and Technology to produce economic intelligence that would allow America to keep track of 'what our competition is doing' and remain in a position to 'confront it or confound it'. The FBI drew up a new National Security Threat List, adding 'issue-oriented' guidelines to its traditional list of countries carrying out espionage in America. The adapted guidelines were intended to allow FBI agents to act against countries, like Britain and other allies, which would not necessarily appear on the previous list but which might still be involved in the theft of 'industrial, proprietary, economic information and technology, the loss of which would undermine the US strategic position'. William Sessions, the then FBI Director, said the new issues were being added to the list 'to preserve the economic vitality of this country and to ensure the continued competitiveness of the United States in the international marketplace'. The new threat list led to a dramatic increase in the detection of foreign economic espionage against American companies, with the number of cases jumping from 10 to 500 in the space of nine months. Robert Gates told Congress that nearly twenty countries regularly spy on American companies. Although the resultant damage to US industry is hard to quantify, one estimate put it as high as $100 billion a year.

Few people bothered to point out that America, like all those nasty so-called allies who were stealing US secrets, had a long history of economic espionage of its own. During the 1950s the CIA carried out economic espionage only against the Soviet Bloc and Communist China – responsibility for the rest of the world fell to the State Department's Office of Intelligence and Research. Co-ordinated economic reports were produced by the Economic Intelligence Committee, a subcommittee of the Intelligence Advisory Committee – an early American equivalent of Britain's JIC. But in the mid-1960s the CIA expanded its economic intelligence effort worldwide, setting up an Office of Economic Research within the Directorate of Intelligence. The National Security Agency – America's equivalent of GCHQ – also carried out commercial intelligence. One former US Air Force signals specialist who worked at a US signals-intelligence base in Britain in the 1960s described how he had to watch printouts of commercial telexes, picking out those that referred to specific companies or commodities. 'I was provided with a list of about a hundred words I had to look out for. I had to keep a watch for commercial traffic, details of commodities that big companies were selling like iron and steel and gas. Some weeks the list of words to watch for contained dozens of names of big companies.'

In the 1970s and '80s both the NSA and the CIA expanded their operations against foreign governments and companies. One of the CIA's eleven national intelligence officers was given specific responsibility for economic intelligence. The agency began to make more use of open-source economic databases, and NSA computers took over the role of searching international telexes for key companies, commodities and transactions. Under Admiral Stansfield Turner, CIA Director in the late 1970s and early 1980s, a secret programme was set up to brief selected companies on industrial and economic intelligence from countries with which they did business. The quid pro quo was that the companies were to allow the CIA to debrief their executives on return from foreign trips. Under a separate programme operated through the Commerce Department, American companies were provided with declassified economic intelligence.

Howard Teicher, the National Security Council's Middle East Director in the mid-1980s, said the NSA used its base at Menwith Hill in Yorkshire, England, to monitor the al-Yamamah deal under which Saudi Arabia agreed to buy £20 billion worth of British military equipment, including the Tornado fighter. Teicher said Tornado and Panavia, the name of the company that marketed the aircraft, were among key words fed into the NSA computers monitoring communications between Britain and Saudi Arabia. 'Information related to the specific aircraft would have been priority targets,' he said. 'We were certainly aware that by preventing a foreign government from selling something that we hoped an American entity would be able to sell, it would contribute to our commercial interest.'

Gates continued his predecessors' expansion of economic intelligence-gathering, producing a new National Security Directive (NSD-69) which made world economics a major target, and launching a sustained recruitment drive to supplement the CIA's already large pool of economics experts. David Overton, a senior CIA economist, said: 'We have always had the largest contingent in the US government of people doing economic analysis. The Treasury Department's effort in this area is much smaller than ours. We're adding at the margin to a staff already big to begin with.'

In 1993 James Woolsey, Gates's successor, said economic intelligence was 'the hottest current topic in intelligence policy' and claimed that the CIA had already saved 'several billion dollars worth of US contracts'. But angry claims from within the EU at the beginning of the 21st century that the NSA's Echelon system was being used to give American companies an advantage over their European competitors were denied by US intelligence chiefs. General Michael Hayden, NSA Director, told the US Senate in 2002 that NSA did collect economic intelligence but not to help US companies. 'We do conduct collection for economic intelligence purposes, questions of economic policy of foreign powers . . . questions of significant economic events, like famine or flood or civil disturbances . . . economic developments like the delivery of precursor chemicals to rogue states, the proliferation of weapons of mass destruction, arms sales, drug trafficking, money laundering or sanctions-busting.' George Tenet, CIA Director, addressed the European concerns head on. 'The notion that we collect intelligence to promote American business interests is simply wrong,' he said. 'We do not target foreign companies to support American business interests.' But he went on to say that 'on many occasions' signals intelligence had 'provided information about the intentions of foreign businesses, some operated by governments, to violate US laws or sanctions or to deny US businesses a level playing field. There are instances where we learn that foreign companies or their governments bribe, lie, cheat and steal their way to disenfranchise American companies.' That information was passed on to 'other appropriate agencies', a reference to the US Commerce Department. 'They use that information through their other means and channels to see if they can assist an American company. But we play defence. We never play offence.'

Nevertheless, there are areas, like the al-Yamamah contract, where the lines between defence and offence blur. Contracts worth £20 billion will involve large numbers of jobs and sustain industries that are vital to the economy but which might otherwise go to the wall. This produces a grey area into which the CIA has certainly strayed on a number of occasions. The French decision in early 1995 to expel five CIA agents was the result of pent-up frustration over a year-long period during which American economic intelligence had succeeded in blocking at least two major French contracts, one of them remarkably similar to al-Yamamah.

French Prime Minister Édouard Balladur had flown to Jeddah a year earlier to sign a £6 billion contract under which Saudi Arabia would buy French warships and missiles as well as replacing the Saudi state airline's fleet of American aircraft with the French-led Airbus. The deal was never signed. The

NSA and the CIA had found out the details, and a high-pressure campaign by the US government, including a telephone call from President Clinton to King Fahd, had persuaded the Saudis to buy airliners from the American companies Boeing and McDonnell Douglas and to put the rest of the contract on hold. US intelligence could justify its intervention by pointing to the 'sweeteners' that are inevitable in such contracts and saying that it was only 'levelling out the playing field'. But the French were not impressed. They were even less happy when a few months later the CIA discovered that bribes had been paid to Brazilian officials to gain a £1.4 billion contract for a satellite surveillance system that would measure the health of the Amazon rainforest and detect drug-trafficking. Washington put pressure on the Brazilian government, and the American corporation Raytheon walked away with a contract that had been due to go to the French electronics company Thomson CSF. But the French pointed out, convincingly, that in order to have alternative, acceptable contracts ready for the Saudi and Brazilian deals, the Americans must have given Boeing, McDonnell Douglas and Raytheon the secret financing terms of the original contracts. There was at least prima facie evidence that the CIA had been indulging in straightforward commercial espionage.

The DGSE took its revenge by revealing that America was quite as ready to indulge in such devious activities as anyone else. The French press was briefed that a CIA 'Mata Hari' had been caught red-handed offering cash bribes to an official who knew France's secret negotiating position in the GATT world trade talks. One of the five CIA agents expelled by France was a woman working with non-diplomatic cover who chatted up an adviser to Balladur at a cocktail party. She became his mistress, and subsequently offered him money for details of the French negotiating position. American officials admitted that the French allegations were true. One CIA analyst said, 'We have been involved in GATT and every trade negotiation I know of. We take tasks from the US negotiators to find out the positions. We usually have someone who is right there. We tell our negotiators: "Here's what the other side left out or is holding back".'

But the ethical and practical problems remain unresolved. There is a clear need to include economic factors in strategic intelligence reports. Indeed, one of the key criticisms of the CIA during the post-Cold War debate was that it had failed to pick up on the parlous state of the Soviet economy that led Mikhail Gorbachev, initially with the support of the KGB, to introduce the *perestroika* process that would lead eventually to the collapse of the Soviet system. There can be no arguments against the collection of this sort of economic intelligence. The real ethical and moral concerns centre around commercial espionage. In America, where the debate over such issues has been most pronounced, there has been widespread support for the FBI's new role in countering commercial espionage by foreign intelligence services against American companies. Moves by both Congress and the White House to force the intelligence agencies to take reciprocal action have met with less support. 'The agency's new-found enthusiasm for analysis of certain economic issues is disturbing,' said Jay Young, a former senior CIA analyst. The agency's obsession with 'economic competitiveness' analysis and the creation of the Office of Resources, Trade and Technology represented 'an almost desperate bid' by the CIA to demonstrate its relevance in the post-Cold War era, Young said. Nor is it clear to what use the agency can legally or ethically put such information once it has acquired it. It can scarcely give it to one US company without risking accusations of favouritism from rival firms. Many big multinational companies provide jobs in a number of countries. Should the CIA, for example, give commercial secrets to foreign multinationals that provide American jobs? Stansfield Turner has suggested making the information public, to avoid worrying about who the intelligence should be given to. That would certainly create the level playing field that the US agencies claim is all they want. But declassifying any information collected by the intelligence agencies can compromise the individual sources or methods used to collect it, and to do so on such a grand scale seems certain to cause damage.

And what of the much vaunted special relationship in intelligence, the UKUSA Accord? How would that stand up to a situation where, as they did with the French projects, the CIA and the NSA scuppered a deal like al-Yamamah? The Cold War may have ended, but UKUSA's division of the world into intelligence fiefdoms has left both the American and British agencies dependent on each other – albeit the British more heavily so than the

Americans. The relationship between the US and French intelligence agencies was always less close than the UKUSA arrangement, but it was useful to both sides. The highly public row over the CIA's clumsy attempts to uncover the French GATT negotiating position threatened to damage it almost beyond repair. If such a row were to erupt between America and Britain, how could UKUSA survive?

Commercial espionage is likely to create other headaches as well. The intervention of the intelligence agencies in the market verges on the sort of protectionism that America and Britain spend much of their time attacking. Uncompetitive businesses would gain while efficient companies suffered. The end effect of levelling the international playing field would be to create an uneven one at home. Economic intelligence will continue to be needed, as it has been continuously throughout the past century, for assessment of the strategic threat and for the shaping of government economic policy. But commercial intelligence – spying on foreign companies in order to help your own keep ahead of the game – is a waste of resources that would be better spent on other new roles such as countering international organised crime, fighting terrorism, or preventing what is perhaps the most dangerous of the new threats, the acquisition by maverick states or terrorist groups like al-Qa'eda of nuclear, chemical or biological weapons.

Twenty Five

Poisonous Snakes

We have slain a large dragon, but we live now in a jungle filled with a bewildering variety of poisonous snakes, and in many ways the dragon was easier to keep track of.

> James Woolsey, former CIA Director, on the end of the Cold War.

Counter-proliferation is now a key role for Britain's intelligence and security services. During the Cold War, America and the former Soviet Union kept a very tight control over their weapons systems. Both sold large amounts of conventional weaponry to client states, particularly in Africa and the Middle East, but were much more careful in their sales of weapons of mass destruction, chemical, biological, radiological, nuclear (CBRN) weapons, making them relatively easy to track. The collapse of communism changed this situation completely. When the Soviet Union began to break up, it caused immense problems for those seeking to keep track of the more than 30,000 nuclear warheads scattered across its territory. Strategic missiles based in Belarus, Ukraine and Kazakhstan left these newly independent states as nuclear powers in their own right. With financial problems widespread across the former Soviet Union, there were concerns that scientists or servicemen with access to the weapons might be prepared to sell them off to the highest bidder: to the Russian *Mafiya*, to terrorists, or to rogue states like Iraq, Iran or North Korea.

Three things happened to reduce this threat. Firstly, in a major clandestine operation, the Russian armed forces managed to remove all the tactical nuclear weapons back to Russian soil. Then the US Congress passed the 1991 Threat Reduction Act – the so-called Nunn-Lugar programme – pumping more than a billion dollars into the former Soviet Union to help dismantle nuclear weapons and ensure their security and safety. Finally, Belarus, Kazakhstan and Ukraine were persuaded to sign up to the nuclear non-proliferation treaty and, in exchange for financial compensation, to return the strategic missiles based on their soil to Russia. But the problems of security remained immense. 'US government officials and support contractors who have visited some of these facilities can give you hair-raising accounts of the lack of adequate physical security,' Thomas Cochran, senior scientist for the National Resources Defense Council, told the US Senate. At some Russian sites, the first thing US inspectors had to do was install locks. Intercontinental ballistic missiles were on static sites well protected by minefields, electric fences and highly trained armed guards. Tactical weapons, being mobile, were far less secure. Some were guarded only by civilians and passive defences. The country's financial problems meant that the real value of wages was plummeting. Government workers were not being paid on time. Rations supplies were erratic. Theft from military bases reached epidemic proportions as servicemen sold off anything they could – including weapons – to make money. Scientists at Russia's leading military nuclear establishment complained directly to the then president Boris Yeltsin over the government's repeated failure to pay them. Low morale and lack of funds also led to poor levels of maintenance, and in some cases electricity supplies to nuclear reactors were cut off because the authorities had not paid the bills. This culminated in a series of incidents including a decision by the Moscow regional electricity authority to switch off power to the country's strategic nuclear-missile command centre. There was very nearly a meltdown of nuclear reactors on board four submarines when the Murmansk naval base was cut off for non-payment of bills. In the latter case, a catastrophe was averted only when armed servicemen forced the electricity supplier to restore power at gunpoint.

During the early 1990s, there were suggestions that the easy availability of nuclear materials from the former Soviet Union might make such weapons attractive to terrorists. Many experts argued that the production of a nuclear weapon requires a level of technology and the ability to hide extensive scientific facilities that would not normally be available to terrorists. That is not strictly speaking true of terrorists who are prepared to die in any attack. If they were able to obtain sufficient quantities of highly enriched uranium, fortunately still not easy but equally not impossible, they could create an atomic explosion relatively easily and with very little equipment. The most likely purchasers for former Soviet weapons-grade material were seen as maverick states such as Iran, Iraq or North Korea. 'A few countries whose interests are inimical to the US are attempting to acquire nuclear weapons – Iran and Iraq being two of our greatest concerns,' one CIA officer told the Senate. 'Knowledge of weapon designs is sufficiently widespread that the former weapon secrecy no longer offers adequate protection. Today, there is basically only one obstacle to a committed nation: acquisition of fissile material.' One example of an attempt to obtain materials for a covert nuclear weapons programme was uncovered by British intelligence in 1998. GCHQ intercepts of Iranian diplomatic messages led to a joint operation by MI6 and Customs and Excise to thwart delivery of British technology for use in ballistic missiles. Robin Cook, the then Foreign Secretary, said MI6 and GCHQ had 'tracked Iran's nuclear weapons programme, and enabled us to disrupt Iranian attempts to procure British technology'. They had also 'played a crucial role in revealing Saddam Hussein's biological and chemical weapons programmes, and his continuing ambitions to stockpile these weapons of mass destruction.' Timothy McCarthy, a former UN weapons inspector, said the Iraqis had attempted to acquire materials and technical know-how for weapons of mass destruction from the former Soviet Union. 'Saddam Hussein has sought multiple routes to the acquisition of nuclear, chemical and biological weapons,' he said. 'They [the Iraqis] have sought to exploit weaknesses in the international arms control system. They found the former Soviet Union a hospitable climate in terms of the acquisition of both technical know-how and materials.'

In the wake of the 1991 Gulf War, the UN set up a Special Commission, UNSCOM, to investigate the extent of the Iraqi chemical, biological and nuclear weapons programmes. It produced a lot of information but a great deal was kept secret from it, in particular the extent of Saddam's biological weapons campaign. He had managed to keep this completely hidden from the inspectors until 1995 when his son-in-law Hussein Kamil defected to the West. Kamil was a former Director of the Military Industrialisation

Commission, which had run the programme to produce weapons of mass destruction. Following his defection, the Iraqis released more than two million documents relating to the various programmes. It also admitted that it had produced 183 different biological weapons at a number of sites across Iraq and that it had actually deployed biological weapons. Two other Iraqi MI6-controlled defectors – Jabir Salim, the head of *Mukhabarat* operations in eastern Europe, and Sami Salih, who was in charge of Iraq's sanctions-busting operations – provided details of what equipment and materials Saddam was seeking for his WMD programme and where he was hiding missiles from the UN inspectors. Intelligence on the Iraqi weapons programmes collected after December 1998, when UNSCOM withdrew its staff because of the Iraqi obstruction, largely came from British sources. GCHQ takes the lead over the NSA in covering the Middle East and MI6 always had better sources in Iraq than the CIA, including a number of long-term penetration agents within the regime. But US imagery intelligence collection – if not imagery interpretation – is superior, largely due to its expensive satellites and U-2 spy planes.

A dossier released by the British government in September 2002 and based on intelligence passed to the Joint Intelligence Committee by MI5, MI6, GCHQ and the MoD's Joint Air Reconnaissance Intelligence Centre showed that UN sanctions were not preventing Saddam from pushing forward with his chemical, biological and nuclear weapons programmes. Oil-smuggling through Syria, Turkey and Iran brought in around $3 billion in 2001 alone. Intelligence obtained by MI6, in part from Abbas al-Janabi, the senior aide to Saddam's eldest son Uday who defected to Britain in 1998, showed that Saddam saw weapons of mass destruction as being vital to Iraq's status as a Middle East power and to his own ability to continue to wield power. He did not hesitate to use them on the Kurds and the Shia population in the south, the so-called Marsh Arabs. A senior Iraqi officer, a British long-term penetration agent at the heart of the Iraqi military establishment, told MI6 in August 2002 that Saddam's al-Hussein missile units could deploy within 45 minutes and that command and control arrangements were in place to fire the missiles with chemical or biological warheads. Intelligence also showed that he still had around 20 missiles, adaptations of the Soviet Scud army-level surface-to-surface missile, which have a range of more than 400 miles. Evidence obtained by GCHQ, MI5 and MI6 showed that Saddam had succeeded in obtaining a number of materials that could be used in the production of chemical and biological weapons. Although the main chemical weapons plant at al-Muthanna had been completely destroyed by UNSCOM and had not been rebuilt, other plants formerly associated with the chemical warfare programme, including the key site at Fallujah-2, near Habbaniyah, had been. New chemical weapons plants had been built with illegal assistance from another unnamed country. Biological plants at Fallujah (where ricin was believed to have been produced), al-Dawrah, al-Hakam and Abu Ghraib were fully operational. Saddam was also trying to obtain key material, technology and capability for his nuclear weapons programme, including the ability to turn uranium ore into Highly Enriched Uranium. If he had succeeded, then Iraq could have produced a nuclear weapon in less than two years.

Although Saddam has fallen, the Middle-East, where Iran is still trying to obtain nuclear weapons and faces Israel, already a nuclear power, is just one of three main flashpoints that are the most likely breeding grounds for any nuclear war. The other two are the Korean peninsula, where concerns over Pyongyang's nuclear capabilities have led to protracted disagreements with Washington; and the Indian subcontinent, where there has been a series of confrontations between India and Pakistan over the border area of Kashmir. Throughout the early 1990s, Pakistan made concerted efforts to improve its nuclear expertise. In July 1996, an official at the Pakistani High Commission in London was deported after a joint investigation by the counter-proliferation units of MI5 and GCHQ. For five years Mohammed Saleem had been running a network of British post-graduate students whose families originated in Pakistan. They were all studying nuclear technology at British universities to acquire expertise useful to Islamabad's nuclear weapons programme.

By the mid-1990s, there were serious concerns that a number of terrorist groups were very happy to use weapons of mass destruction, be they chemical, biological or nuclear. The early 1990s had seen a sea change in the way terrorists behaved. Even before the Japanese *Aum Shinru Kyo* sect used Sarin nerve gas to attack commuters on the Tokyo underground in March 1995 and the discovery of similar plans by fundamentalist Christian/white supremacist groups in the United States, MI5 had made a dramatic reappraisal of the threat from terrorist groups. In the spring of 1994, the British Cabinet Civil Contingency Unit carried out a full-scale rehearsal of the steps to be taken in the event of a nuclear terrorist attack, an exercise involving the police, the SAS and the civilian emergency services. In a speech in London in October 1995, Stella Rimington, the then Director-General of MI5, warned that new types of terrorists posed completely different and far more worrying threats than their predecessors. 'The clarity which the Cold War brought has gone,' she said. 'As is all too evident, the collapse of centralised controls in parts of the former Soviet Union as well as in the Balkans has provoked regional instability. From that may come new sources of terrorism and heightened risks from the spread of chemical, nuclear and biological weapons. New types and sources of terrorist violence have emerged. They work in relatively unstructured groups, make no claim for their attacks, and appear to have as their aim the creation of maximum alarm and insecurity.'

The threat from these new types of terrorist was far less easy to quantify than the relatively straightforward behaviour of, for instance, the Provisional IRA or the Palestinian hijackers of the 1970s. While few in the West agreed with their violent methods, the use of 'spectaculars', terrorist attacks specifically designed to lead to television and newspaper coverage that drew attention to their aspirations, was easy to understand and even to identify with. These terrorists were unhappy with specific aspects of the society in which they lived and were using violence to force the changes they required. The aim was not to kill per se, but to extract the maximum publicity, to publicise the cause, and to wear down resistance to their demands. Excessive violence was regarded as counter-productive. When it occurred – often because the cellular structure adopted by such groups had led to a temporary loss of control over maverick individuals – it tended to alienate their supporters and even many within the groups themselves. But the new types of terrorists do not operate under the same set of assumptions. They do not see themselves as part of society, and they have no regard for anyone other than members of their own sect. Anyone who is not a believer is seen as expendable, making mass indiscriminate violence not only morally acceptable but in fact compulsory – a divine duty incumbent on any true believer. Since the early 1980s, when they first came to prominence, Islamic fundamentalist groups have committed only eight per cent of all terrorist acts, yet they have been responsible for nearly 30 per cent of all those killed. A further problem for the security and intelligence services is that the lack of any identification with Western society makes Islamic fundamentalist terrorism far less easy to understand and predict.

The 1994 hijacking by Algerian fundamentalists of an Air France A300 Airbus provided a good example of both these phenomena. The initial assumption was that this was an attempt by the terrorists to draw attention to the civil war taking place in their homeland – much in the manner of the spate of Palestinian hijackings of the late 1960s and early 1970s. By this reasoning, the main value of the attack would come from the worldwide publicity achieved during long-drawn-out negotiations for the release of the hostages. In fact, the terrorists planned to fly the aircraft into the Eiffel Tower and to kill as many people as possible. They would have done so had the French authorities not discovered the plan and carried out a successful assault on the aircraft as it stood on the ground at Marseilles airport. Then in 1995, Philippines police broke up a network of terrorists who were planning to plant bombs on a dozen US airliners and blow them up simultaneously over the Pacific. Abdul Hakim Murad, one of the captured co-conspirators, was a Pakistani national linked to the failed 1993 attempt to blow up the World Trade Centre in New York. He described to his Philippine captors how he had attended flight schools in New York, Texas, California and North Carolina, gaining a commercial pilot's licence 'in preparation for a suicide mission'. He had intended to seize a small plane, fill it with explosives and fly it into the CIA's Langley headquarters with the intention of killing several thousand people. The Philippines interrogation report sent to the FBI stated: 'It is a suicidal mission that he is very much willing to execute.'

Information gathered in the raids led to the conviction of Ramzi Ahmed Yousef – the mastermind behind the attack on the World Trade Centre. It emerged that Yousef had spent some time staying in a Pakistani guesthouse belonging to a Saudi national. Osama bin Laden was the son of a Yemeni builder who had become head of a large construction firm linked to the Saudi royal family. He studied at Jeddah University where he came under the influence of a prominent Palestinian, Dr Abdullah Azzam, a man regarded as the inspiration behind the fundamentalist Palestinian terror group Hamas. During the Soviet occupation of Afghanistan, bin Laden used his family fortune to help Azzam to set up an organisation to fund and organise Mujahideen operations against the Soviet troops. The Afghan Bureau had links to the Saudi and Egyptian governments, and the Pakistani Inter-Service Intelligence (ISI). But in 1988, bin Laden fell out with Azzam over the latter's support for Ahmad Shah Masood – the Western-backed Mujahideen leader. It was then that he set up another organisation to fund Mujahideen operations which he called al-Qa'eda (the Base).

During the 1990s, al-Qa'eda set out to help any Muslims who were fighting against regimes they felt were not following fundamentalist Islamic teachings. These included Saudi Arabia, which had failed to honour its promise to force foreign troops to leave once Iraq was expelled from Kuwait as well as Egypt and Algeria. It also sent former Mujahideen to assist Muslim forces fighting in the Balkans, Kashmir, Dagestan, Chechnya, the Philippines, and Indonesia. But at the same time it plotted a *jihad* or holy war against America and US interests around the world. As early as December 1992, bin Laden had sent al-Qa'eda terrorists to act as advisors to the leader of the Somalia National Alliance leader General Mohamed Farah Aideed, who was trying to counter a UN military operation designed to restore order in Somalia. He would later claim responsibility for the deaths in October 1993 of 18 US soldiers in an operation to capture two of Aideed's key lieutenants. By now a Pakistani crackdown on terrorist organisations had forced bin Laden to move his bases to the Sudan, where, on top of a personal fortune put at around £200 million, he had a number of businesses providing funds for al-Qa'eda. He used this money to set up three terrorist training camps and to hire an Arab scientist to help him to develop nuclear and chemical weapons. Then in 1996, a man claiming to be a leading al-Qa'eda member, Jamal Ahmed al-Fadl, turned up at a US embassy in Africa offering information on al-Qa'eda. 'I have information about people,' he said. 'They want to do something against your government. Maybe they will try to do something in the United States and they may try to fight the United States Army outside, and also they may try to make a bomb against some embassy.'

The CIA set up a special operation, known as the Bin Laden Issue Station and codenamed Alex, within its counter-terrorism centre to track bin Laden and al-Qaʿeda activities, and in May 1996, under pressure from America, Sudan expelled bin Laden, confiscating some of his personal fortune. He moved al-Qaʿeda and its training camps to Afghanistan where the Islamic fundamentalist Taliban was just beginning to take control of the country. A month later, a lorry bomb exploded at a military barracks in Saudi Arabia, killing 19 US servicemen. An example of the second of al-Fadl's predicted attacks had taken place. Protected by US intelligence, al-Fadl provided a detailed account of how al-Qaʿeda operated, which could soon be checked against information obtained from a new, extraordinarily valuable source that was about to come on line.

In November 1996, Dr Saad al-Fagih, a Saudi-born surgeon living in London, bought a satellite telephone and more than 3,000 hours of pre-paid calls from a New York-based company and had it sent to bin Laden in Afghanistan. Over the next two years, bin Laden and his deputy, Mohammed Atif, used it to keep in touch with al-Qaʿeda terrorists and sympathisers around the world. A large number of calls were made to Britain, many of them to the home of Khalid al-Fawwaz, the UK representative of al-Qaʿeda, who lived in the London suburb of Dollis Hill, but allegedly also to more than 20 other telephone numbers. The main other countries contacted using the satellite telephone were Yemen, Sudan, Iran, Azerbaijan, Pakistan and Saudi Arabia. They were all made via a satellite over the Indian Ocean monitored by GCHQ via its Morwenstow satellite-intercept station.

Information from conversations on that telephone and others linked to it, married to al-Fadl's information, allowed British and American intelligence to build up a highly detailed picture of al-Qaʿeda's organisation. Bin Laden was intent on waging a holy war against America and the West. He totally controlled al-Qaʿeda. He was advised by a consultative council – the *Shura Majlis*. This ruling group controlled four separate committees, the most important of which was the military committee, which ran the training camps and planned and prepared the operations. It was headed by Mohammed Atif.

The operations used a classic cellular structure with no-one knowing more than he needed to know (there were no women in the organisation).

Al-Qa'eda had begun to spread its influence among other Islamic fundamentalist groups, financing their operations, albeit only after every detail of the plan had been confirmed by bin Laden and Atif, it was acting as an umbrella organisation for a wide range of radical terrorist organisations, an anti-American terrorist front. In return for the financing and crucially training, the groups carried out their terrorist attacks in al-Qa'eda's name as well as their own in what amounted to the establishment of a series of al-Qa'eda franchises. The training function, carried out in its own camps, allowed al-Qa'eda to influence the active members of each of the groups, effectively infiltrating them and spreading its influence still further. These included the two main Egyptian fundamentalist groups, the Islamic Group of Egypt and Egyptian Islamic Jihad, from whom many of al-Qa'eda's members were drawn. But they also spanned the world to include: the Moro Islamic Liberation Front (MILF) and the Abu Sayyaf Group (ASG) in the Philippines; *Jemaah Islamiah* – the Indonesian group believed to be behind the Bali bombing in October 2002; the Algerian Armed Islamic Group (GIA) and a number of Kashmiri groups. These included *Harakat-ul Jihad, Harakat-ul Mujahideen* and *Hizbi-al-Islami*. There were close links to Hamas and Hizbullah. Al-Qa'eda also spread its influence among Muslim groups in Europe and even America itself.

It was clear that al-Qa'eda was rapidly becoming the single most dangerous terrorist threat to America and the West in general. By June 1998, intelligence from a number of sources indicated that bin Laden was considering attacks on the United States mainland, on New York and Washington. At this stage, the biggest terrorist threat to Britain remained dissident Irish republican groups. But among foreign terrorist groups al-Qa'eda was far and away the most important target and dominated the counter-terrorist agendas of both MI6 and GCHQ. Then on 7 August 1998 it struck again, this time driving lorry bombs up to the US embassies in Kenya and Tanzania, killing 224 people of whom only 12 were US citizens. The third of the al-Fadl warnings had come true. President Clinton ordered cruise missile strikes against a pharmaceuticals factory in Sudan thought to belong to al-Qa'eda and one of the Afghan training camps where bin Laden and key associates were due to hold a meeting. It was to be an intelligence disaster. Not only did the owner of the pharmaceuticals factory come forward to claim he was nothing to do with bin Laden, but the terrorist leader had left the Afghan training camp six hours before the missile struck. If he was not already wondering about the remarkable coincidence that the camp should be attacked on the same day he and his key advisors were holding a meeting there, he soon learned that it was no coincidence. An American official leaked the ability to tap bin Laden's satellite telephone to the US media. A few weeks after the attacks, bin Laden stopped using the telephone in what Michael Hayden, the NSA Director, describes as 'a setback of inestimable consequences in the war against terrorism'.

But if that particular telephone was no longer in use, GCHQ had built up a directory of contact numbers for other telephones. Some of these would have been discarded by the terrorists as insecure, but enough would have remained to start building up a picture of the fresh network of telephones. GCHQ had also monitored faxes being sent to the house in Dollis Hill, including one in the wake of the Nairobi bombing which, with the assistance of MI6, led back to one of the bombers. Mohamed Rashid Daoud al-Owhali, a Saudi citizen, was extradited to America and, along with three accomplices, jailed for life for his part in the bombing.

By late 1998, it was already clear not only that bin Laden was exploring the use of every kind of weapon, including if possible nuclear weapons, but that he was determined to take his attacks to the United States mainland. In September of that year, there was a report that al-Qa'eda terrorists planned to fly an aircraft filled with explosives into a US airport. Over the next few months, intelligence showed that al-Qa'eda was trying to set up an operations cell inside the United States with the intention of attacking targets in New York and Washington and that bin Laden was offering a bounty for the assassination of four senior intelligence officials. One intelligence assessment stated that bin Laden was 'actively planning against US targets' and that a number of reports showed he was 'keenly interested in striking the US on its own soil'. Tenet told his deputies that despite their successes against al-Qa'eda 'we all acknowledge that retaliation is inevitable and that its scope may be far larger than we have previously experienced. We are at war. I want no resources or people spared in this effort either inside CIA or the community.' There were continuing reports throughout 1999 from the intelligence and security services of a number of countries that al-Qa'eda was planning attacks on the United States.

By the late 1990s, a large network of intelligence and security agencies around the world was co-operating on terrorist issues. Based on a European network set up before the Gulf War, it had been extended to include a number of friendly Arab countries, Russia and other member states of the former Soviet Union, and countries in the Far East, including the Philippines, Malaysia and Singapore. This ensured that a number of attempts to mount attacks around the millennium were foiled and the suspects arrested. One of the most prominent of these foiled attacks was a plan to take the battle to the United States itself, bombing Los Angeles International Airport. This was thwarted when the main suspect was arrested as he attempted to enter America from Canada. A second attack was to be aimed at American and Israeli tourists visiting Christian holy sites in Jordan in order to celebrate the millennium. Palestinian militants intended to use 16 tons of TNT to flatten the 400-room Radisson Hotel in central Amman, which was fully booked, largely by Americans, Israelis and Europeans who intended to visit Jordan to celebrate the dawn of the millennium. Other targets in Jordan included two Christian holy sites and two border crossings into Israel. The plot had been more than three years in the making but had been given added impetus when the terrorists obtained the backing of al-Qa'eda.

They needed funding to carry out the attacks and through an intermediary made contact with Abu Zubaydah, a key member of the al-Qa'eda leadership, who was responsible for setting up links to other Islamic militant groups around the world. He screened members of the group at his guesthouse in Peshawar, Pakistan, before sending them to one of the al-Qa'eda training camps in Afghanistan. Abu Zubaydah laid down very strict ground rules designed to keep the possibility of interception of messages between himself and the group to the minimum. One member of the group should be allocated to maintain the communications link with al-Qa'eda. No other members of the group were to contact him. The allocated representative had to vouch for everyone involved, who must all be enthusiastic volunteers. No-one was to be coerced into taking part in the operation. All the group's targets and the timing of the attacks must be approved by al-Qa'eda. Raed Hijazi, one of the leaders of the group told his interrogators how, after completing his training in the use of explosives, he was taken to one side by Abu Zubaydah. He was given a piece of paper on which were written the words: 'In the name of God the Merciful, the Compassionate. I promise to ally myself to Osama bin Laden for the sake of God.' After reading it out aloud, he was told he was now authorised to act in bin Laden's name 'anywhere in jihad territories'. But despite the security measures, the Jordanian police were tracking the plot. They were listening in when, at the end of November 1999, Abu Zubaydah gave the go-ahead for the attacks to take place on '*al-yowm al-fiyah*', the day of the millennium. In the early hours of 5 December 1999, the Jordanian police raided the Amman house in which the terrorists were planning their attack and arrested a dozen men. Nine months later, a military court convicted 22 terrorists of involvement in the planned attacks. Six of them were sentenced to death, including Raed Hijazi and Abu Zubaydah, both of whom were sentenced in absentia.

A month later, a group of al-Qa'eda terrorists met in Malaysia. Those attending included Khalid al-Midhar, who was a known al-Qa'eda player, plus another as yet unknown man, Nawaq al-Hamzi. The Malaysian authorities told the CIA that they were at the meeting. Contrary to subsequent claims by the FBI that they were not told of the meeting and therefore could not have known that al-Midhar was a threat, the CIA briefed FBI officers on the meeting and passed them a copy of al-Midhar's passport, which included a US visa, for further investigation. But the CIA did not put either man on a US State Department watch list, which would have prevented their being allowed to enter the United States. With a major international operation against al-Qa'eda now in force, the arrests continued throughout 2000, foiling an attempted attack on tourists visiting the Frankfurt Christmas Market, and into 2001. In a direct spin-off from the success of the Jordanian arrests, MI5 mounted Operation Auden, a three-month surveillance operation in London on suspected GIA terrorists linked to al-Qa'eda. On 13 February 2001, six Arabs were arrested in dawn raids by Special Branch. Subsequent searches of six houses and an Islamic library uncovered more computer disks, leading to further raids in Manchester and Birmingham. Among those arrested was Abu Qatada, also known as Omar Abu Omar, a Palestinian cleric regarded as the spiritual head of al-Qa'eda's European network, who had been sentenced to 15 years imprisonment in absentia by the Jordanian courts for his part in the foiled millennium attacks. Despite the fact that Abu Qatada was on income support, police found £180,000 in sterling, US dollars, Spanish pesetas and German marks in his west-London house. The British and German arrests were followed by a series of further arrests in Italy, Germany, Spain and India, where an al-Qaʻeda group had been planning a bomb attack on the US embassy in New Delhi.

The al-Qaʻeda support network in Britain and a number of other countries across Europe operated at several different levels. There was a first tier of people who were simply supporters of the cause, attracted by the evangelical approach adopted by militant clerics like Abu Qatada in a number of mosques in towns with large concentrations of Muslims. They represented the vast majority who would live normal law-abiding lives and never do anything other than visit the mosque, attend demonstrations and make the odd provocative statement. A second, much smaller, tier was made up of people who had attended one of the training camps in Afghanistan. Many of those who attended the camps would go on to fight alongside the Taliban but would baulk at the idea of taking part in terrorist activities. The third tier was made up of the very few who were selected from among those attending the camps as being suitable for the terrorist operations that al-Qaʻeda mounted itself. These came under the direction of Mohammed Atif, the head of the military committee, who was in charge of planning all operations until he was killed during the allied attacks on Afghanistan.

As the Bush administration took over in early 2001, officials attempted to press upon it the importance of dealing with al-Qaʻeda, a conviction that had been reinforced by the killing of 17 US sailors in the attack on the USS *Cole* off Yemen in October 2000. Richard Clarke, head of the White House Counter-Terrorism Group, outlined a series of proposals aimed at breaking up al-Qaʻeda. In a presentation entitled: 'Response to al-Qaʻeda: Roll back', Clarke advocating freezing al-Qaʻeda funds around the world, cutting off funding from bogus charities and giving aid and assistance to countries where al-Qaʻeda was funding terrorist insurgencies, like the Philippines, Uzbekistan and Yemen. But the key to the plan was large-scale use of special-forces operations inside Afghanistan to bring down aerial strikes on the al-Qaʻeda camps and massively increased funding for the Northern Alliance to destroy the

Taliban. Amid arguments and discussions over the administration's defensive priorities, which were obsessively centred around plans for a national missile defence system, none of this would be done until after the 11 September attacks.

The failure to predict the al-Qaʿeda attacks has been described as a greater intelligence failure than the US inability to predict the Japanese attack on Pearl Harbor and with some justification. Certainly, the FBI appears to have been about as inept as it could possibly have been. The CIA was criticised for its failure to place the names of al-Midhar and al-Hamzi on the State Department watch list until shortly before the attacks and for its inability to infiltrate al-Qaʿeda. In the wake of the attacks, one former officer claimed that his ex-colleagues did not go anywhere where they might get diarrhoea. The CIA did, however, have major problems dealing with al-Qaʿeda and other terrorist organisations. This was partly because of the ban on recruiting anyone with an 'unsavoury' background, a distinct handicap when attempting to infiltrate a terrorist organisation. But the biggest problem by far was the agency's relationship with Pakistan's ISI secret service. For reasons that remain inexplicable, even in the context of their genesis during the Soviet occupation of Afghanistan, the CIA had an agreement with the ISI that it would not conduct unilateral operations inside Afghanistan. Given that the ISI was one of the chief sponsors of the Taliban, it is hardly surprising that this agreement seriously hampered CIA operations against al-Qaʿeda. Fortunately, the intelligence relationship with Britain is so strong that this did not matter as much as it might otherwise have done. As had happened before when the US agencies were barred from doing something, the British stepped in to help. Unlike the CIA, MI6 was traditionally strong in Afghanistan and had a number of agents there, apparently including some inside al-Qaʿeda and the Taliban. Jim Pavitt, the CIA's Deputy Director of Operations, expressed irritation at suggestions that the agency had ignored Afghanistan during the 1990s. 'If you hear somebody say, and I have, the CIA abandoned Afghanistan after the Soviets left and that we never paid any attention to that place until September 11th,' Pavitt said. 'I would implore you to ask those people how we knew who to approach on the ground, which operations, which warlord to support, what information to collect. Quite simply we were there well before September 11th.'

The biggest problem was the tightly run cellular structure of al-Qa'eda. This meant that not even having well-placed agents inside the organisation would necessarily translate into knowing what form its next operation would take. Some members of the al-Qa'eda hit squads who carried out the 11 September attacks were unaware other aircraft were to be hijacked and may even have had no idea of what was to happen to the aircraft they were on, Pavitt said. 'The terror cells that we're coming up against are typically small and all terrorist personnel participating in those cells, perpetrating the acts of terror, all those personnel were carefully screened. The number of personnel who knew vital information, targets, timing, the exact methods to be used had to be smaller still. Against that degree of control, that kind of compartmenta-tion, that depth of discipline and fanaticism, I personally doubt, and I draw upon my 30 years of experience in this business, that anything short of one of the knowledgeable inner circle personnel or hijackers turning himself in to us would have given us sufficient foreknowledge to have prevented the horren-dous slaughter that took place on the 11th.'

The British inquiry, carried out by the parliamentary Intelligence and Security Committee, largely absolved MI5, MI6 and GCHQ of any blame. But its main conclusion, that 'the scale of the threat and the vulnerability of Western states to terrorists with this degree of sophistication and a total disre-gard for their own lives was not understood', raised a lot of eyebrows among the intelligence and security agencies. That the committee could conclude this is scarcely credible. For a number of years, anyone who knew anything about terrorism was aware that: a) there were a number of modern groups, particu-larly but not exclusively fundamentalist Muslim groups, who did not care what the general public thought of them and were very happy to kill as many people as possible, and b) al-Qa'eda represented the biggest threat of all. More importantly it is impossible to reconcile the committee's conclusion with the first paragraph on the same page of its report, which quotes John Scarlett, the JIC Chairman, as saying that there was an 'acute awareness in the period before 11 September that Osama bin Laden and his associates represented a very serious threat' and were planning a terrorist 'spectacular' inside America that summer with the intention of causing 'massive casualties'.

The intelligence on the attack had begun in March 2001 when one source claimed a group of al-Qaʻeda terrorists, one of whom was living in America, were planning an attack on America the following month. As such it was similar to operations reported during the late 1990s and never carried out. But in April it was backed up by evidence from other sources. Although no attack materialised, the intelligence 'chatter' about an impending attack continued and between May and July 2001, GCHQ and NSA intercepted more than thirty telephone calls and emails appearing to indicate that a terrorist attack was imminent. But none gave any hint as to when and where the attack might take place. By June, suspects linked to al-Qaʻeda were being tracked on the move to Britain, Canada, and America, and a number of al-Qaʻeda terrorists were said to be preparing for 'martyrdom'.

Scarlett told the Intelligence and Security Committee that at one high-level meeting in June 'considerable anxieties were expressed at the lack of specific intelligence. Attacks, probably against US interests, were imminent but their nature and target were unknown'. One agent who had recently been in Afghanistan reported that 'everyone is talking about an impending attack'. A US intelligence briefing for senior administration officials in July, predicted that bin Laden would 'launch a significant terrorist attack against US and/or Israeli interests in the coming weeks. The attack will be spectacular and designed to inflict mass casualties against US facilities or interests. Attack preparations have been made. Attack will occur with little or no warning'.

If the FBI had been doing its job properly, it is arguable that the attacks would not have succeeded. Despite all the above warnings, and its own internal knowledge that suspected terrorists were taking flying lessons in which they had shown no interest in learning how to land an aircraft, it had told the Federal Aviation Authority that there was no threat that required security surrounding domestic flights to be improved. After the attacks, it exacerbated those errors by participating in a series of leaks designed to try to spread the blame for the failure to predict the attacks. That created a climate where the leakage of top secret intelligence appeared inconsequential.

The ability of the NSA and GCHQ to intercept al-Qaʻeda's communications had been seriously hampered, albeit fortunately not eliminated, by the 1998 leaking of details of bin Laden's satellite telephone number. Now there was a further leak of signals-intelligence source material from the congressional committee investigating the attacks. The NSA had allegedly intercepted two telephone calls referring to the attacks but had failed to transcribe them until the day after the attacks. The motivation behind the leak was apparently the NSA's reluctance to declassify the two messages. The leak was specifically designed to force declassification by placing them in the public domain. But the leaking of the exact text of the two conversations almost certainly ensured not only that the telephones concerned would never be used again but that other telephones which had been commonly used for communication with those two telephones would also be considered compromised and would also not be used again. The leak had only served to hamper efforts to keep track of al-Qaʻeda. To make matters worse, the messages were in fact intercepted and transcribed by GCHQ and not the NSA, so the leak risked damaging the trans-Atlantic intelligence exchange which, given Britain's greater expertise at dealing with Arabic-language intercepts, is vital to US efforts to track al-Qaʻeda terrorists. Michael Hayden expressed some of the anger felt over the incident within NSA and GCHQ when he told the Congressional panel that such leaks meant that 'efforts measured in millions of dollars and thousands of man-years are turned to naught overnight'. The person who leaked the information no doubt thought the American people needed to know that the two messages had been intercepted. But the revelation did not show any error. Given the millions of telephone calls and email conversations intercepted every day by NSA and GCHQ, the speed with which these two conversations were transcribed was extremely good, indicating that they were given a high priority, although not the highest priority. This was because the telephones were previously listed as 'possibly al-Qaʻeda related' but their specific ownership was unclear. What is clear is that the stupid and irresponsible leak from the US inquiry did nothing to make the American people, or indeed anyone else, any safer from al-Qaʻeda terrorists.

Despite all of the difficulties, the increased terrorist threat has been a blessing in disguise for the intelligence services, leading to increased budgets and better acceptance by the politicians of what the spies have to say. The Intelligence and Security Committee's belief that the intelligence services did not know al-Qaʻeda was planning, and capable of, the murder of large numbers of Americans seems to have been a result of the testimony of the ministers concerned, rather than the intelligence agencies. The committee's conclusion was immediately preceded by a quote from a speech by David Blunkett, Home Secretary, to the House of Commons. He told MPs that the nature and level of the threat was 'different from what was previously envisaged' and that the intelligence assessment had 'underestimated what potentially might happen and the level of the threat, particularly to the US'. Like the committee's own conclusion, this is worryingly at odds with the real situation as described by John Scarlett. It is interesting to note that the various ministers admitted to the committee that, since the attacks, they were attaching 'greater emphasis . . . to intelligence and intelligence-related matters . . . than previously had been the case'. They clearly had not been paying enough attention before the attacks as indeed, the FBI and CIA errors notwithstanding, appears to have been the position with the US administration. In the wake of the report's publication, David Omand, a former Director of GCHQ, was appointed as Intelligence and Security Coordinator inside the Cabinet Office, a move seen in part as designed to increase the influence and credibility of the intelligence and security services at the heart of government.

Twenty Six

Secrets and Lies

The publication in September 2002 of a British government dossier on Saddam Hussein's nuclear, chemical and biological weapons,* designed to justify the 2003 war on Iraq, was to cause immense damage to the credibility of the intelligence services. They initially opposed the publication on the grounds that it risked inadvertently revealing sources of intelligence, preventing their future use and, in the case of human sources, dissuading others from coming forward with information. Eventually, they reluctantly agreed to participate, only to find their concerns over publication justified, if not quite for the reasons they originally cited. A number of issues raised in the dossier became controversial, largely because of the inability of the allies to find any of the so-called weapons of mass destruction.

The controversy over intelligence and the war focused on four issues. The first was the now infamous claim that Iraq could deploy some of its weapons within 45 minutes, which was highlighted by a BBC report that it was used to 'sex up' the dossier; the second, the existence or non-existence of the weapons; the third, the allegation that Iraq had attempted to obtain uranium ore from Niger; and the finally, the alleged link between Iraq and al-Qaʻeda.

The most controversial of these issues in Britain was the so-called 45-minute claim. The claim, which was to be mentioned repeatedly in the government's Iraq dossier and was at the centre of its attempts to justify the war in Iraq, came from a highly placed MI6 source in Baghdad. He was an Iraqi general – an 'agent-in-place' – and, according to Sir Richard Dearlove, then head of MI6, 'an established and reliable source who was certainly in a position to know'. It is worth noting that according to the Intelligence and Security Committee, 'Iraq was a hard target, but MI6 successfully ran a

---

* Not to be confused with the second, 'dodgy' dosier, of which more later.

number of agents against Iraq and Saddam's regime. These agents provided intelligence over a wide range of topics, although MI6 acknowledged that coverage of some subjects was stronger than on others.'

The intelligence relating to the 45-minute claim arrived in MI6 on 29 August, 2002, just as the government was preparing to release its dossier on Iraqi weapons of mass destruction, which was to be based on 'sanitised' assessments by the JIC (Joint Intelligence Committee). With interest in Iraqi WMD at an all-time high, the standard MI6 'CX' report was sent the next day to a number of 'customers' including the JIC itself, the MoD, and the Prime Minister. It contained several pieces of intelligence, including the claim that it would take an average of 20 minutes to deploy chemical and biological weapons (CBW). The maximum time was 45 minutes.

Interestingly, the source did not specify precisely what the context for these timings was and no-one in either MI6 or the JIC Current Intelligence Group on Iraq seemed to know. But among old hands within the Defence Intelligence Staff section working on artillery and missile systems, the figures rang some very loud bells. They appeared to be straight out of the old Soviet artillery and rocket troops manual. The most likely delivery systems the Iraqis would use to deliver chemical or biological weapons were all Soviet-made mortar, artillery and missile systems. These were: 120mm heavy mortars, 155mm heavy howitzers; Soviet-made BM21 Katyusha multiple rocket launchers; and the al-Hussein surface-to-surface missile. This was an Iraqi version of the Scud missile, which was the Soviet army-level surface-to-surface missile system. In common with all other Soviet workers, Red Army troops were given 'norms' for the time it should take them to perform particular tasks. The 'norm' for the time it should take to resupply a self-propelled artillery battery with shells from front line storage sites and for that battery to be ready to fire was less than 20 minutes. The same 'norm' for a Scud missile launcher was 45 minutes.

At this point, it is probably worth mentioning the debate over whether or not the 45-minute claim referred to battlefield weapons. John Scarlett, JIC Chairman, made this distinction in testimony to the Hutton Inquiry, as did the Intelligence and Security Committee in its report into the intelligence on Iraqi 'weapons of mass destruction'. But within the context of realistic Iraqi capabilities, the term 'battlefield weapons' was redundant. The Iraqis did have

L29 unmanned aerial vehicles, which could have been used to disperse chemical or biological agents in spray form. Chemical or biological weapons might also have been dropped from manned aircraft like the MiG21 ground attack aircraft. But with the US Air Force and the RAF enforcing no-fly zones over much of Iraq, it was highly unlikely that any Iraqi aircraft, whether manned or otherwise, could stay in the air for more than a few minutes. The main long-range threat came from the al-Hussein missiles, which had a range of more than 400 miles, and it was these missiles which the dossier cited as being capable of hitting any target within Israel or the two British Sovereign Base Areas in Cyprus.

Saddam had used the missiles in a strategic role during the 1991 Gulf War, firing around 50 at Israel in a failed attempt to drag it into the war and split the coalition. But they were essentially Scud missiles, designed for attacks on enemy rear echelon forces. Around 40 were used in this way during the 1991 war, and during the 2003 Iraq War, that is how Iraqi forces used the small number of al-Hussein missiles they are believed to have fired, attacking US and British troops at rear bases in Kuwait. Not only were the al-Hussein missiles battlefield weapons, the 45-minute claim was a specific reference to the time it should take to resupply the launchers with warheads and for the missiles to be ready to fire.

There was a certain amount of debate between the JIC, the DIS and MI6 over whether or not the draft dossier should make clear precisely what the 45 minutes was believed to mean. At first the suggestion from within the JIC was that it should point out that the weapons had to be already stored on the front line and the original form of words chosen was: 'Intelligence indicates that, from forward-deployed storage sites, chemical and biological munitions could be with military units and ready for firing within 45 minutes.'

But there was a widespread nervousness within the intelligence community about the way its material was being used, and eventually the argument from within the DIS and MI6 – that since the source had not spelt it out in his report, no assumptions on what it meant should appear in the draft dossier – won the day. As a result the claim was couched in careful terms, but the important qualification that the weapons should be ready in 'forward-deployed storage sites' was not made. It was only the first of a series of mistakes that would lead eventually, albeit indirectly, to the death of the government weapons scientist Dr David Kelly, three separate inquiries, and a dramatic loss of public confidence in the honesty of the Blair government and the competence of the intelligence services.

It was in fact very important to make clear that the weapons had to be already prepared and actually waiting on the front line. The presence of the UNSCOM weapons inspectors had forced Iraq to adopt a 'just-in-time' policy with regard to its chemical and biological weapons. It would maintain the programmes, and the ability to produce the weapons, but no large stocks of weapons, because that would mean static storage sites which UNSCOM would want to inspect, as well as technicians and guards it could interview. There was no need to keep stocks of biological weapons, which could be produced within days. Chemical weapons might take longer, as much as months in the cases of Sarin and VX gas, and there was some suspicion that Iraq might have retained small stocks of VX gas, which had been declared but never accounted for.

It is not clear whether the Prime Minister spotted the 45-minute claim when it first landed on his desk in the shape of the original CX report from MI6. But it had certainly caught his eye in the days following its first mention in a draft of the dossier circulated on 9 September 2002. At this stage it was only mentioned twice and, since it was not qualified, couched in very cautious terms. The 9 September draft said the intelligence merely 'suggested' that Iraq could deploy chemical or biological weapons within 45 minutes.

But amid the confusing, and often uncertain, intelligence reports on Iraq it was a detail that Mr Blair and his advisers, not least Alastair Campbell, his Director of Communications, knew the public would understand. There is no doubt that as far as they were concerned, it was the sound bite that would sell the war to some of the many people who remained unconvinced, not least a large number of backbench Labour MPs. It would only take Saddam 45 minutes to fire his chemical or biological weapons. Put at its simplest, as Mr Campbell knew the tabloid headline writers would, British bases in Cyprus were '45 minutes from doom'.

That this possibility was at the forefront of the minds of Mr Blair and his advisers was demonstrated by an email from Jonathan Powell, the Prime Minister's Chief of Staff, in which he asked Mr Campbell, 'What will be the headline in the *Standard* on the day of publication?' The need to ensure a suitable headline in the London *Evening Standard* resulted from the fact that although it is essentially a local newspaper serving the capital and its immediate environs, the *Standard*'s various editions land on the desks of the editors of the London-based national media throughout the day as they make decisions on what their own headlines should be. It therefore has influence out of all proportion to its own limited circulation.

We know that the likely impact of the 45-minute claim was in the minds of not just Campbell and Powell but also of Blair himself, because Campbell told the Hutton Inquiry that it was the Prime Minister who insisted that the claim had a prominent place in the dossier. James Dingemans, counsel to the inquiry, put it to Campbell that he 'plainly had selected 45 minutes as a message worth including in the Prime Minister's foreword'. Campbell replied: 'Well, more to the point the Prime Minister had. I had a discussion with the Prime Minister, I think with David Manning [Blair's then foreign policy adviser], with Jonathan Powell, certainly with John Scarlett, and I started to work upon what the Prime Minister wanted to say, and certainly that was one of the points that he felt was worth covering.'

So Campbell began writing Blair's foreword and, on his orders, placing the unqualified 45-minute claim at the very heart of its evidence against Saddam. The Prime Minister said in his foreword that the JIC assessment revealed that Saddam's 'military planning allows for some of the WMD to be ready within 45 minutes of an order to use them'. This was true, if the weapons were already prepared and on the front line, but the foreword failed to make this clear. It was also far firmer than the JIC was initially willing to be. The next draft, dated 16 September, mentioned the claim four times. The main body of the draft remained cautious, saying that the Iraqi military 'may be able to deploy these weapons within 45 minutes'. But the executive summary and Blair's new foreword were in no doubt, and the very much firmer line taken by the Prime Minister was also about to be imposed on the rest of the draft dossier.

On 17 September, Campbell emailed Scarlett with 16 different queries on the JIC draft, including at point 10 the differences between the main body of the report and that of the summary and the Prime Minister's foreword. 'Page 17, 2 lines from the bottom, "may" is weaker than in the summary,' Campbell wrote. The following day, Scarlett responded to all of Campbell's points and, on the issue of the 45-minute claim, said: 'The language you queried on the old page 17 has been tightened.' Scarlett told Lord Hutton that the executive summary and not the body of the report was the JIC judgement, thereby justifying the decision to harden the language in the body of the draft dossier rather than tone down the Prime Minister's foreword. But put simply, *could* had become *can*.

The truth is that the presentation of the 45-minute claim in its final form, as agreed by Scarlett, was the worst of all possible worlds. There were two alternative views. Either the 45 minutes referred to weapons that were already prepared and on the front line, in which case this needed to be made clear and the wording could be unequivocal, or it was not clear what it meant and the wording should have been cautious. Scarlett's acceptance of Campbell's suggestion left the wording very firm without any qualification at all.

This was of course precisely what the Prime Minister and Campbell wanted. Lord Hutton was correct in concluding that neither knew that it referred to 'battlefield weapons', or more accurately weapons that were already prepared and on the front line. But the truth was arguably worse. They did not care. Neither Blair nor Campbell thought to ask, and it is worth pointing out that to do so would have excluded the soundbite that they hoped would sell the need for a war to the many doubters. As a result, the 45 minutes appeared in the dossier in a form that left its actual meaning unclear not just to the layman but even to experts like Dr Kelly and other military intelligence analysts working on Iraqi nuclear, chemical and biological weapons programmes.

The inquiry heard evidence that Dr Kelly and a number of DIS officials were very unhappy about the 45-minute claim. Brian Jones, head of the DIS directorate that dealt with chemical and biological weapons, said he and his staff regarded it as 'unreliable'. The day after Scarlett 'tightened' the wording around the 45-minute claim, it was discussed at a meeting in the Old War Office chaired by Dr Jones and attended by Dr Kelly and a number of government experts on Iraqi chemical and biological weapons. One of those attending was a witness known only as Mr A, a Foreign Office adviser, who said the meeting produced 25 separate points that the DIS officers felt should be changed, with David Kelly playing a driving role in the discussions.

There was considerable debate about of the 45-minute claim. They were all experts on chemical or biological weapons and not on artillery or missile systems, so none of them understood what it meant. The dossier did make clear that it would take weeks not minutes for Iraq to produce chemical or biological weapons. But nevertheless they remained concerned that the 45-minute claim was misleading and given undue prominence. 'I think all of us touched on the subject in one way or another,' Mr A told the inquiry. 'It was a statement which seemed to rather beg more questions than it answered . . . and if your assessment causes you to immediately ask questions, then we felt that it was not perhaps a statement that should be included.' The changes they recommended were taken into account but they made no recommendation with regard to the 45-minute claim. It was not their area of expertise. Nevertheless both Dr Kelly and Dr Jones continued to express concern to their bosses about the claim. Extraordinarily, no one within the DIS management structure thought to make it clear to either man that the claim did not fall within their area of expertise but was simply about the operation times for various artillery and missile systems. If it had been explained, of course, both men would have pointed out that it was so lacking in context as to appear to be deliberately misleading.

The failure to brief Dr Kelly and Dr Jones was sadly not the only example of incompetent man-management within the MoD to be exposed by the affair. Dr Kelly's eminence among experts on biological weapons, and particularly Iraqi biological weapons, is not in doubt. He was a key adviser to the intelligence services on the subject and had played a crucial role not only in determining what capabilities in this field Saddam might and might not have, but also in the MI6 debriefing of Vladimir Pasechnik after his defection to Britain. It was Dr Kelly who realised the extent of the Russian biological weapons programme, which went far beyond what the then Russian President Boris Yeltsin had admitted. Yet on the 45-minute claim no one seems to have been listening to him. He eventually decided to go to the media, taking his concerns to the BBC. The MoD mishandling of Dr Kelly – after he came forward to admit to being the source for a BBC report that some within the intelligence services were unhappy with the use of the 45-minute claim – was abysmal. The distortion of the 45-minute claim was not the only area of change where the Prime Minister or his advisers altered the emphasis of the dossier. At the same time as Dr Kelly, Dr Jones and the DIS analysts were meeting to discuss the dossier, across Whitehall, Powell was sending an email to Campbell and Scarlett. This was the same email that asked what the headline would be in the Evening Standard. It went on to refer to page 19 of the 16 September draft, which said: 'Saddam is prepared to use chemical and biological weapons, if he believes his regime is under threat.' This was 'a bit of a problem', Powell said. 'It backs up the argument that there is no CBW threat and we will only create one if we attack him. I think you should redraft the paragraph.' Scarlett agreed to remove it without consulting the JIC. When asked why, he told Lord Hutton that he had the authority to do so and that there was intelligence to back up the change. It remains unclear what that intelligence was.

The other major change to the dossier came in its title, which in the final draft produced on 16 September was Iraq's Programme for Weapons of Mass Destruction. Given the doubts over whether or not there were any Iraqi stocks of chemical or biological weapons, the use of the word programme was crucial. But the title of the actual dossier published on 24 September was Iraq's Weapons of Mass Destruction. It remains unclear who changed this, although it seems likely that the key players would have been Campbell and Scarlett.

It is tempting to say that, post-Hutton, the 45-minute claim no longer really matters. But the simple truth is that it does. Its misuse will colour our perceptions of how much we can trust our intelligence services for a long time to come, although nowhere near as much as the inability of America and Britain to find all those stocks of biological and chemical weapons that Tony Blair and George Bush kept talking about. So why was the intelligence that formed the basis for the dossier, and the politicians' statements, so terribly wrong?

The answer, surprisingly given the amount of controversy it provoked, is that it wasn't. Britain's intelligence services – unlike the Prime Minister, who repeatedly talked about 'Saddam's weapons of mass destruction' – were unable to say for sure whether there were any stocks. The title of the JIC's final draft dossier was, as we have seen, Iraq's Programme for Weapons of Mass Destruction. The section on 'the current situation' in the JIC's final draft spoke mostly of capabilities and programmes. It did refer vaguely to evidence of 'recent production of chemical and biological agents' but its only mention of actual stocks of weapons was the possibility that Saddam 'might' have quantities of VX gas, about 1.5 tonnes, already prepared.

The Iraqi 'just-in-time' policy meant there was no need to keep stocks of biological weapons, which could be produced very quickly. Dr Kelly, the real expert in this area, said it would take days. The JIC's final draft was more cautious and said weeks. It did not mention any current stocks of biological weapons. Chemical weapons would take longer to produce and there was a possibility that some might exist, it said. 'Iraq could produce quantities of mustard gas within weeks and of Sarin and VX within months,' the final JIC draft said: 'In the case of VX, it might have already have done so.' If we ignore the misleading suggestion inherent in the 45-minute claim, that was all it provided as evidence for the actual existence of stocks of chemical and biological weapons. It tallied in fact with David Kelly's assessment that there was a 30 per cent chance of some stocks of chemical weapons. The clear implication of the JIC assessment was that there was no firm evidence of any other stocks of chemical or biological weapons.

Predictably, perhaps, this was one of the things that Campbell picked up in the 16-point email he sent to Scarlett on 17 September. Attention focused on point 10 of this email, his request that the 45-minute claim be hardened up. But the previous point referred to the uncertainty over the stocks of VX gas. Campbell complained that 'the *might* reads very weakly'. In stark contrast to his willingness to harden up the 45-minute claim, Scarlett was very firm that as regards the stocks of VX gas, the intelligence services 'cannot improve on the use of *might*'.

This was of course entirely the proper reaction. But Campbell's request led to further discussion among the intelligence analysts producing the JIC assessments, and it was decided that the lack of reliable evidence as to whether or not Iraq had any VX gas was such that even this tenuous claim should be removed from the dossier. This was a thoroughly worthy action but it had precisely the reverse effect to that desired. It removed the implication that this was as much as the intelligence services could say about Iraq's stocks of weapons and, combined with the much looser language used by the politicians, gave the false impression that Britain's intelligence services believed that Iraq did have stocks of chemical and biological weapons. The simple truth is that the British intelligence services had no firm evidence that Saddam had any stocks of chemical and biological weapons and the actual dossier did not claim that he did.

There was a third area of controversy arising out of the dossier. This concerned its claim that 'there is intelligence that Iraq has sought the supply of significant quantities of uranium from Africa'. That this should become a controversial remark is astonishing. The country concerned was soon revealed to be Niger, which had a record of selling uranium to Iraq. Given that Iraq had already bought uranium from Niger and that it is the third largest producer of uranium behind Canada and Australia, neither of which was likely to sell any uranium to Saddam, the suggestion that he had merely tried to buy uranium from Niger should not have been at all contentious. But a series of events led to the claim becoming highly controversial.

The first was the decision by George Bush to say, in his State of the Union address to the American people on 28 January 2003, that British intelligence 'has learned that Saddam Hussein recently sought significant quantities of uranium from Africa'. This was in fact true. But it subsequently emerged that the CIA had given the UN's atomic watchdog, the International Atomic Energy Authority, documents purporting to prove the Niger link which were shown to be amateurish fakes. A number of US press reports blamed MI6. But British intelligence officials said they did not see the documents until they were passed to the UN, and they then immediately recognised them as fakes. The CIA had also sent a former US ambassador, the husband of one of its own staff, to Niger to determine whether or not Iraq had tried to buy uranium. Leaving aside the naïvety of this move – he apparently asked a number of Niger officials and all of them unsurprisingly assured him it was not true – the source for the MI6 intelligence was completely different from that of the faked documents.

The problem for MI6 was that it could not pass the CIA its 'different and credible' evidence, which came from two other intelligence services, at least one of which was French, because the originating services would not allow it to do so. It would therefore have been a breach of the protocols governing exchange of intelligence for MI6 to pass the evidence to the CIA. The likelihood that the US administration might use the intelligence to exonerate President Bush, by leaking it to the American media, thereby risking the source, was almost certainly a key factor in the reluctance of the intelligence services concerned to allow MI6 to give the Americans the evidence, some of which was documentary (and not faked). But in the case of the French, it is of course possible that they were also very happy to see the Americans embarrassed. The intelligence was also backed up by a GCHQ intercept showing that an Iraqi official had visited Niger during the period in question and the Intelligence and Security Committee, which saw the evidence, judged the MI6 decision to continue insisting it was true to be 'reasonable'.

The fourth controversial claim relating to intelligence on Iraq – that Saddam Hussein was in league with Osama bin Laden and his al-Qa'eda terrorists – was complete nonsense. The *Mukhabarat* made an attempt in early 1998 to forge a relationship with bin Laden, on the basis that he was a Saudi opposition figure, but the links are believed to have foundered on the inherent incompatibilities between a fundamentalist Shi'ite organisation and an agnostic Sunni Muslim government. Whether or not the link continued beyond 1998, intelligence analysts on both sides of the Atlantic insist that there was insufficient evidence to justify claims by Colin Powell, the US Secretary of State, to the UN Security Council that a network of al-Qa'eda agents was operating with Saddam's connivance inside Baghdad. The alleged link was not mentioned in the British dossier because MI6 did not believe a word of it. Indeed, when Tony Blair suggested – in support of the US claim – that there was a link, but it was just not clear what it was, he was hauled back by his intelligence advisers who told him that even this fairly ambiguous statement could not be justified.

As regards the 'sexing up' of the British dossier, Lord Hutton's final judgement – seen by many as a whitewash – was extraordinarily harsh on the BBC, which was simply reporting what a very good source was telling it, and let Blair and Campbell off the hook. If David Kelly believed it to be true that the 45-minute claim was used to make the dossier 'sexier' and that Campbell was behind this, then the BBC was entitled to report it. In fact, it did not use Campbell's name, that was done by Andrew Gilligan, the BBC Radio 4 *Today* programme Defence Correspondent responsible for the story, in a column in the *Mail on Sunday*. But as long as he was reporting what his source said – and the transcript of David Kelly's conversation with another BBC reporter Susan Watts, suggests strongly that Dr Kelly did believe this to be so – it was again perfectly proper behaviour. Gilligan was not entitled to report that the government 'probably knew' that the 45-minute figure was wrong. Dr Kelly had not told him this. The 45-minute figure was not wrong. It was merely misrepresented, and neither Blair nor Campbell were aware of this. But as we have already seen, in many ways the truth was even worse. Neither man was interested in the detail of what the 45 minutes meant. To them, it already had an instantly understandable meaning that could be used to sell the need for war.

Gilligan at least admitted his error to the Hutton Inquiry. The government admitted not one single mistake. There were very serious errors in the handling of Dr Kelly once he came forward to admit to meeting Gilligan, some of which were pointed out by Lord Hutton. But what about the government's use of the intelligence in the dossier? What of Dr Kelly's claim that the 45-minute claim was used to make the dossier sexier? We know that it was presented completely out of context. Sir Richard Dearlove admitted to Lord Hutton that it was given 'undue prominence'. The Intelligence and Security Committee concluded that its use was 'unhelpful to an understanding of the issues'. But perhaps the most astute of all the judgements passed so far remains that of David Kelly in his taped interview with Susan Watts when she asked him about the 45-minute claim:

I knew the concern about that statement. It was a statement that was made and it just got out of all sense of proportion . . . They were desperate for information. They were pushing hard for information which could be released. That was one that popped up and it was seized on, and it was unfortunate that it was.

The intelligence services, and not the government, were to blame for the way in which the 45-minute claim was placed in the draft dossier without any attempt to put it into its proper context. But at that stage it was couched in very careful terms and not particularly highlighted. The conclusions of both Lord Hutton and the Intelligence and Security Committee that Blair and Campbell did not then use the 45-minute claim to 'sex up' the dossier were so naïve as to appear perverse. Merely ensuring that it was in the Prime Minister's foreword, placing it where journalists looking for a useful soundbite would latch on to it, amounted to using it to 'sex up' the dossier.

According to Campbell's own testimony, Blair was responsible for that. For the journalists to use it in an unequivocal way, it had to be expressed in very hard terms both in the foreword and the body of the dossier. Campbell ensured that this happened and he did not do this carelessly. He was the head of the government's spin machine, a former tabloid journalist with an instinctive understanding of what would and would not make news. He was, of course, simply doing his job – making sure that the message the government wanted to put across was passed on to the public – and he did it well. Think back to Jonathan Powell's email asking what the headline would be in the *Evening Standard*. The headline the *Standard* used was '45 MINUTES TO ATTACK', and its influence could clearly be seen in the headline in the biggest selling British daily newspaper the *Sun*, precisely the headline 10 Downing Street wanted to see – '45 MINUTES FROM DOOM'.

Apparently flushed with the success of this propaganda operation, Campbell went on, in February 2003, to publish a second dossier, through his grandly named Coalition Information Centre – a throwback to the old black propaganda operations of the early Cold War – in which he used intelligence material without consulting the agencies. The agencies' anger over this action, which could easily have compromised intelligence sources, was compounded when the CIC was found to have plagiarised academic papers from the internet. Campbell subsequently apologised personally to Sir Richard Dearlove over the second dossier, but its publication only served to emphasise the way in which some within government were prepared to misuse intelligence in order to persuade doubters to back the war.

The Intelligence and Security Committee, like Lord Hutton, may have failed to get to the bottom of the government's misuse of the intelligence, but the oversight it has provided since its creation in 1994 has been a useful advance for the British intelligence system. Its absolution of the government of any 'sexing up' of the dossier and its main conclusion on the 11 September attacks aside, the committee has earned a good reputation for pointing out potential problems. These include the risk that too much focus on al-Qaʻeda will leave gaps in other areas of intelligence collection or that failure to provide funding to keep pace with US technological advances in spy satellites will damage the transatlantic intelligence links. But far too much information is still kept secret. As the research for this book shows, a great deal of what the intelligence community tries to keep secret is already in the public domain. The committee should be able to hold open hearings like its counterparts in America, and the intelligence services need to grow up a little in their censoring of the committee's reports. There can, for example, be no possible security reason for preventing Parliament and indeed the taxpayer from knowing the precise budgets of each agency. But these have been carefully replaced by rows of asterisks in each of the committee's annual reports. GCHQ in particular seems incapable of allowing even the most basic conclusions from being constantly interrupted by a stream of asterisks, the most ludicrous example being in the committee's report on the 11 September attacks where it is recorded that al-Qa'eda terrorists 'tended to speak Arabic, *** ***. However there is a recognised shortage of linguists *** ***.' It doesn't take an expert in linguistics to work out that the two missing languages are probably Urdu and Pashto. But even if they aren't, al-Qa'eda surely knows what languages its terrorists speak.

Britain's spies have had to learn to be more open about what they do since the end of the Cold War. This is partly because an increasing amount of their work is being exposed to scrutiny in the courts – an MI5 officer tracking down a terrorist or a major criminal is now as likely to call in the lawyers as he is a surveillance team, for the simple reason that he or she needs to ensure that the evidence stands up in court. But the need to protect budgets will also be a key factor in pushing our spies into being more open in order to show that they are worth the hundreds of millions of pounds they receive from the Exchequer. The war on terror may have put an end to the drastic financial cutbacks that were a feature of the 1990s, but paradoxically the more efficient Britain's spies are in countering the terrorist threat, the more likely it is that the temptation to cut their budgets will return.

The other problem they face is pressure from within the European Union for moves away from the close relationship with the US intelligence agencies, epitomised by the European Parliament's investigation of the so-called Echelon system and attempts to set up an integral intelligence organisation as part of the European Security and Defence Initiative. Fortunately, once politicians come to power and see the scope of the transatlantic intelligence exchange they usually realise how foolish Britain would be to turn instead to the European agencies. The British agencies have very good relationships with many of their European counterparts, particularly the French internal security service, *Direction de la Surveillance du Territoire* (DST), which is rated extremely highly by both MI5 and MI6. But they have made it clear that membership of the European Union will not affect the exchange arrangements with their American counterparts. 'In modern times, relations with the French and German services have always been good, and I don't think they have been much affected by our membership of the EU,' a senior intelligence officer said. 'For us, the Americans are still the most important partner, just because their capacity is so much greater than for example the Germans' capacity. If you said, "Let's substitute the relationship with the Germans for the Americans," you would lose quite a lot. The Americans are just better at it.'

That conclusion can only have been reinforced by the differences with France and Germany over the 2003 Iraq War. There are of course occasional difficulties in the alliance with America, as was demonstrated by the Bush administration's fraudulent use of intelligence to 'prove' a link between al-Qa'eda and Saddam Hussein. The willingness of politicians to distort intelligence in order to 'prove' their own prejudices, a problem which the 45-minute claim showed, is not unique to America, is irritating but unlikely to outweigh the value of the trans-Atlantic alliance.

But if the war on terror is to be won, British and American intelligence officers will increasingly need to share intelligence with countries that would never have figured on distribution lists in the past. They are also likely to have to share intelligence with the politicians and the public in order to persuade them to back often dangerous military action. While the protection of sources must remain paramount, Britain's spies will have to be much more open about what they do and, where possible, the intelligence they have collected. They are rightly regarded as being among the best, if not the best, in the world. But intelligence, however high-quality, is no good on its own. If it is not passed on to the people making the decisions it will be no use at all.

Appendix I

This extract from a joint MI5–MI6 report given to the KGB by John Cairncross, the so-called Fifth Man, gave details of a previously undisclosed network of Soviet agents in Britain during the late 1930s and early 1940s.

The Green Case

The following case is cited to illustrate the methods used by Soviet military intelligence to obtain intelligence data and should, in view of comments about the work of the Counter-Intelligence Department, be studied carefully.

Oliver Charles Green was born in Birmingham in 1904. He left school at 14 and went to work at a printing house, where he stayed until 1937. It has been established that by 1933 he was already a member of the Communist Party of Great Britain. In 1937, Green joined the International Brigade in Spain, serving there until he was wounded, after which he was given the special job of compiling references for troops of the English battalion, with particular emphasis on their political reliability and the possibility of their promotion to leadership posts. Green also worked on a history of the International Brigade.

At the start of 1938, Green went back to Birmingham and some time later moved to 293a Edgware Road NW9 where he went back into printing. In May 1941, he began working for Hendon ARP as an ambulance driver. When Green returned from Spain, it was suggested that he might get involved in undercover work, under the leadership of someone from London. Since he was not in contact with any well-known members of the Communist Party and was not working in a job that gave him access to secret material, he was not suspected of involvement with Soviet Intelligence.

In 1941, Green was arrested for forging petrol coupons and a search of his house revealed a dark room. The police found two rolls of film for a Leica which, once they'd been developed and enlarged, proved to be photographs of weekly summaries from military intelligence, secret documents intended to be seen by a fairly wide range of people. The address of an English soldier named Elliott, living in Smedleys Hydro, Matlock, was found in a notebook, owned by Green. Elliott was a well-known Communist of several years' standing who had also served with the International Brigade in Spain and had access to the weekly summaries from military intelligence from which Green extracted information.

Green was sent to prison and confessed that he had been working for Soviet Intelligence. Subsequently he gave a full and frank account of his methods. He said that initially he had been approached by an officer in the Brigade who suggested he become a spy in France. He agreed. However, he was also picked to carry out intelligence work in England on behalf of the USSR. He agreed to this as well, was given £40 and told to go back to England and wait to receive a letter signed by 'Johnny'. There would be a meeting once he received the letter. He was given full instructions on how to approach the rendezvous and how to establish contact with and ascertain the identity of the person he was to meet, on previously agreed signals for danger and on his precise movements for two hours before and after the meeting. In the run-up period, he fitted out his flat on the Edgware Road, bought the necessary equipment for the Leica, including special lenses for photographing documents and, although not an experienced photographer, managed to become an expert in the field in only nine days.

Organisation

Green knew two leaders of the organisation by sight but not by name (it has been established that they were Russian and members of staff at the Russian trade representation). The people connected with the organisation were always British subjects. Green handed his documents to the person with whom he had made contact at the very beginning. These documents were extracts from his recruits' reports and the film was not developed. Meetings were always held outside and only once, under exceptional circumstances, did Green visit the flat of one of his confederates. Green knew the head of the organisation as 'the boss'. 'The boss', or the legal rezident, received all Green's reports, edited them and added information received from other souces. He also gave instructions about the politics and nature of the information to be gathered and provided the money passed on to Green in one-pound notes. As well as pocket money, Green was given £500 (which were hidden away) for use in dire necessity (for example, the occupation of Great Britain or the departure of the Soviet Embassy). Radio was used as a means of communication more frequently than the diplomatic bag.

Agents

All the agents recruited by Green were British subjects, soldiers in the British Army, a worker at an aviation plant, a merchant seaman, a source with access to an aviation plant though not working there, a member of a government department and a pilot. If there was any suggestion that someone was suspected by counter-intelligence, they were not recruited (all members of the Communist Party came into this category). If any member of the Communist Party was likely to be put forward, it was suggested that he gradually distance himself from party work and from the party. That's how Green went about it. His recruits were sited in different parts of the country and this forced him to travel around the country. He was forbidden to use his own car but ignored the ban and it was forging petrol coupons that led to his being exposed.

Meetings

Meetings always took place out of doors, watches were always synchronised and there were detailed plans for movement during the two hours before and after a meeting. Flexibility was a major goal of the organisation and well-thought out steps were taken to ensure they were not watched. Simple but effective signals for recognising one another and danger signals were also used. Green said that the number of agents he would meet in a month was no more than 15 and, in extreme circumstances, he could see every agent once a fortnight. Agents and informants recruited by an operative are not necessarily run by the same operative.

Timeliness of reports

Green himself was responsible for the timeliness of the reports he put together and transmitted. Great attention was paid to training agents and 'the boss' gave Green secret material to help him. Training was on an ideological basis.

Radio equipment and operators

Several transmitters were located in various regions and used in turn. The operators had no difficulty obtaining instructions. Power transmitters were still not used. Transmissions were made about once a fortnight, late in the evening or early in the morning when there were very few people listening to the radio. The wavelength was constantly changed and transmission was automatic – which is the best way of tapping out by hand. Green claimed that automatic high speed was used to save time and prevent transmissions being overheard by radio amateurs. This has not been fully substantiated. There were several back-up transmitters.

Using undeveloped film

Undeveloped film was used as a way of ensuring the safety of information and of organisational and other issues. Reports to 'the boss' were always made on undeveloped film no more than eight-inches long. Green always carried an electric torch so that in an emergency he could shine it on the film. Two photographs were always made of each report: the second, undeveloped, negative was always kept until the first report reached its destination. Once photographed, agents' reports were destroyed.

Green's organisation: its objectives

The primary aim was to gather political information. After the fall of France, England had a choice: either: 1) a Fascist government in England that might declare war on Russia or: 2) the Germans would seize England, which would lead, at the very least, to the recall of the Russian Embassy in England and therefore to the urgent need for diversionary and espionage operations against a new enemy. If the Russian Embassy and the legal resident of the Counter-Intelligence Department did leave England, Green was to take charge of operations. Espionage would proceed in the usual way and the Communist Party would carry out acts of sabotage on Green's instructions. Five or six months before the Germans invaded Russia, Green was asked to gather information from British intelligence sources on German armaments and battle order. Green was also to transmit any information about the British Army's weapons but it was stressed that information about Germany was the priority.

Green did not think the Communist Party (of Great Britain) was engaged in underground work akin to his own. He was wrong but it is interesting to note since it provides one more testimony that Russian intelligence was working independently of the (British) Communist Party, although it is most probable that the leading members of the party were involved.

Appendix II

Armed Forces Intelligence Departments During the First and Second World Wars

Directorate of Military Operations in 1907

MO1   Imperial Defence: Strategy and Operations

MO2   Foreign Intelligence: Europe and the Near East

MO3   Foreign Intelligence: Asia and the Americas

MO4   Topography of potential foreign theatres of operation

MO5   Special Duties (covert intelligence and counter-intelligence operations)

MO6   Medical information on foreign theatres of operation

Of the three intelligence sections, MO5 took the lead in intelligence operations. The role of MO2 and MO3 was more analytical, and was defined as: 'Collection, preparation and distribution of information concerning the military geography, resources and armed forces of all foreign countries. Supply of information regarding India and adjoining territories. Questions relating to the defence of India, other than those concerning coastal defences. Correspondence with military attachés. Examination of foreign journals and literature generally.'

Directorate of Military Intelligence in 1918

MIR   Russian section (responsible for intelligence on Russia, Siberia, central Asia, Persia, Afghanistan, China, Japan and Siam; information emanating from India; and liaison with the General Staff (India)

MI1   Secretariat (responsible for organisation; distribution of military policy regarding submarine cables and wireless telegraphy; preparation, distribution and security of War Office cyphers; interior economy of the directorate; interrogation of prisoners of war in the United Kingdom)

MI2	Military information concerning the Americas (except Canada), Spain, Portugal, Italy, Liberia, Tangier, the Balkan States, the Ottoman Empire, Arabia, Sinai, Abyssinia, Egypt, Sudan and West Persia
MI3	Military information concerning France, Belgium, Morocco, Austria, Hungary, Switzerland, Germany, Luxembourg, Holland, Norway, Sweden and Denmark
MI4	Geographical section
MI5	Counter-espionage
MI6	Legal and Economic section
MI7	Press Control
MI8	Cable Censorship
MI9	Postal Censorship
MI10	Military attachés

Directorate of Military Intelligence in World War II

MI1	Administration and Personnel
MI2	Intelligence on northern and eastern Europe, USSR, Middle East and Asia
MI3	Intelligence on western Europe and the Americas
MI4	Maps (transferred to Directorate of Military Operations in 1940)
MI5	Security Service (Civilian organisation)
MI6	Secret Intelligence Service (Civilian Organisation)
MI7	Press (transferred to Ministry of Information in 1940)
MI8	Signals Intelligence
MI9	PoW Intelligence
MI10	Technical Intelligence (became part of MI16 at end of war); Road Intelligence (from end of war)
MI11	Field Security
MI12	Postal and Telegraph Censorship (abandoned, reluctantly, at end of war)
MI14	Intelligence on Germany
MI15	Photographic Intelligence (transferred to Air Ministry in 1943); Air Defence Intelligence (from 1943)

MI16   Scientific and Technical Intelligence (formed at end of war)
MI17   Co-ordination/JIC
MI19   Interrogation of enemy prisoners/debriefing of refugees

Naval Intelligence Division in World War II

NID1   Germany and northern Europe
NID2   Americas
NID3   Mediterranean; Middle East; north-east and east Africa
NID4   Far East
NID5   Geographical Handbooks
NID6   Topographical
NID7   Constructional Engineering and Technical Matters
NID8   Operational Intelligence Centre
NID9   Y Service
NID10   Codes and Cyphers
NID11   PoW Intelligence
NID12   Special Navy Section, Bletchley Park
NID14   Secretariat
NID15   Liaison with other naval departments
NID16   Soviet Union
NID17   Liaison with JIC and SIS
NID18   Naval Intelligence Section, Washington DC
NID19   Information; press cuttings; liaison with government departments and BBC
NID20   Vichy France; Iberia; north-west, west and southern Africa
NID21   Contacts

Air Intelligence in World War II

AI (JIC)   Liaison with JIC and Inter-Services Security Board
AI1   Receipt and dissemination of intelligence. Air attachés
AI1a   Administration and Personnel
AI1b   Air Ministry Weekly Bulletin
AI1c   Liaison with MI6
AI1d   Liaison with MI5

AI1f	Liaison with Free French, Czech, Norwegian and Polish intelligence services
AI1g	Technical Intelligence
AI1k	PoW interrogation
AI1p	Recruitment and selection of personnel
AI1s	Internal Security
AI3a	Political and Strategic Intelligence
AI3b	Germany; Italy; France; Spain; Portugal; Switzerland; Bulgaria; Romania; Hungary; and Yugoslavia.
AI3c	Liaison with Ministry of Economic Warfare on target intelligence and enemy fuel resources
AI3d	Russia; Finland; Sweden; Japan; China; Thailand; Dutch East Indies; Turkey; Iraq; Iran; Afghanistan; Egypt
AI3(USA)	USA and Latin America
AI3e	German Air Force
AI4a	Airfields and communications of all countries
AI4b	Middle East
AI5	Photo-reconnaissance
AI6	Photo-reconnaissance
AI9	Liaison with MI9
AI10	Liaison with GC&CS

Appendix III

Extracts from an MI5 handbook on watching and tailing a suspect handed over to the KGB by Anthony Blunt during the Second World War.

OBSERVATION

Observation is a very onerous and exacting profession. Screen sleuths of the Secret Service thriller or detective novel appeal to the uninitiated, but in actual practice there is little glamour and much monotony in such a calling as 'observation'. A successful watcher is a rarity and though 'many are called, few are chosen,' even then not more than a very small proportion of those engaged in such work can be considered first class.

After many years experience of watching and following, the writer is forced to the conclusion that the ideal watcher is born and not made, and unless he has a natural flair for the work he will never rise above a mediocre standard. At various times hundreds of men have been interviewed as prospective trainees but very few have been accepted, for the reason that when tried out they are found to lack the one essential qualification, viz., patience, and to have engaged them would have unfair to tried men who would be called to carry passengers every time a tricky spot of watching became necessary.

The ideal watcher should not be more than 5ft 7ins or 5ft 8ins in height, looking as unlike a policeman as possible. It is a mistake to use men who are too short as they would be just as conspicuous as tall men. A watcher should be a rather nondescript type: good eyesight is essential, also good hearing as it is often possible to overhear a suspect's conversation. He should be active and alert, as it frequently occurs that a suspect hastily boards, or alights from a fast-moving vehicle. Above all a watcher must be a quick thinker, capable of acting on the spur of the moment.

A watcher must adapt himself to the locality in which he is called upon to

A spots him coming – walks on apace,
B crosses over to take up the chase

keep observation, e.g., He must wear old clothes, cap, muffler, etc., in the slum quarters, and be better dressed for the West End where he frequently has to enter hotels, blocks of residential flats or office buildings. In short, it is the watcher's job to carry on in such a manner as not to bring undue notice to himself from local residents.

The use of facial disguise is not recommended. It may be considered essential in Secret Service films but in practice it is to be deplored. A false moustache or beard is easily detected, especially under the high lights of a restaurant, pub or in a tube train.

In many cases, close observation is the only means of discovering a suspect's contacts and obtaining the essential evidence for prosecution. BUT the watching must be conducted with care in every case. Careless watching is not only useless but may result in serious harm to an important case. Unskilful observation is of the greatest benefit to the suspect when he is aware he is under observation, for, if he is clever, he will cover his tracks by assuming the actions and demeanour of an innocent person, and as a consequence the chance will be lost of obtaining incriminating evidence. On the other hand the accurate reporting of a suspect's movements has sometimes reacted to his advantage at his ultimate interrogation, when, in any case, it will be realised much reporting is essential for testing the accuracy of the suspect's statements.

OBSERVATION TIPS AND WRINKLES

Picking up the Suspect

From his address: If a full
description is available together
with a recent photograph the
job is simplified. If there is no
description then one must
adopt a process of elimination
to find the right person from
among all the residents – often
a long procedure.

Take up a position some
distance from the address, on
the same side if possible, or
some distance away on the
other side. Be careful to be out
of view of the suspect's rooms.

Following in the Street

Keep about 25-30 yards behind
the quarry and when on the
move by foot it is preferable to
keep on the opposite pavement,
except in very busy streets.

S turns the corner, B takes the lead,
A watches B till it's safe to proceed

Whenever possible have two watchers, one on the same side of the street, and
the other on the opposite.

Shorten the distance from the suspect before reaching a corner, and at the
corner take a detour, wide if possible, in order to avoid the suspect if he halts
suddenly and turns around.

Be prepared for the suspect to board a moving vehicle such as a bus, tram
or train, or hailing a cruising taxi, or any other such device to shake off a 'tail'.

The watcher must be prepared to think and act one jump ahead of the
suspect, and if the latter does board a bus and mounts to the top, one watcher

should take a seat or stand just inside the platform. If the suspect goes inside a bus one watcher should take a seat immediately behind him if possible, even at the risk of being noticed, and the second watcher should then be prepared to cover the first and carry on alone if the first is obliged to drop out.

On the Underground

When travelling by Underground and booking a fare, if the suspect's destination cannot be overheard, take a ticket from a slot machine and have plenty of spare change ready at the other end to pay the excess if necessary. Pay the collector a little extra rather than argue with him and lose your suspect. On escalators, especially where they lead directly on to platforms or street exits, gradually close up on the suspect. When he is suspicious, a subject will often board a train just before the doors close, making himself the last one on the train, or he may alight at the last moment; so do not give him any rope on such occasions.

Entering Blocks of Flats or Offices

When entering buildings or blocks of flats again use common sense. If possible precede the suspect, enter the lift and take a position at the back: do not accompany a suspect in a small lift, or where it is worked automatically, but judge the floor he uses from the action of the lift and the place at which it stops by by making a rapid mounting of the stairs. A

Wherever he's listing, top floor or basement, take care he can't peep at you on the pavement

subsequent observation with the knowledge thus acquired will often get the suspect housed.

In a Restaurant

If a suspect uses a restaurant or café it is essential to see his contacts. If he feeds alone then entry and exit should follow each other rapidly. If he makes a contact then a full description of the person should be memorised with a view to subsequent picking up from such a description. If it is necessary to remain in a hotel, restaurant or café, be sure to be in a position to make a hurried exit – have such exits acted, have the bill ready for payment with plenty of loose change – don't be delayed at the cash desk.

Housing Suspects

When housing contacts of suspects be certain of the number, name of the road or street, and the district – this is not easy in these days of blackout. Ascertain if possible whether the contact entered by key, knocking or ringing, or by communal doorway, as this may give some indication whether he resides at or visits this address: be prepared to take up observation early next day to confirm your suspicions. If the address is in a quiet street, observation has to be maintained from a distance, so be in a situation to keep watch on a definite mark or be able to get a silhouette of anyone leaving the doorway.

Following by Taxi

If a taxi is used to follow a suspect or contact, then it is desirable immediately to take the number of the cab being followed. Choose, if possible, a modern cab for following and enthuse a little extra activity into the driver in order that he may avoid the suspect's detecting the following cab in mirrors or from the rear window. Keep your driver keen at traffic lights or traffic congestion and generally co-opt his help. Concoct a suitable tale which may go down well with the cabby, such as a divorce case, absconding husband or wife and promise the driver a good tip.

Travelling by Train

Travel by train in wartime is difficult, but much the same procedure should be adopted in the free and easy times. If possible, overhear the suspect's destination when he books and be guided accordingly as to booking a ticket, position to occupied in the train and and the tactics to be used at the destination. Close or free observation will depend on the circumstances of travel, but invariably it has been found that close observation on the heels of the suspect produces the best results.

If the suspect gets away or has to be picked up by a relief at his destination, take note of the time of departure of the train, its scheduled time of arrival, how the suspect is travelling, e.g., what class, how near from the front or rear, his baggage, whether light or heavy and any other encumbrances: and a full description of him, including his dress.

In the Post Office

There are excellent opportunities for investigation, which may have important bearing on the case. If the suspect goes to a writing desk it is often possible to get a brief glance at the addresses should the suspect write a telegram, address a letter or postcard. If he goes to the counter, the watcher can learn a lot if he gets close behind him.

Posting a Letter

Immediately after he posts a letter take a loosely folded newspaper and thrust it through the aperture of the letter-box in such a way that it will open out as it falls on

This is too small a lift, so better beware, S asked for his floor, best use the stair

the letters that have been posted; this will facilitate the identification of the correspondence posted by the suspect.

Observation Reports

The utmost care should be exercised in writing up observation reports. It cannot be too strongly emphasised that success or failure of a case depends in great measure on the exact times of a suspect's meetings with contacts, and the time spent in his or her company.

In instructions to watchers the following points should be brought out for their daily reports.

(1) The hours when observation was commenced, interrupted, and finished.

(2) All incidents, etc. however trivial.

(3) The addresses of people contacted – these are important.

(4) Suspect's demeanour under observation.

(5) Full description of contacts.

(6) Follow-up enquiries as soon as possible after locating a contact.

(7) The daily reports should be written out at the first opportunity after the duty has been completed. When two watchers are employed on the same case they must compile their reports without collaboration.

Avoiding Recognition by Suspects

Perhaps to wind up, it would be as well to mention the best methods experience has found to counter observation. Frequently a watcher has been 'dogged' and here once again a watcher will use his common sense. He will probably walk home, walk round a block, return home, leave again and start off in another direction from his most direct route. He will know his own neighbourhood intimately and use such knowledge to alternate his means of conveyance by bus, tram or train, but always gradually making towards his objective and ascertaining at the same time if he has a 'tail'. If he finds he has, then it is his best plan to act normally but not to go anywhere near to his particular 'job'. A good watcher will change his clothes daily if possible; change his route to and from home frequently; will not form habits such as that of drinking in one public house at a particular time; will not frequent a particular restaurant or café; will be discreet on the telephone and will not mention names or addresses unless told to do so; he will make his notes with care and above all will cultivate a good memory.

Finally REMEMBER

Observation cannot be mastered from textbooks or lectures. Hard practical training in the street is the only way to bring out a man's aptitude for the job – generally a long process.

DON'T BELITTLE THE PERSON YOU ARE FOLLOWING. IF HE DOES APPEAR SIMPLE APPEARANCES ARE OFTEN DECEPTIVE.

Bibliography

Adams, James, *The New Spies: Exploring the Frontiers of Espionage* (Hutchinson, London, 1994)

Aid, Matthew M. and Wiebes, Cees, *Secrets of Signals Intelligence during the Cold War and Beyond* (Frank Cass, London, 2001)

Aldrich, Richard J. (ed.), *British Intelligence, Strategy and the Cold War, 1945–51* (Routledge, London, 1992)

Aldrich, Richard J, *Espionage, Security and Intelligence in Britain 1945–1970* (MUP, Manchester, 1998)

Aldrich, Richard J., *The Hidden Hand: Britain, America and Cold War Secret Intelligence* (John Murray, London, 2001)

Aldrich, Richard J. and Hopkins, Michael F. (eds), *Intelligence, Defence and Diplomacy: British Policy in the Post-War World* (Frank Cass, London, 1994)

Aldrich, Richard J, Rawnsley, Gary D. and Rawnsley, Ming-Yeh T. (eds), *The Clandestine Cold War in Asia 1945–65* (Frank Cass, London, 2000)

Alvarez, David (ed), *Allied and Axis Signals Intelligence in World War II* (Frank Cass, London, 1999)

Alvarez, David, *Secret Messages: Codebreaking and American Diplomacy 1930–1945* (University Press of Kansas, Lawrence, 2000)

Andrew, Christopher, *Secret Service: The Making of the British Intelligence Community* (William Heinemann, London, 1985)

Andrew, Christopher and Dilks, David (eds), *The Missing Dimension: Governments and Intelligence Communities in the Twentieth Century* (Macmillan, London, 1984)

Andrew, Christopher and Mitrokhin, Vasili, *The Mitrokhin Archive: The KGB and the West* (Allen Lane, London, 1999)

Andrew, Christopher and Noakes, Jeremy, *Intelligence and International Relations 1909–1945* (University of Exeter, 1987)

Bamford, James, *The Puzzle Palace* (Sidgwick & Jackson, London, 1982)

Bamford, James, *Body of Secrets* (Century, London, 2001)

Blake, George, *No Other Choice: An Autobiography* (Jonathan Cape, London, 1990)

Borovik, Genrikh, *The Philby Files* (Little, Brown, London, 1994)

Bower, Tom, *The Perfect English Spy: Sir Dick White and the Secret War 1935-90* (William Heinemann, London, 1995)

Bower, Tom, *The Red Web: MI6 and the KGB Master Coup* (Aurum Press, London, 1989)

Boyle, Andrew, *The Climate of Treason* (Coronet, London, rev. edn, 1980)

Brook-Shepherd, Gordon, *Iron Maze: The Western Secret Services and the Bolsheviks* (Macmillan, London, 1998)

Brook-Shepherd, Gordon, *The Storm Birds: Soviet Post-War Defectors* (Weidenfeld & Nicolson, London, 1988)

Brook-Shepherd, Gordon, *The Storm Petrels* (Collins, London, 1977)

Budiansky, Stephen, *Battle of Wits* (Viking, London, 2000)

Cairncross, John, *An Agent for the Duration: Memoirs of the Fifth Man* (St Ermin's Press, London, 1996)

Cavendish, Anthony, *Inside Intelligence* (Collins, London, 1990)

Cecil, Robert, *A Divided Life: A Biography of Donald Maclean* (Bodley Head, London, 1988)

Clayton, Anthony, *Forearmed: A History of the Intelligence Corps* (Brasseys, London, 1993)

Connor, Ken, *Ghost Force: The Secret History of the SAS* (Weidenfeld & Nicolson, London, 1998

Davis, Philip, *British Intelligence: A Bibliography* (ABC Clio, Oxford, 1996)

Deacon, Richard, *A History of the British Secret Service* (Muller, London, 1969)

Dear, I C B (ed.), *The Oxford Companion to the Second World War* (OUP, Oxford, 1995)

Dorrill, Stephen, *MI6: Fifty Years of Special Operations* (Fourth Estate, London, 2000)

Fergusson, Thomas G, *British Military Intelligence 1870-1914: The Development of a Modern Intelligence Organization* (Arms and Armour Press, London, 1984)

Foot, M. R. D., and Langley, J. M., *MI9 Escape and Evasion 1939-1945* (Bodley Head, London, 1979)

Geraghty, Tony, *BRIXMIS: The Untold Exploits of Britain's Most Daring Cold War Spy Mission* (HarperCollins, London, 1996)

Geraghty, Tony, *The Irish War* (HarperCollins, London, 1998)

Gill, Peter, *Policing Politics: Security Intelligence and the Liberal Democratic State* (Frank Cass, London, 1994)

Haswell, Jock, *British Military Intelligence* (Weidenfeld & Nicolson, London, 1973)

Herman, Michael, *Intelligence Power in Peace and War* (CUP, Cambridge, 1996)

Herman, Michael, *Intelligence Services in the Information World* (Frank Cass, London, 2001)

Hesketh, Roger, *Fortitude: The D-Day Deception Campaign* (St Ermin's Press, London, 1999)

Hinsley, F. H., et al, *British Intelligence in the Second World War* (HMSO, London, 1979-1990)

Hinsley, F. H., and Stripp, Alan (eds), *Codebreakers: The Inside Story of Bletchley Park* (OUP, Oxford, 1993)

Hoffman, Bruce, *Inside Terrorism* (Victor Gollancz, London, 1998)

Hollingsworth, Mark, and Fielding, Nick, *Defending the Realm: MI5 and the Shayler Affair* (Andre Deutsch, London, 1999)

Jackson, Robert, *High Cold War* (PSL, London, 1998)

Jones, R. V., *Most Secret War* (Hamish Hamilton, London, 1978)

Jones, R. V., *Reflections on Intelligence* (Mandarin, London, 1990)

Judd, Alan, *The Quest for C: Mansfield Cumming and the Founding of the Secret Service* (HarperCollins, London, 1999)

Kemp, Anthony, *The SAS at War* (John Murray, London, 1991)

Kemp, Anthony, *The SAS: Savage Wars of Peace 1947 to the Present* (John Murray, London, 1994)

Knightley, Phillip, *Kim Philby: KGB Masterspy* (Andre Deutsch, London, 1988)

Knightley, Phillip, *The Second Oldest Profession: The Spy as Bureaucrat, Patriot, Fantasist and Whore* (Andre Deutsch, London, 1986)

Lacquer, Walter, *A World of Secrets: The Uses and Limits of Intelligence* (Basic, New York, 1985)

Lanning, Hugh and Norton-Taylor, Richard, *A Conflict of Loyalties: GCHQ 1984–1991* (New Clarion Press, Cheltenham, 1991)

Lashmar, Paul, *Spy-Flights of the Cold War* (Sutton, London, 1996)

Lloyd, Mark, *The Guinness Book of Espionage* (Guinness, London, 1994)

Lustgarten, Laurence and Leigh, Ian, *In From the Cold: National Security and Parliamentary Democracy* (OUP, Oxford, 1994)

McKay, C. G., *From Information to Intrigue: Studies in Secret Service based on the Swedish Experience, 1939–45* (Frank Cass, London, 1993)

McNab, Andy, *Immediate Action* (Bantam, London, 1995)

Masterman, J. C., *The Double-Cross System of the War of 1939–45* (Yale University Press, London and New Haven, 1972)

Mitrokhin, Vasiliy, *KGB Lexicon: The Soviet Intelligence Officer's Handbook* (Frank Cass, London, 2002)

Modin, Yuri, *My Five Cambridge Friends* (Headline, London, 1994)

Parritt, Lt-Col B. A. H., *The Intelligencers: The Story of British Military Intelligence up to 1914* (Templer Press, Ashford, 1971)

Philby, Kim, *My Silent War* (MacGibbon & Kee, London, 1968)

Philby, Rufina, *The Private Life of Kim Philby* (St Ermin's Press, London, 1999)

Porter, Bernard, *The Origins of the Vigilant State: The London Metropolitan Police Special Branch before the First World War* (Weidenfeld & Nicolson, London, 1987)

Porter, Bernard, *Plots and Paranoia: A History of Political Espionage in Britain 1790–1988* (Unwin Hyman, London, 1989)

Rennie, James, *The Operators: On the Streets with 14 Company* (Century, London, 1996)

Richelson, Jeffrey T., *A Century of Spies* (OUP, Oxford, 1995)

Richelson, Jeffrey T., *Foreign Intelligence Organizations* (Ballinger, Cambridge, MA, 1988)

Richelson, Jeffrey T., and Ball, Desmond, *The Ties That Bind* (Unwin Hyman, Boston, 2nd edn, 1990)

Ring, Jim, *We Come Unseen: the Untold Story of Britain's Cold War Submarines* (John Murray, London, 2001)

Robertson, K. G. (ed), *British and American Approaches to Intelligence* (Macmillan, London, 1987)

Robertson, K. G., *Secrecy and Open Government: Why Governments want you to know* (Macmillan, London, 1999)

Robertson, K.G. (ed.), *War, Resistance & Intelligence: Essays in Honour of MRD Foot* (Leo Cooper, London, 1999)

Smith, Michael, *The Emperor's Codes: Bletchley Park and the Breaking of Japan's Secret Ciphers* (Bantam, London, 2000)

Smith, Michael, *Foley: The Spy Who Saved 10,000 Jews* (Hodder & Stoughton, London, 1999)

Smith, Michael, *New Cloak, Old Dagger: How Britain's Spies Came In from the Cold* (Victor Gollancz, London, 1996)

Smith, Michael, *Station X: The Codebreakers of Bletchley Park* (Channel 4 Books, London, 1998)

Smith, Michael and Erskine, Ralph (eds), *Action This Day: Bletchley Park from the Breaking of the Enigma Code to the Birth of the Modern Computer* (Bantam, London, 2001)

Sparrow, Elizabeth, *Secret Service: British Agents in France 1792–1815* (Boydell, London, 1999)

Sontag, Sherry and Drew, Christopher, *Blind Man's Bluff: The Untold Story of American Submarine Espionage*, (HarperCollins, New York, 1998)

Stafford, David, *Spies Beneath Berlin* (John Murray, London, 2002)

Stafford, David, *Churchill and Secret Service* (John Murray, London, 1997)

Steers, Bob (ed.), *FSS: Field Security Section* (Robin Steers, London, 1996)

Stripp, Alan, *Codebreaker in the Far East* (Frank Cass, London, 1989)

Thurlow, Richard, *The Secret State: British Internal Security in the Twentieth Century* (Blackwell, Oxford, 1994)

Tomlinson, Richard, *The Big Breach* (Cutting Edge, Edinburgh, 2001)

Urban, Mark, *The Man Who Broke Napoleon's Codes* (Faber & Faber, London, 2001)

Urban, Mark, *UK Eyes Alpha* (Faber & Faber, London, 1996)

Verrier, Anthony, *Through the Looking Glass: British Foreign Policy in the Age of Illusions* (Jonathan Cape, London, 1983)

Welchman, Gordon, *The Hut Six Story* (Allen Lane, London, 1982)

West, Nigel, *The Friends: Britain's Post-War Secret Intelligence Operations* (Weidenfeld & Nicolson, London, 1988)

West, Nigel, *GCHQ: The Secret Wireless War 1900–86* (Weidenfeld & Nicolson, 1986)

West, Nigel, *A Matter of Trust: MI5 1945–72* (Coronet, London, 1982)

West, Nigel, *MI5: British Security Service Operations 1909–45* (Bodley Head, London, 1981)

West, Nigel, *MI6: British Secret Intelligence Service Operations 1909–1945* (Weidenfeld & Nicolson, London, 1983)

West, Nigel, and Tsarev, Oleg, *The Crown Jewels* (Harper Collins, London, 1998)

Whitwell, John, *British Agent* (Frank Cass, London, 1996)

Wiebes, Cees, *Intelligence and the War in Bosnia 1992–1995* (LIT, London, 2003)

Wright, Peter, *Spycatcher: The Candid Autobiography of a Senior Intelligence* Officer (Viking, New York, 1987)

Wright, Peter, *The Spycatcher's Encyclopedia of Espionage* (William Heinemann, Melbourne, 1991)

Index